Learning and Behavior

This book reviews how people and animals learn and how their behaviors are changed as a result of learning. It describes the most important principles, theories, controversies, and experiments that pertain to learning and behavior that are applicable to diverse species and different learning situations. Both classic studies and recent trends and developments are explored, providing a comprehensive survey of the field. Although the behavioral approach is emphasized, many cognitive theories are covered as well, along with a chapter on comparative cognition. Real-world examples and analogies make the concepts and theories more concrete and relevant to students. In addition, most chapters provide examples of how the principles covered have been applied in behavior modification and therapy. Thoroughly updated, each chapter features many new studies and references that reflect recent developments in the field. Learning objectives, bold-faced key terms, practice quizzes, a chapter summary, review questions, and a glossary are included.

The volume is intended for undergraduate or graduate courses in psychology of learning, (human) learning, introduction to learning, learning processes, animal behavior, (principles of) learning and behavior, conditioning and learning, learning and motivation, experimental analysis of behavior, behaviorism, and behavior analysis.

Highlights of the new edition include:

- A new text design with more illustrations, photos, and tables;
- *In the Media*, *Spotlight on Research*, and *Applying the Research* boxes that highlight recent applications of learning principles in psychology, education, sports, and the workplace;
- Discussions of recent developments in the growing field of neuroscience;
- Coverage of various theoretical perspectives to the study of learning—behavioral, cognitive, and physiological;
- Expanded coverage of emerging topics such as the behavioral economics of addictions, disordered gambling, and impulsivity;
- New examples, references, and research studies to ensure students are introduced to the latest developments in the field;
- A website at www.routledge.com/cw/Mazur where instructors will find a test bank, PowerPoint slides, and Internet links. Students will find practice quizzes, definitions of key terms, chapter outlines, and Internet sources for additional information.

James E. Mazur is Emeritus Professor of Psychology at Southern Connecticut State University, USA.

Learning and Behavior

Eighth Edition

James E. Mazur

Routledge
Taylor & Francis Group

NEW YORK AND LONDON

Eighth edition published 2017
by Routledge
711 Third Avenue, New York, NY 10017

and by Routledge
2 Park Square, Milton Park, Abingdon, Oxon, OX14 4RN

Routledge is an imprint of the Taylor & Francis Group, an informa business

First edition published 1990 by Prentice-Hall
Seventh edition published 2012 by Taylor & Francis

Library of Congress Cataloging in Publication Data
Names: Mazur, James E., 1951– author.
Title: Learning and behavior / James E. Mazur.
Description: Eighth edition. | New York, NY : Routledge, 2017. |
    Includes bibliographical references and index.
Identifiers: LCCN 2016026434 | ISBN 9781138689947 (hardback : alk. paper)
Subjects: LCSH: Learning, Psychology of. | Conditioned response. |
    Behavior modification. | Psychology, Comparative.
Classification: LCC BF318 .M38 2017 | DDC 153.1/5—dc23
LC record available at https://lccn.loc.gov/2016026434

ISBN: 978-1-138-68994-7 (hbk)
ISBN: 978-1-315-45028-5 (ebk)

Typeset in Bembo and Helvetica Neue
by Apex CoVantage, LLC

Printed and bound in the United States of America by Sheridan

In memory of my parents, Ann and Lou Mazur, who responded to my early interests in science with encouragement, understanding, and patience.

Contents

Detailed Contents

Preface

The purpose of this book is to introduce the reader to the branch of psychology that deals with how people and animals learn and how their behaviors are later changed as a result of this learning. This is a broad topic, for nearly all of our behaviors are influenced by prior learning experiences in some way. Because examples of learning and learned behaviors are so numerous, the goal of most psychologists in this field has been to discover general principles that are applicable to many different species and many different learning situations. What continues to impress and inspire me after many years in this field is that it is indeed possible to make such general statements about learning and behavior. This book describes some of the most important principles, theories, controversies, and experiments that have been produced by this branch of psychology in its first century.

This text is designed to be suitable for introductory or intermediate-level courses in learning, conditioning, or the experimental analysis of behavior. No prior knowledge of psychology is assumed, but the reading may be a bit easier for those who have had a course in introductory psychology. Many of the concepts and theories in this field are fairly abstract, and to make them more concrete and more relevant, I have included many real-world examples and analogies.

Roughly speaking, the book proceeds from the simple to the complex, with respect to both the difficulty of the material and the types of learning that are discussed. Chapter 1 discusses the behavioral approach to learning and contrasts it with the cognitive approach. It also describes some of the earliest theories about the learning process; then it presents some basic findings about the neural mechanisms of learning. Chapter 2 discusses innate behaviors and the simplest type of learning, habituation. Many of the terms and ideas introduced here reappear in later chapters on classical conditioning, operant conditioning, and motor-skills learning. The next two chapters deal with classical conditioning. Chapter 3 begins with basic principles and ends with some therapeutic applications. Chapter 4 describes more recent theoretical developments and experimental findings in this area.

The next three chapters discuss the various facets of operant conditioning: Chapter 5 covers the basic principles and terminology of positive reinforcement, Chapter 6 covers schedules of reinforcement and applications, and Chapter 7 covers negative reinforcement and punishment. Chapters 8 and 9 have a more theoretical orientation. Chapter 8 presents differing views on such fundamental questions as what constitutes a reinforcer and what conditions are necessary for learning to occur. Chapter 9 takes a more thorough look at generalization and discrimination, and it also examines research on concept learning.

Chapter 10 surveys a wide range of findings in the rapidly growing area of comparative cognition. Chapter 11 discusses two types of learning that are given little or no emphasis in many texts on learning—observational learning and motor-skills learning. A substantial portion of human learning involves either observation or the development of new motor skills. Readers might well be puzzled or disappointed (with some justification) with a text on learning that includes no mention of these topics. Finally, Chapter 12 presents an overview of behavioral research on choice.

This book includes a number of learning aids for students. Each chapter begins with a list of learning objectives and ends with a summary of the main points covered. Each chapter also includes practice quizzes and review questions to help students determine if they are learning and understanding the key points. The book also includes a glossary of all important terms. The website for this text has a number of additional resources. For instructors, there is a test bank of multiple-choice and short-essay questions, PowerPoint slides for use in class, and Internet resources. For students, there are online quizzes for each chapter, definitions of key terms, chapter outlines, and Internet links related to many of the topics covered in the text.

New to this eighth edition are boxes in each chapter that highlight topics that should be of special interest to students. The boxes are focused on three themes: *In the Media*, covering topics related to learning and behavior that have been covered by various media sources, *Spotlight on Research*, taking a closer look at current research on specific topics, and *Applying the Research,* presenting real-world applications of the principles described in the text. This edition also includes many new figures and illustrations to help students understand and remember important concepts, principles, experimental procedures, and applications. To enhance the relevance of this material for today's students, a number of older and somewhat technical topics from previous editions have been removed, and there are more examples of how behavioral and cognitive principles of learning can be observed in people's everyday behaviors. Most of the chapters include sections that describe how the theories and principles of learning have been used in the applied field of behavior modification.

I owe thanks to many people for the help they have given me as I wrote this book. Many of my thoughts about learning and about psychology in general were shaped by my discussions with the late Richard Herrnstein—my teacher, advisor, and friend. I am most grateful to Debra Riegert and Rachel Severinovsky of Taylor and Francis for all the advice and assistance they provided me throughout the work on this edition. Thanks go to the reviewers of various editions of this book:

Matthew C. Bell, Mark Branch, Thomas Brown, Maureen Bullock, Gary Brosvic, Valerie Farmer-Dougan, April Fugett, Adam Goodie, Kenneth P. Hillner, Peter Holland, Ann Kelley, Melinda Leonard, Kathleen McCartney, Harold L. Miller, Jr., David Mostofsky, Thomas Moye, Jack Nation, Erin Rasmussen, David Schaal, James R. Sutterer, Edward Wasserman, Steve Weinert, and Joseph Wister. In addition, I thank Marge Averill, Stan Averill, John Bailey, Chris Berry, Paul Carroll, David Coe, David Cook, Susan Herrnstein, Margaret Makepeace, Margaret Nygren, Steven Pratt, and James Roach for their competent and cheerful help on different editions of this book. Finally, I thank my wife, Laurie Averill, who drew many of the illustrations and gave me plenty of valuable help on this and previous editions.

J. E. M.

About the Author

James E. Mazur obtained his B.A. in Psychology from Dartmouth College in 1973 and his Ph.D. in Experimental Psychology from Harvard University in 1977. He taught at Harvard as an assistant professor and associate professor from 1980 to 1988, and since then he has taught at Southern Connecticut State University, where he was honored with the title of CSU Professor in 2010. He is now Professor Emeritus and continues to teach part-time. He has conducted research on operant conditioning and choice for over 40 years. He has been a reviewer and associate editor for several journals, and he served as editor for the *Journal of the Experimental Analysis of Behavior*. He has published numerous journal articles and chapters on such topics as reinforcement schedules, conditioned reinforcement, self-control, risk taking, procrastination, and mathematical models of choice.

CHAPTER 1

History, Background, and Basic Concepts

Learning Objectives

After reading this chapter, you should be able to

- describe the early theories of memory proposed by the Associationists and the early memory studies of Hermann Ebbinghaus
- explain the behavioral and cognitive approaches to studying learning and how they differ
- explain the advantages and disadvantages of using animals in psychological research
- discuss intervening variables and the debate over whether they should be used in psychology
- explain how our sensory receptors respond to "simple sensations" and how feature detectors in the visual system respond to more complex patterns
- list three main types of changes that can take place in the brain as a result of a learning experience, and present evidence for each type

If you know nothing about the branch of psychology called *learning*, you may have some misconceptions about the scope of this field. I can recall browsing through the course catalog as a college freshman and coming across a course offered by the Department of Psychology with the succinct title "Learning." Without bothering to read the course description, I wondered about the contents of this course. Learning, I reasoned, is primarily the occupation of students. Would this course teach students better study habits, better reading, and better note-taking skills? Or did the course examine learning in children, covering such topics as the best ways to teach a child to read, to write, to do arithmetic? Did it deal with children who have learning disabilities? It was difficult to imagine spending an entire semester on these topics, which sounded fairly narrow and specialized for an introductory-level course.

My conception of the psychology of learning was wrong in several respects. First, a psychology course emphasizing learning in the classroom would probably have a title such as "Educational Psychology" rather than "Learning." My second error was the assumption that the psychology of learning is a narrow field. A moment's reflection reveals that students do not have a monopoly on learning. Children learn a great deal before ever entering a classroom, and adults must continue to adapt to an ever-changing environment. Because learning occurs at all ages, the psychological discipline of learning places no special emphasis on classroom learning. Furthermore, since the human being is only one of thousands of species on this planet that have the capacity to learn, the psychological discipline of learning is by no means restricted to the study of human beings. For reasons to be explained, a large percentage of all psychological experiments on learning have used nonhuman subjects. Though they may have their faults, psychologists in the field of learning are not chauvinistic about the human species.

Although even specialists have difficulty defining the term *learning* precisely, most would agree that it is a process of change that occurs as a result of an individual's experience. Psychologists who study learning are interested in this process wherever it occurs—in adults, school children, other mammals, reptiles, and even insects. This may sound like a large subject, but the field of learning is even broader than this because psychologists study not only the *process* of learning but also the *product* of learning—the long-term changes in one's behavior that result from a learning experience.

An example may help to clarify the distinction between process and product. Suppose you glance out the window and see a raccoon near some garbage cans in the backyard. As you watch, the raccoon gradually manages to knock over a garbage can, remove the lid, and tear open the garbage bag inside. If we wanted to study this raccoon's behavior, many different questions would probably come to mind. Some questions might deal with the learning process itself: Did the animal open the can purely by accident, or was it guided by some "plan of action"? What factors determine how long the raccoon will persist in manipulating the garbage can if it is not immediately successful in obtaining something to eat? These questions deal with what might be called the **acquisition** phase, or the period in which the animal is acquiring a new skill.

Once the raccoon has become skillful at opening garbage cans, we can ask questions about its long-term performance. How frequently will the raccoon visit a given backyard, and how will the animal's success or failure affect the frequency of its visits? Will its visits occur at the most advantageous times of the day or week? Such questions concern the end product of the learning process, the raccoon's new behavior patterns. This text is entitled *Learning and Behavior*, rather than simply *Learning*, to reflect the fact that the psychology of learning encompasses both the acquisition process and the long-term behavior that results.

THE SEARCH FOR GENERAL PRINCIPLES OF LEARNING

Because the psychology of learning deals with all types of learning and learned behaviors in all types of creatures, its scope is broad indeed. Think, for a moment, of the different behaviors you performed in the first hour or two after rising this morning. How many of those behaviors would not have been possible without prior learning? In most cases, the decision is easy to make. Getting dressed, washing your face, making your bed, and going to the dining room for breakfast are all examples of behaviors that depend mostly or entirely on previous learning experiences. The behavior of eating breakfast depends on several different types of learning, including the selection of appropriate types and quantities of food, the proper use of utensils, and the development of coordinated hand, eye, and mouth movements. It is hard to think of human behaviors that do not depend on prior learning.

Considering all of the behaviors of humans and other creatures that involve learning, the scope of this branch of psychology may seem hopelessly broad. How can any single discipline hope to make any useful statements about all these different instances of learning? It would make no sense to study, one by one, every different example of learning that a person might come across, and this is not the approach of most researchers who study learning. Instead, their strategy has been to select a relatively small number of learning situations, study them in detail, and then try to generalize from these situations to other instances of learning. Therefore, the goal of much of the research on learning has been to develop general principles that are applicable across a wide range of species and learning situations.

B. F. Skinner, one of the most influential figures in the history of psychology, made his belief in this strategy explicit in his first major work, *The Behavior of Organisms* (1938). In his initial studies, Skinner chose white rats as subjects and lever pressing as a response. An individual rat would be placed in a small experimental chamber containing little more than a lever and a tray into which food was occasionally presented after the rat pressed the lever. A modern version of such a chamber is shown in Figure 1.1. In studying the behavior of

Figure 1.1 An experimental chamber in which a rat can receive food pellets by pressing a lever.

rats in such a sparse environment, Skinner felt that he could discover principles that govern the behavior of many animals, including human beings, in the more complex environments found outside the psychological laboratory. The work of Skinner and his students will be examined in depth beginning in Chapter 5, so you will have the opportunity to decide for yourself whether Skinner's strategy has proven to be successful.

Attempts to discover principles or laws with wide applicability are a part of most scientific endeavors. For example, a general principle in physics is the law of gravity, which predicts, among other things, the distance a freely falling object will drop in a given period of time. If an object starts from a stationary position and falls for t seconds, the equation $d = 16t^2$ predicts the distance (in feet) that the object will fall. The law of gravity is certainly a general principle because in theory it applies to any falling object, whether a rock, a baseball, or a skydiver. Nevertheless, the law of gravity has its limitations. As with most scientific principles, it is applicable only when certain criteria are met. Two restrictions on the equation are that it applies (1) only to objects close to the earth's surface and (2) only as long as no other force, such as air resistance, plays a role. Therefore, the law of gravity can be more accurately studied in the laboratory, where the role of air resistance can be minimized through the use of a vacuum chamber. For similar reasons, principles of learning and behavior are often best studied in a laboratory environment. Every chapter in this book will introduce several new principles of learning and behavior, nearly all of which have been investigated in laboratory settings. To demonstrate that these principles have applicability to more natural settings, each chapter will also describe real-world situations in which these principles play an important role.

Within the field of psychology, researchers have studied the topic of learning in several different ways. The remainder of this chapter gives an overview of these different approaches, plus a brief history of the field and some background information that will help you to understand the topics covered in later chapters. We will begin with some of the earliest recorded thoughts about learning and memory, and then we will examine and compare two modern approaches to learning—the behavioral and cognitive approaches. Finally, this chapter will introduce a third approach to studying learning—the neuroscience approach—which examines what happens in the brain and in individual nerve cells when we learn.

THE ASSOCIATIONISTS

Aristotle

The Greek philosopher Aristotle (c. 350 B.C.) is generally acknowledged to be the first **Associationist**. He proposed three principles of association that can be viewed as an elementary theory of memory. Aristotle suggested that these principles describe how one thought leads to another. Before reading about Aristotle's principles, you can try something Aristotle never did: You can conduct a simple experiment to test these principles. Before reading further, take a few moments to try the demonstration in Box 1.1.

Aristotle's first principle of association was **contiguity**: The more closely together (contiguous) in space or time two items occur, the more likely will the thought of one item lead to the thought of the other. For example, the response *chair* to the word *table* illustrates association by spatial contiguity since the two items are often found close together. The

BOX 1.1   APPLYING THE RESEARCH

A Demonstration of Free Association

This exercise, which should take only a minute or two, can be called a study of free association. Take a piece of paper and a pencil, and write numbers 1 through 12 in a column
down the left side of the paper. Below is a list of words also numbered 1 through 12.
Reading one word at a time, write down the first one or two words that come to mind.

1. apple
2. night
3. thunder
4. bread
5. chair
6. bat
7. girl
8. dentist
9. quiet
10. sunset
11. elephant
12. blue

Once you have your list of responses to the 12 words, look over your answers and try
to develop some rules that describe how you came up with your responses. Can you
guess any of Aristotle's three principles?

response *lightning* to the word *thunder* is an example of association by temporal contiguity.
Other examples of association by contiguity are *bread-butter* and *dentist-pain*.

Aristotle's other two principles of association were **similarity** and **contrast**. He stated
that the thought of one concept often leads to the thought of similar concepts. Examples
of association by similarity are *apple-orange* or *blue-green*. By the principle of contrast, Aristotle meant that an item often leads to the thought of its opposite (e.g., *night-day*, *girl-boy*,
sunset-sunrise). Most people who try this simple free-association experiment conclude that
Aristotle's principles of association have both strengths and weaknesses. His list of factors
that affect the train of thought seems incomplete, but it is not bad as a first step in the development of a theory about the relationship between experience and memory.

The British Associationists: Simple and Complex Ideas

For some philosophers who wrote about Associationism several centuries after Aristotle, this
topic assumed a much greater significance: Associationism was seen as a theory of all knowledge. The **British Associationists** included John Locke (1690), James Mill (1829), and

John Stuart Mill (1843). These writers are also called Empiricists because of their belief that every person acquires all knowledge empirically, that is, through experience. This viewpoint is typified by John Locke's statement that the mind of a newborn child is a *tabula rasa* (a blank slate) onto which experiences make their marks. The Empiricists believed that every memory, every idea, and every concept a person has is based on previous experiences.

The opposite of **Empiricism** is **Nativism**, or the position that some ideas are innate and do not depend on an individual's past experience. For instance, Immanuel Kant (1781) believed that the concepts of space and time are inborn and that through experience new concepts are built on the foundation of these original, innate concepts. As we will see many times throughout this book, modern research has uncovered numerous examples that support Nativism and contradict the extreme Empiricist position that all knowledge is learned through experience. Nevertheless, we can grant that some concepts are innate, but many concepts are developed through experience.

The British Empiricists offered some hypotheses both about how old concepts become associated in memory and about how new concepts are formed. According to the Associationists, there is a direct correspondence between experience and memory. Experience consists of sensations, and memory consists of ideas. Furthermore, any sensory experience can be broken down into simple sensations. For instance, if a person observes a red box-shaped object, this might be broken down into two simple sensations: *red* and *rectangular*. Later, the person's memory of this experience would consist of the two corresponding simple ideas of *red* and *rectangular* (see Figure 1.2a). A simple idea was said to be a sort of faint replica of the simple sensation from which it arose.

Now suppose that the person repeatedly encounters such a red box-shaped object. Through the principle of contiguity, an association should develop between the ideas of *red* and *rectangle*, as shown in Figure 1.2b. Once such an association is formed, if the person experiences the color red, this will not only invoke the idea of red, but by virtue of the association the idea of rectangular will be invoked as well (Figure 1.2c).

Of course, the Associationists realized that many of our concepts are more complex than the simple ideas of *red*, *rectangular*, *thunder*, and *lightning*. In an attempt to come to grips with the full range of memories and knowledge that all people have, some Associationists speculated about the formation of complex ideas. James Mill (1829) proposed that if two or more simple sensations are repeatedly presented together, a product of their union may be a **complex idea**. For instance, if the sensations *red* and *rectangular* occur together repeatedly, a new, complex idea of *brick* may form. Figure 1.2d shows one way to depict Mill's hypothesis graphically. Once such a complex idea is formed, it can also be evoked by the process of association when the sensation of either *red* or *rectangle* occurs. Mill went on to say that complex ideas could themselves combine to form larger **duplex ideas**. In the following passage, Mill (1829) describes the formation of a hierarchy of ideas of increasing complexity:

> Some of the most familiar objects with which we are acquainted furnish instances of these unions of complex and duplex ideas. Brick is one complex idea, mortar is another complex idea; these ideas, with ideas of position and quantity, compose my idea of a wall. . . . In the same manner my complex idea of glass, and wood, and others, compose my duplex idea of a window; and these duplex ideas, united together, compose my idea of a house, which is made up of various duplex ideas.
>
> (pp. 114–116)

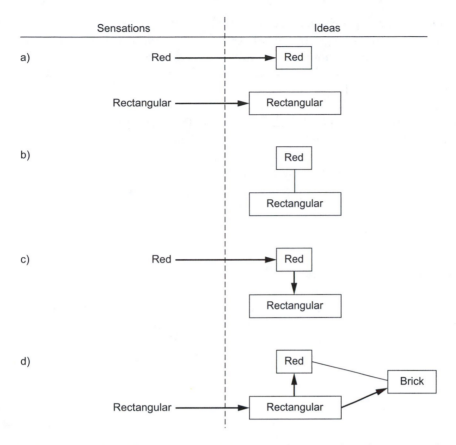

Figure 1.2 Some principles of Associationism. (a) One-to-one correspondence between simple sensations and simple ideas. (b) After repeated pairings of the two sensations, an association forms between their respective ideas. (c) Once an association is formed, presenting one stimulus will activate the ideas of both. (d) With enough pairings of two simple ideas, a complex idea encompassing both simple ideas is formed. The complex idea may now be evoked if either of the simple stimuli is presented.

There are both strengths and weaknesses in this hypothesis. Some types of learning do seem to progress from simple to complex concepts. For example, only after children understand the concepts of *addition* and *repetition* are they taught the more complex concept of *multiplication*, and it is often introduced as a procedure for performing repeated additions. However, other concepts do not seem to follow as nicely from Mill's theory, including his own example of the concept of *house*. A 2-year-old may know the word *house* and use it appropriately without knowing the "simpler" concepts of *mortar*, *ceiling*, or *rafter*. With *house* and many other complex concepts, people seem to develop at least a crude idea of the entire concept before learning all of the components of the concept, although according to Mill's theory this should not be possible. Thus, although it appears to have validity in some cases, Mill's theory is at best incomplete.

Another Associationist, Thomas Brown (1820), tried to expand Aristotle's list by adding some additional principles. For example, he proposed that the *length of time* two sensations coexist determines the strength of the association, and the *liveliness* or vividness of the sensations also affects the strength of the association. According to Brown, intense stimuli or emotional events will be more easily associated and better remembered. He also proposed that a stronger association will also occur if the two sensations have been paired *frequently* or if they have been paired *recently*.

The ideas of the Associationists can be called the earliest theories of learning, for they attempted to explain how people change as a result of their experiences. However, the Associationists never conducted any experiments to test their ideas. In retrospect, it is remarkable that despite an interest in principles of learning spanning some 2,000 years, no systematic experiments on learning were conducted until the end of the nineteenth century. This absence of research of learning was not a result of technological deficiencies because the first experiments on learning were so simple that they could have been performed centuries earlier.

Ebbinghaus's Experiments on Memory

Hermann Ebbinghaus (1885) was the first to put the Associationists' principles to an experimental test. In his memory experiments, Ebbinghaus served as his own subject. This is not an acceptable arrangement by modern standards because his performance could have been biased by his expectations. Yet despite this potential problem, all of his major findings have been replicated by later researchers using modern research procedures.

To avoid using stimuli that had preexisting associations (such as *coffee-hot*), Ebbinghaus invented the *nonsense syllable*—a meaningless syllable consisting of two consonants separated by a vowel (e.g., HAQ, PIF, ZOD). He would read a list of nonsense syllables out loud at a steady pace, over and over. Periodically, he would test his memory by trying to recite the list by heart, and he would record the number of repetitions needed for one perfect recitation. He then might allow some time to pass and then try to learn the list to perfection a second time, again recording how many repetitions were needed. He could then calculate his *savings*—the decrease in the number of repetitions needed to relearn the list. For example, if he needed 20 repetitions to learn a list the first time, but only 15 repetitions to relearn the list at a later time, this was a savings of 5 repetitions, or 25%.

A few examples will show how Ebbinghaus tested the Associationists' principles. One of Thomas Brown's principles was that the frequency of pairings affects the strength of an association. Obviously, this principle is supported by the simple fact that with enough repetitions Ebbinghaus could learn even long lists of nonsense syllables. However, one of Ebbinghaus's findings provided additional support for the frequency principle. If he continued to study a list beyond the point of one perfect recitation (e.g., for an additional 10 or 20 repetitions), his savings after 24 hours increased substantially. In other words, even after he appeared to have perfectly mastered a list, additional study produced better performance in a delayed test. Continuing to practice after performance is apparently perfect is called **overlearning**, and Ebbinghaus demonstrated that Brown's principle of frequency applies to periods of overlearning as well as to periods in which there is visible improvement during practice.

Another of Thomas Brown's principles was recency: The more recently two items have been paired, the stronger will be the association between them. Ebbinghaus tested this principle by varying the length of time that elapsed between his study and test periods. As shown

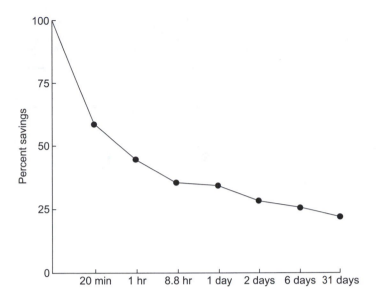

Figure 1.3 Ebbinghaus's forgetting curve. The percentage savings is shown for various time intervals between his initial learning and relearning of lists of nonsense syllables. (After Ebbinghaus, 1885)

in Figure 1.3, he examined intervals as short as 20 minutes and as long as 1 month. This graph is an example of a **forgetting curve**, for it shows how the passage of time has a detrimental effect on performance in a memory task. The curve shows that forgetting is rapid immediately after a study period, but the rate of additional forgetting slows as more time passes. The shape of this curve is similar to the forgetting curves obtained by later researchers in numerous experiments with both humans and animals, although the time scale on the x-axis varies greatly, depending on the nature of the task and the species of the subjects. Forgetting curves of this type provide strong confirmation of Brown's principle of recency.

A final example will show how Ebbinghaus tested Aristotle's principle of contiguity. He reasoned the strongest associations in his lists should be between adjacent syllables, but there should also be measurable (though weaker) associations between nonadjacent items. He devised an ingenious method for testing this idea, which involved rearranging the items in a list after they were memorized and then learning the rearranged list. His technique is illustrated in Table 1.1.

The designations I1 through I16 refer to the 16 items as they were ordered in the original list (List 0). Once this list is memorized, there should be a strong association between I1 and I2, a somewhat weaker association between I1 and I3 (since these were separated by one item in the original list), a still weaker association between I1 and I4, and so on. There should be similar gradations in strength of association between every other item and its neighbors.

The rearranged list, called List 1 in Table 1.1, was used to test for associations between items one syllable apart. Notice that every adjacent item in List 1 was separated by one syllable in the original list. If there is any association between I1 and I3, between I3 and I5, and so on, then List 1 should be easier to learn than a totally new list. In a similar fashion, List 2

Table 1.1 Ebbinghaus's rearranged list experiment. An original list of 16 nonsense syllables (represented here by the symbols I1 through I16) was rearranged to test for possible associations between items separated by one syllable (List 1) or associations between items separated by two syllables (List 2).

List 0 (Original list)	List 1 (1 item skipped)	List 2 (2 items skipped)
I1	I1	I1
I2	I3	I4
I3	I5	I7
I4	I7	I10
I5	I9	I13
I6	I11	I16
I7	I13	I2
I8	I15	I5
I9	I2	I8
I10	I4	I11
I11	I6	I14
I12	I8	I3
I13	I10	I6
I14	I12	I9
I15	I14	I12
I16	I16	I15

tests for associations between items that were two syllables apart in the original list. Ebbinghaus found that if List 0 was simply relearned after 24 hours, the savings amounted to about 33%. In comparison, he found an average savings of 11% if List 1 was studied 24 hours after List 0 and a savings of 7% if List 2 was used. Although the amount of savings with these rearranged lists was not large, the pattern of results was orderly: As the number of skipped syllables increased in the rearranged lists, the amount of savings was diminished. These results therefore support the principle of contiguity because they show that the strength of an association between two items depends on their proximity in the original list.

The Influence of the Associationists and Ebbinghaus

Several themes from the Associationists and Ebbinghaus can still be seen in the work of present-day psychologists. During the twentieth century, two major approaches to the study of learning arose—the behavioral and cognitive approaches. Many researchers from both the behavioral and cognitive traditions have adopted the idea that learning involves the formation of associations, as the next several chapters will show. Both behavioral and cognitive psychologists continue to be interested in how factors such as contiguity, similarity among stimuli, repetition, and the passage of time affect what we learn and what we remember. They continue to investigate how people (and animals) learn complex concepts and novel ideas. Now that we have surveyed the contributions of these early thinkers, we can turn to the modern-day learning researchers who followed them.

BEHAVIORAL AND COGNITIVE APPROACHES TO LEARNING

The field of learning is frequently associated with a general approach to psychology called **behaviorism**, which was the dominant approach to the investigation of learning for the first half of the twentieth century. During the 1960s, however, a new approach called **cognitive psychology** began to develop, and one of the reasons for its appearance was that its proponents were dissatisfied with the behavioral approach. This book considers both perspectives, but it places more emphasis on the behavioral approach. Two of the most notable characteristics of the behavioral approach are (1) a heavy reliance on animal subjects and (2) an emphasis on external events (environmental stimuli and overt behaviors) and a reluctance to speculate about processes inside the organism that cannot be seen.

The Use of Animal Subjects

A large proportion of the studies described in this text used animals as subjects, especially pigeons, rats, and rabbits. Researchers in this field frequently choose to conduct their experiments with nonhuman subjects for a number of reasons. First, in research with humans, subject effects can sometimes pose serious problems. A **subject effect** occurs when those who are participating in an experiment change their behavior because they know they are being observed. Whereas people may change the way they behave when they know a psychologist is watching, subject effects are unlikely to occur with animal subjects. Most studies with animal subjects are conducted in such a way that the animal does not know its behavior is being monitored and recorded. Furthermore, it is unlikely that an animal subject will be motivated to either please or displease the experimenter.

A second reason for using animal subjects is convenience. The species most commonly used are easy and inexpensive to care for, and animals of a specific age and sex can be obtained in the quantities the experimenter needs. Once animal subjects are obtained, their participation is as regular as the experimenter's: Animal subjects never fail to show up for their appointments, which is unfortunately not the case with human participants.

Probably the biggest advantage of domesticated animal subjects is that their environment can be controlled to a much greater extent than is possible with either wild animals or human subjects. This is especially important in experiments on learning, where previous experience can have a large effect on a subject's performance in a new learning situation. When a person tries to solve a brainteaser as part of a learning experiment, the experimenter cannot be sure how many similar problems the subject has encountered in his or her lifetime. When animals are bred and raised in the laboratory, however, their environments can be constructed to ensure they have no contact with objects or events similar to those they will encounter in the experiment.

A final reason for using animal subjects is that of comparative simplicity. Just as a child trying to learn about electricity is better off starting with a flashlight than a cell phone, researchers may have a better chance of discovering the basic principles of learning by examining creatures that are less intelligent and less complex than human beings. The assumption here is that although human beings differ from other animals in some respects, they are also similar in some respects, and it is these similarities that can be investigated with animal subjects.

One disadvantage of research with animals is that many of the most advanced human abilities cannot be studied with animals. Although there has been some research with animals on skills such as language and problem solving (see Chapter 10), most behavioral psychologists would agree that some complex abilities are unique to human beings. The difference between behavioral psychologists and cognitive psychologists seems to be only that cognitive psychologists are especially interested in those complex abilities that only human beings possess, whereas behavioral psychologists are typically more interested in learning abilities that are shared by many species. This is nothing more than a difference in interests, and it is pointless to argue about it.

A second argument against the use of animal subjects is that human beings are so different from all other animals that it is not possible to generalize from animal behavior to human behavior. This is not an issue that can be settled by debate; it can only be decided by collecting the appropriate data. As will be shown throughout this book, there is abundant evidence that research on learning with animal subjects produces findings that are also applicable to human behavior.

A third concern about the use of animals as research subjects is an ethical one. Is it right to use animals in research and, if so, under what conditions? This complex and controversial issue is discussed in the next section.

Ethical Issues and Animal Research

In recent years there has been considerable debate about the use of animals as research subjects. Viewpoints on this matter vary tremendously. At one extreme, some of the most radical animal rights advocates believe that animals should have the same rights as people and that no animals should be used in any type of research whatsoever (Regan, 1983). Others, both animal welfare advocates and members of the general public, take less extreme positions but believe that steps should be taken to minimize and eventually phase out the use of animals in research.

In response to such arguments, scientists have emphasized that many of the advances in medicine, including vaccines, surgical techniques, and prescription drugs, would not have been possible without research on animals. They warn that if research with animals were to stop, it would severely impede progress in medical research and hamper efforts to improve the health of the world population. In psychology, researchers have documented the many benefits that have resulted from animal research in the treatment of disorders ranging from anxiety and depression to drug addictions and memory loss (N. E. Miller, 1985). They argue that progress in dealing with mental health problems would be jeopardized if animals were no longer used as subjects in psychological research (Baldwin, 1993; Brennan, Clark, & Mock, 2014).

Because of ethical concerns, many new regulations have been put in place in an effort to improve the well-being of animal subjects. In the United States, most colleges, universities, and research centers that use animal subjects are required to have an Institutional Animal Care and Use Committee (IACUC) to oversee all research projects involving animals. The IACUC must review each project with animal subjects before it begins to ensure that all governmental regulations are met and that the animals are well cared for. Any pain or discomfort to the animals must be minimized to the extent possible. For example, if an animal undergoes surgery, appropriate anesthesia must be used. Regulations also require that all research animals have adequate food and water; clean and well-maintained living environments with appropriate temperature, humidity, and lighting conditions; and the continual availability of veterinary care.

It should be clear that recent research has been governed by increasingly strict regulations designed to ensure the humane treatment of animal subjects. Older studies were conducted during times when there were fewer regulations about animal research. Nevertheless, it is probably safe to say that even before the advent of tighter regulations, the vast majority of the experiments were done by researchers who took very good care of their animals because they realized that one of the best ways to obtain good research results is to have subjects that are healthy and well treated.

The Emphasis on External Events

The term *behaviorism* was coined by John B. Watson (1919), who is often called the first behaviorist. Watson criticized the research techniques that prevailed in the field of psychology at that time. A popular research method was introspection, which involves reflecting on, reporting, and analyzing one's own mental processes. Thus, a psychologist might attempt to examine and describe his thoughts and emotions while looking at a picture or performing some other specific task. A problem with introspection was that it required considerable practice to master this skill, and, even then, two experienced psychologists might report different thoughts and emotions when performing the same task. Watson recognized this weakness, and he argued that verbal reports of private events (sensations, feelings, states of consciousness) should have no place in the field of psychology.

Watson's logic can be summarized as follows: (1) We want psychology to be a science; (2) sciences deal only with events everyone can observe; therefore, (3) psychology must deal only with observable events. According to Watson, the observable events in psychology are the stimuli that a person senses and the responses a person makes; they are certainly not the subjective reports of trained introspectionists.

Whereas Watson argued against the use of unobservable events as psychological data, B. F. Skinner criticized the use of unobservable events in psychological theories. Skinner (1950) asserted that it is both dangerous and unnecessary to point to some unobservable event, or **intervening variable**, as the cause of behavior. Consider an experiment in which a rat is kept without water for a certain number of hours and is then placed in a chamber where it can obtain water by pressing a lever. We would probably find an orderly relationship between the independent variable, the number of hours of water deprivation, and the dependent variable, the rate of lever pressing. The rule that described this relationship is represented by the arrow in Figure 1.4a.

Skinner has pointed out that many psychologists would prefer to go further, however, and postulate an intervening variable such as *thirst*, which is presumably controlled by the hours of deprivation and which in turn controls the rate of lever pressing (see Figure 1.4b). According to Skinner, this intervening variable is unnecessary because it does not improve our ability to predict the rat's behavior—we can do just as well simply by knowing the hours of deprivation. The addition of the intervening variable needlessly complicates our theory. Now our theory must describe two relationships: the relationship between hours of deprivation and thirst, and that between thirst and lever pressing.

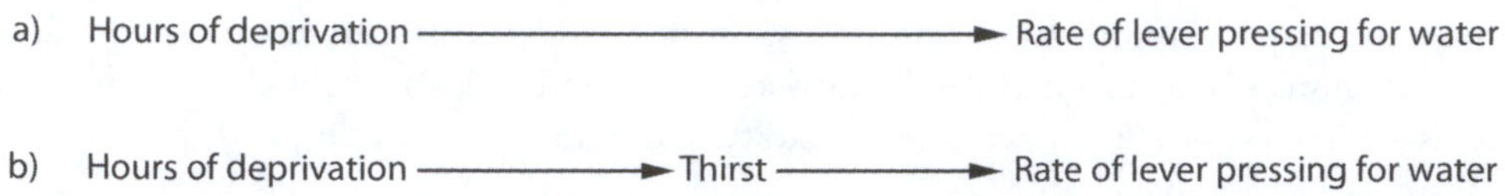

a)   Hours of deprivation ─────────────────────────────► Rate of lever pressing for water

b)   Hours of deprivation ───────────► Thirst ───────────► Rate of lever pressing for water

Figure 1.4 (a) A schematic diagram of a simple theory of behavior with no intervening variables. (b) The same theory with an intervening variable added. In this example, the intervening variable, thirst, is unnecessary, for it only complicates the theory. (From N.E. Miller, 1959, Liberalization of basic S-R concepts, in S. Koch, *Psychology: The study of a science,* Vol. 2. © McGraw-Hill Education. Reprinted by permission.)

Skinner also argued that the use of an intervening variable such as thirst is dangerous because we can easily fool ourselves into thinking we have found the cause of a behavior when we are actually talking about a hypothetical and unobservable entity. Suppose that when a father is asked why his son does not do his homework, he answers, "Because he is lazy." In this case, laziness, an unobservable entity, is offered as an explanation, and accepting this explanation could prematurely curtail any efforts to improve the problem behavior. After all, if the cause of a behavior is inside the person, how can we control it? However, Skinner proposed that the causes of many behaviors can be traced back to the external environment, and by changing the environment, we can change the behavior. Perhaps the boy spends all afternoon playing video games, eats dinner with the family at a fairly late hour, and then is too tired to do his assignments. If so, the parents might be able to change the boy's behavior by requiring him to complete his homework before playing any video games. In short, the potential for controlling a behavior may be recognized if an intervening variable such as laziness is rejected and an external cause of the behavior is sought.

Neal Miller (1959), another behavioral psychologist, disagreed with Skinner's position that intervening variables are always undesirable. Miller suggested that intervening variables are often useful when several independent and dependent variables are involved. As shown in Figure 1.5, he noted that besides hours of water deprivation, two other independent variables that could affect the rat's lever pressing might also increase if it were fed dry food or if it were given an injection of a saline solution. Furthermore, the rate of lever pressing is only one of many dependent variables that might be affected by water deprivation, dry food, or a saline injection. Two other dependent variables are the volume of water consumed and the amount of quinine (which would give the water a bitter taste) that would have to be added to make the rat stop drinking.

Miller argued that once these additional independent and dependent variables are considered, to account for the rat's behavior we would need a theory with nine cause-and-effect relationships, as symbolized by the nine crossing arrows in Figure 1.5a. This fairly complicated theory could be simplified by including the intervening variable, thirst. We can assume that each of the three independent variables affects an animal's thirst, and thirst controls each of the three dependent variables. Figure 1.5b shows that once the intervening variable, thirst, is included in this way, only six cause-and-effect relationships (represented by the six arrows in the figure) have to be described. In other words, when there are multiple independent and dependent variables to consider, the theory with the intervening variable is actually simpler (because there are fewer cause-and-effect relationships to account for).

Some psychologists have also pointed out that intervening variables are commonplace in other, firmly established sciences. For instance, many familiar concepts from physics

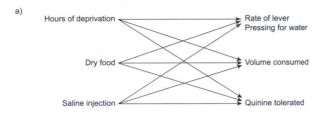

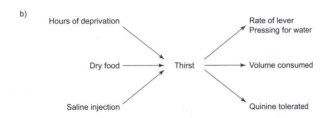

Figure 1.5 (a) The arrows represent the nine relationships between independent and dependent variables that must be defined by a theory without intervening variables. (b) The arrows represent the six relationships the theory must define if it includes the intervening variable of thirst. Neal Miller argued that the second theory is superior because it is more parsimonious. (From N.E. Miller, 1959, Liberalization of basic S-R concepts, in S. Koch, *Psychology: The study of a science,* Vol. 2. © McGraw-Hill Education. Reprinted by permission.)

(gravity, magnetism, force) are intervening variables since they are not directly observable. Some psychologists have therefore reasoned that progress in psychology would be needlessly restricted if the use of intervening variables were disallowed (Nicholas, 1984).

As Miller's position shows, it is not correct to say that all behaviorists avoid using intervening variables. As a general rule, however, cognitive psychologists tend to use intervening variables more freely and more prolifically than do behavioral psychologists. The debate over the use of intervening variables has gone on for decades, and we will not settle it here. My own position (though hardly original) is that the ultimate test of a psychological theory is its ability to predict behavior. If a theory can make accurate predictions about behaviors that were previously unpredictable, then the theory is useful, regardless of whether it contains any intervening variables. In this book, we will encounter many useful theories of each type.

PRACTICE QUIZ 1: CHAPTER 1

1. Aristotle's three principles of association were _____, _____, and _____.

2. Ebbinghaus's forgetting curve shows that the rate of forgetting in the first few minutes after studying is _____ than the rate of forgetting a week later.

3. Animals have been used as research subjects more often by _____ psychologists than by _____ psychologists.

4. According to John B. Watson, if psychology is to be a science it must focus on observable events, namely _____ and _____.

5. According to B. F. Skinner, theories in psychology should not include _____.

ANSWERS

1. contiguity, similarity, contrast 2. faster 3. behavioral, cognitive 4. stimuli, responses 5. intervening variables

BRAIN AND BEHAVIOR

What happens in the nervous system when two stimuli are repeatedly paired and a person begins to associate the two? How do our sensory systems allow it to recognize complex stimuli such as bricks, automobiles, or people's faces? Neuroscientists, who study the brain and nervous system, have attempted to answer these questions and many others like them, with varying degrees of progress so far. The rest of this chapter gives a brief overview of some of this research. To understand this material you need to have some understanding of how neurons (nerve cells) function, so the following section provides a short summary of the basic points.

The Basic Characteristics of Neurons

The nervous systems of all creatures on earth are composed of specialized cells called neurons, whose major function is to transmit information. The human brain contains many billions of neurons, and there are many additional neurons throughout the rest of the body. Although they vary greatly in size and shape, the basic components of all neurons, and the functions of those components, are quite similar.

Figure 1.6 shows the structure of a typical neuron. The three main components are the **cell body**, the **dendrites**, and the **axons**. The cell body contains the nucleus, which regulates the basic metabolic functions of the cell, such as the intake of oxygen and the release of carbon dioxide. In the transmission of information, the dendrites and the cell body are on the receptive side; that is, they are sensitive to certain chemicals called **transmitters** that are released by other neurons. When its dendrites and cell body receive sufficient stimulation, a neuron is said to "fire"—it exhibits a sudden change in electrical potential lasting only a few milliseconds (thousandths of a second). The more stimulation a neuron receives, the more rapidly it fires: It may fire only a few dozen times a second with low stimulation but several hundred times a second with high stimulation. The axons are involved on the transmission side. Each time a neuron fires, enlarged structures at the ends of the axons, the axon terminals, release a transmitter that may stimulate the dendrites of other neurons. Therefore, within a single neuron, the flow of activity typically begins

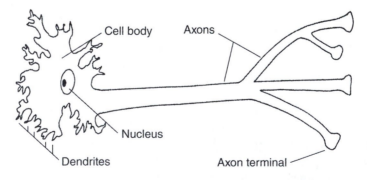

Figure 1.6 A schematic diagram of a neuron.

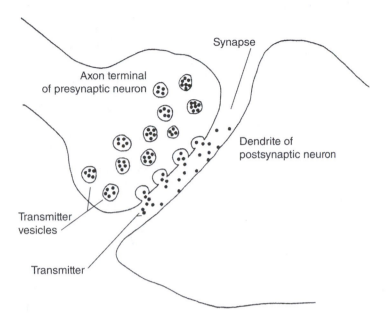

Figure 1.7 A schematic diagram of a synapse between two neurons. The chemical transmitter released by the axon terminal of the presynaptic neuron causes changes in the dendrite of the postsynaptic neuron that makes the neuron more likely to fire (in an excitatory synapse) or less likely to fire (in an inhibitory synapse).

with the dendrites, travels down the axons, and ends with release of transmitter by the axon terminals.

The term **synapse** refers to a small gap between the axon terminal of one neuron (called the *presynaptic neuron*) and the dendrite of another neuron (called the *postsynaptic neuron*). As Figure 1.7 shows, the presynaptic neuron releases its transmitter into the synapse. This transmitter can affect the postsynaptic neuron in one of two ways. In an *excitatory synapse*, the release of transmitter makes the postsynaptic neuron more likely to fire. In an *inhibitory synapse*, the release of transmitter makes the postsynaptic neuron less likely to fire. A single neuron may receive inputs, some excitatory and some inhibitory, from thousands of other neurons. At any moment, a neuron's firing rate reflects the combined influence of all its excitatory and inhibitory inputs.

Simple Sensations

One theme of the Associationists that has been uniformly supported by subsequent brain research is the hypothesis that our sensory systems analyze the complex stimulus environment that surrounds us by breaking it down into "simple sensations." The nervous system's only contact with the stimuli of the external environment comes through a variety of specialized neurons called **receptors**. Instead of dendrites that are sensitive to the transmitters of other neurons, receptors have structures that are sensitive to

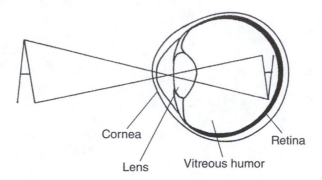

Figure 1.8 How light from an object in the environment enters the eye and is focused on the retina as an inverted image.

specific types of external stimuli. In the visual system, for example, receptors sensitive to light are located on the retina. As shown in Figure 1.8, light entering the eye is focused by the cornea and lens and is projected onto the retina. A miniature inverted image of the visual world is focused on the retina, which lines the inside surface of the eyeball. Some of the receptors on the retina are called cones (because of their shape), and different cones are especially sensitive to different colors in the spectrum of visible light. In the normal human eye, there are three classes of cones, which are most effectively stimulated by light in the red, green, and blue regions of the spectrum, respectively. A red-sensitive cone, for example, is most responsive to red light, but it will also exhibit a weaker response when stimulated by other colors in the red region of the spectrum, such as orange, violet, and yellow. Although we have only three types of cones, we can distinguish many subtle differences in color because they produce different patterns of activity in the three types of cones. A particular shade of yellow, for example, will produce a unique pattern of activity: The red and green cones may be activated to approximately the same extent, and the blue cones will exhibit very little activity. Since no other color will produce exactly the same pattern of activity in the cones, this pattern is the visual system's method of encoding the presence of a particular shade of yellow. We can think of the cones as receptors that decompose the complex visual world into what the Associationists called "simple sensations."

Similarly, all of our other senses have specialized receptors that are activated by simple features. The skin contains a variety of tactile receptors, some sensitive to pressure, some to pain, some to warmth, and some to cold. In the auditory system, single neurons are tuned to particular sound frequencies so that one neuron might be most sensitive to a tone with a frequency of 1,000 cycles/second. This neuron would be less sensitive to tones of higher or lower pitches. Regarding the sense of taste, most experts believe that all gustatory sensations can be decomposed into four simple tastes: sour, salty, bitter, and sweet (and possibly a fifth, savory). Some very exacting experiments by von Bekesy (1964, 1966) showed that individual taste receptors on the tongue are responsive to one and only one of these simple tastes. In summary, the evidence from sensory physiology is clear: All sensory systems begin by breaking down incoming stimuli into simple sensations.

Feature Detectors

Whereas our visual systems start by detecting the basic features of a stimulus—color, brightness, and location—each of us can recognize complex visual patterns, such as the face of a friend or a written word. The same is true of our other senses. We do not simply hear sounds of different pitches and intensities; we can perceive spoken sentences, automobile engines, and symphonies. When we eat, we do not just detect the basic tastes; we perceive the complex tastes of a pepperoni pizza or a strawberry sundae. How do our nervous systems start with simple sensations and arrive at these much more complex perceptions?

In their groundbreaking research, Hubel and Wiesel (1965, 1979) found neurons in the brain that can be called **feature detectors** because each neuron responded to a specific visual stimulus. Using an anesthetized monkey or cat, Hubel and Wiesel would isolate a single neuron somewhere in the visual system and record its electrical activity while presenting a wide range of visual stimuli (varying in color, size, shape, and location in the visual field) to the animal. The question Hubel and Wiesel wanted to answer was simple: What type of feature detector is this neuron? That is, what type of visual stimuli will make the neuron fire most rapidly?

Hubel and Wiesel found several different types of feature detectors in the visual cortex, an area in the back of the head, just beneath the skull. One class of cells, which they called **simple cells**, fired most rapidly when the visual stimulus was a line of a specific orientation, presented in a specific part of the visual field. For example, one simple cell might fire most rapidly in response to a line at a 45-degree angle from the horizontal. If the orientation of the line were changed to 30 or 60 degrees, the cell would fire less rapidly, and with further deviations from 45 degrees, the cell would respond less and less. Other simple cells responded to lines of other orientations.

It is not hard to imagine how neural signals from the rods and cones on the retina could combine to produce a line detector. Imagine that a simple cell in the cortex receives (through a chain of intervening neurons) excitatory inputs from individual receptors that are positioned in a row on the surface of the retina. A line of just the right angle will stimulate this entire row of retinal cells, and so there will be a very strong input to the simple cell in the visual cortex. Lines of other orientations will only stimulate a few of the retinal cells, so there will be less stimulation (and less response) of the simple cell in the visual cortex. So far, no one has actually managed to trace the "wiring diagram" for a simple cell, but it is clear from Hubel and Wiesel's results that some such integration of information must occur between the retina and the line-detecting cells in the visual cortex. Hubel and Wiesel also found more complex feature detectors in the visual cortex. Some cells responded only to shapes with two edges intersecting at a specific angle. For instance, one cell might respond to the corner of a rectangle—two edges forming a 90-degree angle. Another cell might be most responsive to part of a triangle—two edges forming an angle of, say, 45 degrees.

When Hubel and Wiesel (1963) examined cells in the visual cortex of newborn kittens with no previous visual experience, they found feature detectors similar to those found in adult cats (though the neurons of kittens were more sluggish in their response). This shows that individual neurons in a kitten's visual cortex are prewired to respond to specific visual features (lines, angles) before the kitten has seen any visual patterns whatsoever. A Nativist might call this an example of "innate knowledge": The newborn kitten already knows how to extract information from the visual world. However, feature detectors are also affected by experience. Blakemore and Cooper (1970) found that kittens raised in an environment with large vertical stripes on the walls had more vertical line detectors as adult cats, and those raised in an environment with horizontal lines had more horizontal line detectors. Therefore, both heredity and environment contribute to the types of visual feature detectors found in the adult animal.

The most complex visual detectors ever reported are cortical neurons in macaque monkeys that could be called "hand detectors" and "face detectors" (Desimone, Albright, Gross, & Bruce, 1984). For instance, the face detectors responded vigorously to human or monkey faces, whereas a variety of other stimuli (shapes, textures, pictures of other objects) evoked little or no response. Extrapolating from these remarkable findings, does this mean that the brain has individual neurons in the visual system for every complex stimulus one can recognize, such as the face of a friend or a 2010 Porsche? Current research suggests that the answer is "no." From studies on human visual perception, there is evidence from both infants and adults that large parts of the visual cortex are activated when people perceive human faces, and it is the entire pattern of brain activity that allows us to recognize a face (Nichols, Betts, & Wilson, 2010). And although human face perception may be different in some ways from other types of object perception, many different areas of the brain are involved when we perceive other objects as well (Konen & Kastner, 2008). Yet even with modern brain-imaging technology and extensive research on this topic, there is much that neuroscientists still do not understand about what takes place in the brain when a person recognizes a familiar object.

The Neuroscience of Learning

There are several possible ways in which the brain might change during learning. One possibility is that learning involves chemical changes at the level of individual synapses that alter flow of communication among neurons. A second possibility is that neurons may grow new axons and/or new dendrites as a result of a learning experience so that new synaptic connections are formed. A third possibility is that completely new neurons are grown during a learning experience. Let us examine each of these possibilities.

Chemical Changes

There is now plenty of evidence that some changes in the brain do not depend on the growth of new synapses but rather on chemical changes in already existing synapses. For example, say the neurons in a slice of rat brain tissue are given a brief burst of electrical stimulation; this action can produce long-lasting increases in the strength of existing connections between neurons. The increase in the strength of excitatory synapses as a result of electrical stimulation is called **long-term potentiation**, and the effect can last for weeks or months (Bliss & Lomo, 1973). Long-term potentiation has also been observed in human brain tissue removed during the course of surgical procedures (Chen et al., 1996) and even in the intact brains of humans (Heidegger, Krakow, & Ziemann, 2010). Long-term potentiation has been demonstrated in brain areas that are implicated in the storage of long-term memories, such as the hippocampus and the cerebral cortex. For this reason, some investigators believe that long-term potentiation may be a basic process through which the brain can change as a result of a learning experience. There is growing evidence that it may play a role in the learning of new associations (Wang & Morris, 2010).

What type of chemical changes could cause an increase in the strength of a synaptic connection? One possibility is that as a result of a learning experience, the axon terminal of the presynaptic neuron develops the capacity to release more transmitter. Another possibility is that the cell membrane of the postsynaptic neuron becomes more sensitive to the transmitter, so its response to the same amount of transmitter is greater. In experiments on long-term potentiation, researchers have found evidence that both presynaptic and postsynaptic changes may be involved (Bourne, Chirillo, & Harris, 2013; Meis, Endres, & Lessmann, 2012). It seems that the mammalian brain has at its disposal a number of different chemical mechanisms for altering the strengths of the connections between neurons.

Growth of New Synapses

There is now abundant evidence that learning experiences can lead to the growth of new synaptic connections between neurons. Some of the earliest evidence for the hypothesis that new synapses are developed as a result of experience came from studies in which animals were exposed to enriched living environments. Rosenzweig and his colleagues (Rosenzweig, 1966; Rosenzweig, Mollgaard, Diamond, & Bennet, 1972) placed young rats in two different environments to determine how early experience influences the development of the brain. Some rats were placed in an environment rich in stimuli and in possible learning experiences. These animals lived in groups of 10 to 12, and their cages contained many objects to play with and explore—ladders, wheels, platforms, mazes, and the like. Other rats were raised in a much more impoverished environment. Each animal lived in a separate, empty cage, and it could not see or touch other rats. These rats certainly had far fewer sensory and learning experiences. After the rats spent 80 days in these environments, Rosenzweig and colleagues found that the brains of the enriched rats were significantly heavier than those of impoverished rats. Differences in weight were especially pronounced in the cerebral cortex, which is thought to play an important role in the learning process. Many recent studies have found evidence that growth in specific parts of the cerebral cortex and other brain areas can result from a variety of different learning experiences, ranging from rats learning mazes (Lerch et al., 2011) to people learning to juggle (Draganski et al., 2004). It seems clear that learning experiences can produce growth in brain tissue.

What types of changes at the cellular level accompany these differences in overall brain size? Microscopic examinations have revealed a variety of changes in the brain tissue of rats exposed to enriched environments, including more branching of dendrites (indicating more synaptic connections between axons and dendrites) and synapses with larger surfaces. Other studies have found that exactly where neural changes take place in the brain depends on what the learning task involved. Spinelli, Jensen, and DiPrisco (1980) trained young kittens to flex one foreleg to avoid a shock to that leg. After a few brief sessions with this procedure, there was a substantial increase in the amount of dendritic branching in the area of the cortex that controlled the movement of that foreleg. Studies like this provide compelling evidence that relatively brief learning experiences can produce significant increases in the number, size, and complexity of synaptic connections.

Many neuroscientists believe that the growth of new dendrites and synaptic connections underlies the formation of long-term memories (Kolb & Gibb, 2008). In humans, studies have shown that dramatic arborization, or the branching of dendrites, occurs in the months before birth and in the first year of life. At the same time, other connections between neurons disappear. It is not clear how much of this change is due to maturation and how much to the infant's learning experiences. It appears, however, that as a child grows and learns, numerous new synaptic connections are formed and other unneeded connections are eliminated. These neural changes continue at least until the adolescent years (Huttenlocher, 1990).

Growth of New Neurons

In the past, it was generally believed that except before birth and possibly during early infancy, no new neurons can grow in the brains of animals. According to this view, all learning takes the form of changes in existing neurons (through chemical changes or synaptic growth), and any neurons that are lost due to illness or injury cannot be replaced. Today, however, there is convincing evidence that this traditional view of neural growth is incorrect and that new neurons continue to appear in the brains of adult mammals (Fuchs & Flügge, 2014). For example, research with adult macaque monkeys has found new neurons developing in several areas of the cerebral cortex (Gould, Reeves, Graziano, & Gross, 1999). The growth of new neurons, called **neurogenesis**, has also been observed in other species, and in some cases this growth appears to be related to learning experiences. For instance, in one experiment, some rats learned tasks that are known to involve the hippocampus, and other rats learned tasks that do not involve the hippocampus. For the first group of rats, after the learning period, new neurons were found in a nearby area of the brain that receives inputs from the hippocampus. For the second group of rats, no new neurons were found in this area. These results suggest that new neurons can grow during a learning experience and that exactly where they grow may depend on the specific type of learning that is involved (Gould, Beylin, Tanapat, Reeves, & Shors, 1999).

Studies of adult humans have shown that their brains also continue to produce new neurons and that neurogenesis may play an important part in the functioning of the adult brain. If a person's level of neurogenesis is unusually low, this may be related to various types of psychological disorders. Adults suffering from clinical depression have decreased levels of neurogenesis, and antidepressant medications appear to increase neurogenesis (Boldrini et al., 2013). After a brain injury, neurogenesis may help restore some level of brain functioning in the damaged area. There is evidence that after such an injury, new brain cells grow through mitosis (cell division), and they appear to develop some of the same physical characteristics and neural connections as the neurons that were damaged (Kokaia & Lindvall, 2003).

Where Are "Complex Ideas" Stored in the Brain?

Before concluding this brief survey of the physiological approach to learning, let us take one final look at James Mill's concept of complex ideas. What happens in the brain when a child learns the concept *house* or when a kitten learns to recognize and respond appropriately to a snake? Although the answer to this question is not yet known, a number of different possibilities have been proposed.

One hypothesis is that every learning experience produces neural changes that are distributed diffusely over many sections of the brain. This hypothesis was supported by some classic experiments by Karl Lashley (1950). After training rats to run through a maze, Lashley removed sections of the cerebral cortex (different sections for different rats) to see whether he could remove the memories of the maze. If he could, this would show where the memories about the maze were stored. However, Lashley's efforts to find the location of these memories were unsuccessful. When a small section of cortex was removed, this had no effect on a rat's maze performance, no matter which section was removed. When a larger section of cortex was removed, this caused a rat's performance in the maze to deteriorate, no matter which section was removed. Lashley concluded that memories are stored diffusely throughout the brain and that removing small sections of the brain will not remove the memory. Many later studies have also provided support for the view that large sections of the brain undergo change during simple learning experiences and that many brain regions are also involved when these learning experiences are remembered at a later time (Shimamura, 2014; Tomie, Grimes, & Pohorecky, 2008).

A very different hypothesis is that the information about individual concepts or ideas is localized, or stored in small, specific sections of the brain. For example, some psychologists have suggested that the cerebral cortex may contain many unused or dormant neurons. Through an animal's learning experiences, one (or a few) of these dormant neurons might come to respond selectively to a particular complex object (Konorski, 1967). To take a simple example, after an animal has had experience with a complex object such as an apple, some cortical neuron might develop excitatory inputs from detectors responsive to the apple's red color, roughly spherical shape, specific odor, and other characteristics. In this way, an animal that at birth had no complex idea of an apple might develop the ability to recognize apples as a result of its experience.

Some evidence supporting this idea came from the pioneering research of Penfield (1959), who electrically stimulated areas of the cerebral cortex of human patients during brain surgery. When Penfield stimulated small areas of the cortex, his patients, who were anesthetized but awake, reported a variety of vivid sensations, such as hearing a specific piece of music or experiencing the sights and sounds of a circus. Although it might be tempting to conclude that the electrical stimulation had triggered a site where specific memories of the past were stored, Penfield's findings can be interpreted in many ways, and their significance is not clear.

Better evidence for localized memories comes from reports of people who suffered damage to small sections of the brain as a result of an accident or stroke. Brain injury can, of course, produce a wide range of psychological or physical problems, but in a few individuals the result was a loss of very specific information. For example, one man had difficulty naming any fruit or vegetable, whereas he had no trouble identifying any other types of objects (Hart, Berndt, & Caramazza, 1985). Another person could not name objects typically found in a room, such as furniture and walls (Yamadori & Albert, 1973). Another could no longer remember the names of well-known celebrities, but he had no problem with the names of other famous people, such as historical and literary figures (Lucchelli, Muggia, & Spinnler, 1997). There is also evidence from brain-imaging studies that specific but different areas of the brain are activated when people look at pictures of animals versus pictures of tools (Chouinard & Goodale, 2010). These findings suggest that specific concepts are stored in specific areas of the brain and that concepts belonging to a single category are stored close together.

The debate over whether the neural representation of complex ideas is localized or distributed has gone on for many years, and it has not yet been resolved. It is possible that both hypotheses are partially correct, with some types of learning producing changes in fairly specific parts of the brain and others producing changes over large portions of the brain. Modern-day neuroscientists continue to investigate the question asked by James Mill over a century and a half ago: What are complex ideas, and how does the human brain acquire them and retain them? If and when neuroscientists eventually discover exactly how the brain stores information about complex concepts and ideas, this will be a milestone in the psychology of learning.

PRACTICE QUIZ 2: CHAPTER 1

1. In communication between neurons, a chemical transmitter is released by the _____ of one neuron and received by the _____ of another neuron.
2. There are three types of cones in the human retina that respond to three different types of stimuli: _____, _____, and _____.
3. The "simple cells" in the visual cortex found by Hubel and Wiesel respond specifically to _____.
4. Three main types of changes that can occur in the brain as a result of a learning experience are _____, _____, and _____.
5. By removing different parts of the brains of rats after they learned a maze, Lashley concluded that memories are stored _____.

ANSWERS

1. axon terminals, dendrites 2. red, green, and blue 3. lines of specific orientations 4. chemical changes, growth of new synapses, growth of new neurons 5. diffusely throughout the brain

---

SUMMARY

The field of learning is concerned with both how people and animals learn and how their long-term behavior changes as a result of this learning. The earliest ideas about learning were developed by the Associationists, who proposed principles about how the brain forms associations between different thoughts and ideas. Aristotle proposed the principles of contiguity, similarity, and contrast. James Mill developed a theory of how two or more simple ideas can be combined to form more complex ideas. Hermann Ebbinghaus conducted some of the first studies on learning and memory using lists of nonsense syllables as his stimuli and repeating the lists to himself until he memorized them. He demonstrated several basic principles of learning, including contiguity, recency, and overlearning.

Two main approaches to studying learning are the behavioral and cognitive approaches. Behavioral psychologists have often used animal subjects because they are interested in general principles of learning that are shared by many species, because animals are less complex than human subjects, and because animal environments can be controlled to a greater degree. Critics of animal research have questioned whether we can generalize from animals to people, and they have raised ethical concerns about the use of animal subjects. Behaviorists have argued that psychology should deal only with observable events, whereas cognitive psychologists regularly use intervening variables such as hunger, memory, and attention. B. F. Skinner argued that intervening variables make scientific theories more complex than necessary. However, Neal Miller showed that if a theory includes many independent variables and many dependent variables, then using intervening variables can actually simplify a theory.

Specialized sensory neurons in the eyes, ears, and other sense organs respond to very simple sensory properties, much as the Associationists suggested. Neurons in the eye respond to specific colors, and neurons in the ear respond to specific pitches of sound. In the brain, the inputs from many sensory neurons are often combined, so that individual neurons may respond to features such as edges, angles, and corners of a visual stimulus. How the nervous system combines all this information so that we can perceive and identify objects in our environments is still not well understood, but there is evidence that object recognition involves patterns of brain activity across large sections of the brain.

Neuroscientists assume that whenever an individual learns something new, there is a physical change somewhere in the brain or nervous system. Some axon terminals may begin to produce neurotransmitters in greater quantities, some dendrites may become more sensitive to existing neurotransmitters, new synapses may form between neurons, and completely new neurons may grow. There is solid evidence for each of these different types of changes. Lashley's early research with rats suggested that many different sections of the brain are changed during a simple learning experience. However, research on humans with brain injuries suggests that some types of information may be stored in fairly small, specific areas of the brain.

Review Questions

1. Describe Aristotle's three principles of association and some of the additional principles proposed by Brown. Illustrate these principles by giving some examples from your own life of words or concepts that you tend to associate.

2. What procedure did Ebbinghaus use to study memory? How did his results offer evidence for the principles of frequency, recency, and contiguity?

3. What are some of the advantages and disadvantages to using animals as subjects in research on learning?

4. Why did B. F. Skinner believe that intervening variables should not be used in psychological theories? In your opinion, what is the biggest disadvantage of using intervening variables? What do you consider the biggest advantage?

5. Describe some research results that provide evidence that learning can result in chemical changes in the brain, the growth of new synaptic connections, and the growth of new neurons.

REFERENCES

Aristotle. (ca. 350 B.C.). De memoria et reminiscentia. In J.A. Smith (Trans.) & W.D. Ross (Ed.), *The works of Aristotle* (Vol. 3). Oxford: Clarendon Press. (English translation published 1931.).

Baldwin, E. (1993). The case for animal research in psychology. *Journal of Social Issues, 49*, 121–131.

Blakemore, C., & Cooper, G.F. (1970). Development of the brain depends on the visual environment. *Nature, 228*, 477–478.

Bliss, T.V.P., & Lomo, T. (1973). Long-lasting potentiation of synaptic transmission in the dentate area of the anaesthetized rabbit following stimulation of the perforant path. *Journal of Physiology, 232*, 331–356.

Boldrini, M., Santiago, A.N., Hen, R., Dwork, A.J., Rosoklija, G.B., Tamir, H., & . . . Mann, J.J. (2013). Hippocampal granule neuron number and denate gyrus volume in antidepressant-treated and untreated major depression. *Neuropsychopharmacology, 38*, 1068–1077.

Bourne, J.N., Chirillo, M.A., & Harris, K.M. (2013). Presynaptic ultrastructural plasticity along CA3→CA1 axons during long-term potentiation in mature hippocampus. *The Journal of Comparative Neurology, 521*, 3898–3912.

Brennan, P., Clark, R., & Mock, D. (2014). Time to step up: Defending basic science and animal behaviour. *Animal Behaviour, 94*, 101–105.

Brown, T. (1820). *Lectures on the philosophy of the human mind* (Vols. 1 and 2). Edinburgh, UK: James Ballantyne.

Chen, W.R., Lee, S.H., Kato, K., Spencer, D.D., Shepherd, G.M., & Williamson, A. (1996). Long-term modifications of synaptic efficacy in the human inferior and middle temporal cortex. *Proceedings of the National Academy of Sciences, 93*, 8011–8015.

Chouinard, P.A., & Goodale, M.A. (2010). Category specific neural processing for naming pictures of animals and naming pictures of tools: An ALE meta-analysis. *Neuropsychologia, 48*, 409–418.

Desimone, R., Albright, T.D., Gross, C.G., & Bruce, C. (1984). Stimulus-selective properties of inferior temporal neurons in the macaque. *Journal of Neuroscience, 4*, 2051–2062.

Draganski, B., Gaser, C., Busch, V., Schuierer, G., Bogdahn, U., & May, A. (2004). Neuroplasticity: Changes in grey matter induced by training. *Nature, 427*, 311–312.

Ebbinghaus, H. (1885). *Memory*. Leipzig, Germany: Duncker.

Fuchs, E., & Flügge, G. (2014). Adult neuroplasticity: More than 40 years of research. *Neural Plasticity*, Article ID 541870.

Gould, E., Beylin, A., Tanapat, P., Reeves, A., & Shors, T.J. (1999). Learning enhances adult neurogenesis in the hippocampal formation. *Nature Neuroscience, 2*, 260–265.

Gould, E., Reeves, A.J., Graziano, M.S., & Gross, C.G. (1999). Neurogenesis in the neocortex of adult primates. *Science, 286*, 548–552.

Hart, J., Berndt, R.S., & Caramazza, A. (1985). Category-specific naming deficit following cerebral infarction. *Nature, 316*, 439–440.

Heidegger, T., Krakow, K., & Ziemann, U. (2010). Effects of antiepileptic drugs on associative LTP-like plasticity in human motor cortex. *European Journal of Neuroscience, 32*, 1215–1222.

Hubel, D.H., & Wiesel, T.N. (1963). Receptive fields of cells in striate cortex of very young, visually inexperienced kittens. *Journal of Neurophysiology, 26*, 994–1002.

Hubel, D.H., & Wiesel, T.N. (1965). Binocular interaction in striate cortex of kittens reared with artificial squint. *Journal of Neurophysiology, 28*, 1041–1059.

Hubel, D.H., & Wiesel, T.N. (1979). Brain mechanisms in vision. *Scientific American, 241*, 150–162.

Huttenlocher, P.R. (1990). Morphometric study of human cerebral cortex development. *Neuropsychologia, 28*, 517–527.

Kant, I. (1781/1881). *Kritik der reinen Vernunft*. Riga [*Critique of pure reason*]. (F. Max Muller, Trans.). London: Henry G. Bohn.

Kokaia, Z., & Lindvall, O. (2003). Neurogenesis after ischaemic brain insults. *Current Opinion in Neurobiology, 13*, 127–132.

Kolb, B., & Gibb, R. (2008). Principles of neuroplasticity and behavior. In D.T. Stuss, G. Winocur, & I.H. Robertson (Eds.), *Cognitive neurorehabilitation: Evidence and application* (2nd ed., pp. 6–21). New York: Cambridge University Press.

Konen, C.S., & Kastner, S. (2008). Two hierarchically organized neural systems for object information in human visual cortex. *Nature Neuroscience, 11*, 224–231.

Konorski, J. (1967). *Integrative activity of the brain: An interdisciplinary approach*. Chicago, IL: University of Chicago Press.

Lashley, K.S. (1950). In search of the engram: Physiological mechanisms in animal behavior. In J.F. Danielli & R. Brown (Eds.), *Symposium of the Society for Experimental Biology* (pp. 454–482). Cambridge, MA: Cambridge University Press.

Lerch, J.P., Yiu, A.P., Martinez-Canabal, A., Pekar, T., Bohbot, V.D., Frankland, P.W., & . . . Sled, J.G. (2011). Maze training in mice induces MRI-detectable brain shape changes specific to the type of learning. *NeuroImage, 54*, 2086–2095.

Locke, J. (1690). *An essay concerning humane understanding: In four books*. London: Thomas Bassett.

Lucchelli, F., Muggia, S., & Spinnler, H. (1997). Selective proper name anomia: A case involving only contemporary celebrities. *Cognitive Neuropsychology, 14*, 881–900.

Meis, S., Endres, T., & Lessmann, V. (2012). Postsynaptic BDNF signalling regulates long-term potentiation at thalamo-amygdala afferents. *Journal of Physiology, 590*, 193–208.

Mill, J. (1829). *Analysis of the phenomena of the human mind*. London: Baldwin & Cradock.

Mill, J.S. (1843). *A system of logic, ratiocinative and inductive, being a connected view of the principles of evidence, and the methods of scientific investigation*. London: J. W. Parker.

Miller, N.E. (1959). Liberalization of basic S-R concepts: Extensions to conflict behavior, motivation, and social learning. In S. Koch (Ed.), *Psychology: A study of a science* (Vol. 2, pp. 196–292). New York: McGraw-Hill.

Miller, N.E. (1985). The value of behavioral research with animals. *American Psychologist, 40*, 423–440.

Nicholas, J.M. (1984). Lessons from the history of science. *Behavioral and Brain Sciences, 7*, 530–531.

Nichols, D.F., Betts, L.R., & Wilson, H.R. (2010). Decoding of faces and face components in face-sensitive human visual cortex. *Frontiers in Perception Science, 1*(29), 1–13.

Penfield, W. (1959). The interpretive cortex. *Science, 129*, 1719–1725.

Regan, T. (1983). *The case for animal rights*. Berkeley, CA: University of California Press.

Rosenzweig, M.R. (1966). Environmental complexity, cerebral change, and behavior. *American Psychologist, 21*, 321–332.

Rosenzweig, M.R., Mollgaard, K., Diamond, M.C., & Bennet, T.E.L. (1972). Negative as well as positive synaptic changes may store memory. *Psychological Review, 79*, 93–96.

Shimamura, A.P. (2014). Remembering the past: Neural substrates underlying episodic encoding and retrieval. *Current Directions in Psychological Science, 23*, 257–263.

Skinner, B.F. (1938). *The behavior of organisms*. New York: Appleton-Century-Crofts.

Skinner, B.F. (1950). Are theories of learning necessary? *Psychological Review, 57*, 193–216.

Spinelli, D.H., Jensen, F.E., & DiPrisco, G.V. (1980). Early experience effect on dendritic branching in normally reared kittens. *Experimental Neurology, 62*, 1–11.

Tomie, A., Grimes, K.L., & Pohorecky, L.A. (2008). Behavioral characteristics and neurobiological substrates shared by Pavlovian sign-tracking and drug abuse. *Brain Research Reviews, 58*, 121–135.

von Bekesy, G. (1964). Sweetness produced electrically on the tongue and its relation to taste theories. *Journal of Applied Physiology, 19*, 1105–1113.

von Bekesy, G. (1966). Taste theories and the chemical stimulation of single papillae. *Journal of Applied Physiology, 21*, 1–9.

Wang, S.H., & Morris, R.G.M. (2010). Hippocampal–neocortical interactions in memory formation, consolidation, and reconsolidation. *Annual Review of Psychology, 61*, 49–79.

Watson, J.B. (1919). *Psychology from the standpoint of a behaviorist.* Philadelphia, PA: Lippincott.

Yamadori, A., & Albert, M.L. (1973). Word category aphasia. *Cortex, 9*, 112–125.

CHAPTER 2

Innate Behavior Patterns and Habituation

When any animal is born, it is already endowed with a variety of complex abilities. Its immediate survival depends on the ability to breathe and to pump blood through its veins. If it is a mammal, it has the ability to regulate its temperature within narrow limits. If its survival depends on the ability to flee from predators, it may start to walk and run within minutes after birth. Newborn animals are also equipped with a range of sensory capacities. One major purpose of this chapter is to provide examples of the types of behavioral abilities that an animal may already possess as it enters the world. There are good reasons for examining innate behavior patterns in a book about learning. First, many learned behaviors are derivatives, extensions, or variations of innate behaviors. Second, many of the features of learned behaviors (e.g., their control by environmental stimuli, their mechanisms of temporal sequencing) have parallels in inborn behavior patterns. Besides surveying different types of innate behaviors, this chapter will also examine the phenomenon of habituation, which is often said to be the simplest type of learning.

One characteristic that is common to many behaviors, both learned and unlearned, is that they appear to be purposive, or goal directed. As we will see, this is true of some of our most primitive reflexes as well as our most complex skills. For this reason, it will be useful to begin this chapter with some concepts from **control systems theory**, a branch of science that deals with goal-directed behaviors in both living creatures and inanimate objects.

CHARACTERISTICS OF GOAL-DIRECTED SYSTEMS

Control systems theory provides a general framework for analyzing a wide range of goal-directed systems. The terminology used here is based on the work of McFarland (1971). A simple example of an inanimate goal-directed system is a house's heating system. The goal of the heating system is to keep the house temperature above some minimum level, say 65°F. If the house temperature drops below 65°F, the heating system "spontaneously" springs into action, starting the furnace. Once the temperature goal is reached, the heating system turns off. Of course, we know there is nothing magical about this process. The activity of the heating system is controlled by a thermostat, which relies on the expansion and contraction of metal components to open or close a switch that turns the furnace off or on.

The thermostat is an example of a fundamental concept in control systems theory, the **comparator**. As shown in Figure 2.1, a comparator receives two types of input, called the *reference input* and the *actual input*. The reference input is often not a physical entity but a conceptual one (the temperature that, when reached, will be just enough to open the switch and stop the furnace). On the other hand, the actual input measures some actual physical characteristic of the present environment, in this case, the air temperature in the vicinity of the thermostat.

Any comparator has rules that it follows to determine, based on the current actual input and reference input, what its output will be. In the case of a thermostat, the output is an on/off

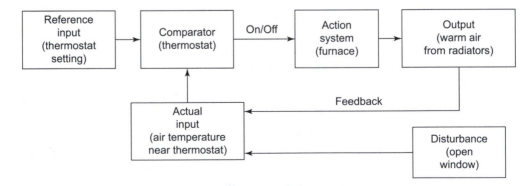

Figure 2.1 Concepts of control systems theory as applied to a house's heating system.

command to the furnace, which is an example of an *action system*. The rules that the thermostat follows might be these: (1) If the air temperature becomes one degree lower than the reference input, turn on the furnace; (2) if the air temperature becomes one degree higher than the reference input, turn off the furnace. With a setting of 65°F, these rules would keep the air temperature between 64°F and 66°F.

The product of the action system is simply called the *output*—the entry of warm air from the radiators in this example. As Figure 2.1 shows, the output of the action system feeds back and affects the actual input to the comparator. For this reason, such a goal-directed system is frequently called a *feedback system* or a *closed-loop system*. However, the actual input can also be affected by other factors, such as the *disturbance* depicted in Figure 2.1, an open window. A window open on a cold day can disrupt this feedback system by keeping the house cold even if the furnace runs continuously.

This example illustrates six of the most important concepts of control systems theory: comparator, reference input, actual input, action system, output, and disturbance. We will encounter many examples of goal-directed behaviors in this book, and it will often be useful to try to identify the different components of the feedback loop in these examples. The next section is the first of many in this text that will make use of the concepts of control systems theory.

REFLEXES

A **reflex** is a stereotyped pattern of movement of a part of the body that can be reliably elicited by presenting the appropriate stimulus. You are probably familiar with the patellar (knee-jerk) reflex: If a person's leg is supported so that the foot is off the ground and the lower leg can swing freely, a light tap of a hammer just below the kneecap will evoke a small kicking motion from the leg. As with all reflexes, the patellar reflex involves an innate connection between a stimulus and a response. The stimulus in this example is the tapping of the tendon below the kneecap, and the response is the kicking motion.

A normal newborn child displays a variety of reflexes. A nipple placed in the child's mouth will elicit a sucking response. If the sole of the foot is pricked with a pin, the child's knees will flex, pulling the feet away from the painful stimulus. If an adult places a finger in the child's palm, the child's fingers will close around it in a grasping reflex. Some of the newborn's reflexes disappear with age. Others, such as the constriction of the pupils and the closing of the eyes in response to a bright light or coughing in response to a throat irritation, persist throughout life.

If you ever accidentally placed your hand on a hot stove, you probably exhibited a flexion reflex—a rapid withdrawal of the hand caused by a bending of the arm at the elbow. The response is very rapid because the association between sensory and motor neurons occurs directly in the spinal cord. Figure 2.2 depicts a cross section of the spinal cord and some of the neural machinery involved in this reflex. The hand contains sensory neurons sensitive to pain, and their lengthy axons travel all the way into the spinal cord before synapsing with other neurons. In the flexion reflex, one or more small neurons, called *interneurons*, separate the sensory neurons from motor neurons. The motor neurons have cell bodies within the spinal cord, and their axons exit through the front of the spinal cord, travel back down the arm, and synapse with individual muscle fibers in the arm. When excited, the muscle fibers

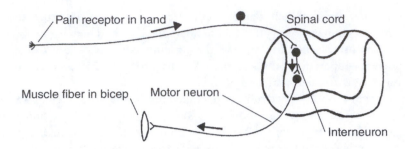

Figure 2.2 A cross section of the spinal cord, along with the components of the spinal withdrawal reflex.

contract, thereby producing the response. The physiology of this reflex is sometimes called the **spinal reflex arc**, after the shape of the path of neural excitation shown in Figure 2.2. Not one but many such sensory neurons, interneurons, and motor neurons are involved in producing the reflexive response.

There is more to the flexion reflex than the simple stimulus–response relation shown in Figure 2.2, however. Even this basic reflex is actually a simple feedback system. Within the muscles of the arm are structures called stretch receptors, which serve as the comparators of the feedback system. We will not go into detail about how this happens, but the stretch receptors compare (1) the goal or reference input—the commands sent from the motor neurons to the muscle fibers telling them to contract—and (2) the actual amount that the muscles have contracted. Just because some motor neurons have sent their commands to the muscle, this does not guarantee that the arm is safely withdrawn from the dangerous object. There might be a disturbance—an obstruction that impedes the movement of the arm. If the muscles have not contracted sufficiently for any such reason, the stretch receptors begin to stimulate the motor neurons (which in turn stimulate the muscle fibers more vigorously), and this stimulation continues until the contraction is completed. In short, the comparators (the stretch receptors) continue to stimulate the action system (the motor neurons and muscle fibers) until the goal (a successful muscle contraction) is achieved. Feedback can play a crucial role in even the simplest reflexive behaviors.

TROPISMS

Whereas a reflex is the stereotyped movement of a part of the body, a **tropism** is a movement or change in orientation of the entire animal. The first to study tropisms was Jacques Loeb (1900), who called tropisms forced movements to suggest that no intelligence, will, or choice was involved. Later researchers (e.g., Fraenkel & Gunn, 1940) grouped tropisms into two major categories: kineses (plural of **kinesis**) and taxes (plural of **taxis**).

Kineses

A common example of a kinesis is the humidity-seeking behavior of the wood louse. This creature, though actually a small crustacean, resembles an insect, and it spends most of its time under a rock or a log in the forest. The wood louse must remain in humid areas in order to survive; if the air is too dry, it will die of dehydration in a matter of hours. Fortunately for the wood louse, nature has provided it with a simple yet effective technique for finding and remaining in moist areas. To study the wood louse's strategy, Fraenkel and Gunn (1940) placed several wood lice in the center of a chamber in which the air was moist at one end and dry at the other. They found that the wood lice usually kept walking when they were in the dry end of the chamber, but they frequently stopped for long periods of time in the moist end. As a result, wood lice tended to congregate in the moist end of the chamber.

What distinguishes a kinesis from a taxis is that in a kinesis the direction of the movement is random in relation to a stimulus. The wood louse does not head directly toward a moist area or away from a dry one because it has no means of sensing the humidity of a distant location—it can only sense the humidity of its present location. Nevertheless, its tendency to keep moving when in a dry area and stop when in a moist area is generally successful in keeping the creature alive. Kineses can also help to keep creatures away from predators. For instance, one species of slugs displays rapid movement when exposed to a chemical produced by a predatory beetle and less movement when the chemical is not present (Armsworth, Bohan, Powers, Glen, & Symondson, 2005).

The wood louse's humidity-seeking behavior is another example of a feedback system. Although we do not know exactly how the wood louse measures humidity, its behavior tells us that it must have a comparator that can detect the actual input (current humidity) and compare it to the reference input (the goal of high humidity). The action system in this case is the creature's locomotion system, that is, the motor neurons, muscles, and legs that allow it to move about. Locomotion is, of course, the output of this action system, but there is no guarantee that locomotion will lead to the goal of high humidity. The wood louse may move about incessantly if it finds itself in a dry location, but if there are no humid areas nearby, the goal of high humidity will not be reached.

Taxes

Unlike kineses, in a taxis, the direction of movement bears some relationship to the location of the stimulus. One example of a taxis is a maggot's movement away from any bright light source. If a bright light is turned on to the maggot's right, it will promptly turn to the left and move in a fairly straight line away from the light. The maggot accomplishes this directional movement by using a light-sensitive receptor at its head end. As the maggot moves, its head repeatedly swings left and right, and this oscillating movement allows it to compare the brightness of light in various directions and to move toward the direction where the light is less intense.

A more sophisticated taxis is exhibited by the ant, which can use the sun as a navigational aid when traveling to or from its home. On a journey away from home, the ant travels in a straight path by keeping the sun at a constant angle to its direction of motion. To return home, the ant changes the angle by 180 degrees. The ant's reliance on the sun can be demonstrated by providing it with an artificial sun that the experimenter can control. If this light source is gradually moved, the ant's direction of travel will change to keep its orientation constant with respect to the light (Schneirla, 1933).

SEQUENCES OF BEHAVIOR

So far we have discussed innate behaviors that consist of either a brief movement or a continuous series of adjustments. The innate behavior patterns we will now examine are more complex, for they consist of a series of different movements performed in an orderly sequence.

Fixed Action Patterns

A **fixed action pattern** is a sequence of behaviors that has the following characteristics: (1) It is a part of the repertoire of all members of a species, and it may be unique to that species; (2) suitable experiments have confirmed that the animal's ability to perform the behavior is not a result of prior learning experiences; and (3) the behaviors occur in a rigid order regardless of whether they are appropriate in a particular context. Once a fixed action pattern is started, it will continue to completion.

As an example of a fixed action pattern, Eibl-Eibesfeldt (1975) described the nut-burying behavior of a particular species of squirrel:

> The squirrel *Sciurus vulgaris L.* buries nuts in the ground each fall, employing a quite stereotyped sequence of movement. It picks a nut, climbs down to the ground, and searches for a place at the bottom of a tree trunk or a large boulder. At the base of such a conspicuous landmark it will scratch a hole by means of alternating movements of the forelimbs and place the nut in it. Then the nut is rammed into place with rapid thrusts of its snout, covered with dirt by sweeping motions and tamped down with the forepaws.
>
> (p. 23)

Although all members of the species exhibit this behavior pattern, this does not prove that the behavior is innate. Each squirrel may learn how to bury nuts by watching its parents early in life. To determine whether the behavior pattern is innate, Eibl-Eibesfeldt conducted a deprivation experiment in which all possible means of learning the behavior were removed. A squirrel was separated from its parents at birth and raised in isolation so that it had no opportunity to observe other squirrels burying nuts (or doing anything else, for that matter). In addition, the squirrel received only liquid food and it lived on a solid floor, so it had no experience in handling food or in digging or burying objects in the ground. The animal was kept well fed so that it had little chance of discovering that storing away food for a time of need is a good strategy. When the squirrel was full grown, Eibl-Eibesfeldt finally gave it some nuts, one at a time. At first the squirrel ate the nuts until apparently satiated. When given additional nuts, it did not drop them but carried them around in its mouth as it searched about the cage. It seemed to be attracted by vertical objects, such as a corner of the cage, where it might drop the nut. Obviously, it could not dig a hole in the floor, but it would scratch at the floor with its forepaws, push the nut into the corner with its snout, and make the same covering and tamping-down motions seen in the burying sequence of a wild squirrel. This careful experiment demonstrates conclusively that the squirrel's nut-burying repertoire is innate. The caged

Figure 2.3 An oystercatcher attempts to roll a supernormal egg back to its nest.

squirrel's scratching, covering, and tamping-down motions in the absence of dirt show how the components of a fixed action pattern will occur in their usual place in the sequence even when they serve no function.

It usually takes a fairly specific stimulus, called a **sign stimulus**, to trigger a fixed action pattern. In the case of the squirrel, the sign stimulus is clearly the nut, but without further experiments we cannot tell which features—its size, shape, color, and so on—are essential ingredients for eliciting the response. For other fixed action patterns, systematic investigation has revealed which features of a stimulus are important and which are irrelevant. In humans, Provine (1989) has found evidence that contagious yawning (the tendency to yawn when someone else yawns) is a fixed action pattern that may occur if we see the entire face of a yawning person. Seeing only the yawner's eyes or only the mouth is not enough to elicit contagious yawning.

A surprising finding is that sometimes an unrealistic stimulus can elicit a stronger response than the actual sign stimulus itself. One example is provided by the oyster-catcher, a bird that lays white eggs with brown spots. If one of its eggs rolls out of its nest, the bird will retrieve it with stereotyped head and neck movements. However, if given a choice between one of its own eggs and a replica that is four times as large, it prefers this supernormal stimulus to the normal one and strains to bring this "egg" to its nest (Figure 2.3).

Reaction Chains

Whereas fixed action patterns continue until completion once started, in a **reaction chain** the progression from one behavior to the next depends on the presence of the appropriate stimulus. If the stimulus is not present, the chain of behaviors will be interrupted. On the other hand, if a stimulus for a behavior in the middle of a chain is presented at the outset, the earlier behaviors will be omitted.

An interesting example of a reaction chain is provided by the hermit crab. The hermit crab has no shell of its own; instead, it lives in the empty shells of mollusks. Frequently during its life, the hermit crab grows too large for its present shell and must find a larger one. Reese (1963) identified at least eight separate behaviors that usually occur in a sequence as a crab searches for and selects a new shell. A crab that needs a new shell exhibits a high level of locomotion. Eventually the crab spots a shell visually, at which point it approaches the shell and touches it. The crab grasps the shell with its two front legs, then climbs on top of it. Its cheliped (claw) is used to feel the texture of the surface— a rough texture is preferred. The crab then climbs down and rotates the shell in its legs, exploring the external surface. When the aperture of the shell is located, this too is explored by inserting the cheliped as far as possible. If there is sand or other debris in the aperture, it is removed. Once the aperture is clear, the crab turns around and inserts its abdomen deeply into the shell and then withdraws it, evidently to determine whether the size of the interior is acceptable. If the shell is suitable, the crab turns the shell upright, enters it once again, and then goes on its way.

The steps of this response chain are diagrammed in Figure 2.4, which emphasizes a key point about reaction chains: Each response usually produces the stimulus for the next

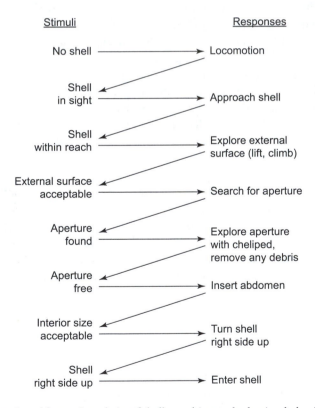

Figure 2.4 The hermit crab's reaction chain of shell searching and selecting behaviors. The behaviors form a chain because each successive behavior usually leads to the stimulus for the next behavior in the chain.

response in the chain. For instance, the first response, locomotion, eventually leads to the sight of a shell, which is the stimulus for the second response, approach. The response of approach brings the shell within reach, which is the stimulus for the third response, lifting, and so on. However, unlike fixed action patterns, the behaviors of a reaction chain do not always occur in the full and complete sequence. The sequence can stop at any point if the stimulus required for the next step is not there. For example, Reese (1963) found that shells filled with plastic would elicit the first five behaviors in Figure 2.4, but since the aperture was not open, the sixth behavior did not occur and the crab would eventually walk away. Conversely, the beginning steps of the sequence may be omitted if the stimulus for a behavior in the middle of the sequence occurs. When crabs were presented with a suitable shell with the aperture directly in front of them, they would often omit the first five behaviors of the sequence and proceed with the last. This dependence on external stimulus support makes reaction chains more variable, but at the same time more adaptable, than fixed action patterns.

INNATE HUMAN ABILITIES AND PREDISPOSITIONS

Although human beings have a variety of reflexes, plus a few fixed action patterns and other inborn behaviors, these innate responses certainly constitute a very small portion of what we do. As noted in Chapter 1, almost all of our daily behaviors are products of our learning experiences. Because learning plays such a large role in human behavior, some philosophers, such as the British Empiricists, have maintained that all human behavior is based on prior learning. (Recall John Locke's statement that the mind of a child at birth is a *tabula rasa*, or blank slate.) This viewpoint about the all-important role of experience was shared by many psychologists, including the behaviorist John B. Watson (1925), whose bold statement about the importance of upbringing is often quoted:

> Give me a dozen healthy infants, well-formed, and my own specified world to bring them up in and I'll guarantee to take any one at random and train him to become any type of specialist I might select—doctor, lawyer, artist, merchant-chief, and yes, even beggar-man and thief, regardless of his talents, penchants, tendencies, abilities, vocations, and race of his ancestors. I am going beyond the facts and I admit it, but so have advocates of the contrary, and they have been doing it for thousands of years.
>
> (p. 82)

Watson believed that the environment could play such a dominant role in determining what type of adult a child will become because he thought heredity had little or nothing to do with how people behave. In *The Blank Slate*, Steven Pinker (2002) argued that this point of view, though widely held in modern society, is incorrect and that heredity plays a much larger role than is commonly assumed. Pinker surveyed evidence from various areas of scientific research, including neurophysiology, genetics, psychology, and anthropology, to support his contention that all human beings have in common a large set of inborn abilities, tendencies, and predispositions, which collectively might be called "human nature." He maintained that the human brain is not simply a batch of uniform, undifferentiated neurons that are waiting to be shaped by whatever the environment presents. He reviewed evidence that neurons in different parts of the brain are specialized to perform certain functions or to respond to the environment in certain preestablished ways.

As one example, it is well known that certain parts of the human brain play a critical role in our ability to use language. A section of the cerebral cortex called Wernicke's area is essential for language comprehension: If this area is damaged through accident or illness, a person cannot understand spoken language. Another area of the cerebral cortex, Broca's area, is necessary for speech production, and if this area is damaged, a person loses the ability to speak in coherent sentences. Pinker maintains that the presence of neurons specifically designed to respond to human speech is what allows young children to learn language so easily. Although chimpanzees, dolphins, and a few other species can be taught to use human-like language to a certain degree (as described in Chapter 10), no other species comes close to what young children can do.

A strategy used by Pinker (and by other scientists) to support the claim that a particular characteristic of human beings is innate is to demonstrate that this characteristic is found in people everywhere on earth. We cannot conduct deprivation experiments with people as Eibl-Eibesfeldt (1975) did with a squirrel, but we can demonstrate that people living in vastly different cultures and environments all exhibit a particular characteristic. There are many different languages on earth, but all human societies have verbal language, and all human languages have nouns, verbs, adjectives, and adverbs. Although different languages use different word orders, there are certain commonalities in the way sentences are structured (Baker, 2001). Children of all cultures babble before they learn to speak, and even deaf children babble at an early age (Lenneberg, 1967). These and other cross-cultural universals have been used as evidence for an innate human ability to acquire language. However, some researchers have argued that upon closer inspection, the similarities across human languages are not really as universal as they may appear (Evans & Levinson, 2009), and this issue has not been settled.

One other aspect of human behavior that may be innate is the range of emotions people experience, how emotions are reflected in their facial expressions, and how others interpret these facial expressions. The psychologist Paul Ekman has found that facial expressions can be understood by people from cultures around the world (Ekman, 1973; Ekman & Matsumoto, 2011). Ekman showed people from many different cultures photographs of faces that depicted six different emotions (happiness, disgust, surprise, sadness, anger, and fear) and asked them to classify the emotion of the person in the photograph. Regardless of where they lived, people showed a high degree of accuracy in classifying the emotions shown in the photographs. Ekman and his colleagues have also suggested that there is a cross-cultural ability to recognize basic emotions through a person's vocalizations, such as screams or laughs (Sauter, Eisner, Ekman, & Scott, 2010). Some of Ekman's hypotheses remain controversial, but many psychologists now agree that there is cross-cultural uniformity in how people express emotions and interpret facial expressions. However, learning is also involved because some types of facial expressions are culture specific. For example, in China, sticking out your tongue is a way of showing surprise, and this is not so in Western societies.

BOX 2.1   SPOTLIGHT ON RESEARCH

We Have a Lot in Common: Human Universals

Scientists who study human behavior have concluded that people around the world share many basic characteristics besides simple reflexes. The anthropologist Donald E. Brown (1991) has compiled a list of **human universals**—abilities or behaviors that are found in all known human cultures. The list contains about 400 items, and it includes some very specific behaviors such as dance, music, death rituals, hygienic care, jokes, and folklore, as well as some major characteristics of human life, such as marriage, inheritance rules, tool making and tool use, government, sanctions for crimes, and division of labor. Learning and experience clearly affect just about every item on Brown's list: Dance, music, and folklore vary tremendously from culture to culture. So do a society's type of government, what is considered a crime and how people are punished, what types of tools people make, and how labor is divided among individuals. However, Brown's point is that every human society has some type of dance, some type of government, some type of division of labor, and so on (Figure 2.5). He maintains that because these characteristics of human existence are found in all cultures, even those that are completely isolated from the modern world, they most likely reflect innate human tendencies. Over the years, other researchers have suggested possible additions to Brown's original list based on new findings about cross-cultural similarities in human behavior (e.g., Aknin et al., 2013; Saucier, Thalmayer, & Bel-Bahar, 2014).

Figure 2.5 Dance is a human universal. (Filipe Frazao/Shutterstock.com)

Deciding that a particular behavioral tendency or characteristic is innate is not an easy matter. The fact that a behavioral characteristic is found in all human cultures does not, by itself, constitute proof that the characteristic is innate. Another possibility is that the behavior is seen in people everywhere because the environment places similar constraints on people everywhere. For example, one could argue that division of labor is advantageous in all environments because it is more efficient for an individual to become an expert in one line of work than to try to master dozens of different skills. Perhaps future research on human genetics will help sort out which of these universal human characteristics are hereditary, which are the products of similar environments, and which are a combination of the two. Whatever the case may be, Brown's list of human universals is interesting to contemplate because it shows, in a world full of people with vastly different lifestyles, interests, beliefs, and personalities, how much all people have in common.

Can you think of other human universals besides those mentioned above? Take a few moments and try to list a few examples of behaviors, practices, or customs that are found in all human cultures. You can then compare your examples with Brown's complete list, which can be found at: http://condor.depaul.edu/mfiddler/hyphen/humunivers.htm.

HABITUATION

Habituation is defined as a decrease in the strength of a response after repeated presentation of a stimulus that elicits the response. Here is a typical example. For his vacation, Dick has rented a cottage on a picturesque lake deep in the woods. The owner of the cottage has advised Dick that although the area is usually very quiet, members of the fish and game club just down the shore often engage in target practice for a few hours during the evening. Despite this forewarning, the first loud rifle shot elicits a startle reaction from Dick—he practically jumps out of his chair, his heart beats rapidly, and he breathes heavily for several seconds. After about half a minute, Dick has fully recovered and is just returning to his novel when he is again startled by a second gunshot. This time, the startle reaction is not as great as the first one: Dick's body does not jerk quite as dramatically, and there is not so large an increase in heart rate. With additional gunshots, Dick's startle response

PRACTICE QUIZ 1: CHAPTER 2

1. In control systems theory, the comparator compares the _____ and the _____, and if they do not match, the comparator signals the _____.
2. In the flexion reflex, pain receptors in the hand have synaptic connections with _____, which in turn have synapses with _____.
3. A kinesis is a _____ movement in response to a stimulus, and a taxis is a _____ movement in response to a stimulus.
4. The main difference between fixed action patterns and reaction chains is that _____.
5. Abilities or behaviors that are found in all known human cultures are called _____.

ANSWERS

1. actual input, reference input, action system 2. interneurons, motor neurons 3. random, directional 4. the behavior sequence occurs in a rigid order in fixed action patterns, but it is more flexible in reaction chains 5. human universals

decreases until it has habituated completely; that is, the noise no longer disrupts his concentration on his novel.

Another behavior that often displays habituation is the **orienting response**. If a new sight or sound is presented to a dog or other animal, the animal may stop its current activity, lift its ears and its head, and turn in the direction of the stimulus. If the stimulus is presented repeatedly but is of no consequence, the orienting response will disappear. Similarly, if an infant is played a tape recording of an adult's voice, the infant will turn its head in the direction of the sound. If, however, the same word is played over and over, the infant will soon stop turning toward the sound. Therefore, both animals and humans will typically exhibit an orienting response to a novel stimulus, and they will both exhibit habituation of the orienting response if the same stimulus is presented many times.

The function that habituation serves for the individual should be clear. In its everyday activities, a creature encounters many stimuli, some potentially beneficial, some potentially dangerous, and many neither helpful nor harmful. It is to the creature's advantage to be able to ignore the many insignificant stimuli it repeatedly encounters. Being continually startled or distracted by such stimuli would be a waste of the creature's time and energy. A study by Dielenberg and McGregor (1999) shows how animals can habituate to a fear-provoking stimulus if the stimulus repeatedly proves to be insignificant. Rats were presented with a cat collar that contained a cat's odor, and the response of the rats was to run into a hiding place and remain there for quite a while. However, Figure 2.6 shows that after several presentations of the cat collar, the rats' hiding times decreased and came close to those of the control group of rats that were exposed to a cat collar that had no cat odor on it.

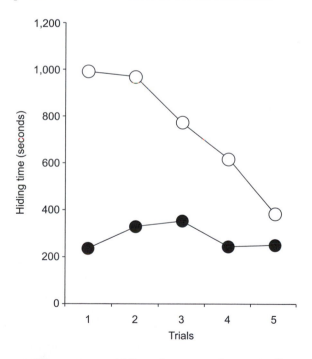

Figure 2.6 The amount of time rats spent hiding when exposed to a cat collar with cat odor exhibits habituation over successive days of exposure. The filled circles are from a control group of rats exposed to a cat collar that had no cat odor. (From Dielenberg, R.A. & McGregor, I.S., 1999, Habituation of the hiding response to cat odor in rats, *Journal of Comparative Psychology*, 113, 376–387. © American Psychological Association. Adapted with permission.)

Because habituation is a simple yet very useful type of learning, it is not surprising that it can be found throughout the animal kingdom. Habituation can be seen in hydra, whose diffuse networks of neurons are among the most primitive nervous systems found on our planet (Rushford, Burnett, & Maynard, 1963). There have even been reports of habituation in protozoa (one-celled organisms). In one study, Wood (1973) found a decline in the contraction response of the protozoan *Stentor coeruleus* with repeated presentations of a tactile stimulus. At the same time, its responsiveness to another stimulus, a light, was undiminished.

General Principles of Habituation

We have seen that habituation occurs in species ranging from one-celled organisms to human beings. Furthermore, it is not just the existence of habituation but its properties that are similar in such diverse species. In a frequently cited article, Thompson and Spencer (1966) listed some of the main principles of habituation that have been observed in people and in a wide variety of other species.

1. Course of Habituation. Habituation of a response occurs whenever a stimulus is repeatedly presented, but it is usually a gradual process that progresses over a number of trials. The decrements in responding from trial to trial are large at first but get progressively smaller as habituation proceeds.

2. Effects of Time. If after habituation the stimulus is withheld for some period of time, the response will recover. The amount of recovery depends on how much time has elapsed. We might say that habituation is "forgotten" as time passes. Suppose that after Dick's startle response to the gunshots has habituated, there are no more gunshots for 30 minutes, but then they begin again. Dick is likely to exhibit a weak startle reaction to the first sound of gunshot after the break. (Thus, there is some savings over time, but also some forgetting.) In comparison, if there were no further shooting until the following evening, Dick's startle reaction after this longer time interval would be larger.

3. Relearning Effects. Habituation may disappear if the stimulus is not presented for a long period of time, but if the same stimulus then begins again, the rate of habituation should be faster the second time. Later, if there is a third or fourth series of stimulus presentations, the habituation should be faster each time. To use Ebbinghaus's term, there will be savings from the previous periods of habituation. For example, although Dick's initial startle response to the sound of gunfire on the second evening of his vacation might be almost as large as on the first evening, the response should disappear more quickly the second time.

4. Effects of Stimulus Intensity. We have already seen that a reflexive response is frequently stronger with a more intense stimulus. Such a response is also more resistant to habituation. Habituation proceeds more rapidly with weak stimuli, and if a stimulus is very intense, there may be no habituation at all.

5. Effects of Overlearning. As in Ebbinghaus's experiments, further learning can occur in habituation even if the response to a stimulus has completely disappeared. Thompson and Spencer called this *below-zero habituation* because it occurs at a time when there is no observable response to the stimulus. Suppose that after 20 gunshots, Dick's startle response has completely disappeared. After a 24-hour interval, however, he might show little savings from the previous day's experience. In comparison, if there were 100 gunshots on the first evening, Dick would probably show less of a startle response on the second evening. In other words, although the additional 80 gunshots produced no additional changes in Dick's behavior at the time, they did increase his long-term retention of the habituation.

6. Stimulus Generalization. The transfer of habituation from one stimulus to new but similar stimuli is called generalization. For example, if on the third evening the sounds of the gunshots are somewhat different (perhaps because different types of guns are being used), Dick may have little difficulty ignoring these sounds. The amount of generalization depends on how similar the new stimulus is to the habituated stimulus.

Developmental psychologists can use habituation (along with stimulus generalization), as a tool to determine exactly which stimuli an infant finds similar, and in doing so they can learn a lot about infants' sensory and cognitive abilities. For example, Johnson and Aslin (1995) presented 2-month-old infants with a display that featured a dark rod moving from side to side behind a white box (Figure 2.7). At first, the infants would look at this display for many seconds, but after repeated presentations, this orienting response habituated. Then, the infants were tested with two new stimuli: a solid rod moving back and forth with no box in front and a broken rod moving back and forth. The infants showed more generalization of habituation to the solid rod than to the broken rod. Based on this finding, Johnson and Aslin concluded that the infants treated the original stimulus as a solid rod (not a broken rod) moving behind the box, even though the middle part of the rod could not be seen.

Many experiments have used similar procedures to examine a wide range of skills in human infants, including their ability to recognize visual stimuli (Singh et al., 2015), to discriminate different musical excerpts (Flom & Pick, 2012), and to analyze cause and effect in a chain of events (Kosugi, Ishida, Murai, & Fujita, 2009). This strategy of using habituation to measure surprise or changes in attention has proven to be a valuable technique for studying the perceptual and mental abilities of infants, even those less than a month old.

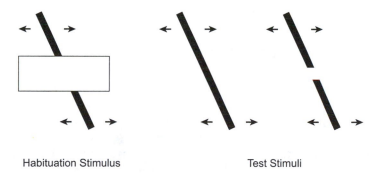

Habituation Stimulus   Test Stimuli

Figure 2.7 In a study by Johnson and Aslin (1995), infants were repeatedly shown the stimulus on the left until their orienting responses to the stimulus habituated. They were then tested for generalization, using each of the two stimuli on the right.

BOX 2.2   SPOTLIGHT ON RESEARCH

Habituation and Psychological Functioning

Although habituation is a very simple type of learning, it is a useful and important one. A creature that was unable to habituate to insignificant stimuli would probably have a difficult time attending to more important stimuli. In fact, there is some evidence that the speed at which human infants and children habituate to repetitive stimuli is related to their mental abilities later in life. Laucht, Esser, and Schmidt (1994) found that infants who displayed faster habituation to repetitive stimuli at 3 months of age obtained, on average, slightly higher scores on intelligence tests when they were 4½ years old. Even before birth, the human fetus exhibits habituation to such stimuli as vibration or sounds, and one study found that a fetus's rate of habituation was related to performance on tests of cognitive functioning 6 months after birth (Gaultney & Gingras, 2005).

Other studies have compared rates of habituation in human adults who are or are not suffering from various psychological disorders such as schizophrenia or severe depression. In some research, habituation was measured in brain activity as the people were repeatedly presented with visual images of faces or other objects. The findings were that habituation in some brain areas, such as the cerebellum and the visual cortex, was slower in individuals with schizophrenia or depression than in the normal population (Williams, Blackford, Luksik, Gauthier, & Heckers, 2013). Slower habituation in people with depression was also found when the habituation was measured in simple overt behaviors such as the eyeblink reflex.

These are correlational studies, not experiments, so it would be a mistake to try to draw any conclusions about cause and effect from them. Still, this research does suggest that the ability to habituate to repetitive, unimportant stimuli early in life may be one predictor of later mental abilities and that this very simple type of learning may be related to overall mental health.

Neural Mechanisms of Habituation

What takes place in a creature's nervous system when it habituates to a stimulus? To investigate this question, some scientists have studied fairly primitive creatures, a strategy known as the **simple systems approach**. A good example is the work of Eric Kandel and his colleagues (Abbott & Kandel, 2012; Castellucci, Pinsker, Kupfermann, & Kandel, 1970), who have spent several decades studying both the behavior and the nervous system of *Aplysia*, a large marine snail. They chose to study this animal because its nervous system is relatively simple—it contains only a few thousand neurons compared to the billions in a mammal's nervous system. Kandel and his coworkers investigated the process of habituation in one of *Aplysia*'s reflexes, the gill-withdrawal reflex. If *Aplysia*'s siphon (described as a "fleshy spout") is touched lightly,

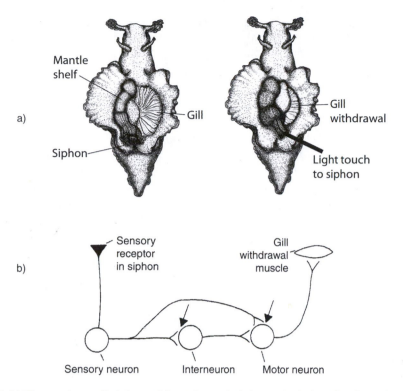

Figure 2.8 (a) The marine snail *Aplysia*. If the siphon is lightly touched, the gill reflexively withdraws beneath the hard mantle. (b) A small portion of the neural circuitry involved in *Aplysia*'s gill-withdrawal reflex. Habituation occurs because after repeated stimulation the sensory neurons release less neurotransmitter at the points indicated by the arrows.

its gill contracts and is drawn inside the mantle for a few seconds (Figure 2.8a). The neural mechanisms that control this reflex are well understood. The siphon contains 24 sensory neurons that respond to tactile stimulation. Six motor neurons control the gill–withdrawal response. Each of the 24 sensory neurons has a monosynaptic connection (i.e., a direct connection that involves just one synapse) with each of the six motor neurons. In addition, other axons from the sensory neurons are involved in polysynaptic connections (indirect connections mediated by one or more interneurons) with these same motor neurons. Figure 2.8b depicts a small portion of this neural circuitry.

If the siphon is stimulated about once every minute for 10 or 15 trials, the gill–withdrawal reflex habituates. Complete habituation lasts for about an hour, and partial habituation may be observed for as long as 24 hours. If such trials are given on three or four successive days, long–term habituation (lasting several weeks) can be observed. Through a series of elaborate tests, Kandel's group was able to determine that during habituation, a decrease in excitatory conduction always occurred at the synapses involving the axons of the sensory neurons (the points marked by arrows in Figure 2.8b). There was no change in the postsynaptic neuron's sensitivity to the transmitter. What had changed was the amount of transmitter released by the presynaptic (sensory) neurons: With repeated stimulus presentations, less transmitter was released into the synapse.

Kandel then proceeded to ask questions at a deeper level: What chemical mechanisms are responsible for the depressed transmitter release of the sensory neurons? Each time a neuron fires, there is an influx of calcium ions into the axon terminals, and this calcium current is thought to cause the release of transmitter into the synapse. Klein, Shapiro and Kandel (1980) found that the calcium current grew weaker during habituation, and in the recovery period after habituation, both the calcium current and the response of the postsynaptic (motor) neuron increased at the same rate. The experimenters concluded that a decrease in the calcium current causes a decrease in the amount of transmitter released into the synapse, which in turn decreases the excitation of the motor neuron, producing a weakened gill-withdrawal response.

The work of Kandel and associates nicely illustrates the potential advantages of the simple systems strategy in physiological research on learning. Because of the comparative simplicity of *Aplysia*'s neural networks, researchers have been able to pinpoint the neural changes responsible for habituation. This research shows that, at least in some cases, learning depends on changes at very specific neural locations, not on widespread changes in many parts of the nervous system. Furthermore, this learning involved no anatomical changes, such as the growth of new axons, but merely changes in the effectiveness of already established connections between neurons.

Because the nervous system of a typical mammal is so much more complex than that of *Aplysia*, it is much more difficult to identify the individual neurons that undergo change during habituation to a stimulus. Nevertheless, substantial progress has been made in locating the brain locations involved in habituation, at least in certain specific cases. Michael Davis (1989) has conducted extensive research on one such specific case: habituation of a rat's startle response to a sudden loud noise. The startle response is measured by testing a rat in a chamber that sits on springs so that the rat's movement when it is startled shakes the chamber slightly, and this movement is measured by a sensor. Through many careful studies, Davis and colleagues were able to trace the entire neural circuit involved in a rat's startle response (Davis, Gendelman, Tischler, & Gendelman, 1982). The circuit begins in the auditory nerve, works its way through auditory pathways to the brainstem, then proceeds to motor pathways that controlled the muscles involved in the startle response. Davis found that habituation of the startle reflex takes place in the early portions of this circuit—the auditory pathways. Although the exact neurons responsible for the habituation have not been identified, these findings are similar to those from *Aplysia* in two respects. First, the neurons that undergo change during habituation are on the sensory side of the circuit. Second, the changes take place within the reflex circuit itself, rather than being the result of new inputs from neurons elsewhere in the nervous system.

Other studies with mammals extend but also complicate the physiological picture of habituation. In some cases of habituation, higher sections of the brain seem to be involved, including the auditory cortex. Using guinea pigs, Condon and Weinberger (1991) found that if the same tone was presented repeatedly, individual cells in the auditory cortex "habituated"; that is, they decreased their sensitivity to this tone, but not to tones of higher or lower pitch.

With modern brain-imaging techniques, such as **positron emission tomography (PET)** and **functional magnetic resonance imaging (fMRI),** it has become possible to identify brain areas that are involved in habituation in humans. With fMRI, researchers can measure the activity of different parts of the brain in real time, as a person performs some task or is presented with some stimulus. For instance, one study using fMRI found habituation in many different parts of the brain, including the cerebral cortex and the hippocampus, when people were repeatedly shown the same pictures of human faces (Fischer et al., 2003). Other brain areas show habituation when people are presented with repeated speech sounds (Joanisse, Zevin, & McCandliss, 2007). PET scans have displayed changes in the cerebellum as a person's startle response to a loud noise habituates (Timmann et al., 1998). There is growing evidence that many different areas of the brain and nervous system can undergo habituation when the same stimulus is repeatedly presented.

Neuroscientists use the term *plasticity* to refer to the nervous system's ability to change as a result of experience or stimulation. All in all, the physiological studies of habituation demonstrate that plasticity is possible in many different levels of the nervous system. Although simple chemical changes such as neurotransmitter depletion may be responsible for some types of habituation, in other cases the neural mechanisms appear to be quite complex (Thompson, 2014).

Habituation in Emotional Responses: The Opponent-Process Theory

Richard Solomon and John Corbit (1974) proposed a theory of emotion that has attracted a good deal of attention. The theory is meant to apply to a wide range of emotional reactions. The type of learning they propose is quite similar to the examples of habituation we have already examined: In both types of learning, an individual's response to a stimulus changes simply as a result of repeated presentations of that stimulus. However, according to the **opponent-process theory** of Solomon and Corbit, with stimulus repetition, some emotional reactions weaken while others are strengthened.

The Temporal Pattern of an Emotional Response

Imagine that you are a premedical student taking a course in organic chemistry. You received a C+ on the midterm, and your performance in laboratory exercises was fair. You studied hard for the final exam, but there were some parts of the exam that you could not answer. While leaving the examination room, you overheard a number of students say that it was a difficult test. Later you receive your grades for the semester, and you learn to your surprise that your grade in organic chemistry was an A–! You are instantly ecstatic and you tell the good news to everyone you see. You are too excited to do any serious work, but as you run some errands, none of the minor irritations of a typical day (long lines, impolite salespeople) bother you. By evening, however, your excitement has settled down, and you experience a state of contentment. The next morning you receive a call from the registrar's office. There has been a clerical error in reporting the grades, and it turns out that your actual grade in organic chemistry was B–. This news provokes immediate feelings of dejection and despair. You reevaluate your plans about where you will apply to medical school, and you wonder whether you will go at all. Over the course of a few hours, however, your emotional state gradually recovers and returns to normal.

This example illustrates all of the major features of a typical emotional episode as proposed by opponent-process theory. Figure 2.9 presents a graph of your emotional states

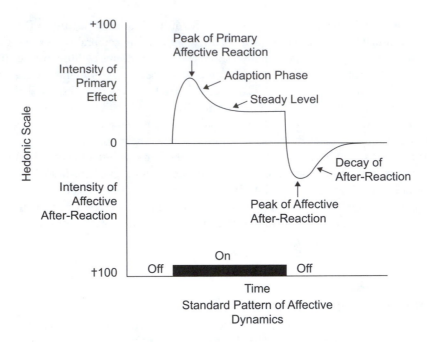

Figure 2.9 The typical pattern of an emotional response according to the opponent-process theory. The solid bar shows the time during which an emotion-eliciting stimulus is present. The solid bar shows the time during which an emotion-eliciting stimulus is present. (From Solomon, R.L., & Corbit, J.D., 1974, An opponent-process theory of motivation: I. Temporal dynamics of affect, *Psychological Review, 81*, 119–145. © American Psychological Association. Reprinted with permission.)

during this imaginary episode. The solid bar at the bottom marks the time during which some emotion–eliciting stimulus is present. In this example, it refers to the time when you believed your grade was an A−. The y-axis depicts the strength of an individual's emotional reactions both while the stimulus is present and afterward. (The response to the stimulus itself is always plotted in the positive direction, regardless of whether the emotion is "pleasant" or "unpleasant.") According to the theory, the onset of such a stimulus produces the sudden appearance of an emotional reaction, which quickly reaches a peak of intensity (the initial ecstasy in this example). This response then gradually declines to a somewhat lower level, or plateau (your contentment during the evening). With the offset of the stimulus (the telephone call), there is a sudden switch to an emotional after-reaction that is in some sense the opposite of the initial emotion (the dejection and despair). This after-reaction gradually declines, and the individual's emotional reaction returns to a neutral state.

As an example where the initial reaction was unpleasant, Solomon and Corbit described a study in which dogs received a series of shocks (Church, LoLordo, Overmier, Solomon, & Turner, 1966). When a shock began, the dogs would show obvious signs of fear and distress, and their heart rates rose rapidly from a resting state of about 120 beats/minute to about 200 beats/minute and then began to decline. At the termination of the shock, a typical dog's behavior was characterized as "stealthy, hesitant, and unfriendly" (1966, p. 121). These after-reactions may not sound like the opposite of fear, but they were certainly different from the initial reaction, and there was a rebound effect in which the dogs' heart rates dropped to about 90 beats/minute and then returned to normal after a minute or so.

The a-Process and b-Process

Solomon and Corbit proposed that many emotional reactions follow the pattern shown in Figure 2.9. They theorized that this pattern is the result of two opposing internal processes that they called the a-process and the b-process. The **a-process** is largely responsible for the initial emotional response, and the b-process for the after-reaction. The left half of Figure 2.10 shows how these two processes supposedly combine to produce the pattern in Figure 2.9. Solomon and Corbit described the a-process as a fast-acting response to a stimulus that rises to a maximum and remains there as long as the stimulus is present. When the stimulus ends, the a-process decays very quickly (see the middle left graph in Figure 2.10). In the heart–rate study with dogs, the a-process would be some hypothetical internal mechanism (perhaps the flow of adrenaline) that produces, among other responses, an increase in heart rate. The opposing **b-process** is supposedly activated only in response to the activity of the a-process, and it is more sluggish both to rise and to decay. The middle left graph in Figure 2.10 also shows the more gradual increase and decrease in the b-process. In the heart–rate example, the b-process would be some internal mechanism causing a decrease in heart rate.

Note in Figure 2.10 that the b-process begins to rise while the stimulus (the shock) is still present. Solomon and Corbit proposed that when both the a- and b-processes

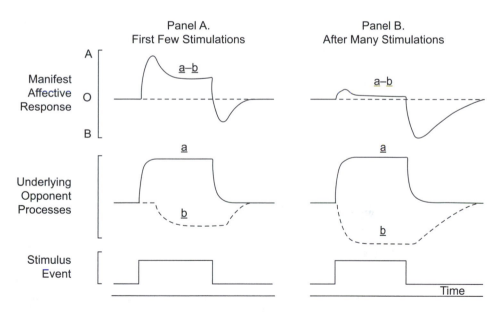

Figure 2.10 According to opponent-process theory, a person's emotional reaction (or "manifest affective response") is jointly determined by the underlying a- and b-processes. The proposed time course of these processes during the first few presentations of an emotion-eliciting stimulus is shown on the left. The right side shows the predicted patterns after many repetitions of the same stimulus. (From Solomon, R.L., & Corbit, J.D., 1974, An opponent-process theory of motivation: I. Temporal dynamics of affect, *Psychological Review, 81*, 119–145, © American Psychological Association. Reprinted with permission.)

are active to some degree, the resulting emotional response can be predicted by simple subtraction. That is, the action of the a-process will be countered to some extent by the action of the b-process, and the emotional response will be weaker. This is why there is a drop in the initial emotional reaction from the peak to the plateau. When the stimulus ends and the a-process quickly decays, all that remains is the b-process, which produces the emotional after-reaction. You should see how the two processes in the middle left graph of Figure 2.10 combine to produce the pattern in the upper left graph.

The Effects of Repeated Stimulation

One of the most important parts of the opponent-process theory concerns how the pattern of an emotional response changes with repeated presentations of the same stimulus. To put it simply, the theory states that with repeated exposures to a stimulus, the initial emotional response exhibits a sort of habituation—it becomes progressively smaller—while at the same time there is a marked increase in the size and duration of the after-reaction. The top right graph in Figure 2.10 shows the predicted pattern of an emotional response after many stimulations. The middle right graph shows that, according to the theory, this change is the result of an increase in the size of the b-process. Whereas the a-process does not change, the b-process is strengthened with use and weakened with disuse. With repeated stimulations, the b-process rises more quickly, reaches a higher maximum, and is slower to decay after the stimulus is terminated.

In support of these predictions Solomon and Corbit described what happened to the emotional responses and heart rates of the dogs in the experiment of Church et al. (1966). After several sessions, there was little, if any, increase in heart rate during the shock. However, after shock termination, heart rates decreased by as much as 60 beats/minute, and they took from 2 to 5 minutes (instead of 1 minute or less) to return to normal. The dogs' overt behaviors also changed: During the shocks, the researchers noted that one dog "appeared pained, annoyed, anxious, but not terrified. . . . Then, when released suddenly at the end of the session, the dog rushed about, jumped up on people, wagged its tail, in what we called at the time 'a fit of joy.' Finally, several minutes later, the dog was its normal self: friendly, but not racing about" (Solomon & Corbit, 1974, p. 122).

In short, with extended experience, the changes in the dogs' heart rates and overt behaviors were similar: The reaction to the shock was smaller than before, but the after-reaction was larger and lasted longer.

Other Emotional Reactions

Solomon and Corbit (1974) claimed that their theory describes many different types of emotional experiences. They discussed the emotional responses of parachutists on their initial jumps and on later jumps, as reported by S. M. Epstein (1967). Overall, the emotional experiences of parachutists resemble those of the dogs in the heart-rate study. Novice parachutists appear terrified during a jump; after the jump, they look stunned for a few minutes and then return to normal. Experienced parachutists appear only moderately anxious during a jump, but afterward they report feelings of exhilaration and euphoria that can last for hours. They claim that this feeling of euphoria is one of the main reasons they continue to jump.

As another example, Solomon and Corbit discussed the powerful reactions people have to addictive drugs such as opiates. After a person's first opiate injection, an intense feeling of pleasure (a "rush") is experienced. This peak of emotion declines to a less intense state of pleasure. As the effect of the drug wears off, however, the aversive after-reactions set in—nausea, insomnia, irritability, anxiety, inability to eat, and other physical problems, along with feelings of craving for the drug. The withdrawal symptoms can last for hours or a few days.

For an experienced opiate user, the pattern changes. The injection no longer brings an initial rush, but only mild feelings of pleasure, if any. This decrease in the effects of a drug with repeated use is called **tolerance**, and it is observed with many drugs besides opiates. According to the opponent-process theory, drug tolerance is the product of a strengthened b-process. The stronger b-process also explains why, with repeated opiate use, the withdrawal symptoms become more severe, and they may last for weeks or longer. Solomon and Corbit proposed that opponent-process theory provides a framework for understanding not only opiate use but all addictive behaviors (such as smoking, alcoholism, and the use of barbiturates and amphetamines). We will see in Chapter 4, however, that other researchers who study drug use disagree with the details of the opponent-process theory.

A Brief Evaluation

The predictions that opponent-process theory makes about the pattern of emotional responses have been tested in numerous experiments. In many cases the theory's predictions have been supported (e.g., Vargas-Perez, Ting-A-Kee, Heinmiller, Sturgess, & van der Kooy, 2007), but sometimes they have not (Newton, Kalechstein, Tervo, & Ling, 2003). To its credit, the theory has been applied to a diverse range of human behaviors, including the effects of exercise (Lochbaum, 1999), the depression that can follow the loss of a loved one (Moss, 2013), and how people experience the sensations of pain followed by relief when the pain ends (Leknes, Brooks, Wiech, & Tracey, 2008).

Recent research on the brain mechanisms of drug addiction supports the assumptions of opponent-process theory about the weakening of the a-process (the pleasures derived from a drug dose) and the strengthening of the b-process (the withdrawal symptoms, Koob & Le Moal, 2008). Some studies with rats have identified specific sections of the brain that appear to be involved in both the initial positive reaction to opiates and the negative after-reactions (Radke, Rothwell, & Gewirtz, 2011), and these findings provide neuroanatomical support for the basic ideas of opponent-process theory. Research on brain changes in drug addiction is consistent with the idea that addicts are motivated to keep using drugs not so much because they continue to provide pleasure but rather because they provide temporary relief from the unpleasant withdrawal symptoms (Baker, Piper, McCarthy, Majeskie, & Fiore, 2004).

Critics of opponent-process theory have pointed out that the different examples used by Solomon and Corbit exhibit vastly different time courses. In the heart-rate studies with dogs, the b-process lasts only seconds or a few minutes. In an addiction, the b-process may continue for months. Is it likely that the same physiological mechanisms are involved in emotional events whose durations differ by a factor of 10,000 or more? The critics have argued that there may be nothing more than a superficial resemblance among the different examples Solomon and Corbit present.

In defense of opponent-process theory, we might assert that as long as emotional responses conform to the predictions of the theory, it does not matter whether these patterns are based on a single physiological mechanism or on a dozen different ones. On a strictly descriptive level, the major characteristics of emotional episodes emphasized by opponent-process theory (the peak, the plateau, the aftereffect, the changes with repeated stimulation) appear to be fairly well documented by case histories, systematic observations, and experiments. Whether or not these patterns share a common physiological mechanism, the theory captures some characteristics of emotional responses that seem to be quite general. This may be the theory's greatest virtue. The broad viewpoint provided by opponent-process theory allows us to see commonalities among our emotions that would probably go unnoticed in a more myopic analysis of individual emotional responses.

SUMMARY

One of the simplest types of innate behaviors is the reflex, which is a simple response to a specific stimulus, such as blinking when a bright light is shined in the eye. Kineses are random movements in response to a specific stimulus, whereas taxes are directed movements (such as an ant using the sun as a compass). Fixed action patterns are sequences of behavior that always occur in a rigid order, whereas reaction chains are more flexible sequences that can be adapted to current circumstances. The concepts of control systems theory, which describe a comparison between the actual state of the world and a goal state, are helpful in analyzing these innate behavior patterns. Few innate behavior patterns have been found in humans, but there is evidence that humans may have quite a few innate abilities and predispositions, including language skills, how emotions are displayed in facial expressions, and a variety of other social behaviors.

Habituation is the decline and eventual disappearance of a reflexive response when the same stimulus is repeatedly presented. Habituation gives a creature the ability to ignore unimportant, repetitive events. In both simple and complex creatures, habituation exhibits the same set of properties, such as forgetting, overlearning, and stimulus generalization. Research with simple creatures such as the snail *Aplysia*, as well as with mammals, has traced the physiological and chemical changes that occur in the brain during habituation and specific brain structures involved in habituation in a few cases.

The opponent-process theory of Solomon and Corbit states that many emotional reactions consist of an initial response called the a-process and a later, opposing response called the b-process. Repeated presentations of the same stimulus strengthen the b-process, so that the initial reaction grows weaker and the after-reaction grows stronger and lasts longer. This theory has been applied to a wide variety of emotional reactions, including drug addiction, the emotions involved in parachute jumping, and responses to painful or aversive stimuli.

Review Questions

1. Describe an example of each of the following innate behavior patterns: reflex, kinesis, taxis, fixed action pattern, and reaction chain. Select one of these examples and show how it can be analyzed using the concepts of control systems theory.

2. What types of evidence do scientists use to support claims that human beings are born with certain abilities and predispositions? Which examples of innate human predispositions do you find most convincing, and which do you find less convincing? Explain your reasoning.

3. If you bought a clock for your room that made a loud ticking sound, you would probably soon habituate to the sound. Use this example to illustrate the general principles of habituation. Why is this simple type of learning useful?

4. How has habituation been studied in human infants, and what has been found?

5. Draw a diagram that shows the pattern of a typical emotional response to a new stimulus according to opponent-process theory. Now diagram the changed pattern that occurs in response to a stimulus that has been frequently repeated. Use a specific example, such as drug addiction or smoking, to explain the diagrams.

REFERENCES

Abbott, L.F., & Kandel, E.R. (2012). A computational approach enhances learning in Aplysia. *Nature Neuroscience, 15*, 178–179.

Aknin, L.B., Barrington-Leigh, C.P., Dunn, E.W., Helliwell, J.F., Burns, J., Biswas-Diener, R., & . . . Norton, M.I. (2013). Prosocial spending and well-being: Cross-cultural evidence for a psychological universal. *Journal of Personality and Social Psychology, 104*, 635–652.

Armsworth, C.G., Bohan, D.A., Powers, S.J., Glen, D.M., & Symondson, W.O.C. (2005). Behavioural responses by slugs to chemicals from a generalist predator. *Animal Behaviour, 69*, 805–811.

Baker, M. (2001). *The atoms of language*. New York: Basic Books.

Baker, T.B., Piper, M.E., McCarthy, D.E., Majeskie, M.R., & Fiore, M.C. (2004). Addiction motivation reformulated: An affective processing model of negative reinforcement. *Psychological Review, 111*, 33–51.

Brown, D.E. (1991). *Human universals*. New York: McGraw-Hill.

Castellucci, V., Pinsker, H., Kupfermann, I., & Kandel, E.R. (1970). Neuronal mechanisms of habituation and dishabituation of the gillwithdrawal reflex in *Aplysia. Science, 167*, 1745–1748.

Church, R.M., LoLordo, V.M., Overmier, J.B., Solomon, R.L., & Turner, L.H. (1966). Cardiac responses to shock in curarized dogs. *Journal of Comparative and Physiological Psychology, 62*, 1–7.

Condon, C.D., & Weinberger, N.M. (1991). Habituation produces frequency-specific plasticity of receptive fields in the auditory cortex. *Behavioral Neuroscience, 105*, 416–430.

Davis, M. (1989). Neural systems involved in fearpotentiated startle. *Annals of the New York Academy of Sciences, 563*, 165–183.

Davis, M., Gendelman, D.S., Tischler, M.D., & Gendelman, P.M. (1982). A primary acoustic startle circuit: Lesion and stimulation studies. *Journal of Neuroscience, 2*, 791–805.

Dielenberg, R.A., & McGregor, I.S. (1999). Habituation of the hiding response to cat odor in rats (*Rattus norvegicus*). *Journal of Comparative Psychology, 113*, 376–387.

Eibl-Eibesfeldt, I. (1975). *Ethology* (2nd ed.). New York: Holt, Rinehart & Winston.

Ekman, P. (1973). Cross-cultural studies of facial expression. In P. Ekman (Ed.), *Darwin and facial expression* (pp. 91–168). New York: Academic Press.

Ekman, P., & Matsumoto, D. (2011). Reading faces: The universality of emotional expression. In M.A. Gernsbacher, R.W. Pew, L.M. Hough, & J.R. Pomerantz (Eds.), *Psychology and the real world: Essays illustrating fundamental contributions to society* (pp. 140–146). New York, NY, US: Worth Publishers.

Epstein, S.M. (1967). Toward a unified theory of anxiety. In B.A. Maher (Ed.), *Progress in experimental personality research* (Vol. 4, pp. 2–89). New York: Academic Press.

Evans, N., & Levinson, S.C. (2009). The myth of language universals: Language diversity and its importance for cognitive science. *Behavioral and Brain Sciences, 32*, 429–448.

Fischer, H., Wright, C.I., Whalen, P.J., McInerney, S.C., Shin, L.M., & Rauch, S.L. (2003). Brain habituation during repeated exposure to fearful and neutral faces: A functional MRI study. *Brain Research Bulletin, 59*, 387–392.

Flom, R., & Pick, A.D. (2012). Dynamics of infant habituation: Infants' discrimination of musical excerpts. *Infant Behavior & Development, 35*, 697–704.

Fraenkel, G.S., & Gunn, D.L. (1940). *The orientation of animals: Kineses, taxes, and compass reactions*. Oxford: Oxford University Press.

Gaultney, J.F., & Gingras, J.L. (2005). Fetal rate of behavioral inhibition and preference for novelty during infancy. *Early Human Development, 81*, 379–386.

Joanisse, M.F., Zevin, J.D., & McCandliss, B.D. (2007). Brain mechanisms implicated in the preattentive categorization of speech sounds revealed using fMRI and a short-interval habituation trial paradigm. *Cerebral Cortex, 17*, 2084–2093.

Johnson, S.P., & Aslin, R.N. (1995). Perception of object unity in 2-month-old infants. *Developmental Psychology, 31*, 739–745.

Klein, M., Shapiro, E., & Kandel, E.R. (1980). Synaptic plasticity and the modulation of the calcium current. *Journal of Experimental Biology, 89*, 117–157.

Koob, G.F., & Le Moal, M. (2008). Addiction and the brain antireward system. *Annual Review of Psychology, 59*, 29–53.

Kosugi, D., Ishida, H., Murai, C., & Fujita, K. (2009). Nine- to 11-month-old infants' reasoning about causality in anomalous human movements. *Japanese Psychological Research, 51*, 246–257.

Laucht, M., Esser, G., & Schmidt, M.H. (1994). Contrasting infant predictors of later cognitive functioning. *Journal of Child Psychology and Psychiatry and Allied Disciplines, 35*, 649–662.

Leknes, S., Brooks, J.C.W., Wiech, K., & Tracey, I. (2008). Pain relief as an opponent process: A psychophysical investigation. *European Journal of Neuroscience, 28*, 794–801.

Lenneberg, E.H. (1967). *Biological foundations of language.* New York: Wiley.

Lochbaum, M.R. (1999). Affective and cognitive performance due to exercise training: An examination of individual difference variables. *Dissertation Abstracts International: Section B: The Sciences and Engineering, 59*(10-B), 5611.

Loeb, J. (1900). *Comparative physiology of the brain and comparative psychology.* New York: Putnam's.

McFarland, D.S. (1971). *Feedback mechanisms in animal behavior.* New York: Academic Press.

Moss, R.A. (2013). Psychotherapy and the brain: The dimensional systems model and clinical biopsychology. *Journal of Mind and Behavior, 34*, 63–89.

Newton, T.F., Kalechstein, A.D., Tervo, K.E., & Ling, W. (2003). Irritability following abstinence from cocaine predicts euphoric effects of cocaine administration. *Addictive Behaviors, 28*, 817–821.

Pinker, S. (2002). *The blank slate.* New York: Viking.

Provine, R.R. (1989). Faces as releasers of contagious yawning: An approach to face detection using normal human subjects. *Bulletin of the Psychonomic Society, 27*, 211–214.

Radke, A.K., Rothwell, P.E., & Gewirtz, J.C. (2011). An anatomical basis for opponent process mechanisms of opiate withdrawal. *Journal of Neuroscience, 31*, 7533–7539.

Reese, E.S. (1963). The behavioral mechanisms underlying shell selection by hermit crabs. *Behaviour, 21*, 78–126.

Rushford, N.B., Burnett, A., & Maynard, R. (1963). Behavior in Hydra: Contraction responses of *Hydra pirardi* to mechanical and light stimuli. *Science, 139*, 760–761.

Saucier, G., Thalmayer, A.G., & Bel-Bahar, T.S. (2014). Human attribute concepts: Relative ubiquity across twelve mutually isolated languages. *Journal of Personality and Social Psychology, 107*, 199–216.

Sauter, D.A., Eisner, F., Ekman, P., & Scott, S.K. (2010). Cross-cultural recognition of basic emotions through nonverbal emotional vocalizations. *PNAS Proceedings of the National Academy of Sciences of the United States of America, 107*, 2408–2412.

Schneirla, T.C. (1933). Some important features of ant learning. *Zeitschrift für Vergleichenden Physiologie, 19*, 439–452.

Singh, L., Fu, C.L., Rahman, A.A., Hameed, W.B., Sanmugam, S., Agarwal, P., & . . . Rifkin-Graboi, A. (2015). Back to basics: A bilingual advantage in infant visual habituation. *Child Development, 86*, 294–302.

Solomon, R.L., & Corbit, J.D. (1974). An opponent-process theory of motivation: I. Temporal dynamics of affect. *Psychological Review, 81*, 119–145.

Thompson, R.F. (2014). Habituation: A history. In F.K. McSweeney & E.S. Murphy (Eds.), *The Wiley Blackwell handbook of operant and classical conditioning* (pp. 79–94). Chichester, UK: Wiley-Blackwell.

Thompson, R.F., & Spencer, W.A. (1966). Habituation: A model phenomenon for the study of neuronal substrates of behavior. *Psychological Review, 73*, 16–43.

Timmann, D., Musso, C., Kolb, F.P., Rijntjes, M., Jüptner, M., Müller, S.P., & . . . Weiller, C.I. (1998). Involvement of the human cerebellum during habituation of the acoustic startle response: A PET study. *Journal of Neurology, Neurosurgery & Psychiatry, 65*, 771–773.

Vargas-Perez, H., Ting-A-Kee, R.A., Heinmiller, A., Sturgess, J.E., & van der Kooy, D. (2007). A test of the opponent-process theory of motivation using lesions that selectively block morphine reward. *European Journal of Neuroscience, 25*, 3713–3718.

Watson, J.B. (1925). *Behaviorism.* New York: Norton.

Williams, L.E., Blackford, J.U., Luksik, A., Gauthier, I., & Heckers, S. (2013). Reduced habituation in patients with schizophrenia. *Schizophrenia Research, 151*, 124–132.

Wood, D.C. (1973). Stimulus specific habituation in a protozoan. *Physiology and Behavior, 11*, 349–354.

CHAPTER 3

Basic Principles of Classical Conditioning

Learning Objectives

After reading this chapter, you should be able to

- describe the procedure of classical conditioning and some of the most common ways it is studied in the laboratory
- explain Pavlov's stimulus substitution theory, and describe its strengths and weaknesses
- describe the basic principles of classical conditioning, including acquisition, extinction, spontaneous recovery, conditioned inhibition, generalization, and discrimination
- explain how the timing of the stimuli in classical conditioning affects the results
- give examples of classical conditioning that are found in everyday life
- describe some behavior therapies that are based on classical conditioning, and evaluate their effectiveness

---

PAVLOV'S DISCOVERY AND ITS IMPACT

The Russian scientist Ivan Pavlov is one of the most famous figures in the history of psychology. Pavlov was interested in the various substances secreted by an animal's digestive system to break down the food eaten, including saliva. He used dogs in his research, and he developed a surgical technique that enabled him to redirect the saliva from one of the dog's salivary ducts through a tube and out of the mouth, so that it could be measured (see Figure 3.1). A dog might receive several test sessions on successive days. In each session the animal would be given food, and its salivation would be recorded as it ate. Pavlov's

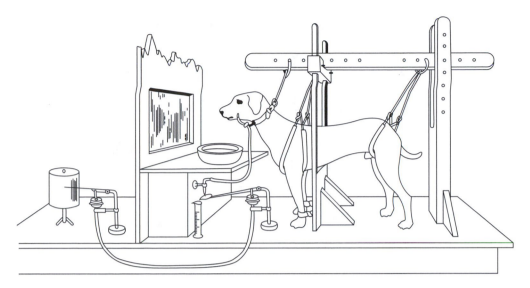

Figure 3.1 Pavlov's salivary conditioning situation. A tube redirects drops of saliva out of the dog's mouth so they can be recorded automatically. (From Yerkes & Morgulis, 1909)

important observation came when studying dogs that had been through the testing procedure several times. Unlike a new dog, an experienced one would begin to salivate even before the food was presented. Pavlov reasoned that some stimuli that always preceded the presentation of food, such as the sight of the experimenter, had developed the ability to elicit the response of salivation. Pavlov concluded that his dogs were exhibiting a simple type of learning: Salivation, which began as a reflexive response to the stimulus of food in the dog's mouth, was now elicited by a new stimulus. This phenomenon is now known as **classical conditioning**. Pavlov discovered many of the findings described in this chapter, and he developed a set of procedures for studying classical conditioning that is still in use today.

The Standard Paradigm of Classical Conditioning

To conduct a typical experiment in classical conditioning, an experimenter first selects some stimulus that reliably elicits a characteristic response. The stimulus of this pair is called the **unconditioned stimulus (US)**, and the response is called the **unconditioned response (UR)**. The term *unconditioned* indicates that the connection between the stimulus and response is unlearned (innate). In Pavlov's experiments on the salivary response, the US was the presence of food in the dog's mouth, and the UR was the secretion of saliva. The third element of the classical conditioning paradigm is the **conditioned stimulus (CS)**, which can be any stimulus that does not initially evoke the UR (e.g., a bell). The term *conditioned stimulus* means that the bell will elicit the response of salivation only after conditioning has taken place.

Figure 3.2 shows the sequence of events on the first trial of classical conditioning and on a later trial. In its simplest form, a classical conditioning trial involves the presentation of the

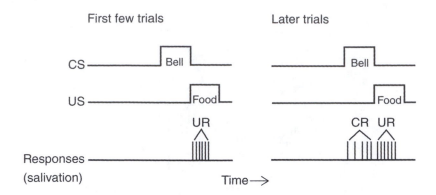

Figure 3.2 Events of a classical conditioning trial both before (left) and after (right) a CR is established.

CS (e.g., a bell) followed by the US (e.g., the food). On the initial trials, only the US will elicit the response of salivation. However, as the conditioning trials continue, the dog will begin to salivate as soon as the CS is presented. Any salivation that occurs during the CS but before the US is referred to as a **conditioned response (CR)** because it is elicited by the CS, not the US.

The Variety of Conditioned Responses

Although classical conditioning can be obtained with many different responses, much of the research has been conducted with a small number of conditioning *preparations* (conditioning situations using a particular US, UR, and species) that can be studied easily and efficiently. The following conditioning preparations are among the most commonly used.

Eyeblink Conditioning

Conditioning of the eyeblink reflex has been studied with humans, rabbits, rats, and other animals. Figure 3.3 shows a modern apparatus for eyeblink conditioning with humans. The US is a puff of air directed at the eye, and the UR is of course an eyeblink. Eyeblinks are recorded by a photocell that measures movement of the eyelid. In eyelid conditioning research with rabbits, the US can be an air puff or a mild electric shock delivered to the skin in the vicinity of the eye, which also reliably elicits an eyeblink as a UR. The CS may be a light, a tone, or some tactile stimulus such as a vibration of the experimental chamber, and the duration of the CS is typically about 1 second. Like the UR, the CR is an eyeblink. Eyeblink conditioning can be slow: It may take over 100 pairings before a CR is observed on 50% of the trials. Research in eyeblink conditioning has helped scientists to map the brain areas and chemical mechanisms involved in conditioning, to diagnose psychological disorders, to study the effects of aging, and in other ways (e.g., Radell & Mercado, 2014).

Figure 3.3 An eyeblink conditioning arrangement. The participant wears a headset that has a tube to direct a puff of air to the eye, a photocell to measure movement of the eyelid, and earphones for the presentation of auditory stimuli.

Conditioned Suppression

In the **conditioned suppression** procedure, also called the *conditioned emotional response* (CER) procedure, the subjects are usually rats, and the US is an aversive event such as a brief electric shock delivered through the metal bars that form the floor of the experimental chamber. A rat is first trained to press a lever at a steady pace by occasionally delivering a food pellet after a lever press. Occasionally, a CS (a light, sound, vibration, etc.) is presented for perhaps a minute, followed by the US, the shock. At first, the rat will continue to press the lever during the 1-minute CS. However, after several trials on which the CS was followed by shock, the rat will slow down or stop its lever pressing when the CS is on, as if it is anticipating the upcoming shock. Therefore the CR in this procedure is the suppression of lever pressing, and it indicates the rat has learned the association between CS and US. As soon as the shock is over, the rat will resume lever pressing at its normal rate. Conditioning in this procedure can be rapid: Strong conditioned suppression can often be found in fewer than 10 trials, and in some cases significant suppression can be observed after just one CS–US pairing.

The Skin Conductance Response

A conditioning preparation called **skin conductance response (SCR)**, sometimes referred to as the *electrodermal response*, uses human participants. The SCR is a change in the electrical conductivity of the skin. To measure a person's SCR, two coin-shaped electrodes are attached to the palm, and they measure momentary fluctuations in the conductivity of the skin (caused by small changes in perspiration). The conductivity of the skin is altered by emotions such as fear or surprise, which is why the SCR is often one measure used in lie detector tests. One stimulus that reliably produces a large increase in skin conductivity is electric shock, and a similar increase in conductivity can be conditioned to any CS that is paired with shock. For instance, the CS might be a tone, the US a shock to the left wrist, and the response an increase in conductivity of the right palm. The SCR is of value to researchers because it can be quickly and reliably conditioned with human participants, and many complex stimuli (such as spoken or written words) can be examined as CSs.

Taste-Aversion Learning

The CS in this procedure is the taste of something the animal eats or drinks, often a food it has never tasted before. After eating or drinking, the animal is given an injection of a poison (the US) that makes it ill. Several days later, the animal is again given the opportunity to consume the food that served as the CS. The animal typically consumes little or none of this food. Therefore, the measure of conditioning is the degree to which the animal avoids the food.

A taste aversion is something that many people experience at least once in their lives. Perhaps there is some type of food that you refuse to eat because you once became ill after eating it. You may find the very thought of eating this food a bit nauseating, even though most people enjoy the food. If you have such a taste aversion, you are not unusual—one study found that more than half of the college students surveyed had at least one taste aversion (Logue, Ophir, & Strauss, 1981).

Pavlov's Stimulus Substitution Theory

Pavlov proposed a theory of classical conditioning that is called the **stimulus substitution theory**. The theory states that in classical conditioning the CS becomes a substitute for the US, so that the response initially elicited only by the US is now also elicited by the CS. At first glance, this theory seems to provide a perfectly satisfactory description of what takes place in many common examples of classical conditioning. In salivary conditioning, at first only the food elicits salivation, but later the CS also elicits salivation. In eyeblink conditioning, both the UR and the CR are eyelid closures. In SCR conditioning, an increase in skin conductance is first elicited by a shock, and after conditioning there is a similar skin conductance response to some initially neutral stimulus.

Despite these apparent confirmations of stimulus substitution theory, today most psychologists believe that the theory is not correct. There are several problems. First, the CR is almost never an exact replica of the UR. For instance, in eyeblink conditioning, the UR to an air puff is a large and rapid eyelid closure, but the CR is a smaller and more gradual eyelid closure. Second, not all parts of the UR become part of the CR. For example, Zener (1937) noted that when a dog is presented with food as a US, many responses, such as chewing and swallowing the food, occur in addition to salivation. However, a well-trained CS such as a bell will usually elicit only salivation, not chewing and swallowing responses. Third, a CR may include some features that are not part of the UR. For instance, using a bell as a CS,

Zener found that many dogs would turn their heads and look at the bell when it was rung. Sometimes a dog would move its entire body closer to the ringing bell. Obviously, these behaviors were not a normal part of the dog's UR to food. Fourth, in some cases the CR is opposite of the UR. For instance, one response to an electric shock is an increase in heart rate, but in studies with guinea pigs, Black (1965) observed conditioned heart rate decreases to a CS paired with shock. As another example, one of the URs to a morphine injection is an increase in body temperature. However, if rats are repeatedly presented with some CS followed by a morphine injection, the CS will later produce decreases in body temperature. Conditioned responses that are the opposite of the UR are called **conditioned compensatory responses**.

In summary, although its simplicity is appealing, stimulus substitution theory does not provide a full and complete description of what occurs in classical conditioning. Classical conditioning is not simply a transfer of a response from one stimulus to another. Because of the problems described here, it is often difficult to predict in advance what the CR will look like in a specific instance. It may resemble the UR, or it may be very different.

Because of the problems with the stimulus substitution approach, other theories have been proposed. According to the **sign-tracking theory** (Costa & Boakes, 2009; Hearst & Jenkins, 1974), the CS does not become a *substitute* for the US but rather a *sign* or signal for the upcoming US. The theory states that animals tend to orient themselves toward, approach, and explore any stimuli that are good predictors of important events, such as the delivery of food. For instance, if a bell is repeatedly paired with food, a dog may exhibit an orienting response: It may raise its ears, look in the direction of the bell, and possibly approach the bell. Therefore, it is not surprising that some components of the orienting response to the CS are retained as part of the CR. In summary, the form of the CR may include features that are part of the animal's natural response to the signal, as well as features of its natural response to the US.

What Is Learned in Classical Conditioning?

Besides recording the behavior of his animals, Pavlov also speculated about what changes might take place in the brain during classical conditioning. He proposed that there is a specific part of the brain, which we can call the *US center*, that becomes active whenever a US (such as food) is presented. Similarly, for every different CS (a tone, a light), there is a separate *CS center*, which becomes active whenever that particular CS is presented. From what we know about the physiology of the sensory systems (Chapter 1), these assumptions seem quite reasonable. Pavlov also assumed that for every UR (say, salivation) there is a part of the brain that can be called a *response center*, which, when activated, sends the neural commands that produce the observed response. There is an innate connection between the US center and the response center (see Figure 3.4). During classical conditioning, some new association develops, so that now the CS activates the response center (and a CR is observed).

As Figure 3.4 shows, there are at least two types of new associations that would give the CS the capacity to elicit a CR. On one hand, a direct association between the CS center and the response center might form during conditioning, which can be called a stimulus–response association, or *S-R association*. On the other hand, an association might

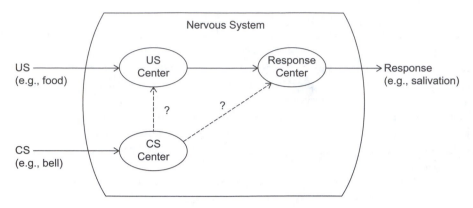

Figure 3.4 Two possible versions of Pavlov's stimulus substitution theory. During classical condition-ing, an association might develop from the CS center to the US center or from the CS center directly to the response center.

form between the CS center and the US center (an association between two stimuli, or *S-S association*). Later, when the CS is presented, the CS center is activated, which activates the US center (through the S-S association), which in turn activates the response center (through the innate association). Pavlov tended to favor the S-S alternative, but he had little data on which to decide between the two.

Later experimenters devised some clever techniques to try to distinguish between these two alternatives. Rescorla (1973) used the following reasoning: If the S-S position is correct, then after conditioning, the occurrence of a CR depends on the continued strength of two associations—the learned association between the CS center and the US center and the innate association between the US center and the response center (see Figure 3.4). If the US-response connection is somehow weakened, this should also weaken the CR since the occurrence of the CR depends on this connection. However, if the S-R position is correct, the strength of the CR does not depend on the continued integrity of the US-response association but only on the direct association between the CS center and the response center. But how can a reflexive US-response association be weakened? Rescorla's solution was to rely on habituation.

Rescorla used a conditioned suppression procedure with rats, with a loud noise as the US, because he knew that there would be habituation to the noise if it were repeatedly presented. The design of the experiment is shown in Table 3.1. In Phase 1, two groups of rats received identical classical conditioning with a light as the CS and the noise as the US. In Phase 2, the habituation group received many presentations of the noise by itself in order to habituate the rats' fear of the noise. The technique of decreasing the effectiveness of the US after an excitatory CS has been created is called *US devaluation*. The control rats spent equal amounts of time in the experimental chamber in Phase 2, but no stimuli were presented, so there was no opportunity for the noise to habituate in this group. In the test phase, both groups were presented with the light by itself for a number of trials, and their rates of lever pressing were recorded. When the light came

Table 3.1 Design of Rescorla's (1973) experiment on S–S versus S–R connections.

Group	Phase 1	Phase 2	Test
Habituation	Light→Noise	Noise (habituation)	Light
Control	Light→Noise	No stimuli	Light

on, lever pressing was greatly suppressed in the control group but not in the habituation group. Rescorla concluded that the strength of the CR depends on the continued strength of the US-response association, as predicted by the S-S position but not the S-R position.

Similar studies have been conducted with human subjects, some using the skin conductance response (SCR) preparation. For example, a CS (such as a picture of some common object) is paired with a loud noise or a shock, and then the intensity of the US is changed. If the US intensity is decreased, SCRs to the CS decrease as well. Conversely, if the intensity of the US is increased, SCRs to the CS also increase (Schultz, Balderston, Geiger, & Helmstetter, 2013; White & Davey, 1989). These results also support the S-S position because they show that the response to the CS changes depending on the current strength of the response to the US. Other research on the associations formed during classical conditioning will be described in Chapter 4.

BASIC CONDITIONING PHENOMENA

Acquisition

The part of a conditioning experiment in which the learner first experiences a series of CS–US pairings, and during which the CR gradually appears and increases in strength, is called the **acquisition phase**. Figure 3.5 shows the results of an acquisition phase in an experiment on eyeblink conditioning with human participants (Gerwig et al., 2010). The participants received three sessions of 100 trials per day, in which a brief tone was followed by an air puff directed at the eye. For the normal adults, the percentage of trials with a CR gradually increased until it leveled off at about 55%. This value—the maximum level of conditioned responding that is gradually approached as conditioning proceeds—is called the *asymptote*. Figure 3.5 also shows the results from a group of adults who had suffered strokes that caused damage to the cerebellum, a part of the brain that plays an important role in eyeblink conditioning. These participants showed weaker levels of conditioned responding, which reached an asymptote of about 30%.

In general, if a stronger stimulus is used as a US (a stronger puff of air, a larger amount of food), the asymptote of conditioning will be higher (a higher percentage of conditioned eyeblinks, more salivation). Strong USs also usually result in faster conditioning; that is, it may take fewer trials for a CR to appear with a strong US than with a weak one. The same is true about the intensity of the CS (e.g., classical conditioning will be faster with a loud tone than with a soft tone).

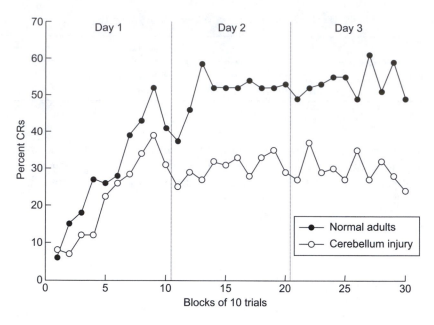

Figure 3.5 The acquisition of eyeblink CRs by normal adults and by those who had suffered strokes that caused damage to the cerebellum. (Adapted from *Behavioural Brain Research*, Vol. 2, Gerwig, M. et al., Evaluation of multiple-session delay eyeblink conditioning comparing patients with focal cerebellar lesions and cerebellar degeneration, 143–151. Copyright 2010, with permission from Elsevier.)

Extinction

A simple technique for producing a reduction and eventual disappearance of the CR is **extinction**, which involves repeatedly presenting the CS without the US. Suppose we followed the acquisition phase with an extinction phase in which the bell was presented for many trials but no food was delivered. The first two panels in Figure 3.6 show, in an idealized form, the likely results of our hypothetical experiment. As the bell is presented trial after trial without food, the amount of salivation gradually decreases, and eventually it disappears altogether. When the extinction phase is completed, we have a dog that behaves like a dog that is just beginning the experiment—the bell is presented and no salivation occurs. We might conclude that extinction simply reverses the effects of the previous acquisition phase. That is, if the animal has formed an association between the CS and the US during the acquisition phase, perhaps this association is gradually destroyed during the extinction phase. This hypothesis seems very reasonable, but it is almost certainly wrong, as explained in the next section.

Spontaneous Recovery, Disinhibition, and Rapid Reacquisition

Suppose that after an acquisition phase on Day 1 and an extinction phase on Day 2, we return the dog to the experimental chamber on Day 3 and conduct another series of extinction trials with the bell. Figure 3.6 shows that on the first several trials of Day 3, we are likely

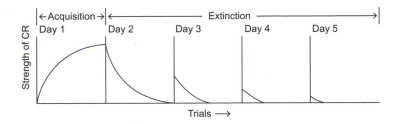

Figure 3.6 Idealized changes in the strength of a CR across one acquisition day followed by 4 days of extinction.

to see some conditioned responding to the bell, even though no CRs were observed at the end of Day 2. Pavlov called this reappearance of conditioned responding **spontaneous recovery**, and he treated it as proof that the CS–US association is not permanently destroyed in an extinction procedure.

Several different theories about spontaneous recovery have been proposed. One popular theory, which we can call the *inhibition theory*, states that after extinction is complete, the subject is left with two counteracting associations (Konorski, 1948). The CS–US association formed during acquisition is called an *excitatory association* because through this association the CS now excites, or activates, the US center. According to this theory, a parallel but *inhibitory association* develops during extinction. When extinction is complete, the effects of the excitatory and inhibitory associations cancel out, so that the US center is no longer activated when the CS is presented. However, the theory states that inhibitory associations (at least newly formed ones) are more fragile than excitatory associations, and they are more severely weakened by the passage of time. Therefore, at the beginning of Day 3, the weakened inhibitory association can no longer fully counteract the excitatory association, and so some CRs are observed. Further extinction trials on Day 3 strengthen the inhibitory association, and so conditioned responding once again disappears.

If we were to conduct further extinction sessions on Days 4, 5, 6, and so on, we might again observe some spontaneous recovery, but typically the amount of spontaneous recovery would become smaller and smaller until it no longer occurred (see Figure 3.6). According to the inhibition theory, this happens because the inhibitory association becomes progressively stronger with repeated extinction sessions.

The inhibition theory is just one of several theories about why spontaneous recovery occurs. Some experiments by Robbins (1990) supported a theory that during extinction, the subject stops "processing" or "paying attention to" the CS. Conditioned responses then disappear because when the animal stops paying attention to the CS, it stops responding to the CS. Later, when the animal is brought back to the conditioning chamber after some time has passed, the animal's attention to the CS is revived for a while, leading to a spontaneous recovery of CRs.

Another theory of spontaneous recovery states that the CS becomes an ambiguous stimulus because it has been associated both with the US and then with the absence of the US (Bouton, 2000; Capaldi, 1966). As you can see, there is disagreement among the experts on exactly what causes extinction and spontaneous recovery. Modern neurophysiological research suggests that several different processes may contribute to extinction, including inhibition and a partial erasure or weakening of the original association (Delamater & West-brook, 2014).

More evidence that extinction is not the complete erasure of previous learning comes from the phenomenon of **disinhibition**. Suppose that an extinction phase has progressed to the point where the CS (a bell) no longer evokes any salivation. Now, if a novel stimulus such as a buzzer is presented a few seconds before the bell, the bell may once again elicit a CR of salivation. Pavlov called this effect disinhibition because he believed that the presentation of a distracting stimulus (the buzzer) disrupts the fragile inhibition that supposedly develops during extinction. According to the inhibition theory, the more stable excitatory association is less affected by the distracting stimulus than is the inhibitory association, and the result is a reappearance of the conditioned salivary response.

The phenomenon of **rapid reacquisition** is a third piece of evidence that extinction does not completely eliminate what was learned in the acquisition phase. Rapid reacquisition is similar to the "savings" that are found in experiments on list learning (Chapter 1) or habituation (Chapter 2). In classical conditioning, if a subject receives an acquisition phase, an extinction phase, and then another acquisition phase with the same CS and the same US, the rate of learning is substantially faster in the second acquisition phase—the reacquisition phase (Bouton, Woods, & Pineño, 2004). Furthermore, if an animal receives repeated cycles of extinction and reacquisition, the rate of learning tends to get faster and faster (Hoehler, Kirschenbaum, & Leonard, 1973).

These three phenomena—spontaneous recovery, disinhibition, and rapid reacquisition—make it very clear that there is no simple way to get a subject to "unlearn" a CR and that no amount of extinction training can completely wipe out all the effects of a classical conditioning experience. Extinction can cause a CR to disappear, and after a while spontaneous recovery may disappear, but the subject will never be exactly the same as before the conditioning began.

Conditioned Inhibition

There is plenty of evidence that, depending on the procedures used in classical conditioning, a CS may become either excitatory or inhibitory (Miller & Spear, 1985). An **excitatory CS** is simply one that elicits a CR. An **inhibitory CS** (also called a **conditioned inhibitor** or a **CS–**) is one that prevents the occurrence of a CR or reduces the size of the CR from what it would otherwise be. Pavlov discovered a fairly simple and effective procedure for changing a neutral stimulus into a conditioned inhibitor. Suppose we repeatedly pair the sound of the buzzer with food until a dog always salivates at the sound of the buzzer. The buzzer can now be called an excitatory CS (or CS+) because it regularly elicits a CR. In the second phase of the experiment, the dog receives two types of trials. Some trials are exactly like those of Phase 1 (buzzer plus food). However, on other trials both the buzzer and a light are presented simultaneously, but no food is delivered. The simultaneous presentation of two or more CSs, such as the buzzer and the light, is called a **compound CS**. After many trials of both types, the dog will eventually salivate on trials with the buzzer alone but not on trials with both the buzzer and the light. It appears that the light has become a conditioned inhibitor: It prevents the response of salivation to the buzzer that would otherwise occur.

One way to provide a convincing demonstration that the light has become a conditioned inhibitor is to show that it can prevent salivation to some other CS, not just to the buzzer with which it was trained. Suppose that a third stimulus, a fan blowing air into the chamber, is paired with food until it reliably elicits salivation. Now, for the first time, the animal receives a trial with a compound CS consisting of the fan and the light. If the light is truly a conditioned inhibitor, it should have the capacity to reduce the salivation produced by any CS, not just by the buzzer with which it was originally presented. In this test, we would find that the light reduced or eliminated the CR to the fan, even though these two stimuli were never presented together before. This shows that the light is a general conditioned inhibitor because it seems to have the ability to block or diminish the salivation elicited by any excitatory CS.

Generalization and Discrimination

After classical conditioning with one CS, other, similar stimuli will also elicit CRs, even though these other stimuli have never been paired with the US. This transfer of the effects of conditioning to similar stimuli is called **generalization**, which is illustrated in Figure 3.7. In this experiment, rabbits received eyeblink conditioning with a 1,200-Hz tone as the CS and a shock near the eye as a US (Liu, 1971). Then the rabbits were tested with tones of five different frequencies, but no US was presented. As can be seen, the 1,200-Hz tone elicited the highest percentage of CRs. The two tones closest in frequency to the 1,200-Hz tone elicited an intermediate level of responding, and the more distant tones elicited the fewest responses. The function in Figure 3.7 is a typical **generalization gradient**. It shows that the more similar a stimulus is to the training stimulus, the greater will be its capacity to elicit CRs.

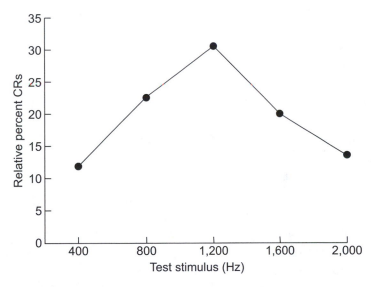

Figure 3.7 A typical generalization gradient. After eyeblink conditioning with a 1,200-Hz tone, rabbits were tested with tones of higher and lower pitches. (From Liu, S. S., 1971, Differential conditioning and stimulus generalization of the rabbit's nictating membrane response. *Journal of Comparative and Physiological Psychology, 77,* 136–142. © American Psychological Association. Reprinted with permission.)

Generalization can be used by advertisers to help them sell their products. Till and Priluck (2000) found that if consumers have a favorable attitude toward a particular brand name of a product, this favorable attitude generalizes to other brands that have similar names and to other products with the same brand name. This can help to explain why many products you see in supermarkets and department stores have names and package designs similar to those of well-known brands.

The opposite of generalization is **discrimination**, in which an individual learns to respond to one stimulus but not to a similar stimulus. We have seen that if a rabbit's eyeblink is conditioned to a 1,200–Hz tone, there will be substantial generalization to an 800–Hz tone. However, if the 800–Hz tone is never followed by food, but the 1,200–Hz tone is always followed by food, the animal will eventually learn a discrimination in which the 1,200–Hz tone elicits an eyeblink and the 800–Hz tone does not. This type of discrimination learning is important in many real-world situations. For instance, it is appropriate for you to have a fear reaction if you are rapidly driving into an intersection and you see that the light has turned red, but not if you see the light is green.

BOX 3.1   SPOTLIGHT ON RESEARCH

Classical Conditioning and the Immune System

As you probably know, the body's immune system is designed to fight off infections. Whenever bacteria, viruses, or foreign cells enter a person's body, the immune system produces antibodies that attack and kill these invaders. There is convincing evidence that the immune system can be influenced by classical conditioning. Ader and Cohen (1975) conducted a landmark study in this area. They gave rats a single conditioning trial in which the CS was saccharin-flavored water and the US was an injection of cyclophosphamide, a drug that suppresses the activity of the immune system. A few days later, the rats were injected with a small quantity of foreign cells (red blood cells from sheep) that their immune systems would normally attack vigorously. One group of rats was then given saccharin-flavored water once again, whereas a control group received plain water. Ader and Cohen found that for rats in the saccharin-water group, the response of the immune system was weaker than for rats in the plain-water group; that is, fewer antibodies were produced by rats in the saccharin-water group. In other words, they found that the saccharin, which normally has no effect on the immune system, now produced a CR, a weakening of the immune system.

The activity of the immune system can also be increased through classical conditioning. Solvason, Ghanata, and Hiramoto (1988) exposed mice to the odor of camphor as a CS, and then they were injected with the drug *interferon* as the US. Interferon normally causes an increase in the activity of natural killer cells in the bloodstream—cells that are involved in combating viruses and the growth of tumors. After a few pairings of the camphor odor and interferon, presenting the camphor odor by itself was enough to produce an increase in activity of the natural killer cells. A similar study with healthy human adults also obtained increases in natural killer cells through classical conditioning (Buske-Kirschbaum, Kirschbaum, Stierle, Jabaij, & Hellhammer, 1994).

Researchers have recognized the potential importance of this phenomenon, and they have begun to understand the brain mechanisms that make conditioning of the immune system possible (Kusnecov, 2014). For people whose immune systems have been temporarily weakened through illness or fatigue, developing psychological techniques to strengthen immune activity could be beneficial. In other cases, decreasing the activity of the immune system may be what is needed. For example, common allergies are the product of an overactive immune system. In one study, people who were allergic to dust mites were given five trials in which flavored water was paired with an antihistamine (a drug that reduces the allergic reaction). Later, when they received a trial with the flavored water but no drug, they showed the same signs of relief from their allergy symptoms as when they actually received the drug (Goebel, Meykadeh, Kou, Schedlowski, & Hengge, 2008). Human research on classical conditioning and the immune system is still fairly limited, but this type of research may eventually produce ways to better control immune system activity for the benefit of the patient.

THE IMPORTANCE OF TIMING IN CLASSICAL CONDITIONING

In all types of classical conditioning, the precise timing of the CS and the US can have a major effect in several ways. The timing of events can affect (1) how strong the conditioning will be, (2) whether a CS will become excitatory or inhibitory, and (3) exactly when the CR occurs.

All of the experiments discussed so far used **short–delay conditioning** in which the CS begins a second or so before the US (as diagrammed in Figure 3.8). This temporal arrangement usually produces the strongest and most rapid conditioning. Studies have shown that it is important for the CS to begin slightly before the US does: In **simultaneous conditioning**, where the CS and US begin at the same moment (see Figure 3.8), conditioned responding is much weaker than in short-delay conditioning (Smith & Gormezano, 1965). This may be so for a few reasons. For one thing, if the US begins at the same moment as the CS, the learner may respond to the US but fail to notice the CS. Also, if

PRACTICE QUIZ 1: CHAPTER 3

1. In eyeblink conditioning, a tone could be used as the _____ and an air puff as the _____; an eyeblink is the _____.
2. A problem with Pavlov's stimulus substitution theory is that the _____ does not always resemble the _____.
3. Rescorla's (1973) experiment supported the theory of S-S associations because after responding to the US (loud noise) was reduced through habituation, responding to the CS _____.
4. Three phenomena that show that extinction is not the complete elimination of a learned association are _____, _____, and _____.
5. After classical conditioning with one CS, the appearance of CRs to new but similar stimuli is called _____.

ANSWERS

1. CS, US, CR and UR 2. CR, UR 3. decreased 4. spontaneous recovery, disinhibition, rapid reacquisition 5. generalization

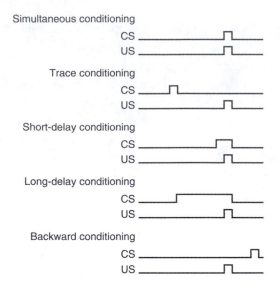

Figure 3.8 The temporal relationships between CS and US in five types of classical conditioning.

the CS does not precede the US, it cannot serve to signal or predict the arrival of the US. As we will see again and again, the predictiveness of a CS is an important determinant of the degree of conditioning the CS undergoes and of whether this conditioning is excitatory or inhibitory. The following rules of thumb, though not perfect, are usually helpful in predicting the outcome of a conditioning arrangement:

- If a CS is a good predictor of the presence of the US, it will tend to become excitatory.
- If a CS is a good predictor of the absence of the US, it will tend to become inhibitory.

Keep these rules in mind when examining the other conditioning arrangements discussed in this section.

As shown in Figure 3.8, **trace conditioning** refers to the case in which the CS and US are separated by some time interval in which neither stimulus is present. The name reflects the idea that since the CS is no longer physically present when the US occurs, the learner must rely on a "memory trace" of the CS if conditioning is to occur. In various studies on classical conditioning, the amount of time elapsing between CS and US presentations, or the *CS–US interval*, was systematically varied. That is, one group might receive a series of conditioning trials with a 2-second CS–US interval, another group with a 5-second CS–US interval, and so on. As the duration of the CS–US interval is increased, the level of conditioning declines systematically (Ellison, 1964).

A similar pattern emerges in **long-delay conditioning**, where the CS begins at least several seconds before the US, but the CS continues until the US is presented (Figure 3.8). In long-delay conditioning, the CS–US interval is the delay between the onsets of the CS and US. Here, too, the strength of the conditioned responding decreases as the CS–US interval increases, but the effects of delay are usually not as pronounced as in trace conditioning (which is understandable since in long-delay conditioning, the learner does not have to rely on memory of the CS).

In long-delay conditioning, Pavlov noted that the timing of the CRs changed over trials. Early in training, a dog would salivate as soon as the CS was presented, although the CS–US interval might be 10 seconds. As conditioning trials continued, however, these early CRs would gradually disappear, and the dog would salivate shortly before the food was presented (8 or 9 seconds after CS onset). This pattern is consistent with the rule that the stimulus that is the best predictor of the US will be the most strongly conditioned. In this example, what stimulus is a better predictor of the US than CS onset? It is the compound stimulus—CS onset plus the passage of about 10 seconds. Therefore, it is this combination that eventually elicits the most vigorous CRs.

The bottom of Figure 3.8 shows the procedure of **backward conditioning**, in which the CS is presented after the US. Even if the CS is presented immediately after the US, the level of conditioning is markedly lower than in simultaneous or short-delay conditioning. This finding illustrates a limitation of the contiguity principle: Besides their temporal proximity, the order of the stimuli is important. Although backward conditioning may result in a weak excitatory association, there is evidence that after more trials, a backward CS becomes inhibitory (Siegel & Domjan, 1971). Once again, the predictiveness rule can serve as a useful guide: In backward conditioning, the CS signals a period of time in which the US will be absent. As long as the CS is present, the learner can be certain that no US will occur.

One hypothesis about classical conditioning that addresses the timing of events is the **temporal coding hypothesis** (Arcediano, Escobar, & Miller, 2005; Matzel, Held, & Miller, 1988). This hypothesis states that in classical conditioning, more is learned than a simple association between CS and US—the individual also learns about the timing of these two events, and this learning affects when the CR occurs. This hypothesis can explain why the CR may occur just before the onset of the US in long-delay conditioning—the individual has learned that a delay of a certain duration separates the onset of the CS and the onset of the US. A variety of experiments have demonstrated the role of temporal coding in both excitatory and inhibitory conditioning. For instance, if animals learn that food is likely to be presented 10 seconds after a CS begins, but food is unlikely to be presented 30 seconds after the CS begins, many CRs occur around the 10-second mark, and very few occur around 30 seconds (Williams, Johns, & Brindas, 2008). Such experiments on the timing of CRs make it very clear that animals learn about temporal relations between CS and US, not just CS–US associations (Kirkpatrick & Church, 2004; Polack, Molet, Miguez, & Miller, 2013).

CS–US Correlations

In all of the conditioning arrangements shown in Figure 3.8, the CS and US are presented on every trial, and the temporal pattern is the same. In the real world, however, things are not always so regular. For example, a sound in the night could be a signal of danger (a burglar in the house), but most of the time it might just be the house creaking. Similarly, for a rabbit in the forest, the rustling of leaves could be a predator, or it could be simply a breeze. Although the relationships among stimuli are variable and uncertain in the real world, it is important for both people and animals to know which stimuli are the most dependable signals of important events, both good and bad. In the laboratory, classical conditioning procedures can be used to evaluate an animal's ability to detect imperfect correlations between stimuli.

A series of experiments by Rescorla (1966, 1968) showed how the probability of the US in the presence of the CS and in its absence combine to determine the strength of the CR. In a conditioned suppression procedure with rats, the CS was a 2-minute tone that was presented at random intervals. In one condition, there was a 40% chance that a shock would occur at some point when the tone was on and a 20% chance of shock when the tone was off. In this case, where the probability of shock was greater in the presence of the tone, the tone became an excitatory CS (lever pressing was suppressed when the tone came on). In another condition, the probability of shock was the same in the presence and absence of the tone (e.g., a 40% chance of shock both when the tone was on and when it was off). In this case, the rats showed no suppression at all to the tone. In a third condition, the probability of shock was lower when the tone was on than when it was off (so the tone signaled a relative level of safety from shock), and in this case the tone became an inhibitory CS.

Based on these results, Rescorla concluded that an important variable in classical conditioning is the correlation between CS and US. If the correlation is positive (the CS predicts a higher-than-normal probability of the US), the CS will become excitatory. If there is no correlation between CS and US (the probability of the US is the same whether or not the CS is present), the CS will remain neutral. If the correlation between CS and US is negative (the CS signals a lower-than-normal probability of the US), the CS will become inhibitory. These results provide another instance where the predictiveness rule is a useful guide: If a CS predicts that the US is likely to occur, the CS will become excitatory; if the CS predicts that the US is not likely to occur, the CS will become inhibitory. This rule is not perfect, but it works well in most cases.

SECOND-ORDER CONDITIONING

So far we have examined only procedures in which a CS is paired with (or correlated with) a US. However, this is not the only way a CS can acquire the ability to elicit a CR. In **second-order conditioning**, a CR is transferred from one CS to another. Pavlov described the following experiment to illustrate this process. First, the ticking of a metronome was used as a CS in salivary conditioning until the sound of the metronome elicited salivation. Because it was paired with the US, the metronome is called a *first-order CS*. Then another stimulus, a black square, was presented and immediately followed by the sound of the metronome on a number of trials, but no food was presented on these trials. After a few trials of this type, the black square began to elicit salivation on its own, even though it was never paired directly with the food (but only with the metronome). In this example, the black square is called a *second-order CS* because it acquired its ability to elicit a CR by being paired with a first-order CS, the metronome.

Second-order conditioning has also been demonstrated with humans. For example, in a procedure called **evaluative conditioning**, people are asked to evaluate different stimuli—to rate how much they like them using a scale that ranges from "very disliked" to "very liked." The first-order CSs are typically words that people consistently rate as being positive (e.g., honest or friendly) or negative (e.g., cruel or arrogant). These words are first-order CSs, not unconditioned stimuli, because they would certainly have no value to someone who

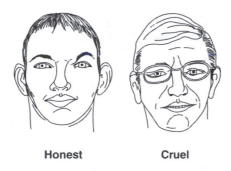

Honest   **Cruel**

Figure 3.9 In evaluative conditioning, initially neutral stimuli such as pictures of faces are paired with positive or negative adjectives. After conditioning, people will have positive or negative reactions to the faces as well.

did not know the English language. For English speakers, these words presumably attained their positive or negative values because they have been associated with good or bad experiences in the past. In one interesting study, pictures of people's faces were the second-order stimuli, and, while looking at some of these faces, the participants heard either positive or negative adjectives (Figure 3.9). The participants later rated the faces as being "liked" if they had been paired with positive adjectives and "disliked" if they had been paired with negative adjectives. These positive or negative ratings of the faces occurred even if the participants could not remember the adjectives that had been paired with individual faces. In other words, participants knew they liked some faces and disliked others, but they could not say exactly why (Baeyens, Eelen, Van den Bergh, & Crombez, 1992).

CLASSICAL CONDITIONING OUTSIDE THE LABORATORY

In everyday life, classical conditioning is important in at least two ways. First, it gives us a way of understanding "involuntary" behaviors, those that are automatically elicited by certain stimuli whether we want them to occur or not. As discussed in the next section, many emotional reactions seem to fall into this category. Second, research on classical conditioning has led to several major treatment procedures for behavior disorders. These procedures can be used to strengthen desired "involuntary" responses or to weaken undesired responses. The remainder of this chapter examines the role of classical conditioning in these nonlaboratory settings.

Classical Conditioning and Emotional Responses

Everyday emotional responses such as feelings of pleasure, happiness, anxiety, or excitement are frequently triggered by specific stimuli. In many cases, the response-eliciting properties of a stimulus are not inborn but acquired through experience. Suppose you open your mailbox and find a card with the return address of a close friend. This stimulus may immediately evoke a pleasant and complex emotional reaction that you might loosely call affection, warmth, or fondness. Whatever you call the emotional reaction, there is no doubt that this particular stimulus—a person's handwritten address on an envelope—would not elicit the response from you shortly after your birth, nor would it elicit the response now if you did not know the person who sent you the letter. The envelope is a CS that elicits a pleasant emotional response only because the address has been associated with your friend. Other stimuli can elicit less pleasant emotional reactions. For many college students, examination periods can be a time of high anxiety. This anxiety can be conditioned to stimuli associated with the examination process—the textbooks on one's desk, a calendar with the date of the exam circled, or the sight of the building where the exam will be held.

Classical conditioning can also affect our emotional reactions to other people. In one study using evaluative conditioning, participants were asked to look at photographs of people's faces, and each photograph was paired with either a pleasant, neutral, or unpleasant odor. When they later had to evaluate their preferences for the people in the photographs (with no odors present), they gave the highest ratings to faces previously paired with pleasant odors and the lowest ratings to those paired with unpleasant odors (Todrank, Byrnes, Wrzesniewski, & Rozin, 1995). This research surely encourages companies that sell mouthwash, deodorant, and perfume.

Applications in Behavior Therapy

Systematic Desensitization for Phobias

One of the most widely used procedures of behavior therapy is **systematic desensitization**, a treatment for phobias that arose directly out of laboratory research on classical conditioning. A phobia is an excessive and irrational fear of an object, place, or situation. Phobias can be quite debilitating. A fear of insects or snakes may preclude going to a picnic or taking a walk in the woods. A fear of crowds may make it impossible for a person to go to the supermarket, to a movie, or to ride on a bus or train.

How do phobias arise? After Pavlov's discovery, classical conditioning was seen as one possible source of irrational fears. In a famous (or, more accurately, infamous) experiment by John B. Watson and Rosalie Rayner (1921), a normal 11-month-old infant named Albert was conditioned to fear a white rat (which Albert initially did not fear) with a loud noise of a hammer hitting a steel bar (which made him cry). After several trials on which the white rat was paired with the noise, Albert would cry when he was presented with the white rat by itself. This fear also generalized to a white rabbit and to other white furry objects, including a ball of cotton and a Santa Claus mask. If this experiment sounds cruel and unethical, rest assured that modern standards would not allow such an experiment to be conducted today. However, the experiment demonstrated how a fear could be acquired through classical conditioning. It also suggests a possible treatment: If a phobia can be acquired through classical conditioning, perhaps it can be eliminated through extinction.

Systematic desensitization is a procedure in which the patient is exposed to the phobic object gradually, so that fear and discomfort are kept to a minimum and extinction is allowed to occur. The treatment has three parts: the construction of a fear hierarchy, training in relaxation, and the gradual presentation of items in the fear hierarchy to the patient. The fear hierarchy is a list of fearful situations of progressively increasing intensity. At the bottom of the list is an item that evokes only a very mild fear response in the patient, and at the top is the most highly feared situation. Once the fear hierarchy is constructed, patients are given a session of deep muscle relaxation, after which they typically report that they feel very calm and relaxed. The therapist then begins with the weakest item in the hierarchy, describes the scene to the patient, and asks the patient to imagine this scene as vividly as possible. For example, in the treatment of a teenager who developed a fear of driving after an automobile accident, the first instruction was to imagine "looking at his car as it was before the accident" (Kushner, 1968). Because the patient is in a relaxed state, and because the lowest item did not evoke much fear to begin with, it usually can be imagined with little or no fear. After a short pause in which the patient is told to relax, the first item is again presented. If the patient reports that the item produces no fear, the therapist moves on to the second item on the list, and the procedure is repeated. The therapist slowly progresses up the list, being certain that the fear of one item is completely gone before going on to the next item.

The results of numerous studies on systematic desensitization involving thousands of patients have been published, and in most of these reports about 80 to 90% of the patients were cured of their phobias—a very high success rate for any type of therapy in the realm of mental health (Paul, 1969). In some cases, real stimuli are used instead of relying on the patient's imagination. Sturges and Sturges (1998) treated an 11-year-old girl with a fear of elevators by systematically exposing her to an elevator (beginning by having her just stand near an elevator and ending with her riding alone on the elevator). In another variation of systematic desensitization, humor was used in place of relaxation training, based on the reasoning that humor would also counteract anxiety. Individuals with an extreme fear of spiders were asked to create jokes about spiders, and they were presented with humorous scenes involving spiders. This treatment proved to be just about as effective as the more traditional relaxation training in reducing spider phobias (Ventis, Higbee, & Murdock, 2001).

BOX 3.2 APPLYING THE RESEARCH

Virtual Reality Therapy

A therapy technique that combines classical conditioning and modern computer technology is **virtual reality therapy**, in which the patient wears a headset that displays realistic visual images that change with every head movement, simulating a three-dimensional environment. One application is in the treatment of phobias. In one case, for example, a man with a fear of flying was exposed to more and more challenging simulations of riding in a helicopter, and eventually his fear of flying diminished. Virtual reality therapy has been successfully used for fears of animals, heights, public speaking, and so on (Baus & Bouchard, 2014; North, North, & Coble, 2002). This technique has several advantages over traditional systematic desensitization. The procedure does not rely on the patient's ability to imagine the objects or situations. The stimuli are very realistic, they can be controlled precisely, and they can be tailored to the needs of each individual patient.

Virtual reality therapy has also been used to treat individuals with post-traumatic stress disorder (PTSD), including combat veterans and others who have been exposed to violence in their lives. In one controlled study, active-duty soldiers with PTSD were randomly assigned to two groups. One group received "treatment as usual"—the standard treatment provided by mental health facilities for PTSD, which included such things as cognitive therapy, relaxation training, thought control, and group therapy. The other group received virtual reality therapy over a period of about 10 weeks, with one or two therapy sessions a week. The patients wore 3-D goggles that depicted scenes and events that were very similar to those they had experienced in combat, such as the sights and sounds of their base camp, engaging in house-to-house searches, and being attacked by enemy forces. As in systematic desensitization, the patients were also given relaxation training, and the stimuli were presented in a graduated sequence, going from mild to increasingly stressful situations. Besides relying on the patients' reports of their anxiety levels during this treatment, the therapists used medical recording equipment to continually measure the patients' arousal and anxiety levels to make sure their emotional reactions did not become too intense. This study found substantial improvement in most of those in the virtual reality group (at least a 30% decrease in PTSD symptoms), and this was significantly better than the group that received treatment as usual (McLay et al., 2011). Other clinical tests have confirmed that virtual reality therapy can be an effective treatment for PTSD (Botella, Serrano, Baños, & Garcia-Palacios, 2015).

In addition to phobias and PTSD, virtual reality therapy has been used with some success for other disorders, including chronic pain, smoking, alcoholism, and drug addictions. Of course, the treatment methods can vary greatly depending on the type of problem being treated. For instance, in the treatment for drug addictions, images of stimuli associated with the drug are repeatedly presented in an effort to reduce the drug cravings produced by these stimuli (see the section on cue-exposure therapy in Chapter 4). As the technology continues to improve and as therapists discover the most effective ways to apply it in conjunction with other treatment methods, it seems likely that the use of computer-generated stimuli will become more widespread in behavior therapy in the future.

Aversive Counterconditioning

The goal of **aversive counterconditioning** is to develop an aversive CR to stimuli associated with an undesirable behavior. For instance, if a person has alcoholism, the procedure may involve conditioning the responses of nausea and queasiness of the stomach to the sight, smell, and taste of alcohol. The term *counterconditioning* is used because the technique is designed to replace a positive emotional response to certain stimuli (such as alcohol) with a negative one. In the 1940s, Voegtlin and his associates treated over 4,000 individuals with alcoholism who volunteered for this distinctly unpleasant therapy (Lemere, Voegtlin, Broz, O'Hallaren, & Tupper, 1942; Voegtlin, 1940). Over a 10-day period, a patient received about a half dozen treatment sessions in which alcoholic beverages were paired with an emetic (a drug that produces nausea). First, the patient received an emetic, and soon the first signs of nausea would begin. The patient was then given a large glass of whiskey and was instructed to look at, smell, and taste the whiskey, and after a few minutes the drug caused the patient to vomit. In later conditioning sessions, other liquors were used to ensure that the aversion was not limited to whiskey. It is hard to imagine a more unpleasant therapy, and the patients' willingness to participate gives an indication both of their commitment to overcome their alcoholism and of their inability to do so on their own.

Figure 3.10 shows the percentages of patients who were totally abstinent for various lengths of time after the therapy. The percentage was high at first but declined as years passed. The diminishing percentages may reflect the process of extinction: If over the years a person repeatedly encounters the sight or smell of alcohol (at weddings, at parties, on television) in the absence of the US (the emetic), the CR of nausea should eventually wear off. At least two types of evidence support the role of extinction. First, patients who received "booster sessions" (further conditioning sessions a few months after the original treatment) were, on average, abstinent for longer periods of time. The reconditioning sessions presumably counteracted the effects of extinction. Second, those who continued to associate with old drinking friends (and were thereby exposed to alcohol) were the most likely to fail.

If the declining percentages in Figure 3.10 seem discouraging, it is important to realize that a similar pattern of increasing relapses over time occurs with other treatments for alcoholism. Furthermore, Voegtlin used a very strict criterion for success—total abstinence. Individuals who drank with moderation after the treatment, or had just one relapse, were counted as failures. Figure 3.10 therefore presents the most pessimistic view possible about the success of this treatment. Despite the evidence for its effectiveness, in recent

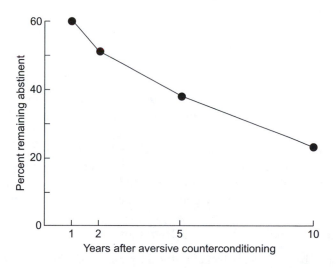

Figure 3.10 The percentages of Voegtlin's clients who remained completely abstinent for various amounts of time following aversive counterconditioning for alcoholism. (Based on Lemere & Voegtlin, 1950)

years aversive counterconditioning has not often been used as a treatment for alcoholism. When used, it is often included as one component of multifaceted treatment programs that also involve family counseling, self-control training, and other techniques (Smith & Frawley, 1990).

Aversive counterconditioning has also been applied to other behavioral problems, including drug use, cigarette smoking, overeating, and sexual deviations. Different aversive stimuli have been used, including electric shock, unpleasant odors, or disgusting mental images. One method that has been used to help people quit smoking cigarettes is called "rapid smoking": The smoker inhales cigarette smoke at a rapid pace, which makes it a sickening experience. This technique has had a respectable success rate (Gifford & Shoenberger, 2009).

In summary, aversive counterconditioning is a procedure that attempts to decrease unwanted behaviors by conditioning aversive reactions to stimuli associated with the behaviors. Its effectiveness is variable. It appears to be a useful procedure for eliminating some sexual deviations, such as fetishes and exhibitionism. When used as a treatment for alcoholism or smoking, some clients have had relapses, but others have remained abstinent for years.

Treatment of Nocturnal Enuresis

Nocturnal enuresis (bedwetting during sleep) is a fairly common problem with children. If it continues at age 5 or older, it can become a frustrating problem for both children and parents. Fortunately, most cases can be cured by a straightforward procedure developed by Mowrer and Mowrer (1938) called the bell-and-pad method. The pad, a water-detecting device, is placed beneath the child's sheets; a single drop of urine will activate the device and ring the bell to wake up the child. The child is instructed in advance to turn off the alarm, go to the toilet and urinate, and then go back to sleep. The bell and pad are used every night until the problem disappears.

In this procedure, the bell is a US that elicits two responses in the child: (1) awakening and (2) the tightening of those muscles necessary to prevent further urination (responses that occur because the child has no difficulty retaining urine when awake). The goal of the procedure is to transfer either or both of these responses to an internal CS—the sensations associated with having a full bladder. For simplicity, let us call the CS a full bladder. By repeatedly pairing a full bladder with the bell, the response of awakening and/or tightening the muscles so as to retain one's urine should eventually be elicited by the full bladder alone, before the bell sounds.

Various studies have found success rates of about 80% for the bell-and-pad method. Relapses are a frequent problem, but they can be readily treated with additional bell-and-pad training. Evidence from a number of different studies has shown that the bell-and-pad method is more effective than other treatments for enuresis (Brown, Pope, & Brown, 2011).

Summary of the Classical Conditioning Therapies

Behavior therapies based on principles of classical conditioning have been used to strengthen, eliminate, or replace behaviors. The bell-and-pad treatment for nocturnal enuresis is an example of a procedure designed to strengthen a behavior (i.e., night-time retention).

Systematic desensitization is used to eliminate the emotional responses of fear and anxiety. Aversive counterconditioning is designed to replace pleasant emotional responses to such stimuli as alcohol and cigarette smoke with aversion. Each of these procedures has its share of failures and relapses, but each can also boast of long-term successes for a significant percentage of those who receive treatment.

SUMMARY

In its simplest form, classical conditioning involves the repeated pairing of a CS with a US that naturally elicits a UR. After repeated pairings, the CS starts to elicit a CR. Pavlov used the salivation response of dogs to study classical conditioning, but in modern research, some common conditioning preparations are eyeblink conditioning, conditioned suppression, the skin conductance response, and taste–aversion learning.

PRACTICE QUIZ 2: CHAPTER 3

1. When the CS and US are separated by some time interval, this is called _____.
2. The temporal arrangement that usually produces the strongest excitatory conditioning is _____ conditioning.
3. In an evaluative conditioning procedure in which pictures of people are paired with either positive or negative adjectives, the adjectives are _____ and the pictures of people are _____.
4. When the effectiveness of aversive counterconditioning for alcoholism weakens over time, this could be an example of the conditioning principle of _____.
5. In the classical conditioning treatment for bedwetting, the US is _____.

ANSWERS

1. trace conditioning 2. short-delay 3. first-order CSs, second-order CSs 4. extinction 5. an alarm that wakes up the child

---

According to Pavlov's stimulus substitution theory, the CS should produce the same response that the US originally did. In reality, however, sometimes the CR is different in form, and sometimes it is actually the opposite of the UR. In the brain, it has been proposed that neural centers for the CS become connected to either the center for the US (an S-S connection) or directly to the center for the response (an S-R connection). Some experiments on US devaluation favor the S-S view.

Throughout the animal kingdom, instances of classical conditioning exhibit the same basic principles, including acquisition, extinction, spontaneous recovery, disinhibition, conditioned inhibition, generalization, and discrimination. The most effective temporal arrangement for conditioning occurs in short-delay conditioning; weaker conditioning usually occurs in simultaneous, long-delay, or trace conditioning. In backward conditioning, the CS may become a conditioned inhibitor. In second-order conditioning, a CR is transferred not from US to CS but from one CS to another.

In everyday life, classically CRs can be seen in our emotional reactions to many different stimuli. In behavior therapy, systematic desensitization is used to extinguish phobias by gradually presenting more and more intense fear-provoking stimuli while the patient is in a relaxed state. Aversive counterconditioning is used to replace positive responses to certain stimuli (e.g., alcohol, cigarettes) with negative responses. The bell-and-pad method is used to train children to avoid bedwetting.

Review Questions

1. Define CS, US, UR, and CR. Use the examples of salivary conditioning and conditioning of the skin conductance response to illustrate these four concepts.
2. What three different types of evidence show that extinction does not simply erase the association that was formed during classical conditioning?
3. Describe one temporal arrangement between CS and US that produces strong excitatory conditioning, one that produces weak excitatory conditioning, and one that produces inhibitory conditioning. Give a reasonable explanation of why each different procedure produces the results that it does.
4. Explain how television advertisers can use classical conditioning to give viewers a positive feeling about their product. How could they use classical conditioning to give viewers a negative reaction to other brands? Can you think of actual commercials that use these techniques?
5. Explain how systematic desensitization is used to treat phobias. Explain how extinction and generalization are important parts of the procedure. Why don't phobias extinguish by themselves, without the need for treatment?

REFERENCES

Ader, R., & Cohen, N. (1975). Behaviorally conditioned immunosuppression. *Psychosomatic Medicine, 37*, 333–340.

Arcediano, F., Escobar, M., & Miller, R.R. (2005). Bidirectional associations in humans and rats. *Journal of Experimental Psychology: Animal Behavior Processes, 31*, 301–318.

Baeyens, F., Eelen, P., Van den Bergh, O., & Crombez, G. (1992). The content of learning in human evaluative conditioning: Acquired valence is sensitive to US revaluation. *Learning and Motivation, 23*, 200–224.

Baus, O., & Bouchard, S. (2014). Moving from virtual reality exposure-based therapy to augmented reality exposure-based therapy: A review. *Frontiers in Human Neuroscience, 8*, 112.

Black, A.H. (1965). Cardiac conditioning in curarized dogs: The relationship between heart rate and skeletal behavior. In W.F. Prokasy (Ed.), *Classical conditioning: A symposium* (pp. 20–47). New York: Appleton-Century-Crofts.

Botella, C., Serrano, B., Baños, R.M., & Garcia-Palacios, A. (2015). Virtual reality exposure-based therapy for the treatment of post-traumatic stress disorder: A review of its efficacy, the adequacy of the treatment protocol, and its acceptability. *Neuropsychiatric Disease and Treatment, 11*, Article ID 2533–2545.

Bouton, M.E. (2000). A learning theory perspective on lapse, relapse, and the maintenance of behavior change. *Health Psychology, 19*, 57–63.

Bouton, M.E., Woods, A.M., & Pineño, O. (2004). Occasional reinforced trials during extinction can slow the rate of rapid reacquisition. *Learning and Motivation, 35*, 371–390.

Brown, M.L., Pope, A.W., & Brown, E.J. (2011). Treatment of primary nocturnal enuresis in children: A review. *Child: Care, Health and Development, 37*, 153–160.

Buske-Kirschbaum, A., Kirschbaum, C., Stierle, H., Jabaij, L., & Hellhammer, D. (1994). Conditioned manipulation of natural killer (NK) cells in humans using a discriminative learning protocol. *Biological Psychology, 38*, 143–155.

Capaldi, E. J. (1966). Partial reinforcement: A hypothesis of sequential effects. *Psychological Review, 73*, 459–477.

Costa, D.S. J., & Boakes, R.A. (2009). Context blocking in rat autoshaping: Sign-tracking versus goal-tracking. *Learning and Motivation, 40*, 178–185.

Delamater, A.R., & Westbrook, R.F. (2014). Psychological and neural mechanisms of experimental extinction: A selective review. *Neurobiology of Learning and Memory, 108*, 38–51. doi:10.1016/j.nlm.2013.09.016

Ellison, G.D. (1964). Differential salivary conditioning to traces. *Journal of Comparative and Physiological Psychology, 57*, 373–380.

Gerwig, M., Guberina, H., Eßer, A.C., Siebler, M., Schoch, B., Frings, M., & . . . Timmann, D. (2010). Evaluation of multiple-session delay eyeblink conditioning comparing patients with focal cerebellar lesions and cerebellar degeneration. *Behavioural Brain Research, 212*, 143–151.

Gifford, E.V., & Shoenberger, D. (2009). Rapid smoking. In W.T. O'Donohue & J.E. Fisher (Eds.), *General principles and empirically supported techniques of cognitive behavior therapy* (pp. 513–519). Hoboken, NJ: Wiley.

Goebel, M.U., Meykadeh, N., Kou, W., Schedlowski, M., & Hengge, U.R. (2008). Behavioral conditioning of antihistamine effects in patients with allergic rhinitis. *Psychotherapy and Psychosomatics, 77*, 227–234.

Hearst, E., & Jenkins, H.M. (1974). *Sign tracking: The stimulus-reinforcer relation and directed action.* Austin, TX: Monograph of the Psychonomic Society.

Hoehler, F.K., Kirschenbaum, D.S., & Leonard, D.W. (1973). The effects of overtraining and successive extinctions upon nictitating membrane conditioning in the rabbit. *Learning and Motivation, 4*, 91–101.

Kirkpatrick, K., & Church, R.M. (2004). Temporal learning in random control procedures. *Journal of Experimental Psychology: Animal Behavior Processes, 30*, 213–228.

Konorski, J. (1948). *Conditioned reflexes and neuron organization.* New York: Cambridge University Press.

Kushner, M. (1968). The operant control of intractable sneezing. In C.D. Spielberger, R. Fox, & D. Masterson (Eds.), *Contributions to general psychology* (pp. 326–365). New York: Ronald Press.

Kusnecov, A.W. (2014). Behavioral conditioning of immune responses: An overview and consideration of clinical applications. In F.K. McSweeney & E.S. Murphy (Eds.), *The Wiley Blackwell handbook of operant and classical conditioning* (pp. 143–163). Chichester, UK: Wiley-Blackwell.

Lemere, F., & Voegtlin, W.L. (1950). An evaluation of the aversion treatment of alcoholism. *Quarterly Journal of Studies on Alcohol, 11*, 199–204.

Lemere, F., Voegtlin, W.L., Broz, W.R., O'Hallaren, P., & Tupper, W.E. (1942). The conditioned reflex treatment of chronic alcoholism: VIII. A review of six years' experience with this treatment of 1526 patients. *Journal of the American Medical Association, 120*, 269–270.

Liu, S.S. (1971). Differential conditioning and stimulus generalization of the rabbit's nictitating membrane response. *Journal of Comparative and Physiological Psychology, 77*, 136–141.

Logue, A.W., Ophir, I., & Strauss, K.E. (1981). The acquisition of taste aversions in humans. *Behavior Research and Therapy, 19*, 319–333.

Matzel, L.D., Held, F.P., & Miller, R.R. (1988). Information and expression of simultaneous and backward associations: Implications for contiguity theory. *Learning and Motivation, 19*, 317–344.

McLay, R.N., Wood, D.P., Webb-Murphy, J.A., Spira, J.L., Wiederhold, M.D., Pyne, J.M., & Wiederhold, B.K. (2011). A randomized, controlled trial of virtual reality-graded exposure therapy for post-traumatic stress disorder in active duty service members with combat-related post-traumatic stress disorder. *Cyberpsychology, Behavior, and Social Networking, 14*, 223–229.

Miller, R.R., & Spear, N.E. (Eds.). (1985). *Information processing in animals: Conditioned inhibition*. Hillsdale, NJ: Erlbaum.

Mowrer, O.H., & Mowrer, W.M. (1938). Enuresis: A method for its study and treatment. *American Journal of Orthopsychiatry, 8*, 436–459.

North, M.M., North, S.M., & Coble, J.R. (2002). Virtual reality therapy: An effective treatment for psychological disorders. In K.M. Stanney (Ed.), *Handbook of virtual environments: Design, implementation, and applications* (pp. 1065–1078). Mahwah, NJ: Erlbaum.

Paul, G.L. (1969). Outcome of systematic desensitization: II. Controlled investigations of individual treatment, technique variations, and current status. In C.M. Franks (Ed.), *Behavior therapy: Appraisal and status* (pp. 105–159). New York: McGraw-Hill.

Polack, C.W., Molet, M., Miguez, G., & Miller, R.R. (2013). Associative structure of integrated temporal relationships. *Learning & Behavior, 41*, 443–454.

Radell, M.L., & Mercado, E.I. (2014). Modeling possible effects of atypical cerebellar processing on eyeblink conditioning in autism. *Cognitive, Affective & Behavioral Neuroscience, 14*, 1142–1164.

Rescorla, R.A. (1966). Predictability and number of pairings in Pavlovian fear conditioning. *Psychonomic Science, 4*, 383–384.

Rescorla, R.A. (1968). Probability of shock in the presence and absence of CS in fear conditioning. *Journal of Comparative and Physiological Psychology, 66*, 1–5.

Rescorla, R.A. (1973). Second order conditioning: Implications for theories of learning. In F.J. McGuigan & D.B. Lumsden (Eds.), *Contemporary approaches to conditioning and learning* (pp. 127–150). New York: Wiley.

Robbins, S.J. (1990). Mechanisms underlying spontaneous recovery in autoshaping. *Journal of Experimental Psychology: Animal Behavior Processes, 16*, 235–249.

Schultz, D.H., Balderston, N.L., Geiger, J.A., & Helmstetter, F.J. (2013). Dissociation between implicit and explicit responses in postconditioning UCS revaluation after fear conditioning in humans. *Behavioral Neuroscience, 127*, 357–368.

Siegel, S., & Domjan, M. (1971). Backward conditioning as an inhibitory procedure. *Learning and Motivation, 2*, 1–11.

Smith, J.W., & Frawley, P.J. (1990). Long-term abstinence from alcohol in patients receiving aversion therapy as part of a multimodal inpatient program. *Journal of Substance Abuse Treatment, 7*, 77–82.

Smith, M.C., & Gormezano, I. (1965). *Conditioning of the nictitating membrane response of the rabbit as a function of backward, simultaneous and forward CS–UCS intervals*. Paper presented at the meeting of the Psychonomic Society, Chicago, IL.

Solvason, H.B., Ghanata, V., & Hiramoto, R.H. (1988). Conditioned augmentation of natural killer cell activity: Independence from nociceptive effects and dependence on interferon-B. *Journal of Immunology, 140*, 661–665.

Sturges, J.W., & Sturges, L.V. (1998). In vivo systematic desensitization in a single-session treatment of an 11-year-old girl's elevator phobia. *Child & Family Behavior Therapy, 20*, 55–62.

Till, B.D., & Priluck, R.L. (2000). Stimulus generalization in classical conditioning: An initial investigation and extension. *Psychology and Marketing, 17*, 55–72.

Todrank, J., Byrnes, D., Wrzesniewski, A., & Rozin, P. (1995). Odors can change preferences for people in photographs: A cross-modal evaluative conditioning study with olfactory USs and visual CSs. *Learning and Motivation, 26*, 116–140.

Ventis, W.L., Higbee, G., & Murdock, S.A. (2001). Using humor in systematic desensitization to reduce fear. *Journal of General Psychology, 128*, 241–253.

Voegtlin, W.L. (1940). The treatment of alcoholism by establishing a conditioned reflex. *American Journal of Medical Science, 199*, 802–810.

Watson, J.B., & Rayner, R. (1921). Studies in infant psychology. *Scientific Monthly, 13*, 493–515.

White, K., & Davey, G.C.L. (1989). Sensory preconditioning and UCS inflation in human "fear" conditioning. *Behaviour Research and Therapy, 27*, 161–166.

Williams, D.A., Johns, K.W., & Brindas, M. (2008). Timing during inhibitory conditioning. *Journal of Experimental Psychology: Animal Behavior Processes, 34*, 237–246.

Yerkes, R.M., & Morgulis, S. (1909). The method of Pavlov in animal psychology. *Psychological Bulletin, 6*, 257–273.

Zener, K. (1937). The significance of behavior accompanying conditioned salivary secretion for theories of the conditioned response. *American Journal of Psychology, 50*, 384–403.

CHAPTER 4

Theories and Research on Classical Conditioning

Learning Objectives

After reading this chapter, you should be able to

- explain the blocking effect and why it is important
- describe the basic concepts of the Rescorla–Wagner model and how it accounts for conditioning phenomena such as acquisition, extinction, blocking, and conditioned inhibition
- summarize research findings on the neural mechanisms of classical conditioning in primitive animals, mammals, and humans
- explain how heredity can influence what animals and people learn through classical conditioning
- discuss the role that classical conditioning plays in drug tolerance and addiction

---

This chapter surveys some major themes and issues in the field of classical conditioning. The chapter is divided into four sections, each of which addresses different questions. The first section covers theories about when and how different types of conditioning will occur: Under what conditions will a stimulus become an excitatory CS, or become an inhibitory CS, or remain neutral? The second section examines classical conditioning from the perspective of neuroscience. We will take a brief look at how classical conditioning alters the functioning of individual neurons and what areas of the brain are involved. The third section, on biological constraints, examines the role that hereditary factors play in associative learning. The final section addresses the question of what form a CR will take. Will the CR be similar to the UR, the opposite of the UR, or something entirely different? This question has important practical implications, as when a stimulus that has been associated with a drug might later elicit a response that either mimics or opposes the reaction to the drug itself.

RESEARCH AND THEORIES ON ASSOCIATIVE LEARNING

One of the oldest principles of associative learning is the principle of frequency: The more frequently two stimuli are paired, the more strongly will a learner associate the two. Thomas Brown first proposed this principle, and it has been a basic assumption of many theories of learning. Because of widespread acceptance of the frequency principle as a fundamental rule of learning, an experiment by Leon Kamin that contradicted this principle attracted considerable attention.

The Blocking Effect

To simplify the description of Kamin's (1968) experiment and others in this chapter, the following notation will be used. We will use capital letters to represent different CSs (e.g., T will represent a tone, and L will represent a light). A plus sign (+) will indicate that a US was presented after a CS. For example, T+ will indicate a trial on which a tone was presented and was followed by a US. The notation TL will refer to a trial on which two CSs, a tone and a light, were presented simultaneously but were not followed by the US.

Kamin's original experiment used rats in a conditioned suppression procedure. Table 4.1 outlines the design of the experiment. There were two groups of rats, a **blocking** group and a control group. In Phase 1, rats in the blocking group received a series of L+ trials (a light followed by shock), and by the end of this phase, L elicited a strong CR (suppression of lever pressing when L was on). In Phase 2, the blocking group received a series of LT+ trials: The light and a tone were presented together, followed by shock. Finally, in the test phase, T was presented by itself (with no shock) for several trials so as to measure the strength of conditioning to the tone.

There was only one difference in the procedure for the control group: In Phase 1, no stimuli were presented at all. Therefore, the first time these rats were exposed to L, T, and shock was in Phase 2. The important point is that both groups received *exactly the same number of pairings of T and shock*. So the frequency principle predicts that conditioning to T should be equally strong in the two groups. However, this is not what Kamin found: Whereas he observed a strong fear response (conditioned suppression) to T in the control group, there was almost no fear response at all to T in the blocking group. Kamin concluded that the prior conditioning with L somehow "blocked" the later conditioning of T. Since Kamin's

Table 4.1 Design of Kamin's blocking experiment.

Group	Phase 1	Phase 2	Test Phase	Results
Blocking	L+	LT+	T	T → no fear
Control	–	LT+	T	T → fear

pioneering work, the blocking effect has been demonstrated in numerous experiments using a variety of conditioning situations with both animals and people.

An intuitive explanation of the blocking effect is not difficult to construct: To put it simply, T was redundant in the blocking group; it supplied no new information. By the end of Phase 1, rats in the blocking group had learned that L was a reliable predictor of the US—the US always occurred after L and never at any other time. Adding T to the situation in Phase 2 added nothing to the rat's ability to predict the US. This experiment suggests that conditioning will not occur if a CS adds no new information about the US.

This experiment demonstrates that conditioning is not an automatic result when a CS and a US are paired. Conditioning will occur only if the CS is informative, only if it predicts something important, such as an upcoming shock. For two psychologists, Robert Rescorla and Allan Wagner (1972), the blocking effect and related findings led them to develop a new theory that has become one of the most famous theories of classical conditioning.

The Rescorla–Wagner Model

The **Rescorla–Wagner model** is a mathematical model about classical conditioning, and for some people the math makes the model difficult to understand. However, the basic ideas behind the theory are quite simple and reasonable, and they can be explained without the math. This section is designed to give you a good understanding of the concepts behind the model without using any equations.

Classical conditioning can be viewed as a means of learning about signals (CSs) for important events (USs). The Rescorla–Wagner model is designed to predict the outcome of classical conditioning procedures on a trial-by-trial basis. For each trial in a conditioning procedure, there could be excitatory conditioning, inhibitory conditioning, or no conditioning at all. According to the model, two factors determine which of these three possibilities actually occurs: (1) the strength of the subject's expectation of what will occur and (2) the strength of the US that is actually presented. The model is a mathematical expression of the concept of surprise: It states that learning will occur only when the learner is surprised, that is, when what actually happens is different from what the learner expected to happen.

You should be able to grasp the general idea of the model if you learn and understand the following six rules:

1. If the strength of the actual US is greater than the strength of the learner's expectation, all CSs paired with the US will receive excitatory conditioning.
2. If the strength of the actual US is less than the strength of the learner's expectation, all the CSs paired with the US will receive some inhibitory conditioning.
3. If the strength of the actual US is equal to the strength of the learner's expectation, there will be no conditioning.
4. The larger the discrepancy between the strength of the expectation and the strength of the US, the greater the conditioning (either excitatory or inhibitory).
5. More salient (more noticeable) CSs will condition faster than less salient (less noticeable) CSs.

6. If two or more CSs are presented together, the learner's expectation will be equal to their total strength (with excitatory and inhibitory stimuli tending to cancel each other out).

To demonstrate how these six rules work, we will now examine several different examples. For all of the examples, imagine that a rat receives a conditioning procedure in which a CS (a light, a tone, or some other signal) is followed by food as a US. In this conditioning situation, the CR is activity, as measured by the rat's movement around the conditioning chamber (which can be automatically recorded by movement detectors). In actual experiments using this procedure, the typical result is that as conditioning proceeds, the rat becomes more and more active when the CS is presented, so its movement can be used as a measure of the amount of excitatory conditioning.

Acquisition

Suppose a light (L) is paired with one food pellet (Figure 4.1). On the very first conditioning trial, the rat has no expectation of what will follow L, so the strength of the US (the food pellet) is much greater than the strength of the rat's expectation (which is zero). Therefore, this trial produces some excitatory conditioning (Rule 1). But conditioning is rarely complete after just one trial. The second time L is presented, it will elicit a weak expectation, but it is still not as strong as the actual US, so Rule 1 applies again, and more excitatory conditioning occurs. For the same reason, further excitatory conditioning should take place on Trials 3, 4, and so on. However, with each conditioning trial, the rat's expectation of the food pellet should get stronger, and so the difference between the strength of the expectation and the strength of the US gets smaller. Therefore, the fastest growth in excitatory conditioning occurs on the first trial, and there is less and less additional conditioning as the trials proceed (Rule 4). Eventually, when L elicits an expectation of food that is as strong as the actual food pellet itself, the asymptote of learning is reached, and no further excitatory conditioning will occur with any additional L and food pairings.

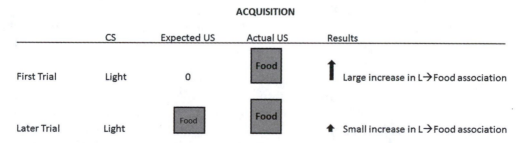

Figure 4.1 According to the Rescorla–Wagner model, during acquisition, the actual US is greater than the expected US, so there is excitatory conditioning (an increase in the strength of the CS–US association). The strength of the expected US is greater on later acquisition trials, so the amount of conditioning is not as great as on the first trial.

BLOCKING AFTER LIGHT HAS BEEN CONDITIONED

CS	Expected US	Actual US	Results
Light & Tone	Food	Food	No change in L→Food association No change in T→Food association

Figure 4.2 According to the Rescorla–Wagner model, the blocking effect occurs because there is no learning on a conditioning trial if the expected US is equal to the actual US.

Blocking

Continuing with this same example, now suppose that after the asymptote of conditioning is reached for L, a compound CS of L and tone (T) are presented together and are followed by one food pellet (Figure 4.2). According to Rule 6, when two CSs are presented, the learner's expectation is based on the total expectations from the two. T is a new stimulus, so it has no expectations associated with it, but L produces an expectation of one food pellet. One food pellet is in fact what the animal receives, so the expected US matches the actual US, and no additional conditioning occurs (Rule 3); that is, L retains its excitatory strength, and T retains zero strength.

This, in short, is how the Rescorla–Wagner model explains the blocking effect: No conditioning occurs to the added CS because there is no surprise—the strength of the learner's expectation matches the strength of the US.

Extinction and Conditioned Inhibition

Suppose that after conditioning with L, a rat receives extinction trials in which L is presented without food (Figure 4.3). The expected US is food, but the actual US is nothing (no food is presented). This is a case where the strength of the expected US is greater than that of the actual US, so according to Rule 2, there will be a decrease in the association between L and food. Further extinction trials will cause more and more decline in the association between L and food.

Now think about a slightly different example. Suppose that after conditioning with L has reached its asymptote, the rat receives trials in which L and T are presented together, but no food pellet is delivered on these trials. This is another case where Rule 2 applies: The strength of the expected US will be greater than the strength of the actual US. According to Rule 2, both CSs, L and T, will acquire some inhibitory conditioning on these extinction trials.

Let us be clear about how this inhibitory conditioning will affect L and T. Because L starts with a strong excitatory strength, the trials without food (and the inhibitory conditioning they produce) will begin to counteract the excitatory strength. This is just another example of extinction. In contrast, T begins the extinction phase with zero strength because it has not been presented before. Therefore, the trials without food (and the inhibitory conditioning they produce) will cause T's strength to decrease below zero—it will become a conditioned inhibitor.

EXTINCTION

<table>
<tr><td>CS</td><td>Expected US</td><td>Actual US</td><td>Results</td></tr>
<tr><td>Light</td><td>Food</td><td>0</td><td>↓ Large decrease in L→Food association</td></tr>
</table>

Figure 4.3 According to the Rescorla–Wagner model, during extinction, the expected US is greater than the actual US, so there is inhibitory conditioning (a decrease in the strength of the CS–US association).

OVERSHADOWING

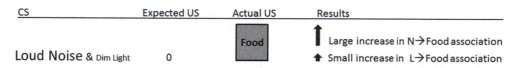

<table>
<tr><td>CS</td><td>Expected US</td><td>Actual US</td><td>Results</td></tr>
<tr><td>Loud Noise & Dim Light</td><td>0</td><td>Food</td><td>↑ Large increase in N→Food association
↑ Small increase in L→Food association</td></tr>
</table>

Figure 4.4 According to the Rescorla–Wagner model, overshadowing occurs because the amount of conditioning depends on the salience of a stimulus. Here, the noise is more salient, so there is a larger increase in the noise–food association than in the light–food association.

Overshadowing

In an experiment with a compound CS consisting of one intense stimulus and one weak one, Pavlov discovered a phenomenon he called **overshadowing**. After a number of conditioning trials, the intense CS would produce a strong CR if presented by itself, but the weak CS by itself would elicit little, if any, conditioned responding. It was not the case that the weak CS was simply too small to become an effective CS, because if it were paired with the US by itself, it would soon elicit CRs on its own. However, when the two CSs were conditioned together, the intense CS seemed to mask, or overshadow, the weaker CS. Overshadowing has been observed in experiments with both animals and humans (Spetch, 1995; Stockhorst, Hall, Enck, & Klosterhalfen, 2014).

The Rescorla–Wagner model's explanation of overshadowing is straightforward (Figure 4.4). According to Rule 5, more salient stimuli will condition faster than less salient stimuli. If, for example, a dim light and a loud noise are presented together and followed by a food pellet, the noise will acquire excitatory strength faster than the light. When the total expectation based on both the noise and the light equals the strength of the actual US, food, conditioning will stop. Because the noise is more salient, it will have developed much more excitatory strength than the light. If the dim light is presented by itself, it should elicit only a weak CR.

The Overexpectation Effect

One characteristic of a good theory is the ability to stimulate research by making new predictions that have not been previously tested. The Rescorla–Wagner model deserves good grades on this count, because hundreds of experiments have been conducted to test the model's predictions. Research on a phenomenon known as the **overexpectation effect** is a good example, because it is a case where the Rescorla-Wagner model makes a prediction that many people find surprising and counterintuitive, yet the prediction turns out to be correct.

Table 4.2 presents the design of an experiment on the overexpectation effect. Two CSs, L and T, are involved. For Phase 1, the notation L+, T+ means that on some trials L is presented by itself and followed by a food pellet, and on other trials T is presented by itself and followed by a food pellet. Consider what should happen on each type of trial. On L+ trials, the strength of the expectation based on L will continue to increase and eventually approach the strength of one food pellet. Similarly, on T+ trials, the strength of the expectation based on T will grow and also approach the strength of one food pellet. At the end of Phase 1, the rat expects one food pellet when L is presented, and it also expects one food pellet when T is presented. In Phase 2, rats in the control group receive no stimuli, so no expectations are changed. Therefore, in the test phase, these rats should exhibit a strong CR to both L and T, and they do.

The results should be quite different for rats in the overexpectation group. In Phase 2, these rats receive a series of trials with the compound stimulus, LT, followed by one food pellet. On the first trial of Phase 2, a rat's total expectation, based on the sums of the strengths of L and T, should be roughly equal to the strength of two food pellets (because both L and T have a strength of about one food pellet). Loosely speaking, we might say that the rat expects a larger US because two strong CSs are presented, but all it gets is a single food pellet (Figure 4.5). Therefore, compared to what it actually receives, the animal has an overexpectation about the size of the US, and Rule 2 states that under these conditions, both CSs will experience some inhibitory conditioning (they will lose some of their associative strength).

Table 4.2 Design of an experiment on the overexpectation effect.

Group	Phase 1	Phase 2	Test Phase	Results
Overexpectation	L+, T+	LT+	L, T	moderate CRs
Control	L+, T+	no stimuli	L, T	strong CRs

OVEREXPECTATION EFFECT
AFTER LIGHT AND TONE HAVE BEEN SEPARATELY CONDITIONED

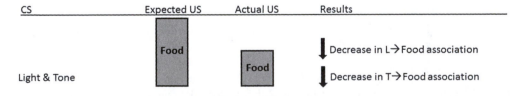

Figure 4.5 According to the Rescorla–Wagner model, the overexpectation effect occurs because when two separately conditioned stimuli are presented together, the expected US is greater than the actual US, so there is inhibitory conditioning (a decrease in the strength of each CS–food association).

With further trials in Phase 2 for the overexpectation group, the strengths of L and T should continue to decrease as long as the total expectation from the two CSs is greater than the strength of one food pellet. In the test phase, the individual stimuli L and T should produce weaker CRs in the overexpectation group because their strengths were decreased in Phase 2. Experiments with both animals and people have confirmed this prediction: CRs are weaker in the overexpectation group than in the control group (Kremer, 1978; Ruprecht, Izurieta, Wolf, & Leising, 2014).

The model's accurate prediction of the overexpectation effect is especially impressive because the prediction is counterintuitive. If you knew nothing about the Rescorla–Wagner model when you examined Table 4.2, what result would you predict for this experiment? Notice that subjects in the overexpectation group actually receive more pairings of L and T with the US, so the frequency principle would predict stronger CRs in the overexpectation group. Based on the frequency principle, the last thing we would expect from more CS–US pairings is a weakening of the CS–US associations. Yet this result is predicted by the Rescorla–Wagner model, and the prediction turns out to be correct.

Summary

The Rescorla–Wagner model might be called a theory about *US effectiveness*: It states that an unpredicted US is effective in promoting learning, whereas a well-predicted US is ineffective. As the first formal theory that attempted to predict when a US will promote associative learning and when it will not, it is guaranteed a prominent place in the history of psychology. The model has been successfully applied to many conditioning phenomena, but it is not perfect. Some research findings are difficult for the model to explain. We will now take a brief look at some of these findings, and at other theories of classical conditioning that are based on different assumptions about the learning process.

Theories of Attention

Some theories of classical conditioning focus on how much attention the learner pays to the CS (e.g., Mackintosh, 1975; Pearce & Hall, 1980). One common feature of these theories is the assumption that the learner will pay attention to informative CSs but not to uninformative CSs. If the learner does not pay attention to a CS, there will be no conditioning of that CS. These theories might also be called theories of *CS effectiveness*, because they assume that the conditionability of a CS, not the effectiveness of the US, changes from one situation to another. A phenomenon called the CS preexposure effect provides one compelling piece of evidence for this assumption.

The **CS preexposure effect** is the finding that classical conditioning proceeds more slowly if a CS is repeatedly presented by itself before it is paired with the US. For example, if a rat receives presentations of a tone by itself, and these are followed by tone-food pairings, conditioning of the tone-food association will take more trials than if there were no tone preexposure trials (Lubow & Moore, 1959). A simple explanation is that because the tone is presented repeatedly but predicts nothing during CS preexposure, the animal gradually pays less and less attention to this stimulus. We might say that the rat learns to ignore the tone because it is not informative, and for this reason it takes longer to associate the tone with the US when conditioning trials begin and the tone suddenly becomes informative.

The problem for the Rescorla–Wagner model is that it does not predict the CS preexposure effect. It is easy to see why. When a new CS is presented by itself, the expected US is zero, and the actual US is zero. Because the expected US equals the actual US, according to the Rescola–Wagner model there should be no learning of any kind. But, evidently, subjects do learn something on CS preexposure trials, and what they learn hinders their ability to develop a CS–US association when the two stimuli are paired at a later time.

Unlike the Rescorla–Wagner model, attentional theories such as those of Mackintosh (1975) and Pearce and Hall (1980) can easily explain the CS preexposure effect: Because the CS predicts nothing during the preexposure period, attention to the CS decreases, and so conditioning is slower when the CS is first paired with the US at the beginning of the conditioning phase. The attentional theories can also account for other basic conditioning phenomena. For example, they can explain the overshadowing effect by assuming that animals pay more attention to the more salient CS.

Experiments designed to compare the predictions of the Rescorla–Wagner model and attentional theories have produced mixed results, with some of the evidence supporting each theory (Balaz, Kasprow, & Miller, 1982; Hall & Pearce, 1983). Perhaps these findings indicate that both classes of theory are partly correct; that is, perhaps the effectiveness of both CSs and USs can change as a result of a subject's experience. If a US is well predicted, it may promote no conditioning (which is the basic premise of the Rescorla–Wagner model). Likewise, if nothing surprising follows a CS, it may become ineffective (the basic premise of the attentional theories).

Comparator Theories of Conditioning

Other theories of classical conditioning, called **comparator theories**, assume that the animal compares the likelihood that the US will occur in the presence of the CS with the likelihood that the US will occur in the absence of the CS (Miller & Schachtman, 1985; Stout & Miller, 2007). Comparator theories differ from those we have already examined in two ways. First, comparator theories do not make predictions on a trial-by-trial basis because they assume that what is important is not the events of individual trials but rather the overall, long-term correlation between a CS and a US. Second, comparator theories propose that the correlation between CS and US does not affect the learning of a CR but rather its performance.

As a simple example, suppose that the probability of a US is 50% in the presence of some CS, but its probability is also 50% in the absence of this CS. The comparator theories predict that this CS will elicit no CR, which is what Rescorla (1968) found, but not because the CS has acquired no excitatory strength. Instead, the theories assume that both the CS and **contextual stimuli**—the sights, sounds, and smells of the experimental chamber—have acquired equal excitatory strengths because both have been paired with the US 50% of the time. Comparator theories also assume that a CS will not elicit a CR unless it has greater excitatory strength than the contextual stimuli. Unlike the Rescorla–Wagner model, however, comparator theories assume that an animal in this situation has indeed learned something about the CS—that the US sometimes occurs in its presence—but the animal will not respond to the CS unless it is a better predictor of the US than the context.

To test comparator theories, one common research strategy is to change the strength of one stimulus and try to show that the conditioned responding changes to another stimulus.

For example, suppose that after conditioning, an animal exhibits only a weak CR to a light because both the light and the contextual stimuli have some excitatory strength. According to comparator theories, one way to increase the response to the light would be to extinguish the excitatory strength of the context by keeping the subject in the context and never presenting the US. If the response to the light depends on a comparison of the light and the context, extinction of the context should increase the response to the light. Experiments of this type have shown that extinction of the context does increase responding to the CS (Matzel, Brown, & Miller, 1987).

In a related experiment by Cole, Barnet, and Miller (1995), one CS was followed by a US every time it was presented, whereas a second CS was followed by a US only 50% of the time. At first, the second CS did not elicit much conditioned responding. However, after responding to the first CS was extinguished, CRs to the second CS increased dramatically. The Rescorla–Wagner model does not predict these effects, because it states that the conditioned strength of one CS cannot change if that CS itself is not presented. According to comparator theories, however, subjects may learn an association between a CS and a US that cannot initially be seen in their performance, but this learning can be unmasked if the strength of a competing CS is weakened.

Research designed to test comparator theories has provided mixed results. Some studies have provided support for this approach (e.g., San-Galli, Marchand, Decorte, & Di Scala, 2011), whereas other studies have supported the predictions of traditional associative learning theories such as the Rescorla–Wagner model (e.g., Dopson, Pearce, & Haselgrove, 2009). Because there is evidence supporting both types of theories, it may be that future theories of classical conditioning will need to take into account both learning and performance variables to accommodate the diverse findings that researchers have obtained.

BOX 4.1   IN THE MEDIA

Classical Conditioning in Advertising

Because classical conditioning can alter a person's feelings about a stimulus, even without the person's awareness, it should come as no surprise that classical conditioning has been used in advertising for a long time. For example, a television commercial may present a certain brand of snack food along with stimuli that most viewers will evaluate positively, such as young, attractive people having a good time. Advertisers hope that viewers will be attracted to the people and that this positive reaction will become conditioned to the product being sold. If the conditioning is successful, you may later have a positive reaction when you see the product in a store, regardless of whether or not you remember the commercial.

In a similar way, many advertisements feature popular celebrities or athletes endorsing products, based on the idea that viewers' positive reactions to the celebrities will transfer from the celebrities to the product. Marketing research suggests that this transfer of positive reactions to the product or brand does indeed occur. In laboratory research, associations can form between CSs that are paired with the same US, and this can also occur in advertising when a celebrity acts as a spokesperson for more than one product. If a celebrity endorses a popular line of athletic shoes and a less familiar brand of other types of athletic equipment, the positive reaction can transfer from one product to the other (Chen, Chang, Besherat, & Baack, 2013).

Some research has shown that the use of a popular celebrity in a commercial can do more than simply give the viewer a vague positive feeling about a product; specific characteristics of the celebrity can become associated with the product. For instance, the handsome and popular actor George Clooney has been a sponsor for a particular brand of expresso. According to Förderer and Unkelbach (2014), viewers of these ads come to associate the specific attributes of Clooney (such as *sexy*, *cosmopolitan*, and *glamorous*) with the product brand. Förderer and Unkelbach refer to this phenomenon as **attribute conditioning** because the attributes or characteristics of one stimulus (the celebrity) are transferred to another stimulus (the product).

Even the music in a commercial can influence people's reactions to the product. In one experiment, college students viewed pictures of pens that differed only in their color, while they listened to music that they either liked or disliked. Later, when asked to choose of one the pens, most showed a preference for the color of pen that was associated with the music they liked (Gorn, 1982).

Classical conditioning can also be used in advertising in the opposite way—to develop negative associations with a competing product. Some ads show people who are frustrated or unhappy when using a competitor's product. Negative advertising is especially common in political commercials. An ad may associate pictures of the other candidate with somber or disturbing music, with images of unpleasant scenes, and with angry or unhappy faces. The goal, of course, is to make voters associate negative emotions with the opponent. Many voters say they dislike these negative ads, and you may wonder why they are used so frequently in political campaigns. The answer is simple: They work.

NEUROSCIENCE AND CLASSICAL CONDITIONING

Our understanding of classical conditioning would be greatly enhanced if we knew exactly what changes take place in the nervous system during the acquisition and subsequent performance of a new CR. This topic has been the focus of intense research efforts for many years, and much has been learned about the neural mechanisms of classical conditioning. This section can provide only a brief survey of some of the major developments.

Some of the research on the neural mechanisms of classical conditioning has been done with primitive creatures. Kandel and his colleagues have been able to study classical conditioning in the gill-withdrawal reflex of *Aplysia* (see Figure 2.8). In this research, the US was a shock to the tail, and the UR was the gill-withdrawal response. The CS was weak stimulation of the siphon, which initially produced only a minor gill withdrawal response. After several pairings of the CS and US, however, the CS began to elicit a full gill-withdrawal response (Carew, Hawkins, & Kandel, 1983). The researchers determined that this CR (the increased response to siphon stimulation) was due to an increase in the amount of transmitter released by the sensory neurons of the siphon. Note that precisely the opposite neural change (decreased transmitter release by the sensory neurons) was found to be responsible for habituation of the gill-withdrawal response (see Chapter 2). However, other changes have been observed in *Aplysia*'s nervous system during classical conditioning as well. Glanzman (1995) found that the dendrites of the postsynaptic neurons in the circuit develop enhanced sensitivity, so they exhibit stronger responses to chemical stimulation. In addition to these chemical changes, repeated classical conditioning trials can produce more permanent, structural changes in *Aplysia*'s nervous system—the growth of new synapses between the sensory neurons in the siphon and motor neurons (Bailey & Kandel, 2009). These are important findings because they show that even in the simple nervous system of *Aplysia*, a variety of chemical and structural changes can take place during a simple learning episode.

With humans and other mammals, research on this topic is proceeding in several different directions. Some studies have examined human participants with damage in specific areas of the brain due to accident or illness; these individuals are trained in a classical conditioning paradigm, such as eyeblink conditioning, to determine the effects of brain damage. Another strategy is to condition people without brain damage while using modern imaging technologies to measure activity in different parts of the brain. With nonhuman subjects, researchers have examined chemical mechanisms and the effects of lesions to different brain areas. Our brief review of this research will focus on five main points.

1. The neural pathways involved in the CR are often different from those involved in the UR. This can be shown through procedures that eliminate one of these responses but not the other. For example, in baboons, a certain part of the hypothalamus appears to be intimately involved in the conditioned heart-rate changes elicited by CSs paired with shock. If this part of the hypothalamus is destroyed, heart-rate CRs disappear, whereas unconditioned heart-rate responses are unaffected (Smith, Astley, DeVito, Stein, & Walsh, 1980).

In rabbit eyeblink conditioning, the **cerebellum**, a part of the brain that is important for many skilled movements, plays a critical role (Tracy, Thompson, Krupa, & Thompson, 2013). As in heart-rate conditioning, different neural pathways are involved in eyeblink URs and CRs. The eyeblink UR to an air puff directed at the eye seems to be controlled by two distinct pathways—a fairly direct pathway in the brainstem and a more indirect pathway passing through the cerebellum. Considerable evidence shows that the eyeblink CR is controlled by this second, indirect pathway. If sections of this pathway in the cerebellum are destroyed, eyeblink CRs disappear and cannot be relearned (Knowlton & Thompson, 1992). If neurons in this same part of the cerebellum are electrically stimulated, eyeblink responses similar to the CR are produced (Thompson, McCormick, & Lavond, 1986). If this divergence of UR and CR pathways is found in other response systems, it would help to explain why the forms of the UR and CR are often different.

2. Many different brain structures may be involved in the production of a simple CR. For example, although the cerebellum is important in rabbit eyeblink conditioning, many other brain areas are involved as well. When humans receive eyeblink conditioning, brain-imaging techniques such as positron emission tomography (PET) reveal increased blood flow in one side of the cerebellum (corresponding to the side of the eye involved in conditioning), but there is increased blood flow in many other parts of the brain as well (Molchan, Sunderland, McIntosh, Herscovitch, & Schreurs, 1994). In other species, several different brain sites have been implicated in heart-rate conditioning, including parts of the amygdala, hypothalamus, and cingulate cortex (Schneiderman et al., 1987).

With humans, fMRI techniques have been used to obtain detailed maps of brain activity when people receive classical conditioning. During classical conditioning with the SCR, fMRIs show complex patterns of activity involving many parts of the brain, which again supports the idea that multiple brain structures are involved in classical conditioning. In one study, pictures of faces were used as CSs, and both pleasant and unpleasant odors were used as USs. Particularly interesting was the finding that even within the same conditioning preparation (pairing faces with odors), the areas of activation were different for pleasant odors and unpleasant odors (Gottfried, O'Doherty, & Dolan, 2002).

3. Different conditioning phenomena may involve different brain locations. This point has been made in a variety of studies with different species. For example, if the hippocampus is removed from a rabbit, the animal will fail to exhibit the blocking effect (Solomon, 1977), but removal of the hippocampus does not prevent the development of conditioned inhibition. In mice, damage to an area near the hippocampus called the entorhinal cortex interferes with the CS preexposure effect (Lewis & Gould, 2007). Another brain area, the amygdala, seems important for associations involving both contextual stimuli and typical CSs (Cummins, Boughner, & Leri, 2014).

4. Different CRs involve different brain locations. For example, whereas the cerebellum is important in eyeblink conditioning, other brain areas are involved in heart-rate conditioning. One study compared a group of people with damage to the cerebellum to a group of people without such brain damage. The people without brain damage quickly learned a conditioned eyeblink response, but those with damage to the cerebellum did not learn this response. However, the air puff itself did elicit an eyeblink UR in those with brain damage, which shows that they had not simply lost motor control of this response (Daum et al., 1993). The deficit appears to be a problem in forming the necessary associations for the eyeblink CR to a neutral stimulus. This does not mean, however, that the people with damage to the cerebellum suffered a general inability to associate stimuli, because measurements of their heart rates and SCRs showed that they had indeed learned the association between CS and the air puff. These results indicate that different parts of the brain are involved in the conditioning of different response systems.

5. Activity and growth in individual neurons seems to be related to the acquisition and production of CRs. For example, one study with adult mice found the sprouting of new axons and the growth of new axon terminals and synapses in the cerebellum during eyeblink conditioning (Boele, Koekkoek, De Zeeuw, & Ruigrok, 2013). Other researchers found that when rabbits were presented with a series of conditioning trials with a CS such as a tone, the activity of certain cells in the cerebellum increased at about the same rate as the eyeblink CR. When the eyeblink CR decreased during extinction, so did the activity of these cells. Moreover, the cellular activity during a single presentation of the CS paralleled the pattern of the eyeblink CR, with the neuron's activity preceding the eyeblink response by about 30 milliseconds. Along with other evidence, this finding suggests that these cells play an important role in the development of the CR (McCormick & Thompson, 1984). Neurons with similar properties have been found in the hippocampus, a brain structure that plays an important role in learning and memory (Berger & Weisz, 1987).

One study used trace conditioning of a fear response (measured by an increased heart rate) with rabbits. For two different groups of rabbits, a CS was followed by shock after a gap of either 10 or 20 seconds. After conditioning, the rabbits received trials in which the CS was presented without shock. The researchers identified individual neurons in the hippocampus whose activity increased after the CS and peaked either 10 or 20 seconds later (matching the CS–US interval with which the rabbits were trained). These neurons, therefore, seemed to be involved in the timing of the CR (McEchron, Tseng, & Disterhoft, 2003).

As we have seen, brain research on clas-

PRACTICE QUIZ 1: CHAPTER 4

1. Kamin's blocking effect was surprising because it seemed to violate the _____ principle of associative learning.
2. According to the Rescorla–Wagner model, excitatory conditioning occurs when the _____ is greater than the _____.
3. According to the Rescorla–Wagner model, extinction is a case where the _____ is greater than the _____, so _____ conditioning occurs.
4. If conditioning to a weak CS is impaired because it is presented along with a more intense CS, this is known as _____.
5. One brain structure that plays an important role in eyeblink conditioning is the _____.

ANSWERS

1. frequency 2. actual US, expected US 3. expected US, actual US, inhibitory 4. overshadowing 5. cerebellum

---

sical conditioning is proceeding on a number of different levels, including research on entire brain structures, on individual neurons, and on chemical mechanisms. Both primitive and more advanced species are being studied. Much is still unknown about the brain mechanisms of classical conditioning, but one point seems certain: Anyone hoping for a simple physiological explanation is going to be disappointed. Classical conditioning, one of the simplest types of learning, appears to involve a very complex system of neural and chemical mechanisms.

BIOLOGICAL CONSTRAINTS ON CLASSICAL CONDITIONING

As discussed in Chapter 1, probably the most fundamental assumption underlying research on animal learning is that it is possible to discover general principles of learning that are not dependent in any important way on an animal's biological makeup. During the 1960s, researchers began to report findings that questioned the validity of the general-principle approach to learning. For the most part, these findings took the form of alleged exceptions to some of the best-known general principles of learning. As this type of evidence began to accumulate, some psychologists started to question whether the goal of discovering general principles of learning was realistic. They reasoned, if we find too many exceptions to a rule, what good is the rule?

This section will examine the evidence against the general-principle approach in the area of classical conditioning, and it will attempt to come to some conclusions about its significance for the psychology of learning. Biological constraints on other types of learning will be discussed in later chapters.

The Contiguity Principle and Taste-Aversion Learning

As discussed in Chapter 1, the principle of contiguity is the oldest and most persistent principle of association, having been first proposed by Aristotle. We saw in Chapter 3 that CS–US contiguity is an important factor in classical conditioning. A popular textbook from the early 1960s summarized the opinion about the importance of contiguity that prevailed at that time: "At the present time it seems unlikely that learning can take place at all with delays of more than a few seconds" (Kimble, 1961, p. 165).

Given this opinion about the importance of contiguity, it is easy to see why the work of John Garcia and his colleagues on long-delay learning attracted considerable attention. Garcia's research involved a classical conditioning procedure in which poison was the US and some novel taste was the CS. In one study (Garcia, Ervin, & Koelling, 1966), rats were given the opportunity to drink saccharin-flavored water (which they had never tasted before), and they later received an injection of a drug that produces nausea in a matter of minutes. For different rats the interval between drinking and the drug injection varied from 5 to 22 minutes. Although these durations were perhaps a hundred times longer than those over which classical conditioning was generally thought to be effective, all rats developed aversions to water flavored with saccharin. Many later experiments replicated this finding, and taste aversions were found even when delays as long as 24 hours separated the CS from the poison US (Etscorn & Stephens, 1973). As a result, some psychologists proposed that taste-aversion learning is a special type of learning, one that does not obey the principle of contiguity. Taste-aversion learning was seen by some as an exception to one of the most basic principles of association.

Biological Preparedness in Taste-Aversion Learning

A crucial assumption underlying most research on classical conditioning is that the experimenter's choice of stimuli, responses, and species of subject is relatively unimportant. Suppose, for example, that an experimenter wishes to test some hypothesis about learning using the salivary conditioning preparation. The subjects will be dogs, and the US will be food powder, but what stimulus should be used as the CS? According to what Seligman and Hager (1972) called the **equipotentiality premise**, it does not matter what stimulus is used; the decision is entirely arbitrary. The equipotentiality premise does not state that all stimuli and all responses will result in equally rapid learning. We know that CSs differ in their salience, and a bright light will acquire a CR more rapidly than a dim light. What the equipotentiality premise does say is that a stimulus (or a response) that is difficult to condition in one situation should also be difficult to condition in other situations. For example, if a dim light is a poor CS in a salivary conditioning experiment, it should also be a poor CS in an eyeblink conditioning experiment. In short, the equipotentiality premise states that a given stimulus will be an equally good (or equally bad) CS in all contexts.

The simplicity of the equipotentiality premise might seem appealing, but plenty of evidence has shown that it is wrong. Garcia and Koelling (1966) conducted an important experiment showing that the same two stimuli can be differentially effective in different contexts. Two groups of rats were each presented with a compound stimulus consisting of both taste and audiovisual components. Each rat received water that had a distinctive flavor, and whenever the rat drank the water, there were flashing lights and a clicking noise. For one group, the procedure consisted of typical taste-aversion learning: After drinking the water, a rat was injected with a poison, and it soon became ill. For the second group, there was no poison; instead, a rat's paws were shocked whenever it drank.

Garcia and Koelling then conducted extinction tests (no shock or poison present) in which the taste and audiovisual stimuli were presented separately. The results were very different for the two groups. The group that received poison showed a greater aversion to the saccharin taste than to the lights and noises. However, exactly the opposite pattern was observed for the group that received the shock. These animals consumed almost as much of the saccharine-flavored water as in baseline, but when drinking was accompanied by the lights and noises, they drank very little.

Figure 4.6 summarizes the results of this experiment, using thick arrows to represent strong associations and thin arrows to represent weak associations. Garcia and his colleagues concluded that because of a rat's biological makeup, it has an innate tendency to associate illness with the taste of the food it had previously eaten. The rat is much less likely to associate illness with visual or auditory stimuli that are present when a food is eaten. On the other hand, the rat is more likely to associate a painful event like shock with external auditory and visual stimuli than with a taste stimulus.

Seligman (1970) proposed that some CS–US associations might be called **prepared associations** because the animal has an innate propensity to form such associations quickly and easily (e.g., a taste–illness association). Other potential associations might be called *contraprepared associations* because even after many pairings, an animal may have difficulty forming an association between the two stimuli (such as taste and shock). It should be clear that

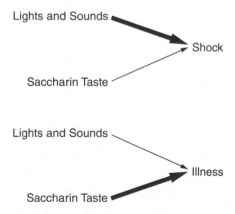

Figure 4.6 In the experiment of Garcia and Koelling (1966), rats acquired a strong association between lights and noises and shock but only a weak association between the taste of saccharin and shock. The opposite was found for rats that had saccharin, lights, and noises paired with a poison.

the concept of preparedness is at odds with the equipotentiality premise. It implies that to predict how effective a particular CS will be, it is not enough to know how effective this CS has been in other contexts. We must also know what US will be used and whether this CS–US pair is an example of a prepared or contraprepared association.

To complicate matters further, the predisposition to associate two stimuli can vary across different species. Although rats may be predisposed to associate taste stimuli with illness, other animals may not be. Wilcoxon, Dragoin, and Kral (1971) compared the behaviors of rats and bobwhite quail that became ill after drinking water that had a distinctive (sour) taste, water with a distinctive (dark blue) color, or water that both tasted sour and was dark blue. As we would expect, rats displayed aversions to the sour taste but not to the blue color. In contrast, quail developed aversions both to the sour water and the blue water, and the blue color was actually the more effective stimulus for these animals. This difference between these species makes sense, because quail rely more on vision in searching for food, whereas rats rely more on taste and smell. Still, these findings show that attempting to generalize about preparedness or ease of learning from one species to another can be a dangerous strategy.

BOX 4.2   SPOTLIGHT ON RESEARCH

Biological Preparedness in Human Learning

People can also develop a strong aversion to a food that is followed by illness, even if the illness follows ingestion of the food by several hours. Logue, Ophir, and Strauss (1981) used questionnaires to ask several hundred college students about any food aversions they might have that developed as a result of an illness that occurred after they ate the food. About 65% reported at least one food aversion. Most said the taste of the food was now aversive to them, but some said that the smell, texture, or sight of the food was also aversive. In many cases, people develop an aversion to some food even though they know that their illness was caused by something completely unrelated to the food, such as the flu or chemotherapy treatment (Bernstein, Webster, & Bernstein, 1982; Scalera & Bavieri, 2009).

Preparedness may also play a part in how people develop fears or phobias (Figure 4.7). Öhman and colleagues have proposed that humans have a predisposition to develop fears of things that have been dangerous to our species throughout our evolutionary history, such as snakes, spiders, and thunder (Öhman & Mineka, 2001). Quite a few experiments have tested this hypothesis, often by pairing shock with pictures of such objects as snakes, spiders, flowers, and mushrooms. Once a fear response has been conditioned, some studies have found greater resistance to extinction in the spider/snake groups compared to the flower/mushroom groups (Öhman, Dimberg, & Ost, 1985; Schell, Dawson, & Marinkovic, 1991). There is also evidence that both adults and young children can detect a snake or spider in a visual array faster than more "neutral" stimuli such as flowers and mushrooms (LoBue & DeLoache, 2008; Öhman, Flykt, & Esteves, 2001).

Figure 4.7 Many people have a fear of spiders, and this might be due to a human biological predisposition. (Cara-Foto/Shutterstock.com)

Dimberg and Öhman (1996) proposed that people are also predisposed to associate angry faces with aversive consequences. Their reasoning is that throughout our evolutionary history, when one person stared with an angry expression toward another person, the angry person often followed this expression with some attempt to hurt or intimidate the other person. As a result, human beings have become prepared to produce a fearful or defensive reaction to an angry face. This hypothesis has been tested with discrimination procedures similar to those used for spiders and snakes, except that angry faces are used in one group and happy or neutral faces are used in a control group. Once again, the results have been varied; some studies found support for the preparedness hypothesis (Dimberg & Öhman, 1983), and others found none (Packer, Clark, Bond, & Siddle, 1991). Overall, the evidence for preparedness in human phobias remains inconclusive. Based on the data that are available, it is possible that both heredity and experience combine to determine what types of fears and phobias people are most likely to develop (Mallan, Lipp, & Cochrane, 2013).

Biological Constraints and the General-Principle Approach

The findings of Garcia and his colleagues were certainly a surprise to traditional learning theorists, but, in retrospect, they have not proven to be damaging to the general-principle approach to learning. It is true that taste–aversion learning can occur with long delays between CS and US, but so can other types of learning. For instance, Lett (1973) found that rats could learn the correct choice in a T-maze even when the delay to the food reinforcer was 60 minutes. Other studies have found learning when stimuli are separated by as much as 24 hours (Capaldi, 1966). Furthermore, contiguity does make a difference in taste-aversion learning, only on a different time scale than more typical learning tasks. To make this point, Figure 4.8 compares the suppressing effects of shock and poison as the delays to these aversive stimuli were increased. The top panel shows the data from rats pressing a lever for food when shocks were used to suppress their responding. As the delay between a response and shock increased, there was less and less suppression of responding. The bottom panel shows the results from a study on taste-aversion learning in which different groups of rats experienced different delays between exposure to a saccharin solution and a poison injection. Observe the similarity in the shapes of the two functions. Both sets of results are consistent with the principle of contiguity—the shorter the interval between a response and an aversive event,

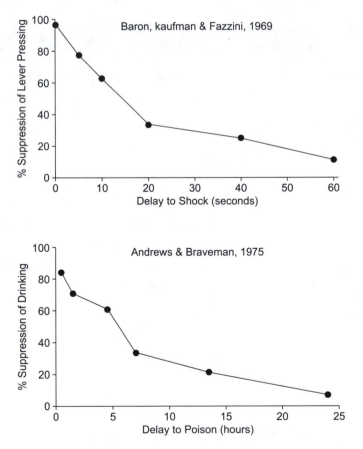

Figure 4.8 The suppression of lever pressing by shocks delivered after different delays (top, based on data from Baron, Kaufman, & Fazzini, 1969) is compared to the suppression of drinking a saccharine solution by poison delivered after different delays (bottom, based on data from Andrews & Braveman, 1975). Notice the different time scales in the two panels.

the stronger the effect of the aversive stimulus. The only major difference between the two experiments is the scale on the x-axis (seconds versus hours). What we need to account for in these two sets of results are just different time scales, not different principles of learning.

At one time, the evidence for biological preparedness in taste-aversion learning (and in other learning situations) was also seen as a problem for the general-principle approach. Notice, however, that the concept of preparedness also deals with differences in the speed of learning or the amount of learning, not in the kind of learning that takes place. It is not impossible for rats to develop an association between a visual stimulus and illness; it simply requires more trials. The same can be said for a taste–shock association. Once again, this alleged evidence against general principles of learning merely amounts to a quantitative difference, not a qualitative one: To account for differences in the speed of learning, we simply need different numbers, not different laws.

Seligman and Hager (1972) had proposed that taste-aversion learning is a unique type of learning that does not obey the laws of traditional learning theory. However, in a review of the findings on this topic, Logue (1979) described considerable evidence that there is actually nothing unique about taste-aversion learning. She noted that many of the most familiar phenomena of classical conditioning, including generalization gradients, extinction, conditioned inhibition, blocking, and second-order conditioning, have all been observed in taste-aversion learning. Later studies also found overshadowing (Nagaishi & Nakajima, 2010) and stimulus preexposure effects (Lubow, 2009) in taste-aversion learning. Based on findings like these, many researchers have concluded that taste-aversion learning violates no traditional principles of learning and requires no new principles of learning. In fact, taste-aversion learning has joined the conditioned suppression and eyeblink paradigms as a commonly used procedure for studying classical conditioning. This fact, perhaps more than any other, should put to rest the notion that taste-aversion learning is inconsistent with the general-principle approach to learning theory.

THE FORM OF THE CONDITIONED RESPONSE

As discussed in Chapter 3, predicting the form of a CR is often difficult. In some cases, the CR is quite similar to the UR, and in others it is the opposite of the UR. When a CR is the opposite of the UR, it is sometimes called a *compensatory CR*, because it tends to compensate for, or counteract, the UR. In this section, we will first investigate how classical conditioning can affect an individual's reaction to a drug. In this area of research, both mimicking and compensatory CRs have been observed. We will then examine some theories that try to explain why CRs assume the variety of forms that they do.

Drug Tolerance and Drug Cravings as Conditioned Responses

A heroin user's first injection produces a highly pleasurable response of euphoria, but with later injections of the same dosage, the intensity of this positive emotional response becomes smaller and smaller. The decrease in effectiveness of a drug with repeated use is called **tolerance**, and it occurs with many drugs. There are a variety of hypotheses about why tolerance occurs (including Solomon and Corbit's opponent-process theory, described in Chapter 2).

Shepard Siegel (1975, 2005) has developed a theory of drug tolerance that is based on classical conditioning. In short, Siegel claims that drug tolerance is due, at least in part, to a compensatory CR that is elicited by CSs that regularly precede a drug administration. These CSs may include the contextual stimuli (environmental surroundings) and stimuli associated with drug administration (needles, drug paraphernalia, etc.). A description of a few of Siegel's experiments will illustrate how he came to these conclusions.

One of the URs produced by the drug morphine is *analgesia*, or a decreased sensitivity to pain. In one experiment with rats, Siegel (1975) found that a decrease in analgesia over successive morphine injections (i.e., tolerance of the analgesic response) was controlled by contextual stimuli. To measure the rats' sensitivity to pain, Siegel would place them on a metal plate that was an uncomfortably warm temperature of about 54°C. When a rat's paws become painfully hot, the rat makes an easily measurable response—it lifts its forepaws and licks them. By timing the latency of this paw-lick response, Siegel could measure a rat's sensitivity to pain.

Rats in a control group received four test trials (separated by 48 hours) on which they were brought into a special experimental room, given an injection of a saline solution (as a placebo), and later placed on the metal surface. The paw-lick latencies for these control subjects were short and roughly the same on all four trials, which shows that pain sensitivity for the control group did not change over trials. The procedure for one experimental group was exactly the same, except that these rats received four morphine injections, not saline injections. On the first trial, the average paw-lick latency for this group was nearly double that of the control group. This result shows that the morphine had its expected analgesic effect. However, the latencies for this group decreased over the next three trials, and on the fourth trial, their latencies were about the same as those of the control group. Therefore, in four trials these rats had developed a tolerance to the morphine—it no longer had an analgesic effect.

According to Siegel's hypothesis, this tolerance occurred because the stimuli that accompanied each morphine injection (the sights, sounds, and smells of the experimental room) were CSs that acquired the capacity to elicit a compensatory CR of *hyperalgesia*, or an increased sensitivity to pain. By Trial 4, this compensatory CR of hyperalgesia completely counteracted the UR of analgesia, so the net effect was no change in pain sensitivity. If this hypothesis was correct, it should be possible to eliminate the tolerance simply by changing the stimuli on the final trial. To accomplish this, a third group of rats received their first three morphine injections in their home cages, but on their fourth trial, they received their morphine injections in the experimental room for the first time. Since this stimulus was completely new, it should elicit no compensatory CRs. As Siegel predicted, these animals showed a strong analgesic response: They looked like rats that had never received a morphine injection before. This big difference between the two morphine groups was obtained simply by *changing the room* in which the morphine was injected.

Some of the most convincing evidence for the compensatory CR theory has come from studies in which the CS is presented without the drug US, and a compensatory CR has been observed directly. Rozin, Reff, Mack, and Schull (1984) showed that for regular coffee drinkers, the smell and taste of coffee can serve as a CS that elicits a compensatory CR counteracting the effects of caffeine. Besides its effects on arousal and alertness, caffeine normally causes an increase in salivation. However, for regular coffee drinkers, this increase in salivation is minimal (a tolerance effect). Rozin and colleagues had regular coffee drinkers drink a cup of coffee that either did or did not contain caffeine (and they were not told which). After drinking coffee with caffeine, these participants showed only a small increase in salivation, as would be expected of habitual coffee drinkers. However, after they drank coffee without caffeine, they showed a substantial decrease in salivation. This decrease was a compensatory CR that was elicited by the stimuli that were usually paired with caffeine (the smell and taste of coffee). In addition, when these coffee drinkers drank a cup of hot apple juice containing caffeine, they showed substantial increases in salivation, which shows that they had not developed a general tolerance to the effects of caffeine—their tolerance was found only when the caffeine was paired with the usual CS, coffee.

Similar evidence for compensatory CRs has been obtained with many other pharmacological agents, including adrenalin and alcohol. One experiment found that the effects of an alcoholic drink can be stronger if a person is in an unfamiliar setting as compared to an environment previously associated with drinking alcohol (Birak, Higgs, & Terry, 2011). Just as the rats' tolerance to morphine disappeared when they were given the drug in a new room in Siegel's (1975) experiment, these people's tolerance to alcohol was diminished when they drank it in a new setting.

If it is generally true that classical conditioning contributes to the phenomenon of drug tolerance, it should be possible to find evidence for this effect in nonlaboratory settings. Siegel, Hinson, Krank, and McCully (1982) presented some evidence from regular heroin users who died, or nearly died, after a heroin injection. Of course, an overdose of heroin can be fatal, but in some cases the dosage that caused a death was one the user had tolerated on the previous day. Siegel proposes that in some cases of this type, the user may have taken the heroin in an unusual stimulus environment, where the user's previously acquired compensatory CRs to the heroin injection would be decreased. He states that survivors of nearly fatal injections frequently report that the circumstances of the drug administration were different from those under which they normally injected the drug.

Another implication of the research on conditioned drug responses is that stimuli in the individual's environment can produce drug cravings and withdrawal symptoms, which make it difficult for a recovering addict to remain abstinent. As Siegel and Ramos (2002) have noted, there is abundant evidence that stimuli previously associated with an addictive substance can elicit cravings, and this has been known for a long time. Well before Pavlov studied classical conditioning, Macnish (1859) described how environmental stimuli can affect an alcoholic:

> Man is very much the creature of habit. By drinking regularly at certain times he feels the longing for liquor at the stated return of these periods—as after dinner, or immediately before going to bed, or whatever the period may be. He even finds it in certain companies, or in a particular tavern at which he is in the habit of taking his libations.
>
> (p. 151)

Because conditioned stimuli can elicit cravings for a drug, some drug treatment programs have included **cue exposure treatment** in which clients are exposed to stimuli normally associated with a drug (but no drug), so that conditioned drug cravings can be extinguished (Drummond, Tiffany, Glautier, & Remington, 1995). For example, in a smoking-cessation program, the smoker might be presented with cigarettes to look at, handle, and light up (but not smoke), so that the cravings associated with these cues can gradually extinguish.

Smoking-related stimuli can also be presented using computer-generated images in virtual environments, and this has been shown to decrease cravings for cigarettes. In one study, Moon and Lee (2009) used functional magnetic resonance imaging (fMRI) to show that areas of the brain that are normally active when a person has nicotine cravings were less active after smokers were given computer-generated stimuli. Cue exposure treatment has been used in the treatment of heroin addictions, alcoholism, and even chocolate cravings (Van Gucht et al., 2008). The success of this approach has been mixed, however. Siegel and Ramos (2002) recommend several ways to make it more effective. One way is to give cue exposure treatment in several different contexts, making them as similar as possible to various real-life situations. (Otherwise, a person who normally smoked a lot at work might well have a relapse when he returned to the work environment.) Also, because spontaneous recovery is a property of classical conditioning, several cue exposure sessions, given over a period of time, may be necessary.

Conditioned Opponent Theories

Schull (1979) proposed an interesting theory about compensatory CRs. He called his theory a **conditioned opponent theory** because he accepted most of the assumptions of the Solomon and Corbit opponent-process theory (Chapter 2) but made one important change. Whereas Solomon and Corbit proposed that the b-process is increased by a nonassociative strengthening mechanism, Schull proposed that any increase in the size of the b-process is based on classical conditioning. To take a specific example, a person's response to an initial heroin injection is a very pleasurable sensation followed by unpleasant withdrawal symptoms. The initial pleasure is the a-process, and the unpleasant after-effect is the b-process. Now, according to Schull, only the b-process can be classically conditioned. Let us assume the stimuli that accompany the heroin injection—the needle, the room, and so on—serve as CSs that, after a few pairings with heroin, begin to elicit the withdrawal symptoms by themselves. These CSs have several effects. First, they tend to counteract the a-process, so a heroin injection no longer produces much of a pleasurable sensation. Second, they combine with the b-process to produce more severe and longer lasting withdrawal symptoms. Third, when no heroin is available, these stimuli can still produce withdrawal symptoms and cravings for the drug. Thus, Schull proposed that classically conditioned stimuli may contribute to many of the debilitating characteristics of drug addiction.

Schull's conditioned opponent theory deals exclusively with the conditioning of b-processes, but Wagner (1981) proposed a general theory that is meant to apply to all CRs, whether or not we would want to call them "b-processes." Wagner called this theory a **sometimes opponent process (SOP)** theory because it predicts that in some cases a CR will be the opposite of the UR, but in other cases a CR will mimic the UR. How can we predict what type of CR we will see in a particular conditioning situation? According to SOP, the CR will mimic the UR if the UR is monophasic, but it will be the opposite of the UR if the UR is biphasic. In essence, the terms *monophasic* and *biphasic* concern whether a b-process can be observed in the UR. For example, the heart-rate UR to shock is biphasic because it consists of an increase in heart rate when the shock is on, followed by a decrease in heart rate below baseline when the shock is terminated. Because the UR exhibits such a "rebound effect," SOP predicts that the CR will be the opposite of the UR, and animal research has demonstrated that this is the case. On the other hand, the UR of an eyeblink to a puff of air is monophasic: The eye closes, then opens, but there is no rebound—the eye does not open wider than it was initially. For this reason, SOP predicts that the CR will mimic the UR in eyeblink conditioning, which is of course the case. A number of studies have found support for the predictions of SOP (e.g., Albert, Ricker, Bevins, & Ayres, 1993; McNally & Westbrook, 2006). Although these conditioned opponent theories are complex, one basic message is clear: Many factors can affect the type of CR that is elicited by any particular CS, so the size and form of the CR may be difficult to predict in advance.

SUMMARY

In Kamin's experiment on the blocking effect, rats first received conditioning trials with a light paired with shock and then trials with both the light and a tone paired with the shock. In the test phase, presenting

the tone alone produced no fear response. To account for this and similar results, the Rescorla–Wagner model states that conditioning will occur only if there is a discrepancy between the strength of the US and the strength of the subject's expectation. This model can account for many conditioning phenomena, such as overshadowing, conditioned inhibition, and the overexpectation effect. However, the model has difficulty explaining certain phenomena such as the CS preexposure effect. Attentional theories of classical conditioning maintain that the effectiveness of a CS decreases if the CS is not informative. Comparator theories propose that subjects may learn a CS–US association but not perform a CR unless the CS is a better predictor of the US than are the contextual stimuli.

Research with simple creatures such as *Aplysia* has discovered specific neural and chemical changes that occur during classical conditioning. Research with vertebrates, including humans, has shown that many brain structures may be involved in the development of a simple CR and that different brain structures seem to be involved for different CRs and different conditioning phenomena.

Animals appear to be biologically prepared to learn certain conditioned associations more easily than others. In taste-aversion learning, animals and people can learn to associate a taste with illness, even if the illness occurs several hours after eating. Rats can quickly learn an association between a taste and illness or between audiovisual stimuli and shock, but they are slow to learn the opposite associations. Although biological constraints cannot be ignored, the same general principles seem to apply to taste-aversion learning as to other forms of classical conditioning.

When a CS has been paired with a drug US, the CS will often elicit compensatory CRs—physiological responses that are the opposite of those produced by the drug—and these compensatory CRs can show up as drug tolerance. Conditioned opponent theories have attempted to explain these compensatory CRs and to predict when a CR will mimic the UR and when it will be the opposite of the UR.

Review Questions

1. Describe Kamin's experiment on the blocking effect. Why was the result surprising?
2. Under what conditions does the Rescorla–Wagner model predict that there will be excitatory conditioning, inhibitory conditioning, or no conditioning? Give a specific example of each case.
3. What are some of the main findings and conclusions that can be drawn from neurophysiological research on classical conditioning?
4. Why were evidence for long-delay taste-aversion learning and other examples of biological constraints on classical conditioning seen as threats to the general-principle approach to learning? How has this issue been settled?
5. What are conditioned compensatory responses? What role do they play in drug tolerance and addiction?

REFERENCES

Albert, M., Ricker, S., Bevins, R.A., & Ayres, J.J.B. (1993). Extending continuous versus discontinuous conditioned stimuli before versus after unconditioned stimuli. *Journal of Experimental Psychology: Animal Behavior Processes, 19*, 255–264.

Andrews, E.A., & Braveman, N.S. (1975). The combined effects of dosage level and interstimulus interval on the formation of one-trial poison-based aversions in rats. *Animal Learning and Behavior, 3*, 287–289.

Bailey, C.H., & Kandel, E.R. (2009). Synaptic and cellular basis of learning. In G.G. Berntson (Ed.), *Handbook of neuroscience for the behavioral sciences* (Vol. 1, pp. 528–551). Hoboken, NJ: Wiley.

Balaz, M.A., Kasprow, W.J., & Miller, R.R. (1982). Blocking with a single compound trial. *Animal Learning and Behavior, 10*, 271–276.

Baron, A., Kaufman, A., & Fazzini, D. (1969). Density and delay of punishment of free-operant avoidance. *Journal of the Experimental Analysis of Behavior, 12*, 1029–1037.

Berger, T.W., & Weisz, D.J. (1987). Rabbit nictitating membrane responses. In I. Gormezano, W.F. Prokasy, & R.F. Thompson (Eds.), *Classical conditioning* (3rd ed., pp. 217–253). Hillsdale, NJ: Erlbaum.

Bernstein, I.L., Webster, M.M., & Bernstein, I.D. (1982). Food aversions in children receiving chemo-therapy for cancer. *Cancer, 50*, 2961–2963.

Birak, K.S., Higgs, S., & Terry, P. (2011). Conditioned tolerance to the effects of alcohol on inhibitory control in humans. *Alcohol and Alcoholism, 46*, 686–693.

Boele, H., Koekkoek, S.E., De Zeeuw, C.I., & Ruigrok, T.H. (2013). Axonal sprouting and formation of terminals in the adult cerebellum during associative motor learning. *Journal of Neuroscience, 33*, 17897–17907.

Capaldi, E.J. (1966). Partial reinforcement: A hypothesis of sequential effects. *Psychological Review, 73*, 459–477.

Carew, T.J., Hawkins, R.D., & Kandel, E.R. (1983). Differential classical conditioning of a defensive withdrawal reflex in *Aplysia californica*. *Science, 219*, 397–400.

Chen, A.C., Chang, R.Y., Besherat, A., & Baack, D.W. (2013). Who benefits from multiple brand celebrity endorsements? An experimental investigation. *Psychology & Marketing, 30*, 850–860.

Cole, R.P., Barnet, R.C., & Miller, R.R. (1995). Effect of relative stimulus validity: Learning or per-formance deficit. *Journal of Experimental Psychology: Animal Behavior Processes, 21*, 293–303.

Cummins, E., Boughner, E., & Leri, F. (2014). Cue-induced renewal of heroin place preference: Involvement of the basolateral amygdala. *Neuroreport: For Rapid Communication of Neuroscience Research, 25*, 297–302.

Daum, I., Schugens, M.M., Ackermann, H., Lutzenberger, W., Dichgans, J., & Birbaumer, N. (1993). Classical conditioning after cerebellar lesions in humans. *Behavioral Neuroscience, 107*, 748–756.

Dimberg, U., & Öhman, A. (1983). The effects of directional facial cues on electrodermal condition-ing to facial stimuli. *Psychophysiology, 20*, 160–167.

Dimberg, U., & Öhman, A. (1996). Behold the wrath: Psychophysiological responses to facial stimuli. *Motivation and Emotion, 20*, 149–182.

Dopson, J.C., Pearce, J.M., & Haselgrove, M. (2009). Failure of retrospective revaluation to influence blocking. *Journal of Experimental Psychology: Animal Behavior Processes, 35*, 473–484.

Drummond, D.C., Tiffany, S.T., Glautier, S., & Remington, B. (Eds.). (1995). *Addictive behaviour: Cue exposure research and theory*. New York: Wiley.

Etscorn, F., & Stephens, R. (1973). Establishment of conditioned taste aversions with a 24-hour CS-US interval. *Physiological Psychology, 1*, 251–253.

Förderer, S., & Unkelbach, C. (2014). The moderating role of attribute accessibility in conditioning multiple specific attributes. *European Journal of Social Psychology, 44*, 69–81.

Garcia, J., Ervin, F.R., & Koelling, R.A. (1966). Learning with prolonged delay of reinforcement. *Psychonomic Science, 5*, 121–122.

Garcia, J., & Koelling, R. (1966). Relation of cue to consequence in avoidance learning. *Psychonomic Science, 4*, 123–124.

Glanzman, D.L. (1995). The cellular basis of classical conditioning in *Aplysia californica*—it's less simple than you think. *Trends in Neuroscience, 18*, 30–36.

Gorn, G.J. (1982). The effects of music in advertising on choice behavior: A classical conditioning approach. *Journal of Marketing, 46*, 94–101.

Gottfried, J.A., O'Doherty, J., & Dolan, R.J. (2002). Appetitive and aversive olfactory learning in humans studied using event-related functional magnetic resonance imaging. *Journal of Neuroscience, 22*, 10829–10837.

Hall, G., & Pearce, J.M. (1983). Changes in stimulus associability during acquisition: Implications for theories of acquisition. In M.L. Commons, R.J. Herrnstein, & A.R. Wagner (Eds.), *Quantitative analyses of behavior: Vol. 3. Acquisition* (pp. 221–239). Cambridge, MA: Ballinger.

Kamin, L.J. (1968). Attention-like processes in classical conditioning. In M.R. Jones (Ed.), *Miami sympo-sium on the prediction of behavior: Aversive stimulation* (pp. 9–33). Miami, FL: University of Miami Press.

Kimble, G.A. (1961). *Hilgard and Marquis' conditioning and learning* (2nd ed.). New York: Appleton-Century-Crofts.

Knowlton, B. J., & Thompson, R. F. (1992). Conditioning using a cerebral cortical conditioned stimulus is dependent on the cerebellum and brain stem circuitry. *Behavioral Neuroscience, 106*, 509–517.

Kremer, E. F. (1978). The Rescorla–Wagner model: Losses in associative strength in compound conditioned stimuli. *Journal of Experimental Psychology: Animal Behavior Processes, 4*, 22–36.

Lett, B. T. (1973). Delayed reward learning: Disproof of the traditional theory. *Learning and Motivation, 4*, 237–246.

Lewis, M. C., & Gould, T. J. (2007). Reversible inactivation of the entorhinal cortex disrupts the establishment and expression of latent inhibition of cued fear conditioning in C57BL/6 mice. *Hippocampus, 17*, 462–470.

LoBue, V., & DeLoache, J. S. (2008). Detecting the snake in the grass: Attention to fear-relevant stimuli by adults and young children. *Psychological Science, 19*, 284–289.

Logue, A. W. (1979). Taste aversion and the generality of the laws of learning. *Psychological Bulletin, 86*, 276–296.

Logue, A. W., Ophir, I., & Strauss, K. E. (1981). The acquisition of taste aversions in humans. *Behavior Research and Therapy, 19*, 319–333.

Lubow, R. E. (2009). Conditioned taste aversion and latent inhibition: A review. In T. R. Schachtman & S. Reilly (Eds.), *Conditioned taste aversion: Behavioral and neural processes* (pp. 37–57). New York: Oxford University Press.

Lubow, R. E., & Moore, A. U. (1959). Latent inhibition: The effect of nonreinforced preexposure to the conditional stimulus. *Journal of Comparative and Physiological Psychology, 52*, 415–419.

Mackintosh, N. J. (1975). A theory of attention: Variations in the associability of stimuli with reinforcement. *Psychological Review, 82*, 276–298.

Macnish, R. (1859). *The anatomy of drunkenness.* Glasgow, Scotland: W. R. McPuhn.

Mallan, K. M., Lipp, O. V., & Cochrane, B. (2013). Slithering snakes, angry men and out-group members: What and whom are we evolved to fear? *Cognition and Emotion, 27*, 1168–1180.

Matzel, L. D., Brown, A. M., & Miller, R. R. (1987). Associative effects of US preexposure: Modulation of conditioned responding by an excitatory training context. *Journal of Experimental Psychology: Animal Behavior Processes, 13*, 65–72.

McCormick, D. A., & Thompson, R. F. (1984). Neuronal responses of the rabbit cerebellum during acquisition and performance of a classically conditioned nictitating membrane-eyelid response. *Journal of Neuroscience, 4*, 2811–2822.

McEchron, M. D., Tseng, W., & Disterhoft, J. F. (2003). Single neurons in CA1 hippocampus encode trace interval duration during trace heart rate (fear) conditioning. *Journal of Neuroscience, 23*, 1535–1547.

McNally, G. P., & Westbrook, R. F. (2006). A short intertrial interval facilitates acquisition of context-conditioned fear and a short retention interval facilitates its expression. *Journal of Experimental Psychology: Animal Behavior Processes, 32*, 164–172.

Miller, R. R., & Schachtman, T. R. (1985). The several roles of context at the time of retrieval. In P. D. Balsam & A. Tomie (Eds.), *Context and learning* (pp. 167–194). Hillsdale, NJ: Erlbaum.

Molchan, S. E., Sunderland, T., McIntosh, A. R., Herscovitch, P., & Schreurs, B. G. (1994). A functional anatomical study of associative learning in humans. *Proceedings of the National Academy of Sciences United States of America, 91*, 8122–8126.

Moon, J., & Lee, J. (2009). Cue exposure treatment in a virtual environment to reduce nicotine craving: A functional MRI study. *CyberPsychology & Behavior, 12*, 43–45.

Nagaishi, T., & Nakajima, S. (2010). Overshadowing of running-based taste aversion learning by another taste cue. *Behavioural Processes, 83*, 134–136.

Öhman, A., Dimberg, U., & Ost, L. G. (1985). Animal and social phobias: Biological constraints on learned fear responses. In S. Reiss & R. R. Bootzin (Eds.), *Theoretical issues in behavior therapy* (pp. 123–178). New York: Academic Press.

Öhman, A., Flykt, A., & Esteves, F. (2001). Emotion drives attention: Detecting the snake in the grass. *Journal of Experimental Psychology: General, 130*, 466–478.

Öhman, A., & Mineka, S. (2001). Fears, phobias, and preparedness: Toward an evolved module of fear and fear learning. *Psychological Review, 108*, 483–522.

Packer, J.S., Clark, B.M., Bond, N.W., & Siddle, D.A. (1991). Conditioning with facial expression of emotion: A comparison of aversive and non-aversive unconditioned stimuli. *Journal of Psychophysiology, 5*, 79–88.

Pearce, J.M., & Hall, G. (1980). A model for Pavlovian learning: Variations in the effectiveness of conditioned but not unconditioned stimuli. *Psychological Review, 87*, 532–552.

Rescorla, R.A. (1968). Probability of shock in the presence and absence of CS in fear conditioning. *Journal of Comparative and Physiological Psychology, 66*, 1–5.

Rescorla, R.A., & Wagner, A.R. (1972). A theory of Pavlovian conditioning: Variations in the effectiveness of reinforcement and nonreinforcement. In A.H. Black & W.F. Prokasy (Eds.), *Classical conditioning II: Current research and theory* (pp. 64–99). New York: Appleton-Century-Crofts.

Rozin, P., Reff, D., Mack, M., & Schull, J. (1984). Conditioned opponent responses in human tolerance to caffeine. *Bulletin of the Psychonomic Society, 22*, 117–120.

Ruprecht, C.M., Izurieta, H.S., Wolf, J.E., & Leising, K.J. (2014). Overexpectation in the context of reward timing. *Learning and Motivation, 47*, 1–11.

San-Galli, A., Marchand, A.R., Decorte, L., & Di Scala, G. (2011). Retrospective revaluation and its neural circuit in rats. *Behavioural Brain Research, 223*, 262–270.

Scalera, G., & Bavieri, M. (2009). Role of conditioned taste aversion on the side effects of chemotherapy in cancer patients. In T.R. Schachtman & S. Reilly (Eds.), Conditioned taste aversion: Behavioral and neural processes (pp. 513–541). New York: Oxford University Press.

Schell, A.M., Dawson, M.E., & Marinkovic, K. (1991). Effects of potentially phobic conditioned stimuli on retention, reconditioning, and extinction of the conditioned skin conductance response. Psychophysiology, 28, 140–153.

Schneiderman, N., McCabe, P.M., Haselton, J.R., Ellenberger, H.H., Jarrell, T.W., & Gentile, C.G. (1987). Neurobiological bases of conditioned bradycardia in rabbits. In I. Gormezano, W.F. Prokasy, & R.F. Thompson (Eds.), *Classical conditioning* (3rd ed., pp. 37–63). Hillsdale, NJ: Erlbaum.

Schull, J. (1979). A conditioned opponent theory of Pavlovian conditioning and habituation. In G.H. Bower (Ed.), *The psychology of learning and motivation* (Vol. 13, pp. 57–90). New York: Academic Press.

Seligman, M.E.P. (1970). On the generality of the laws of learning. *Psychological Review, 77*, 406–418.

Seligman, M.E.P., & Hager, J.L. (1972). *Biological boundaries of learning.* New York: Appleton-Century-Crofts.

Siegel, S. (1975). Evidence from rats that morphine tolerance is a learned response. *Journal of Comparative and Physiological Psychology, 89*, 498–506.

Siegel, S. (2005). Drug tolerance, drug addiction, and drug anticipation. *Current Directions in Psychological Science, 14*, 296–300.

Siegel, S., Hinson, R.E., Krank, M.D., & McCully, J. (1982). Heroin "overdose" death: The contribution of drug-associated environmental cues. *Science, 216*, 436–437.

Siegel, S., & Ramos, B.M.C. (2002). Applying laboratory research: Drug anticipation and the treatment of drug addiction. *Experimental and Clinical Psychopharmacology, 10*, 162–183.

Smith, O.A., Astley, C.A., DeVito, J.L., Stein, J.M., & Walsh, K.E. (1980). Functional analysis of hypothalamic control of the cardiovascular responses accompanying emotional behavior. *Federation Proceedings, 39*, 2487–2494.

Solomon, P.R. (1977). Role of the hippocampus in blocking and conditioned inhibition of the rabbit's nictitating membrane response. *Journal of Comparative and Physiological Psychology, 91*, 407–417.

Spetch, M.L. (1995). Overshadowing in landmark learning: Touch-screen studies with pigeons and humans. *Journal of Experimental Psychology: Animal Behavior Processes, 21*, 166–181.

Stockhorst, U., Hall, G., Enck, P., & Klosterhalfen, S. (2014). Effects of overshadowing on conditioned and unconditioned nausea in a rotation paradigm with humans. *Experimental Brain Research, 232,* 2651–2664.

Stout, S.C., & Miller, R.R. (2007). Sometimes-Competing Retrieval (SOCR): A formalization of the comparator hypothesis. *Psychological Review, 114,* 759–783.

Thompson, R.F., McCormick, D.A., & Lavond, D.G. (1986). Localization of the essential memory-trace system for a basic form of associative learning in the mammalian brain. In S.H. Hulse & B.F. Green, Jr. (Eds.), *One hundred years of psychological research in America* (pp. 125–171). Baltimore, MD: Johns Hopkins University Press.

Tracy, J.A., Thompson, J.K., Krupa, D.J., & Thompson, R.F. (2013). Evidence of plasticity in the pontocerebellar conditioned stimulus pathway during classical conditioning of the eyeblink response in the rabbit. *Behavioral Neuroscience, 127,* 676–689.

Van Gucht, D., Vansteenwegen, D., Beckers, T., Hermans, D., Baeyens, F., & Van den Bergh, O. (2008). Repeated cue exposure effects on subjective and physiological indices of chocolate craving. *Appetite, 50,* 19–24.

Wagner, A.R. (1981). SOP: A model of automatic memory processing in animal behavior. In N.E. Spear & R.R. Miller (Eds.), *Information processing in animals: Memory mechanisms* (pp. 5–47). Hillsdale, NJ: Erlbaum.

Wilcoxon, H.C., Dragoin, W.B., & Kral, P.A. (1971). Illness-induced aversions in rat and quail: Relative salience of visual and gustatory cues. *Science, 171,* 826–828.

CHAPTER 5

Basic Principles of Operant Conditioning

Learning Objectives

After reading this chapter, you should be able to

- describe Thorndike's Law of Effect and experiments on animals in the puzzle box
- discuss how the principle of reinforcement can account for superstitious behaviors
- describe the procedure of shaping and explain how it can be used in behavior modification
- explain B. F. Skinner's free-operant procedure, three-term contingency, and the basic principles of operant conditioning
- define instinctive drift, and explain why some psychologists believed that it posed problems for the principle of reinforcement
- define autoshaping and discuss different theories about why it occurs

---

Unlike classically conditioned responses, many everyday behaviors are not elicited by a specific stimulus. Behaviors such as walking, talking, eating, drinking, working, and playing do not occur automatically in response to any particular stimulus. In the presence of a stimulus such as food, an animal might eat or it might not, depending on the time of day, the time since its last meal, the presence of other animals, and so on. Because it appears that the animal can choose whether to engage in behaviors of this type, people sometimes call them "voluntary" behaviors and contrast them with the "involuntary" behaviors that are part of unconditioned and conditioned reflexes. Some learning theorists state that whereas classical conditioning is limited to involuntary behaviors, operant conditioning influences our voluntary behaviors. The term *voluntary* may not be the best term to use because it is difficult to define in a precise, scientific way, but whatever we call nonreflexive behaviors, this chapter should make one thing clear: Just because there is no obvious stimulus preceding a behavior, this does not mean that the behavior is unpredictable. The extensive research on operant conditioning might be described as an effort to discover general principles that can predict what nonreflexive behaviors an individual will perform and under what conditions.

THE LAW OF EFFECT

Thorndike's Experiments

E. L. Thorndike (1898, 1911) was the first researcher to investigate systematically how an animal's nonreflexive behaviors can be modified as a result of its experience. In Thorndike's experiments, a hungry animal (a cat, a dog, or a chicken) was placed in a small chamber that Thorndike called a **puzzle box**. If the animal performed the appropriate response, the door to the puzzle box would be opened, and the animal could exit and eat some food placed just outside the door. For some animals, the required response was simple: pulling on a rope, pressing a lever, or stepping on a platform. Figure 5.1 shows one of Thorndike's more difficult puzzle boxes, which required a cat to make three separate responses. The first time an animal was placed in a puzzle box, it usually took a long time to escape. A typical animal would move about and explore the various parts of the chamber in a seemingly haphazard way, and eventually it would perform the response that opened the door. Based on his observations, Thorndike concluded that an animal's first production of the appropriate response occurred purely by accident.

To determine how an animal's behavior would change as a result of its experience, Thorndike would return the animal to the same puzzle box many times and measure how long it

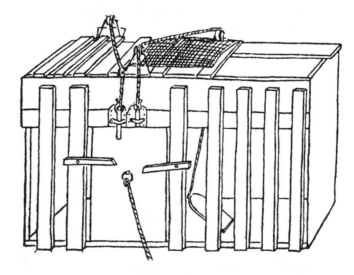

Figure 5.1 One of Thorndike's puzzle boxes. A cat could escape from this box by pulling a string, stepping on the platform, and turning one of the two latches on the front of the door. (From Thorndike, 1898)

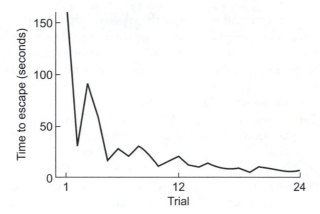

Figure 5.2 The number of seconds required by one cat to escape from a simple puzzle box on 24 consecutive trials. (From Thorndike, 1898)

took the animal to escape each trial. Figure 5.2 presents a typical result from one of Thorndike's cats, which shows that as trials progressed, the cat's time to escape gradually declined (from 160 seconds on the 1st trial to just 7 seconds on the 24th trial). Thorndike attributed this gradual improvement over trials to the progressive strengthening of an S-R connection: The stimulus was the inside of the puzzle box, and the response was whatever behavior opened the door. To account for the gradual strengthening of this connection, Thorndike (1898) formulated a principle of learning that he called the **Law of Effect**: If, in a specific situation, a response is followed by a satisfying state of affairs, the response will become associated with that situation and will be more likely to occur again in that same situation. Thorndike defined a "satisfying state of affairs" as "one which the animal does nothing to avoid, often doing such things as attain and preserve it" (p. 245).

The application of the Law of Effect to the puzzle-box experiments is straightforward: Certain behaviors, those that opened the door, were closely followed by a satisfying state of affairs (escape and food), so when the animal was returned to the same situation it was more likely to produce those behaviors than it had been at first. In modern psychology, the phrase "satisfying state of affairs" has been replaced by the term **reinforcer**, but the Law of Effect (or the principle of **positive reinforcement**) remains as one of the most important concepts of learning theory.

Guthrie and Horton: Evidence for a Mechanical Strengthening Process

Two researchers who followed Thorndike, E. R. Guthrie and G. P. Horton (1946), provided more convincing evidence that the learning that took place in the puzzle box involved the strengthening of whatever behavior happened to be followed by escape and food. They placed cats in a puzzle box with a simple solution: A pole in the center of the chamber had only to be tipped in any direction to open the door. A camera outside the chamber photographed the cat at the same instant that the door swung open, thereby providing a permanent record of exactly how the cat had performed the effective response on each trial. The photographs revealed that after a few trials, each cat settled on a particular method of manipulating the pole that was quite consistent from trial to trial. However, different cats developed different styles for moving the pole; for example, one cat would always push the pole with its left forepaw, another would always bite the pole, and another would lie down next to the pole and roll over into it (Figure 5.3).

In summary, Guthrie and Horton found that after their cats mastered the task, there was relatively little variability from trial to trial for a given cat, but there was considerable variability from one cat to another. These results provide evidence for a particular version of the Law of Effect that Brown and Herrnstein (1975) called the **stop-action principle**. According to this principle, there is a parallel between the action of the camera and the reinforcer in the experiments of Guthrie and Horton. Like the camera, the occurrence of the reinforcer serves to stop the animal's ongoing behavior and strengthen the association between the situation (the puzzle box) and those precise behaviors that were occurring at the moment of reinforcement.

Figure 5.3 These drawings illustrate the sorts of behaviors cats displayed in the puzzle box of Guthrie and Horton. Each cat developed a unique style of moving the pole and used it trial after trial.

The stop-action principle states that because of this strengthening process, the specific bodily position and the muscle movements occurring at the moment of reinforcement will have a higher probability of occurring on the next trial. If the cat repeats the bodily position and movements on the next trial, this will produce a second reinforcer, thereby further strengthening that S-R association even more. This sort of positive feedback process should eventually produce one S-R connection that is so much stronger than any other that this particular response pattern will occur with high probability, trial after trial. For each cat, whatever random behavior happened to get reinforced a few times would become dominant over other behaviors.

Superstitious Behaviors

The mechanical nature of the stop-action principle suggests that behaviors may sometimes be strengthened "by accident." Skinner (1948) conducted a famous experiment, now often called the **superstition experiment**, which made a strong case for the power of accidental reinforcement. Eight pigeons were placed in separate experimental chambers, and grain was presented every 15 seconds regardless of what the pigeons were doing. After a pigeon had spent some time in the chamber, Skinner observed the bird's behavior. He found that six of his eight pigeons had developed clearly defined behaviors that they performed repeatedly between food presentations. One bird made a few counterclockwise turns between reinforcers, another made pecking motions at the floor, and a third repeatedly poked its head into one of the upper corners of the chamber. A fourth bird was observed to toss its head in an upward motion, and two others swayed from side to side. These behaviors occurred repeatedly despite the fact that no behavior was required for reinforcement. Similar results have been found by other researchers who repeated (with some variations) the basic idea of Skinner's experiment (Gleeson, Lattal, & Williams, 1989; Neuringer, 1970).

According to Skinner, whatever behavior happened to be occurring when the reinforcer was delivered was strengthened. If the first reinforcer occurred immediately after a pigeon had tossed its head upward, this behavior of head tossing would be more likely to occur in the future. Therefore, there was a good chance that the next reinforcer would also follow a head-tossing motion. The accidental strengthening process is self-perpetuating because once any one behavior develops a somewhat higher frequency of occurrence than all other behaviors, it has a greater chance of being reinforced, which increases its frequency still further, and so on.

Skinner (1948) proposed that many of the **superstitious behaviors** and rituals that people perform are produced by the same mechanism that caused his pigeons to exhibit such peculiar behaviors: accidental reinforcement. Superstitious behaviors frequently arise when an individual actually has no control over the events taking place, as in card playing or other types of gambling, where winning or losing depends on chance. In laboratory experiments, Matute (1994, 1995) observed superstitious behaviors in situations where people had no control over events. In one case, college students were exposed to unpleasantly loud tones and were told that they could turn off the tones by typing the correct sequence of keys on a keyboard. In reality, the participants had no control over the tones, which went on and off no matter what keys they typed. Nevertheless, most of the students developed superstitious behaviors—they tended to type the same key sequences each time a tone came on. At the end of the experiment, many of the participants said they believed that their typing responses did turn off the tones.

Herrnstein (1966) pointed out that Skinner's analysis is most applicable to idiosyncratic superstitions, like those of a gambler or an athlete. It seems likely that such personal superstitions arise out of a person's own experience with reinforcement. On the other hand, superstitions that are widely held across a society (e.g., the belief that it is bad luck to walk under a ladder, or that the number 13 is unlucky) are probably acquired through communication with others, not through individual experience (Figure 5.4). How some of these common superstitions began is not known, but Herrnstein suggested that they may be the residue of previous contingencies of reinforcement that are no longer in effect. As an example, he cited the belief that it is bad luck to light three cigarettes on a single match. This superstition arose in the trenches during World War I. At that time, there was some justification for this belief because every second that a match remained lit increased the chances of being spotted by the enemy. This danger is not present in everyday life, but the superstition is still passed on from generation to generation. Herrnstein speculated that superstitions may be perpetuated by stories of occasional individuals who violate the rule and meet with an unfortunate fate. Thus, Herrnstein claimed that some superstitions were originally valid beliefs and are now perpetuated by rumor and/or occasional coincidences. It is easy to imagine how some superstitions (such as the one about walking under a ladder) may have begun, whereas the origins of others are less clear.

Figure 5.4 Crossing one's fingers for good luck is a common superstitious behavior. (Misha Beliy/ Shutterstock.com)

Skinner's analysis of his superstition experiment is not the only possible interpretation. Staddon and Simmelhag (1971) conducted a careful replication of the superstition experiment, recorded the pigeons' behaviors more thoroughly than Skinner did, and came to different conclusions. They found that certain behavior patterns tended to occur frequently during the intervals between food deliveries, and they called these interim and terminal behaviors. **Interim behaviors** occurred in the early part of the interval, when the next reinforcer was still some time away. Interim behaviors included pecking toward the floor, turning, and moving along the front wall of the chamber. **Terminal behaviors** tended to occur as the time of food delivery drew near. Two of the most frequent terminal behaviors were orienting toward the food magazine and pecking in the vicinity of the magazine. Staddon and Simmelhag proposed that some of the behaviors that Skinner called "superstitious behaviors" may actually have been interim or terminal behaviors. These behaviors are not produced by accidental reinforcement but are simply innate behaviors that animals tend to perform when the likelihood of reinforcement is low (interim behaviors) or when food is about to be delivered (terminal behaviors). Many other studies have shown that the periodic delivery of food or some other reinforcer can give rise to a variety of stereotyped behaviors that have been collectively called **adjunctive behaviors**. These innate behaviors occur when the next reinforcer is some time away and the animal must do something to "pass the time."

Still, it seems clear that Skinner's analysis of superstitious behaviors was at least partly correct: Sometimes behaviors do increase in frequency because of accidental reinforcement. In the laboratory, experiments with both adults and children have found that they have a tendency to develop superstitious behaviors when free reinforcers were periodically delivered (Sheehan, Van Reet, & Bloom, 2012). These superstitious behaviors tend to increase just before a reinforcer is delivered, and they are distinctly different for different participants. For instance, in a study where a mechanical clown delivered marbles every now and then, one child developed the behavior of kissing the clown on the nose, another child swung his hips, and another puckered his mouth (Wagner & Morris, 1987). Outside the laboratory, many idiosyncratic superstitions can be easily traced to past reinforcement, including those frequently seen in athletes.

BOX 5.1   IN THE MEDIA

Superstitious Behaviors in Sports

Superstitious behaviors are common among athletes. In a study of college football, track, and gymnastics teams, Bleak and Frederick (1998) found that an average player performed about 10 different superstitious behaviors, such as wearing a lucky charm or item of clothing, eating the same meal before each competition, or taping a part of the body that was not injured. Burger and Lynn (2005) found that superstitious behaviors were widespread among professional baseball players in both the United States and Japan. Some superstitious behaviors occur without the athlete's awareness. Ciborowski

(1997) asked college baseball players to describe the behaviors they performed between pitches while batting (e.g., touching parts of the body or clothing, gripping the bat in certain ways, touching the ground or plate with the bat). The players were able to list most of them, but not all. However, when asked how many times they repeated these behaviors, the players' estimates were too low by a factor of four. Amazingly, Ciborowski found that the average player made 82 such movements in one time at bat.

Superstitious behaviors are also frequently seen in sports fans as they watch their favorite teams play. Wann et al. (2013) found that some of the most common superstitions of sports fans are wearing specific types of sports apparel, consuming specific types of food or drink, and choosing either to watch or not watch the action during critical parts of a game. It is easy to imagine how these behaviors could have been accidentally reinforced in the past, when performing the behaviors was followed by a team's success.

THE PROCEDURE OF SHAPING, OR SUCCESSIVE APPROXIMATIONS

Shaping Lever Pressing in a Rat

Imagine that as part of your laboratory work in a psychology course, you are given a rat in an experimental chamber equipped with a lever and a pellet dispenser, and your task is to train the rat to press the lever at a modest rate. You have a remote-control button that, when pressed, delivers one food pellet to a food tray in the chamber. You instructor tells you that an important first step is to establish the sound of the pellet dispenser as a conditioned reinforcer. A **conditioned reinforcer** is a previously neutral stimulus that has acquired the capacity to strengthen responses because that stimulus has been repeatedly paired with food or some other primary reinforcer. A **primary reinforcer** is a stimulus that naturally strengthens any response it follows. Primary reinforcers include food, water, sexual pleasure, and comfort. If you repeatedly expose your rat to the sound of the pellet dispenser followed by the delivery of a food pellet, the sound of the dispenser should become a conditioned reinforcer. You can be sure that this has been accomplished when the rat will quickly return to the food tray from any part of the chamber as soon as you operate the dispenser. The importance of the conditioned reinforcer is that it can be presented immediately after the rat makes any desired response. We have seen that the contiguity between response and reinforcer is very important—whatever behavior immediately precedes reinforcement will be strengthened. With a conditioned reinforcer such as the sound of the pellet dispenser, a response can be immediately reinforced even if it takes the rat several seconds to reach the primary reinforcer, the food.

Once you have established the sound of the pellet dispenser as a conditioned reinforcer, you might just wait until the rat presses the lever and then immediately deliver a food pellet. However, suppose the lever is 5 inches above the floor of the chamber, and it takes an effortful push from the rat to fully depress the lever. Under these circumstances, you might wait for hours and the rat might never depress the lever. And, of course, you cannot reinforce a response that never occurs.

This is where the process of **shaping**, or successive approximations, becomes very useful. A good way to start would be to wait until the rat is below the lever and then reinforce any detectable upward head movement. After 5 or 10 reinforcers for such a movement, the rat will probably be making upward head movements quite frequently. Once this behavior is well established, the procedure of shaping consists of gradually making your criterion for reinforcement more demanding. For example, the next step might be to wait for an upward head movement of at least half an inch before delivering a food pellet. Soon the rat will be making these larger responses regularly. You can then go on to require upward movements of 1 inch, 1.5 inches, and so on, until the rat is bringing its head close to the lever. The next step might be to require some actual contact with the lever, then contact with one forepaw, then some downward movement of the lever, and so on, until the rat has learned to make a full lever press.

Figure 5.5 provides a graphic illustration of how the procedure of shaping makes use of the variability in the subject's behavior. Suppose that before beginning the shaping process, you simply observed the rat's behavior for 5 minutes, making an estimate every 5 seconds about the height of the rat's head above the floor of the chamber. Figure 5.5 provides an example of what you might find: The y-axis shows the height of the rat's head to the nearest half inch, and the x-axis shows the number of times this height occurred in the 5-minute sample. The resulting frequency distribution indicates that the rat usually kept its head about 1.5 inches from the floor, but sometimes its head was lower and sometimes much higher. Given such a distribution, it might make sense to start the shaping process with a requirement that the rat raise its head to a height of at least 2.5 inches before it is reinforced. Figure 5.5 shows how the frequency distribution would probably shift after the shaping process began.

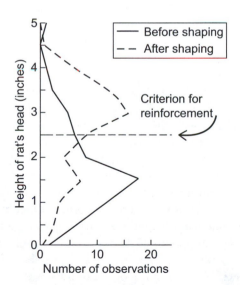

Figure 5.5 Hypothetical distributions showing the height of a rat's head as observed at regular intervals before shaping (solid line) and after selective reinforcement of head heights greater than 2.5 inches (dotted line). Rachlin (1970) presents a similar analysis of the shaping process.

Shaping Behaviors in the Classroom

Shaping can be used to produce totally new behaviors in people as well as in laboratory rats. At many colleges and universities, there are stories about how the students in a large lecture course collaborated to shape the behavior of their professor. In one such story, a professor who usually stood rigidly behind the lectern was reinforced by his students for any movement, and by the end of the hour he was pacing back and forth and gesturing wildly with his arms. In another story, a professor in an introductory psychology course lectured from an elevated stage. The students secretly agreed to reinforce the professor for any movement to the left. The reinforcers they used were listening attentively, nodding their heads in apparent understanding of what he was saying, and taking notes. Whenever the professor moved to the right, however, they stopped delivering these reinforcers—they would stop taking notes, yawn, look bored, and look around the room. This systematic delivery of reinforcers for movement to the left was apparently quite successful, for legend has it that about halfway through the lecture the professor fell off the left side of the stage (which was only about 18 inches high). Stories like this suggest that shaping can work even when the subject is unaware of what is going on.

Shaping as a Tool in Behavior Modification

Not all examples of shaping are as frivolous as those described in the previous section. Shaping is frequently used as a method to establish new or better behaviors in a wide range of settings. As one example, Scott, Scott, and Goldwater (1997) used a shaping technique to improve the performance of a university pole-vaulter. This 21-year-old had been competing in the sport for 10 years, and he had taken part in international events, but there was one aspect of the skill of pole-vaulting that he had difficulty mastering. To obtain the maximum height of a vault, it is important for the athlete to raise his or her arms and the pole as high overhead as possible when the pole is planted in the ground at the moment of takeoff. This vaulter was not extending his arms completely at takeoff, and he knew it, but he could not seem to break this bad habit.

Videotapes of the pole-vaulter showed that on an average attempt, his arms were extended to a height of 2.25 meters. To train him to reach higher, the researchers set up a photoelectric beam and sensor slightly above this point, at 2.30 meters. On every practice trial, a trainer shouted "Reach!" as he was running down the runway, and if his hands broke the photoelectric beam, there was a beep to signal that he had extended his arms to the criterion level. Because this beep was associated with a better performance, it can be called a conditioned reinforcer, just as the sound of the pellet dispenser serves as a conditioned reinforcer for a rat learning a new response. Once the pole-vaulter achieved a success rate of 90% at one hand height, the criterion was gradually increased (to 2.35 meters, then to 2.40 meters, and so on). The improvement took many months of practice, but eventually the vaulter was extending his arms to just about their maximum possible height. From his perspective, the most important result was that with each increase in the height of the photoelectric beam, the height of the bar that he was able to clear rose to a new personal best. Therefore, this systematic shaping procedure produced the results he was trying to attain.

In another example of shaping, therapists used toys and other desired items as reinforcers to get an 8-year-old boy with intellectual disabilities to use a mask that delivered medication he needed to treat a serious respiratory condition (Hagopian & Thompson, 1999). The boy initially resisted using the mask for any length of time, so the therapists started by giving him a reinforcer when he wore the mask for just 5 seconds. The criterion for reinforcement was gradually increased over a period of several weeks until he was using the mask for the full duration of 40 seconds that he needed.

Shaping can be used with groups as well as with individuals. In a program at a drug treatment clinic, cocaine users were given standard methadone treatment, and a shaping procedure was used to gradually decrease their use of cocaine. Over the course of several weeks, patients received vouchers that could be exchanged for items such as movie tickets if their urine samples showed at least a 25% reduction in cocaine metabolites compared to their previous test. Eventually, they could earn vouchers only if there was no sign of cocaine in their urine samples. The researchers found that this shaping procedure was more effective in reducing cocaine use than requiring complete abstinence from the very start of the program (Preston, Umbricht, Wong, & Epstein, 2001). Similar procedures have been used to help people quit smoking (Stoops et al., 2009). Because shaping can help to improve behaviors even under difficult circumstances, it has become a common component of many behavior modification programs.

In some ways, shaping is more of an art than an exact science. Many split-second decisions must be made about which behaviors to reinforce and which not to reinforce, how quickly the criterion for reinforcement should be increased, what to do when the learner has a setback, and so on. However, the procedure of shaping can be made more precise by using a **percentile schedule**. In a percentile schedule, a response is reinforced if it is better than a certain percentage of the last several responses that the learner has made (J. R. Platt, 1973). For example, imagine that a boy in math class does not complete his assignments on time because he is easily distracted. A behavior therapist might use a percentile schedule to shape more and more rapid completion of his work. Suppose the student is told to work on a series of math problems, and at the end of every minute, the boy earns a reinforcer if he completes more problems than he did in 7 of the last 10 minutes. The reinforcers could be points that can later be exchanged for money, snacks, or some other tangible reinforcers. As the boy earns reinforcers, the criterion for future reinforcers should gradually increase, because his performance is always being compared to how well he did in the last 10 minutes.

Percentile schedules have been successfully applied to cases ranging from the academic performance of children with developmental disabilities (Athens, Vollmer, & St. Peter Pipkin, 2007) to increasing activity levels in adults to improve their health (Washington, Banna, & Gibson, 2014). Percentile schedules can also be used in computer software that keeps track of each student's performance and tailors the difficulty of the material to the child's rate of improvement. In this way, slower learners are given additional practice with simpler concepts until they master them, and faster learners are not held back but are given more difficult material to keep them challenged (Figure 5.6).

Figure 5.6 Some types of educational software use shaping procedures that increase the difficulty of the material based on each child's rate of progress. (Money Business Images/Shutterstock.com)

THE RESEARCH OF B. F. SKINNER

Whereas Thorndike deserves credit for the first systematic research on reinforcement, B. F. Skinner was primarily responsible for the increasing interest in this topic during the middle of the twentieth century. Skinner himself discovered many of the most basic and most important properties of reinforcement. In addition, he trained several generations of students whose research has enriched our knowledge about how reinforcement affects the behavior of people and animals.

The Free Operant

In his research on operant conditioning, Skinner modified Thorndike's procedure in a simple but important way. Research with the puzzle box involved a discrete trial procedure: A trial began each time an animal was placed in the puzzle box, and the animal could make one and only one response on each trial. The primary dependent variable was response latency. After each trial, the experimenter had to intervene, physically returning the animal to the puzzle box for the next trial. This procedure was time consuming and cumbersome, and only a small number of trials could be conducted each day. Other early operant conditioning procedures, such as those involving runways or mazes with a reinforcer at the end, shared these same disadvantages.

Skinner's innovation was to make use of a response that the animal could perform repeatedly without the intervention of the experimenter. In experiments with rats, lever pressing is often the operant response. With pigeons, the most common response is the key peck: One or more circular plastic disks, called response keys, are recessed in one wall of the experimental chamber (Figure 5.7), and the bird's pecks at these keys are recorded. Procedures that make use of lever pressing, key pecking, or similar responses are called **free-operant procedures** to distinguish them from the discrete trial procedures of the puzzle box or maze. The distinguishing characteristics of a free-operant procedure are that (1) the operant response can occur at any time and (2) the operant response can occur repeatedly for as long as the subject remains in the experimental chamber. In addition, responses such as lever pressing and key pecking require so little effort that a subject can make thousands of responses in a single session. With so many responses to observe, the experimenter can study the moment-to-moment variations in response rate that occur as a subject learns about the experimental situation or as some external stimulus is changed.

Figure 5.7 A pigeon pecking at a lighted key in a typical operant conditioning chamber. Grain is provided as a reinforcer through the square opening beneath the keys.

The Three-Term Contingency

In its simplest form, a contingency is a rule that states that some event, B, will occur if and only if another event, A, occurs. Simple classical conditioning provides one example: The US will occur if and only if the CS occurs first. It is sometimes said that in operant conditioning, there is a contingency between response and reinforcer—the reinforcer occurs if and only if the response occurs. Skinner pointed out, however, that there are actually three components in the operant conditioning contingency: (1) the context or situation in which a response occurs (i.e., those stimuli that precede the response); (2) the response itself; and (3) the stimulus that follow the response (i.e., the reinforcer). To be more specific, the contingency in operant conditioning usually takes the following form: In the presence of a specific stimulus, often called a **discriminative stimulus**, the reinforcer will occur if and only if the operant response occurs. Because of the three components—discriminative stimulus, response, and reinforcer—Skinner called this relationship a **three-term contingency**.

Suppose a pigeon learns to peck a key for food pellets in a chamber that has a bright yellow light just above the key. When the light is on, each response produces a food pellet, but when the light is off, no food pellets are delivered. If the light is periodically turned on and off during the course of the experiment, the pigeon will learn to discriminate between these two conditions and respond only when the light is on. This type of discrimination learning is important in many real-world situations, because a response that is reinforced in one context may not be reinforced in another. For example, a child must learn that the behavior of telling jokes may be reinforced if it occurs during recess but punished if it occurs during math class. The term **stimulus control** refers to the broad topic of how stimuli that precede a behavior can control the occurrence of that behavior. Chapter 9 will examine this topic in detail.

Basic Principles of Operant Conditioning

Many of the principles of operant conditioning have counterparts in classical conditioning that we have already examined, so a brief discussion of them will suffice here. Thorndike's results (as in Figure 5.2) demonstrate that the **acquisition** of an operant response, like that of a CR, is usually a gradual process. In operant conditioning, the procedure of **extinction** involves no longer following the operant response with a reinforcer, and, as in classical conditioning, the response will weaken and eventually disappear. If the subject is returned to the experimental chamber at some later time, **spontaneous recovery** of the operant response will typically be observed, just as it is observed in classical conditioning.

In the previous section, we saw that **discrimination** learning can occur in operant conditioning as well as in classical conditioning. The opposite of discrimination, **generalization**, is also a common phenomenon in operant conditioning. Let us return to the example of the pigeon that learned to discriminate between the presence and absence of a bright yellow light. Suppose the color of the light changed to green or orange, and no more reinforcers were delivered. Despite this change in color, the pigeon would probably continue to peck at the key for a while until it learned that no more reinforcers were forthcoming. In other words, the pigeon generalized from the yellow light to a light of another color, even though it had never been reinforced for pecking in the presence of this other color. If we tested a number of different colors, we would probably obtain a typical generalization gradient in which responding was most rapid in the presence of yellow and less and less rapid with colors less and less similar to yellow.

Conditioned Reinforcement

As already explained, if a neutral stimulus is repeatedly paired with a primary reinforcer, it can become a conditioned reinforcer. The conditioned reinforcer can then act as a surrogate for the primary reinforcer, increasing the strength of any response that it follows. In an early study on conditioned reinforcement, Skinner (1938) presented rats with repeated pairings of a clicking sound and food. In the second phase of the experiment, food was no longer presented; nevertheless, the rats learned to press a lever when this response produced only the clicking sound. Naturally, since the clicking sound was no longer paired with food, it is not surprising that the lever pressing did not persist for long. To maintain its reinforcing power, a conditioned reinforcer must continue to be paired (at least occasionally) with the primary reinforcer.

Skinner used the term **generalized reinforcers** to refer to a special class of conditioned reinforcers—those that are associated with a large number of different primary reinforcers. Perhaps the best example of a generalized reinforcer is money. The potency of this reinforcer in maintaining the behaviors of workers in our society is clear. Money is a generalized reinforcer (and a powerful one) precisely because it can be exchanged for so many different stimuli that are inherently reinforcing for most people (food, clothing, material possessions, entertainment, etc.). Although money is a powerful reinforcer, it should be clear that its power, like that of all conditioned reinforcers, depends on its continued association with primary reinforcers. If money could no longer be exchanged for any primary reinforcers, it would be difficult to find individuals willing to work simply to obtain their weekly paychecks.

Both laboratory findings and real-world examples of conditioned reinforcers (money; exam grades; praise from a parent, teacher, or boss, etc.) demonstrate the powerful effects that they can have on an individual's behavior. What is still being debated by psychologists, however, is exactly how conditioned reinforcers exert their effects. One basic question is whether conditioned reinforcers affect behavior because they provide information (about the future delivery of a primary reinforcer) or because they add value to the situation (i.e., they add additional reinforcing value above what the primary reinforcer already provides).

To illustrate the difference between providing information and adding value, Rachlin (1976) asked readers to imagine two hotels. In hotel A, a dinner bell rings before each meal. This bell should become a conditioned reinforcer because it is paired with the primary reinforcer, food. In hotel B, a dinner bell also rings before each meal, but the bell also rings at other times, when there is no meal. Which hotel will people prefer? If the bell adds value to the situation, hotel B should be preferred, because the bell rings more often. But, according to Rachlin, it seems obvious that people would prefer hotel A, where the bell provides accurate information about when meals will be served. An experiment with pigeons by Schuster (1969) supported Rachlin's prediction. The pigeons preferred a situation in which the conditioned reinforcers (a light and a buzzer) always signaled food (as in hotel A) over a situation where the light and buzzer were presented extra times without food (as in hotel B). This experiment supports the information theory of conditioned reinforcement—the strongest conditioned reinforcers are those that provide the best information about the delivery of primary reinforcers.

Many other studies on conditioned reinforcement have been conducted, and unfortunately they do not offer a simple answer to the question of exactly what conditioned reinforcers do. Some experiments seemed to provide evidence that conditioned reinforcers do add value to the situation (Bell & Williams, 2013; Williams & Dunn, 1991). Williams (1994) also suggested that conditioned reinforcers may play other roles, including marking and bridging. *Marking* is providing immediate feedback for a particular response, as when the sound of the food dispenser immediately after an appropriate response makes it easier for an animal trainer to shape new behaviors. *Bridging* occurs when a conditioned reinforcer fills the time period between a response and the delivery of a primary reinforcer, which may help the learner to associate the response and the reinforcer.

In a review of the many complex and often conflicting laboratory findings about conditioned reinforcers, Shahan (2010) concluded that most of the results are consistent with the idea that conditioned reinforcers act as "signposts" that "serve to guide rather than strengthen behavior" (p. 279). In other words, he argues in favor of the information hypothesis. However, others continue to argue just as strongly for the reinforcing value hypothesis (e.g., McDevitt & Williams, 2010), so this issue has not been settled.

Response Chains

In Chapter 2, we examined the concept of a reaction chain, which is a sequence of innate behaviors that occur in a fixed order. A similar concept involving learned behaviors is the **response chain**, which is defined as a sequence of behaviors that must occur in a specific order, with the primary reinforcer being delivered only after the final response of the sequence. Some of the clearest examples of response chains are displayed by animals trained to perform complex sequences of behavior for circus acts or other public performances. Imagine a hypothetical performance in which a rat climbs a ladder to a platform, pulls a rope that opens a door to a tunnel, runs through the tunnel to another small platform, slides down a chute, runs to a lever, presses the lever, and finally receives a pellet of food. Ignoring for the moment how the rat could be trained to do this, we can ask what maintains the behavior once it has been learned.

The first response, climbing the ladder, brings the rat to nothing more than a platform and a rope. These are certainly not primary reinforcers for a rat. Skinner would claim, however, that these stimuli act as conditioned reinforcers for the response of climbing the ladder because they bring the animal closer to primary reinforcement than it was before. Besides serving as conditioned reinforcers, the platform and rope also act as discriminative stimuli for the next response of the chain, pulling the rope. The conditioned reinforcer for this response is the sight of the door opening, for this event brings the subject still

Stimuli

Responses

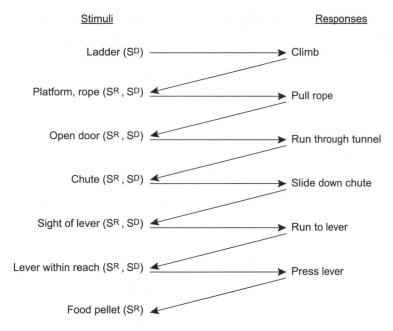

Figure 5.8 The alternating sequence of stimuli and responses in the hypothetical response chain described in the text. Each stimulus within the chain serves as a conditioned reinforcer for the previous response and as a discriminative stimulus for the next response.

closer to primary reinforcement. Like the platform and rope, the open door also serves a second function—it is a discriminative stimulus for the next response, running through the tunnel.

We could go on to analyze the rest of the response chain in a similar fashion, but the general pattern should be clear by now. Each stimulus in the middle of a response chain is assumed to serve two functions: It is a conditioned reinforcer for the previous response and a discriminative stimulus for the next response of the chain. This analysis is depicted graphically in Figure 5.8, where S^D stands for "discriminative stimulus" and S^R stands for "reinforcing stimulus."

How would an animal trainer go about teaching a rat to perform this sequence? One very effective strategy, sometimes called *backward chaining*, is to start with the last response of the chain and work backward. After teaching the rat where to obtain its food reinforcement and establishing the sound of the food dispenser as a conditioned reinforcer, the trainer could start to shape the last response of the chain, pressing the lever. Once this response is well established, the trainer might place the rat on the bottom of the chute. It is very likely that the rat would move from this position to the lever, since the lever will now act as a conditioned reinforcer (having been previously paired with food). By additional shaping, the animal could be trained to slide down the chute to reach the lever, then to travel through the tunnel to reach the chute, and so on. Some shaping with food as a primary reinforcer might be required for some links of the chain (e.g., pulling the rope). Once the response was established, however, the primary reinforcement could be removed and the behavior would be maintained by the conditioned reinforcement provided by the next stimulus of the chain, a stimulus that signaled that the animal was one step closer to the primary reinforcer.

Not surprisingly, the behaviors of a response chain will eventually disappear if the primary reinforcement is eliminated. It is also interesting to observe what happens if one of the conditioned reinforcers in the middle of the chain is eliminated. The general rule is that all behaviors that occur before the "broken link" of the chain will be extinguished, whereas those that occur after the broken link will continue to occur. For example, suppose that pulling the rope no longer opens the door to the tunnel. The response of rope pulling will eventually stop occurring, as will the behavior of climbing the ladder that leads to the platform and rope. On the other hand, if the rat is placed beyond the broken link (inside the tunnel or at the top of the chute), the remainder of the chain should continue as long as the final response is followed by the primary reinforcer.

Because they are the farthest from the primary reinforcer, responses near the beginning of a response chain should be the weakest, or the most easily disrupted. Behavior therapists frequently make use of this principle when attempting to break up a response chain that includes some unwanted behaviors (e.g., walking to the drugstore, buying a pack of cigarettes, opening the pack, lighting a cigarette, and smoking it). Efforts to interrupt this chain should be most effective if applied to the earliest links of the chain.

BOX 5.2   APPLYING THE RESEARCH

Teaching Response Chains

Many everyday activities are examples of response chains. Tasks such as doing the laundry, making your bed, changing a flat tire, installing new software on a computer, preparing a meal, and many others involve sequences of behaviors that must be completed in the right order, and only then is the primary reinforcer obtained (Figure 5.9). Being able to perform response chains like these is an important part of daily life, but some children and adults with autism or other developmental disabilities have difficulty learning them. Educators and behavior analysts have therefore looked for ways to teach response chains effectively.

Backward chaining is one good way to teach a response chain, but it is not the only way. In *forward chaining*, the teacher starts by reinforcing the first response of the chain, then gradually adds the second response, the third response, and so on. For example, in learning to use a laundromat, adolescents with developmental disabilities were first reinforced just for finding an empty washing machine. Next, they were reinforced for finding an empty machine and putting in the soap, then for finding an empty machine, putting in the soap, loading the clothes, and so on (McDonnell & McFarland, 1988).

Figure 5.9 Doing the laundry is an everyday example of a response chain. (Monkey Business Images/Shutterstock.com)

Another training method is the *total task method*: The individual is taught all of the steps of a response chain at once, and the teacher uses prompts to elicit the appropriate response at each step. A *prompt* is an extra discriminative stimulus that makes the correct response more likely to occur. A prompt can be a verbal instruction, physical guidance, or having the teacher model the behavior first, but in all cases the goal is to eventually eliminate the prompt so that the child can perform the task without the guidance of the teacher. This may sound simple enough, but in practice, the teacher must make many decisions about what types of prompts to use and then about how to remove them. One method is the most-to-least approach, where the teacher begins by using the strongest prompts and gradually shifts to weaker ones. For instance, in teaching a child with autism how to build a structure out of Lego blocks, a teacher could use the most-to-least approach by first manually guiding the child's hands each step of the way, then by lightly guiding the child's movements by touching the elbow, and finally by using no physical prompt at all. The opposite method is the least-to-most approach, in which the teacher begins with the least intrusive prompt (such as a light touch on the shoulder) and only proceeds to stronger prompts if they are necessary.

All of these methods for teaching response chains (and many other variations) have been used successfully in teaching life skills to children and adults with severe disabilities (Shrestha, Anderson, & Moore, 2013). A challenge for the teacher or behavior analyst is to determine which methods will work best in a particular case.

BIOLOGICAL CONSTRAINTS ON OPERANT CONDITIONING

Just as biological factors affect what is learned in classical conditioning, they play an important role in operant conditioning. Two phenomena, instinctive drift and autoshaping, both discovered in the 1960s, raised serious questions about the power of reinforcement to modify and control a creature's behavior. The stories of how these phenomena were discovered and the theoretical debates surrounding them provide valuable lessons about the strengths and limitations of the general principles of learning.

Instinctive Drift

Two psychologists who attempted to apply the principles of operant conditioning outside the laboratory were Keller and Marian Breland. After studying with B. F. Skinner, the Brelands became animal trainers and worked with many different species, teaching complex and frequently amusing patterns of behavior. Their animals were trained for zoos, fairs, television commercials, and other public performances. The Brelands' business was successful, and over the years they trained several thousand animals. Despite their successes, however, the Brelands began to notice certain recurrent problems in their use of reinforcement techniques. They referred to these problems as "breakdowns of conditioned operant behavior." In an article entitled "The Misbehavior of Organisms" (Breland & Breland, 1961), they described several of their "failures" in the use of reinforcement.

In one example, they trained a pig to pick up coins, one at a time, and drop them in a piggy bank a few feet away. The pig learned this quite easily, and at first it would go back and forth quickly, carrying the coins and putting them in the piggy bank. But as weeks passed, its behavior became slower and slower, and other, unreinforced behaviors appeared: "He might run over eagerly for each dollar, but on the way back, instead of carrying the dollar and depositing it simply and cleanly, he would repeatedly drop it, root it, drop it again, root it along the way, pick it up, toss it up in the air, drop it, root it some more, and so on. . . . Finally it would take the pig about 10 minutes to transport four coins a distance of about 6 feet. This problem behavior developed repeatedly in successive pigs" (Breland & Breland, 1961, p. 683).

This example differs from the instances of contraprepared associations discussed in Chapter 4. Here, the problem was not in learning the new response but in maintaining it over time. New behaviors appeared that were not reinforced, behaviors that were part of the pig's natural food-gathering repertoires. The Brelands called this phenomenon **instinctive drift**: With extensive experience, the animal's performance drifted away from the reinforced behaviors and toward instinctive behaviors that occur when it is seeking the reinforcer (food) in a natural environment.

A similar problem occurred when the Brelands tried to train a raccoon to pick up coins and place them in a small container. With just one coin, the raccoon learned, with a little difficulty, to pick it up and drop it in the container, after which it received food as a reinforcer. When given two coins simultaneously, however, the raccoon would hold onto the coins for several minutes, frequently rubbing them together, and occasionally dipping them into the container and pulling them out again. These behaviors became more and more prevalent over time, and the swift sequence of depositing the coins that the Brelands desired was never achieved. As with the pigs, the raccoon's intruding behaviors resemble those of its food-gathering repertoire. A raccoon may repeatedly dip a piece of food in a stream before eating it, and the rubbing motions are similar to those it might use in removing the shell from a crustacean. Notice, however, that in the present context these behaviors were inappropriate in two ways: (1) The coins were not food, the container was not a stream, and there was no shell to be removed by rubbing the coins together and (2) the intruding behaviors did not produce food reinforcement—indeed, they actually postponed its delivery.

The Brelands observed many other examples of this sort of instinctive drift, and they claimed that they constituted "a clear and utter failure of conditioning theory" (1961, p. 683). The problem was perfectly clear: Animals exhibited behaviors that the trainers did not reinforce in place of behaviors the trainers had reinforced.

Autoshaping

In 1968, P. L. Brown and Jenkins published an article on a method for training pigeons to peck a key that was easier and less time consuming than manual shaping. Naive pigeons were deprived of food and taught to eat from the grain dispenser. After this, a pigeon was exposed to the following situation: At irregular intervals averaging 60 seconds, the response key was illuminated with white light for 8 seconds; then the key was darkened and food was presented. Although no response was necessary for the delivery of food, after a number of trials all of the pigeons began to peck at the lighted key.

Although autoshaping is a good method for training the response of key pecking, psychologists soon realized the more important theoretical significance of the Brown and Jenkins result. Key pecking had been used in countless experiments because it was considered to be a "typical" operant response—a response that is controlled by its consequences. Yet here was a situation where the key-peck response was not necessary for reinforcement, but it occurred anyway. Why did the pigeons peck at the key? Several different explanations were proposed.

Autoshaping as Superstitious Behavior

Brown and Jenkins suggested that autoshaping might be an example of a superstitious behavior, as discussed earlier in this chapter. It is possible that approaching, making contact, and pecking the lighted key were accidentally reinforced by the food deliveries that soon followed. However, an experiment by Rachlin (1969) suggested that this hypothesis is not correct. Using a procedure similar to that of Brown and Jenkins, Rachlin photographed pigeons on each trial at the moment reinforcement was delivered. The photographs revealed no tendency for the birds to get progressively closer to the key and finally peck it. On the trial immediately preceding the trial of the first key peck, a pigeon might be far from the key, looking in another direction, at the moment of reinforcement. There was no hint of a gradual shaping process at work.

More evidence against the superstition interpretation came from a study in which the food reinforcer was eliminated from any trial on which the pigeon pecked at the lighted key (Williams & Williams, 1969). The results of this experiment were quite remarkable: Even though no food ever followed a key peck, pigeons still acquired the key-peck response and persisted in pecking at the lighted key on about one third of the trials. This experiment showed quite convincingly that key pecking in an autoshaping procedure is not an instance of superstitious behavior.

Autoshaping as Classical Conditioning

Some researchers have proposed that autoshaping is simply an example of classical conditioning intruding into what the experimenter sees as an operant conditioning situation (Moore, 1973). Pigeons eat grain by pecking at the kernels with jerky head movements. We might say that pecking is the pigeon's unconditioned response to the stimulus of grain. According to the classical conditioning interpretation, this response of pecking is transferred from the grain to the key because the lighted key is repeatedly paired with food. One type of evidence supporting this idea came from experiments by Jenkins and Moore (1973) in which a lighted response key was regularly followed by food for some pigeons and by water for other pigeons. In both cases the pigeons began to peck at the lighted key. However, by filming the pigeons' responses, Jenkins and Moore demonstrated that the pigeons' movements toward the key differed depending on which reinforcer was used. When the reinforcer was food, a pigeon's response involved an abrupt, forceful pecking motion made with the beak open wide and eyelids almost closed (Figure 5.10, bottom row). These movements are similar to those a pigeon makes when eating. When the reinforcer was water, the response was a slower approach to the key with the beak closed

Figure 5.10 Photographs of a pigeon's key pecks when the reinforcer was water (top row) and when the reinforcer was grain (bottom row). Notice the different beak and eyelid movements with the two different reinforcers. (From Jenkins, H.M. & Moore, B.R., The form of the auto-shaped response with food or water reinforcers, *Journal of the Experimental Analysis of Behavior, 20,* 163–181. Copyright 1973 by the Society for the Experimental Analysis of Behavior, Inc.)

or nearly closed (Figure 5.10, top row). Sometimes, swallowing movements and a rhythmic opening and closing of the beak were observed. All of these movements are part of the pigeon's characteristic drinking pattern. Jenkins and Moore proposed that these behaviors were clear examples of Pavlov's concept of stimulus substitution. The lighted key served as a substitute for either food or water, and responses appropriate for either food or water were directed at the key.

The term *autoshaping* is now used to refer to any situation in which an animal produces some distinctive behavior in response to a signal that precedes and predicts an upcoming reinforcer. Others have called this phenomenon *sign-tracking* because the animal watches, follows, and makes contact with a signal for an upcoming reinforcer. In this broader sense, autoshaping (or sign-tracking) has been observed in a wide range of species (e.g., Anselme, Robinson, & Berridge, 2013; Morrow, Saunders, Maren, & Robinson, 2015). Many of the examples are consistent with the stimulus substitution theory of classical conditioning because the animal's response to the stimulus that precedes a reinforcer is similar to the response to the reinforcer itself.

Autoshaping as the Intrusion of Instinctive Behavior Patterns

Whereas some studies support for the stimulus substitution interpretation of autoshaping, others do not. Wasserman (1973) observed the responses of 3-day-old chicks to a key light paired with warmth. In an uncomfortably cool chamber, a heat lamp was turned on briefly at irregular intervals, with each activation of the heat lamp being preceded by the illumination of a green key light. All chicks soon began to peck the key when it was green, but their manner of responding was unusual: A chick would typically move very close to the key, push its beak into the key, and rub its beak from side to side in what Wasserman called a "snuggling" behavior. These snuggling responses resembled behaviors a newborn chick normally makes to obtain warmth from a mother hen: The chick pecks at the feathers on the lower part of the hen's body, then rubs its beak and pushes its head into the feathers. The problem for stimulus substitution theory, however, is that the chicks' responses to the heat lamp were very different. There was no pecking or snuggling; instead, a chick would extend its wings (which allowed it to absorb more of the heat) and stand motionless. On other trials, a chick might extend its wings, lower its body, and rub its chest against the floor. There was virtually no similarity between a chick's responses to the key light and its responses to the heat lamp. For this reason, Wasserman concluded that the stimulus substitution account of autoshaping was incorrect.

Other experiments supported Wasserman's conclusion (Bullock and Myers, 2009; Timberlake & Grant, 1975). For example, Timberlake and Grant observed rats when the signal preceding each food pellet was the entry of another rat (restrained on a small moving platform) into the experimental chamber. Since a food pellet elicits biting and chewing responses, the stimulus substitution interpretation of autoshaping predicts that a rat should perform these same biting and chewing responses to the restrained rat, because the rat is a signal for food. Not surprisingly, Timberlake and Grant observed no instances of biting or chewing responses directed toward the restrained rat. However, they did observe a high frequency of other behaviors directed toward the restrained rat, including approach, sniffing, and social contact (pawing, grooming, and climbing over the other rat). Rats often feed in groups, and these social behaviors toward the restrained rat resemble those that might occur during a food-seeking expedition. Timberlake and Grant (1975) suggested the following interpretation:

> As an alternative to stimulus substitution, we offer the hypothesis that autoshaped behavior reflects the conditioning of a system of species-typical behaviors commonly related to the reward. The form of the behavior in the presence of the predictive stimulus will depend on which behaviors in the conditioned system are elicited and supported by the predictive stimulus.
>
> (p. 692)

Timberlake (1993) called this interpretation of autoshaped behaviors a **behavior-systems analysis** to reflect the idea that different reinforcers evoke different systems or collections of behaviors. An animal may have a system of food-related behaviors, a system of water-related behaviors, a system of warmth-seeking behaviors, a system of mating behaviors, and so on. Exactly which behavior from a given system will be elicited by a signal depends on the physical properties of that signal. For instance, in Wasserman's study, the lighted response key (a distinctive visual stimulus about head high) evidently lent itself more readily to snuggling than to wing extension, so that is how the chicks responded.

Summary

Regardless of whether we emphasize the hereditary aspects of autoshaped behaviors or their similarity to classically conditioned CRs, both autoshaped behaviors and instinctive drift seem to pose severe difficulties for operant conditioners. Breland and Breland (1961) summarized the problem nicely: "The examples listed we feel represent clear and utter failure of conditioning theory. . . . The animal simply does not do what it has been conditioned to do" (p. 683).

Reconciling Reinforcement Theory and Biological Constraints

How do those who believe in the general-principle approach to learning, and especially in the principle of reinforcement, respond to these cases where the general principles do not seem to work? When it was first discovered, autoshaping seemed to pose a major problem for the principle of reinforcement because the response occurs again and again, even though it is not required for reinforcement. This seemed to defy the basic concept of reinforcement. However, later analyses suggested that autoshaping is simply an instance of classical conditioning. Although autoshaped responses do not always follow the principle of stimulus substitution (Wasserman, 1973), it is now commonly believed that autoshaping is in fact a good example of classical conditioning. And like taste-aversion learning (Chapter 4), autoshaping has been widely used as a procedure for studying basic principles of classical conditioning (e.g., Balsam, Drew, & Yang, 2002; Locurto, Terrace, & Gibbon, 1981). Autoshaping now appears quite consistent with the general-principle approach to learning after all (but with the principles of classical conditioning rather than operant conditioning).

The evidence on instinctive drift cannot be dealt with so easily. Here, when a trainer tries to reinforce one behavior, other unreinforced behaviors appear and gradually become more persistent. These behaviors are presumably part of the animal's inherited behavioral repertoire. As the Brelands discovered, these behaviors often cannot be eliminated by using standard reinforcement techniques, so it might appear that the principle of reinforcement is simply incorrect—it cannot explain why these behaviors arise and are maintained. How might a psychologist who relies heavily on the concept of reinforcement react to this? The reactions of B. F. Skinner are worth examining. First of all, it is important to realize that Skinner has always maintained that an organism's behavior is determined by both learning experiences and heredity. Well before biological constraints on learning became a popular topic, Skinner had written about the hereditary influences on behavior (Heron & Skinner, 1940; Skinner, 1966). Later, Skinner (1977) stated that he was neither surprised nor disturbed by phenomena such as instinctive drift or autoshaping. He asserted that these are simply cases where phylogenetic (hereditary) and ontogenetic (learned) influences on behavior are operating simultaneously: "Phylogeny and ontogeny are friendly rivals and neither one always wins" (p. 1009). In other words, we should not be surprised that hereditary factors can compete with and sometimes overshadow the reinforcement contingencies as determinants of behavior.

We have seen that if reinforcers are delivered at regular, periodic intervals, a variety of unreinforced behaviors appear between reinforcers, and they are called adjunctive behaviors. In laboratory animals, adjunctive behaviors can take a variety of forms, including aggression, wheel running, and drinking large amounts of water. Adjunctive behaviors have also been observed in humans. In one study, college students played a game of backgammon in which they had to wait for fixed periods of time (and could not watch) as their opponents made their moves. When these waiting periods were long, several behaviors unrelated to playing the game—bodily movement, eating, and drinking—increased in frequency (Allen & Butler, 1990).

Although it might appear on the surface that adjunctive behaviors are distinctly different from typical operant behaviors, appearances can sometimes be deceiving. In a thoughtful review, Killeen and Pellón (2013, p. 1) make a convincing case that "adjunctive behaviors are operants." The details of their arguments are complex and will not be presented here, but one of their points is that adjunctive behaviors follow predictable patterns that depend on the frequency, timing, and number of reinforcers delivered. They also propose that adjunctive behaviors are similar in some ways to superstitious behaviors in the sense that both appear even though there is no contingency between the response and the delivery of reinforcement.

In summary, there is a growing consensus in the field of learning that the research on biological constraints does not forecast the end of the general-principle approach, but rather that it has provided the field with a valuable lesson (Domjan, 2008; Green & Holt, 2003; Logue, 1988). This research shows that an animal's hereditary endowment plays an important part in many learning situations, and the influence of heredity cannot be ignored. However, critics who use these data to claim that the principle of reinforcement should be abandoned appear to be making a serious logical mistake: They conclude that because a theoretical concept cannot explain everything, it is deficient and should be discarded. This reasoning is just as incorrect as claiming that all behaviors are learned, none innate. This chapter (and the next several) provides overwhelming evidence that the delivery of reinforcement contingent upon a response is a powerful means of controlling behavior. No amount of evidence on the hereditary influences on behavior can contradict these findings.

SUMMARY

If a response is followed by a reinforcer, the frequency of that response will increase. Thorndike demonstrated this principle in his experiments with cats in the puzzle box, and he called it the Law of Effect. Using photography, Guthrie and Horton found that whatever motion a cat happened to make at the moment of reinforcement tended to be repeated on later trials. Different cats learned distinctly different styles of making the same response. If a response is strengthened when, by mere coincidence, it is followed by a reinforcer, it is called a superstitious behavior. B. F. Skinner reported seeing superstitious behaviors in a famous experiment with pigeons. Accidental reinforcement may account for the unusual rituals performed by some gamblers and athletes.

> ### PRACTICE QUIZ 2: CHAPTER 5
>
> 1. Thorndike's research with the puzzle box is an example of a _____ procedure, whereas Skinner's research used a _____ procedure.
> 2. The three parts of a three-term contingency are the _____, the _____, and the _____.
> 3. Each stimulus in the middle of a response chain serves as a _____ for the previous response and as a _____ for the next response.
> 4. The procedure in which pigeons start to peck at a lighted response key when it precedes food deliveries is called _____.
> 5. The Brelands used the term instinctive drift to refer to cases where an animal stopped performing _____ behaviors and started performing _____ behaviors as its training progressed.
>
> ### ANSWERS
>
> 1. discrete trial, free-operant 2. discriminative stimulus, operant response, reinforcer 3. conditioned reinforcer, discriminative stimulus 4. autoshaping 5. reinforced, instinctive

The procedure of shaping, or successive approximations, involves reinforcing any small movement that comes closer to the desired response and then gradually changing the criterion for reinforcement until the desired behavior is reached. Shaping is a common part of many behavior modification procedures.

B. F. Skinner used the term *three-term contingency* to describe the three-part relation between a discriminative stimulus, an operant response, and a reinforcer. Responses can be strengthened by either primary reinforcers or conditioned reinforcers. Contingencies between stimuli and responses can have more than three components, as in a response chain, which consists of an alternating series of stimuli and responses, and only the last response is followed by a primary reinforcer.

While using operant conditioning techniques to train animals, Breland and Breland discovered instinctive drift: The animals would begin to display innate behaviors associated with the reinforcers, even though these behaviors were not reinforced. When Brown and Jenkins repeatedly paired a lighted key with food, pigeons eventually began to peck at the key. They called this phenomenon autoshaping. Such examples of biological constraints in operant conditioning do not mean that the principle of reinforcement is incorrect, but they do show that behavior is often controlled by a mixture of learning and hereditary influences.

Review Questions

1. Describe Thorndike's experiments with the puzzle box and how they demonstrated his Law of Effect. What did Guthrie and Horton find when they photographed cats in the puzzle box, and what does this tell us about the principle of reinforcement?

2. Explain how you could use shaping to teach a dog to jump over a tall hurdle.

3. Give a concrete example of how shaping can be used in a behavior modification program with a human learner.

4. Explain how response chains include all of the following: discriminative stimuli, operant responses, conditioned reinforcers, and a primary reinforcer. Describe at least two different techniques for teaching a response chain.

5. What is autoshaping? Describe three different theories about why autoshaping occurs. Which theory do you think is best and why?

REFERENCES

Allen, J.D., & Butler, J.A. (1990). The effect of interplay interval on adjunctive behavior in humans in a game-playing situation. *Physiology and Behavior, 47*, 719–725.

Anselme, P., Robinson, M.F., & Berridge, K.C. (2013). Reward uncertainty enhances incentive salience attribution as sign-tracking. *Behavioural Brain Research, 238*, 53–61.

Athens, E.S., Vollmer, T.R., & St. Peter Pipkin, C.C. (2007). Shaping academic task engagement with percentile schedules. *Journal of Applied Behavior Analysis, 40*, 475–488.

Balsam, P.D., Drew, M.R., & Yang, C. (2002). Timing at the start of associative learning. *Learning and Motivation, 33*, 141–155.

Bell, M.C., & Williams, B.A. (2013). Conditioned reinforcement in chain schedules when time to reinforcement is held constant. *Journal of the Experimental Analysis of Behavior, 99*, 179–188.

Bleak, J.L., & Frederick, C.M. (1998). Superstitious behavior in sport: Levels of effectiveness and determinants of use in three collegiate sports. *Journal of Sport Behavior, 21*, 1–15.

Breland, K., & Breland, M. (1961). The misbehavior of organisms. *American Psychologist, 16*, 681–684.

Brown, P.L., & Jenkins, H.M. (1968). Auto-shaping of the pigeon's key-peck. *Journal of the Experimental Analysis of Behavior, 11*, 1–8.

Brown, R., & Herrnstein, R.J. (1975). *Psychology*. Boston, MA: Little, Brown.

Bullock, C.E., & Myers, T.M. (2009). Stimulus-food pairings produce stimulus-directed touch-screen responding in cynomolgus monkeys (*Macaca fascicularis*) with or without a positive response contingency. *Journal of the Experimental Analysis of Behavior, 92*, 41–55.

Burger, J.M., & Lynn, A.L. (2005). Superstitious behavior among American and Japanese professional baseball players. *Basic and Applied Social Psychology, 27*, 71–76.

Ciborowski, T. (1997). "Superstition" in the collegiate baseball player. *Sport Psychologist, 11*, 305–317.

Domjan, M. (2008). Adaptive specializations and generality of the laws of classical and instrumental conditioning. In R. Menzel (Ed.), *Learning theory and behavior* (pp. 327–340). Oxford: Elsevier.

Gleeson, S., Lattal, K.A., & Williams, K.S. (1989). Superstitious conditioning: A replication and extension of Neuringer (1970). *Psychological Record, 39*, 563–571.

Green, L., & Holt, D.D. (2003). Economic and biological influences on key pecking and treadle pressing in pigeons. *Journal of the Experimental Analysis of Behavior, 80*, 43–58.

Guthrie, E.R., & Horton, G.P. (1946). *Cats in a puzzle box.* New York: Holt, Rinehart & Winston.

Hagopian, L.P., & Thompson, R.H. (1999). Reinforcement of compliance with respiratory treatment in a child with cystic fibrosis. *Journal of Applied Behavior Analysis, 32*, 233–236.

Heron, W.T., & Skinner, B.F. (1940). The rate of extinction in maze-bright and maze-dull rats. *Psychological Record, 4*, 11–18.

Herrnstein, R.J. (1966). Superstition: A corollary of the principles of operant conditioning. In W.K. Honig (Ed.), *Operant behavior: Areas of research and application* (pp. 33–51). New York: Appleton-Century-Crofts.

Jenkins, H.M., & Moore, B.R. (1973). The form of the autoshaped response with food or water reinforcers. *Journal of the Experimental Analysis of Behavior, 20*, 163–181.

Killeen, P.R., & Pellón, R. (2013). Adjunctive behaviors are operants. *Learning & Behavior, 41*, 1–24.

Locurto, C.M., Terrace, H.S., & Gibbon, J. (Eds.). (1981). *Autoshaping and conditioning theory.* New York: Academic Press.

Logue, A.W. (1988). A comparison of taste-aversion learning in humans and other vertebrates: Evolutionary pressures in common. In R.C. Bolles & M.D. Beecher (Eds.), *Evolution and learning* (pp. 97–116). Hillsdale, NJ: Erlbaum.

Matute, H. (1994). Learned helplessness and superstitious behavior as opposite effects of uncontrollable reinforcement in humans. *Learning and Motivation, 25*, 216–232.

Matute, H. (1995). Human reactions to uncontrollable outcomes: Further evidence for superstitions rather than helplessness. *Quarterly Journal of Experimental Psychology: B: Comparative and Physiological Psychology, 48B*, 142–157.

McDevitt, M.A., & Williams, B.A. (2010). Dual effects on choice of conditioned reinforcement frequency and conditioned reinforcement value. *Journal of the Experimental Analysis of Behavior, 93*, 147–155.

McDonnell, J., & McFarland, S. (1988). A comparison of forward and concurrent chaining strategies in teaching laundromat skills to students with severe handicaps. *Research in Developmental Disabilities, 9*, 177–194.

Moore, B.R. (1973). The role of directed Pavlovian reactions in simple instrumental learning in the pigeon. In R.A. Hinde & J. Stevenson-Hinde (Eds.), *Constraints on learning* (pp. 159–188). New York: Academic Press.

Morrow, J.D., Saunders, B.T., Maren, S., & Robinson, T.E. (2015). Sign-tracking to an appetitive cue predicts incubation of conditioned fear in rats. *Behavioural Brain Research, 276*, 59–66.

Neuringer, A.J. (1970). Superstitious key pecking after three peck-produced reinforcements. *Journal of the Experimental Analysis of Behavior, 13*, 127–134.

Platt, J.R. (1973). Percentile reinforcement: Paradigms for experimental analysis of response shaping. In G.H. Bower (Ed.), *The psychology of learning and motivation: Vol 7. Advances in theory and research* (pp. 271–296). New York: Academic Press.

Preston, K.L., Umbricht, A., Wong, C.J., & Epstein, D.H. (2001). Shaping cocaine abstinence by successive approximation. *Journal of Consulting and Clinical Psychology, 69*, 643–654.

Rachlin, H. (1969). Autoshaping of key pecking in pigeons with negative reinforcement. *Journal of the Experimental Analysis of Behavior, 12*, 521–531.

Rachlin, H. (1970). *Introduction to modern behaviorism.* San Francisco, CA: W. H. Freeman.

Rachlin, H. (1976). *Behavior and learning.* San Francisco, CA: W. H. Freeman.

Schuster, R. (1969). A functional analysis of conditioned reinforcement. In D.P. Hendry (Ed.), *Conditioned reinforcement* (pp. 192–234). Homewood, IL: Dorsey Press.

Scott, D., Scott, L.M., & Goldwater, B. (1997). A performance improvement program for an international-level track and field athlete. *Journal of Applied Behavior Analysis, 30*, 573–575.

Shahan, T.A. (2010). Conditioned reinforcement and response strength. *Journal of the Experimental Analysis of Behavior, 93*, 269–289.

Sheehan, K.J., Van Reet, J., & Bloom, C.M. (2012). Measuring preschoolers' superstitious tendencies. *Behavioural Processes, 91*, 172–176.

Shrestha, A., Anderson, A., & Moore, D.W. (2013). Using point-of-view video modeling and forward chaining to teach a functional self-help skill to a child with autism. *Journal of Behavioral Education, 22*, 157–167.

Skinner, B.F. (1938). *The behavior of organisms.* New York: Appleton-Century-Crofts.

Skinner, B.F. (1948). "Superstition" in the pigeon. *Journal of Experimental Psychology, 38*, 168–172.

Skinner, B.F. (1966). The phylogeny and ontogeny of behavior. *Science, 11*, 159–166.

Skinner, B.F. (1977). Herrnstein and the evolution of behaviorism. *American Psychologist, 32*, 1006–1012.

Staddon, J.E.R., & Simmelhag, V.L. (1971). The "superstition" experiment: A reexamination of its implications for the principles of adaptive behavior. *Psychological Review, 78*, 3–43.

Stoops, W.W., Dallery, J., Fields, N.M., Nuzzo, P.A., Schoenberg, N.E., Martin, C.A., & . . . Wong, C.J. (2009). An internet-based abstinence reinforcement smoking cessation intervention in rural smokers. Drug and Alcohol Dependence, 105, 56–62.

Thorndike, E.L. (1898). Animal intelligence: An experimental study of the associative processes in animals. *Psychological Review Monograph Supplement, 2*, 8.

Thorndike, E.L. (1911). *Animal intelligence.* New York: Macmillan.

Timberlake, W. (1993). Behavior systems and reinforcement: An integrative approach. *Journal of the Experimental Analysis of Behavior, 60*, 105–128.

Timberlake, W., & Grant, D.L. (1975). Autoshaping in rats to the presentation of another rat predicting food. *Science, 190*, 690–692.

Wagner, G.A., & Morris, E.K. (1987). "Superstitious" behavior in children. *Psychological Record, 37*, 471–488.

Wann, D.L., Grieve, F.G., Zapalac, R.K., End, C., Lanter, J.R., Pease, D.G., & . . . Wallace, A. (2013). Examining the superstitions of sport fans: Types of superstitions, perceptions of impact, and relationship with team identification. *Athletic Insight: The Online Journal of Sport Psychology, 5*, 21–44.

Washington, W.D., Banna, K.M., & Gibson, A.L. (2014). Preliminary efficacy of prize-based contingency management to increase activity levels in healthy adults. *Journal of Applied Behavior Analysis, 47*, 231–245.

Wasserman, E.A. (1973). Pavlovian conditioning with heat reinforcement produces stimulus–directed pecking in chicks. *Science, 81*, 875–877.

Williams, B.A. (1994). Conditioned reinforcement: Neglected or outmoded explanatory construct? *Psychonomic Bulletin & Review, 1*, 457–475.

Williams, B.A., & Dunn, R. (1991). Preference for conditioned reinforcement. *Journal of the Experimental Analysis of Behavior, 55*, 37–46.

Williams, D.R., & Williams, H. (1969). Automaintenance in the pigeon: Sustained pecking despite contingent non-reinforcement. *Journal of the Experimental Analysis of Behavior, 12*, 511–520.

CHAPTER 6

Reinforcement Schedules

Experimental Analyses and Applications

Learning Objectives

After reading this chapter, you should be able to

- describe the four simple reinforcement schedules and the types of behavior they produce during reinforcement and extinction
- give examples of reinforcement schedules from everyday life
- explain the difference between contingency-shaped and rule-governed behavior
- describe different theories about why there is a postreinforcement pause on fixed-ratio schedules, and explain which theory is best
- discuss explanations of why responding is faster on variable-ratio schedules than on variable-interval schedules
- give examples of how the principles of operant conditioning have been used in behavior modification with children and adults

---

Among B. F. Skinner's many achievements, one of the most noteworthy was his experimental analysis of reinforcement schedules. A **reinforcement schedule** is simply a rule that states under what conditions a reinforcer will be delivered. To this point, we have mainly considered cases in which every occurrence of the operant response is followed by a reinforcer. This schedule is called **continuous reinforcement (CRF)**, but it is only one of an infinite number of possible rules for delivering a reinforcer. In the real world, responses are sometimes, but not always, followed by reinforcers. A salesperson may make many phone calls in vain before finally selling a magazine subscription. A typist may type dozens of pages, comprised of thousands of individual keystrokes, before finally receiving payment for a completed job. A lion may make several unsuccessful attempts to catch a prey before it finally obtains a meal. Recognizing that most behaviors outside the laboratory receive only intermittent reinforcement, Skinner devoted considerable effort to the investigation of how different schedules of reinforcement have different effects on behavior (Ferster & Skinner, 1957).

PLOTTING MOMENT-TO-MOMENT BEHAVIOR: THE CUMULATIVE RECORDER

Skinner constructed a simple mechanical device, the **cumulative recorder**, which records responses in a way that allows any observer to see at a glance the moment-to-moment patterns of a subject's behavior. Figure 6.1 shows how the cumulative recorder works. A slowly rotating cylinder pulls a roll of paper beneath a pen at a steady rate, so the x-axis of the resultant graph, the cumulative record, represents time. If the subject makes no response, a horizontal line is the result. However, each response causes the pen to move up the page by a small increment (in a direction perpendicular to the movement of the paper), so the y-axis represents the cumulative number of responses the subject has made since the start of the session.

As Figure 6.1 shows, a cumulative record tells much more than the overall number of responses. Segments of the record that have a fairly even linear appearance correspond to periods in which the subject was responding at a steady rate—the greater the slope, the faster the response rate. Figure 6.1 also shows how an acceleration or deceleration in response rate would appear in the cumulative record. Finally, small downward deflections in a cumulative

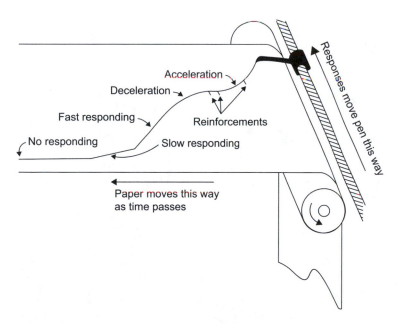

Figure 6.1 A simplified drawing of a cumulative recorder and the type of graph it produces.

record generally indicate those times at which a reinforcer was delivered. With these points in mind, we can now examine how the schedule of reinforcement determines an individual's pattern of responding.

THE FOUR SIMPLE REINFORCEMENT SCHEDULES

Fixed Ratio

The rule for reinforcement in a **fixed–ratio (FR) schedule** is that a reinforcer is delivered after every n responses, where n is the size of the ratio. For example, in an FR 20 schedule, every 20 responses will be followed by a reinforcer. If an animal begins with an FR 1 schedule (which is the same as CRF) and then the ratio is gradually increased, the animal can be trained to make many responses for each reinforcer. For example, many animals will respond for food reinforcement on FR schedules where 100 or more responses are required for each reinforcer. After an animal has performed on an FR schedule for some time and has become acquainted with the requirements of the schedule, a distinctive pattern of responding develops. As Figure 6.2 shows, responding on an FR schedule exhibits a "stop-and-go" pattern: After each reinforcer, there is a pause in responding that is sometimes called a **postreinforcement pause**. Once responding resumes, however, the subject typically responds at a constant, rapid rate until the next reinforcer is delivered.

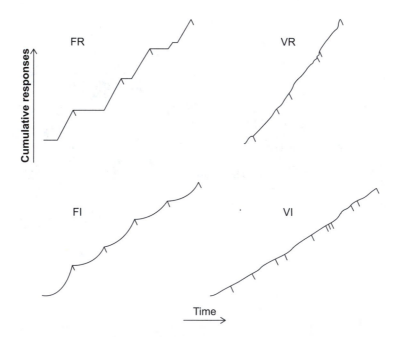

Figure 6.2 Idealized cumulative records showing the typical patterns of behavior generated by the four simple reinforcement schedules.

Outside the laboratory, a good example of FR schedules is the "piecework" method used to pay factory workers in some companies (Figure 6.3). For instance, a worker operating a semiautomatic machine that makes door hinges might be paid $10 for every 100 hinges made. Long ago, I worked in a factory for several summers, and I had the opportunity to observe workers who were paid by the piecework system. Their behavior was quite similar to the FR pattern shown in Figure 6.2. Once a worker started up the machine, he almost always worked steadily and rapidly until the counter on the machine indicated that 100 pieces had been made. At this point, the worker would record the number completed on a work card and then display a postreinforcement pause—he might chat with friends, have a soft drink or a cup of coffee, or glance at a newspaper for a few minutes. After this pause, the worker would turn on the machine and produce another 100 hinges.

With FR schedules, the average size of the postreinforcement pause increases as the size of the ratio increases. For example, the pause will be shorter with an FR 20 schedule than with an FR 200 schedule. In contrast, an individual's rate of responding after the postreinforcement pause remains fairly constant as the size of the ratio increases (Crossman, Bonem, & Phelps, 1987; Powell, 1969). With very large ratios, however, the animal may start to exhibit long pauses at times other than right after reinforcement. The term **ratio strain** is

Figure 6.3 In some jobs, employees are paid on FR schedules: They receive a certain amount of money for every batch of products they complete.

sometimes used to describe the general weakening of responding that is found when large ratios are used.

Variable Ratio

The only difference between an FR schedule and a **variable–ratio (VR) schedule** is that on the latter, the number of required responses is not constant from reinforcer to reinforcer. To be specific, the rule for reinforcement on a VR n schedule is that on average, a subject will receive one reinforcer for every n responses, but the exact number of responses required at any moment may vary widely. When an experiment is controlled by a computer, a VR schedule is sometimes implemented by giving the computer a list of possible ratio sizes from which it selects at random after each reinforcer to determine the number of responses required for the next reinforcer. For example, a list for VR 10 might contain the ratios 1, 2, 3, 4, 5, 6, 10, 19, and 40. In the long run, an average of 10 responses will be required for each reinforcer, but on a given trial, the required number may be as few as 1 or as many as 40.

Figure 6.2 shows a typical cumulative record from a VR schedule. The pattern of responding might be described as rapid and fairly steady. The major difference between FR performance and VR performance is that postreinforcement pauses are typically quite brief on VR schedules (Blakely & Schlinger, 1988). Intuitively, the reason for the shorter postreinforcement pauses on VR schedules seems clear: After each reinforcer, there is always the possibility that another reinforcer will be delivered after only a few additional responses.

Many forms of gambling are examples of VR schedules. Games of chance, such as slot machines, roulette wheels, and lotteries, all exhibit the two important characteristics of VR schedules: (1) A person's chances of winning are directly proportional to the number of times the person plays, and (2) the number of responses required for the next reinforcer is uncertain. It is the combination of these two features that makes gambling an "addiction" for some people; that is, gambling behavior is strong and persistent because the very next lottery ticket or the very next coin in a slot machine could turn a loser into a big winner. Gamblers tend to persist in playing even after long stretches without a win (Horsley, Osborne, Norman, & Wells, 2012).

Although games of chance are among the purest examples of VR schedules outside the laboratory, many other real-world activities, including most sports activities, have the properties of a VR schedule. Consider the behavior of playing golf. As one who is fond of this activity, I know that golf offers many different reinforcers (companionship, exercise, sunshine, fresh air, and picturesque scenery), but one of the strongest reinforcers is the thrill and satisfaction that come from playing well, either through an entire round or on a single shot. Each time a golfer walks to the first tee, a chance exists that this round will be his or her best. The continual possibility of an outstanding round or at least a spectacular shot is probably an important reason why the average golfer keeps returning to the course again and again.

Some other behaviors reinforced on VR schedules include playing practically any competitive sport, fishing, hunting, playing card games or video games, watching the home team play, and going to fraternity parties (Figure 6.4). The delivery of reinforcers for each of these activities fits the definition of a VR schedule: The occasion of the next reinforcer is unpredictable, but in the long run, the more often the behavior occurs, the more rapidly will reinforcers be received.

Figure 6.4 Many sports are examples of variable-ratio schedules. (LuckyImages/Shutterstock.com)

Fixed Interval

In all interval schedules, the presentation of a reinforcer depends both on the subject's behavior and on the passage of time. The rule for reinforcement on a **fixed–interval (FI) schedule** is that the first response after a fixed amount of time has elapsed is reinforced. For example, in an FI 60-second schedule, immediately after one reinforcer has been delivered, a clock starts to time the next 60-second interval. Any responses that are made during those 60 seconds have no effect whatsoever. However, at the 60-second mark, a reinforcer is becomes available, and the next response will produce the reinforcer.

If the subject had either a perfect sense of time or access to a clock, the most efficient behavior on an FI schedule would be to wait exactly 60 seconds, then make one response to collect the reinforcer. However, because no subject has a perfect sense of time and because a clock is usually not provided for the subject to watch, subjects on FI schedules typically make many more responses per reinforcer than the one that is required. Figure 6.2 shows the typical pattern of responding found on FI schedules. As on FR schedules, there is a postreinforcement pause, but after this pause, the subject usually starts by responding quite slowly (unlike the abrupt switch to rapid responding on an FR schedule). As the interval progresses, the subject responds more and more rapidly, and just before reinforcement, the response rate is quite rapid. For obvious reasons, the cumulative record pattern from this class of schedule is sometimes called a *fixed-interval scallop*.

The FI schedule does not have many close parallels outside the laboratory because few real-world reinforcers occur on such a regular temporal cycle. However, one everyday behavior that approximates the typical FI pattern of accelerating responses is waiting for a bus. Imagine that you are walking to a bus stop and that just as you arrive you see a bus leave. Suppose that you are not wearing a watch, but you know that a bus arrives at this stop every 20 minutes so you sit down on a bench and start to read a book. In this situation, the operant response is looking down the street for the next bus. The reinforcer for this response is simply the sight of the next bus. At first, the response of looking for the bus may not occur at all, and you may read steadily for 5 or 10 minutes before your first glance down the street. Your next glance may occur 1 or 2 minutes later, and now you may look down the street every minute or so. After 15 minutes, you may put away the book and stare down the street almost continuously until the bus arrives.

Other situations in which important events occur at regular intervals can produce similar patterns of accelerating behavior. Mawhinney, Bostow, Laws, Blumenfeld, and Hopkins (1971) measured the study behavior of college students in a psychology course, and they found that the pattern of this behavior varied quite predictably, depending on the schedule of examinations. As mentioned earlier, the conditioned reinforcer of a good grade on an exam can be an important reinforcer for studying. All the readings for the course were available only in a special room in the library, and the materials could not be taken out of this room so that the students' study behavior could be measured. At two points in the course, there was a short quiz every class, which approximates a CRF schedule. At two other times in the course, there were no daily quizzes, but a longer exam was given at the end of the third week. This was more like an FI schedule because there was no immediate reinforcer for studying during the early parts of the 3-week period. This arrangement is not exactly like an FI schedule because studying early in the 3-week period presumably had some beneficial effect in terms of the grade on the exam. Despite this difference, Figure 6.5 shows that the patterns of the students' study behavior during the two 3-week periods were similar to typical FI performance: There was little studying during the early parts of the 3-week period, but the amount of studying steadily increased as the exam approached. In contrast,

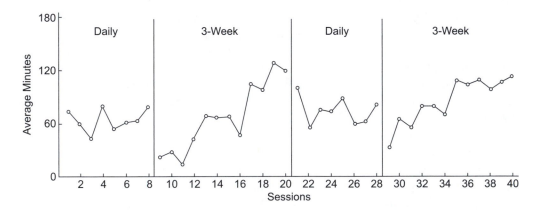

Figure 6.5 The average minutes of study per day by college students when the instructor gave daily quizzes and when a larger exam was given at the end of a 3-week period. (From Mawhinney, V.T., et al., A comparison of students' studying behavior produced by daily, weekly and 3-week testing schedules, *Journal of Applied Behavior Analysis, 4,* 257–264. Copyright 1971 by the Society for the Experimental Analysis of Behavior.)

study behavior was more stable from day to day when the students had daily quizzes. This experiment demonstrates that an instructor's selection of a schedule of quizzes or exams can have a large effect on the study behavior of the students in the course.

Variable Interval

Variable-interval (VI) schedules are like FI schedules except that the amount of time that must pass before a reinforcer is stored varies unpredictably from reinforcer to reinforcer. For example, in a VI 60-second schedule, the time between the delivery of one reinforcer and the storage of another might be 6 seconds for one reinforcer, then 300 seconds for the next, 40 seconds for the next, and so on. As on FI schedules, the first response to occur after a reinforcer is stored collects that reinforcer, and the clock does not start again until the reinforcer is collected.

As Figure 6.2 shows, VI schedules typically produce a steady, moderate response rate. This response pattern seems sensible considering the characteristics of the schedule. Because a reinforcer might be stored at any moment, a long pause after reinforcement would not be advantageous. By maintaining a steady response rate, the subject will collect each reinforcer soon after it is stored, thus keeping the VI clock moving most of the time. On the other hand, a very high response rate, such as that observed on a VR schedule, would produce only a minor increase in the rate of reinforcement.

An example of an everyday behavior that is maintained by a VI schedule of reinforcement is checking for mail. The reinforcer in this situation is simply the receipt of mail. Most people receive mail on some days but not on others, and the days when one will find something reinforcing (e.g., letters, as opposed to junk mail or bills) in the mailbox are usually impossible to predict. The delivery of mail approximates a VI schedule because (1) it is unpredictable; (2) if a reinforcer is stored (the mail has been delivered), only one response is required to collect it; and (3) if the reinforcer has not yet been stored, no amount of responding will bring it forth. The resultant behavior is moderate and steady: Most people check the mail every day, but usually only once a day.

BOX 6.1   IN THE MEDIA

The Scalloped Cumulative Record of the United States Congress

Reinforcement schedules not only control the behavior of individuals; they can also control the behavior of large groups of people. Some behavioral psychologists have noted that both the reinforcement schedule and the performance of the U.S. Congress are similar in some ways to an FI schedule (Critchfield, Haley, Sabo, Colbert, & Macropoulis, 2003; Weisberg & Waldrop, 1972). Each year, Congress begins its session in January, and the session concludes near the end of each year, so there is a roughly fixed period of time in which it must work. Weisberg and Waldrop suggested that one of the main

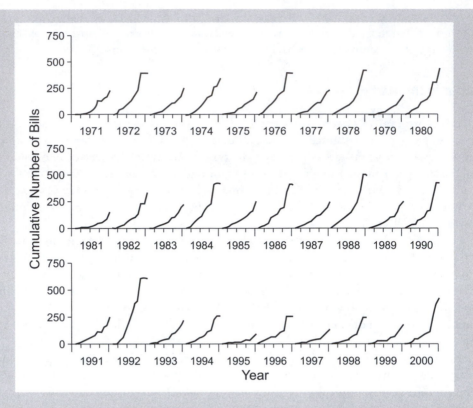

Figure 6.6 A cumulative record of bills passed by the U.S. Congress over a 30-year period. (From Critchfield, T.S., et al., A half century of scalloping in the work habits of the United States Congress. *Journal of Applied Behavior Analysis*, *36*, 2003, 465–486. Copyright 2003 by the Society for the Experimental Analysis of Behavior, Inc.)

behaviors of Congress is to pass legislation, and one of the main reinforcers is adjournment, when members can go home to seek the support of their constituents (so they can be reelected). Based on these assumptions, Critchfield et al. plotted the number of bills passed by Congress over a 30-year period in the form of a cumulative record, with time on the x-axis and cumulative bills passed on the y-axis. As shown in Figure 6.6, the cumulative record of Congress's behavior is a fine example of an FI scallop. In each and every year, the number of bills passed starts at a slow pace and then accelerates as the end of the session approaches.

Critchfield et al. (2003) point out that few real-world examples are exactly the same as laboratory reinforcement schedules, and this is certainly true for congressional behavior. For one thing, there is usually a large amount of preparatory work that must be done before a bill is ready for a vote, so it would be unrealistic to expect that many bills would be passed in the first week of a new session. Also, whereas a laboratory FI schedule actually requires just one response for reinforcement, Congress has a certain amount of work that must be done each year, so there seem to be elements of an FR schedule involved as well. However, the FI features seem to play a dominant role in the case of Congress, as seen in the consistent scalloped pattern.

Another interesting feature of Congress's cumulative record is that more bills are passed in even-numbered years than in odd-numbered years. This is a very consistent trend, which can be seen in the up-and-down heights of the cumulative record in consecutive years. Can you think of an explanation for this pattern? Is there something different about the reinforcers members of Congress receive in even years compared to odd years?

Extinction and the Four Simple Schedules

What happens with the different reinforcement schedules if reinforcement stops? One general finding is that extinction is more rapid after CRF than after a schedule of intermittent reinforcement. This finding is called the **partial reinforcement effect**, an effect that seemed paradoxical to early researchers. Why should a response that is only intermittently followed by a reinforcer be stronger (more resistant to extinction) than a response that has been followed by a reinforcer every time it has occurred? This dilemma has been named **Humphreys's paradox**, after the psychologist who first demonstrated the partial reinforcement extinction effect (Humphreys, 1939).

One explanation of the partial reinforcement effect is called the **discrimination hypothesis** (Mowrer & Jones, 1945). It states that in order for behavior to change once extinction begins, the individual must be able to discriminate the change in reinforcement contingencies. With CRF, where every response has been reinforced, the change to extinction is easy to discriminate, and so it does not take long for responding to disappear. For example, a vending machine usually dispenses reinforcers (snacks, soft drinks) on a schedule of CRF: Each time the correct amount of money is inserted, a reinforcer is delivered. If the schedule is switched to extinction (the machine breaks down), a person will not continue to put money in the machine for long.

Compare this situation to a slot machine, which dispenses reinforcers on a VR schedule. If a slot machine appeared to be functioning normally but could never produce a jackpot, a gambler might continue to pour many coins into the machine before giving up. It would take a long time for the gambler to discriminate the change from a VR schedule to extinction.

Although the discrimination hypothesis may be easy to understand, experimental evidence suggests that a slightly different hypothesis, the **generalization decrement hypothesis** (Capaldi, 1966), is better. Generalization decrement is simply a term for the decreased responding one observes in a generalization test when the test stimuli become less and less similar to the training stimulus. The generalization decrement hypothesis states that responding during extinction will be weak if the stimuli during extinction are different from those that were present during reinforcement, but it will be strong if these stimuli are similar to those encountered during reinforcement.

According to Capaldi, there is a large generalization decrement when the schedule switches from CRF to extinction because the animal has never experienced a situation in which its responses were not reinforced. In other words, the animal quickly stops responding because it has never been taught to keep responding when its initial responses are not reinforced. However, suppose an animal has been reinforced on a VR 50 schedule and now switches to extinction. Here there will be much less generalization decrement because on many occasions in the past the animal has made a long run of unreinforced responses, and eventually a reinforcer was delivered. For this animal, the stimuli present during extinction (long stretches of unreinforced responses) are quite similar to the stimuli present during the VR schedule. For this reason, the animal will probably continue to respond for a longer period of time.

Other Reinforcement Schedules

Although the four simple reinforcement schedules have been the most thoroughly investigated, the number of possible rules for delivering reinforcement is unlimited. Many other reinforcement schedules have been studied by behavioral psychologists. For example, under a **differential reinforcement of low rates (DRL)** schedule, a response is reinforced if and only if a certain amount of time has elapsed since the previous response. If the schedule is DRL 10 seconds, every response that occurs after a pause of at least 10 seconds is reinforced. If a response occurs after 9.5 seconds, this not only fails to produce reinforcement but it resets the 10-second clock to zero, so that now 10 more seconds must elapse before a response can be reinforced. As you might imagine, DRL schedules produce very low rates of responding, but they are not as low as would be optimal. Animals on a DRL schedule often pause slightly less than the required duration; as a result, considerably more than half of their responses go unreinforced (Richards, Sabol, & Seiden, 1993).

The opposite of DRL is the **differential reinforcement of high rates (DRH)** schedule, in which a certain number of responses must occur within a fixed amount of time. For example, a reinforcer might occur each time the subject makes 10 responses in 3 seconds or less. Since rapid responding is selectively reinforced by this schedule, DRH can be used to produce higher rates of responding than those obtained with any other reinforcement schedule. Other common reinforcement schedules combine two or more simple schedules in some way. For instance, in a **concurrent schedule**, the subject is presented with two or more response alternatives (e.g., several different levers), each associated with its own reinforcement schedule. With more than one reinforcement schedule available simultaneously, psychologists can determine which schedule the subject prefers and how much time is devoted to each alternative. Some of these more complex reinforcement schedules will be discussed in later chapters.

FACTORS AFFECTING PERFORMANCE ON REINFORCEMENT SCHEDULES

An individual's behavior on a given reinforcement schedule can be affected by many other factors besides the rule for reinforcement. Some of these factors—*amount of reinforcement*, *rate of reinforcement*, *delay*, and *response effort*—are fairly straightforward. Not surprisingly, both people and animals will display stronger responding on a reinforcement schedule if the reinforcers are large and if they are delivered at a high rate. However, if the reinforcers are delayed, or if each response requires substantial effort, responding will be slower. Another important factor is *reinforcement history*: Research has shown that how an individual responds on one reinforcement schedule depends on what other reinforcement schedules the individual has previously been exposed to. As an example, Weiner (1964) had human participants press a response key to earn points in ten 1-hour sessions. Some participants worked on an FR 40 schedule (on which more rapid responding led to more reinforcers). Other participants worked on a DRL 20-second schedule (on which only pauses longer than 20 seconds were reinforced). Then all participants were switched to an FI 10-second schedule. The participants with FR experience responded rapidly on the FI schedule, but those with DRL experience responded very slowly. These large differences persisted even after 20 sessions with the FI schedule. Similar effects of prior reinforcement history have been found with animals (Macaskill & Hackenberg, 2012; Wanchisen, Tatham, & Mooney, 1989).

Some of these points may seem obvious, but other factors that can affect performance on reinforcement schedules are not so obvious. Next, we will examine some factors that can easily be overlooked.

Behavioral Momentum

When a heavy object starts moving, it acquires momentum and becomes difficult to stop. Nevin (1992) has argued that there is an analogy between the momentum of a moving object and the **behavioral momentum** of an ongoing operant behavior. Nevin has found that a behavior's resistance to change (which is a measure of behavioral momentum) depends on the association between the discriminative stimulus and the reinforcer (i.e., on how frequently the behavior has been reinforced in the presence of a certain discriminative stimulus).

An experiment with pigeons (Nevin, 1974) illustrates the concept of behavioral momentum. The pigeons earned food by pecking on a response key that was sometimes green and sometimes red. VI schedules delivered 60 food presentations per hour when the key was green but only 20 food presentations per hour when the key was red. As expected, the pigeons pecked more rapidly when the key was green. Then, Nevin interrupted the green and red keys with periods during which free food was delivered. When the free food deliveries were very rapid, the pigeons' rates of key pecking decreased by about 60% when the key was green but by over 80% when the key was red. According to Nevin, pecking on the green key had greater momentum because it was associated with a higher rate of reinforcement, so this behavior was less disrupted by the free food deliveries than was pecking on the red key. Studies with humans have also found that behaviors associated with higher rates of reinforcement are harder to disrupt (Milo, Mace, & Nevin, 2010).

Nevin and Grace (2000) proposed that the concept of behavioral momentum has a number of implications for attempts to change behavior outside the laboratory. Behavior therapists frequently want to make sure that a newly trained behavior (e.g., working steadily on one's job during work hours) will persist in the presence of potential disruptors (e.g., distractions by friends, reinforcers for competing behaviors). The newly trained behavior will have more momentum and be more likely to persist despite such potential disruptors if the worker has developed a strong association between the work environment and reinforcement for appropriate work-related behavior.

As another example, the concept of behavioral momentum can help to explain why some undesirable behaviors may relapse when a patient leaves a treatment facility (Podlesnik & Shahan, 2010). For instance, someone who has received treatment for a drug addiction may start taking drugs again when he leaves a treatment center and returns home because the drugs are strongly associated with that environment (the patient's neighborhood and friends). Although he abstained from drugs in the treatment facility, the association between the patient's neighborhood and drugs has not been broken. Because drug-taking behavior has strong momentum when the individual is in his old neighborhood, it may persist in that environment despite the treatment the patient has received elsewhere.

Contingency-Shaped Versus Rule-Governed Behaviors

As we have seen, each reinforcement schedule tends to produce its own characteristic pattern of behavior (Figure 6.2). B. F. Skinner called these patterns **contingency-shaped behaviors** because behavior is gradually shaped into its final form as the individual gains more and more experience with a particular reinforcement schedule (Ferster & Skinner, 1957). However, some laboratory experiments with humans have found behavior patterns that were quite different from those shown in Figure 6.2. For example, under FI schedules, some humans show the accelerating pattern found with animals, others respond very quickly throughout the interval, and others make only a few responses near the end of the interval (Leander, Lippman, & Meyer, 1968). Discrepancies between human and animal behaviors have been found with other reinforcement schedules as well (Lowe, 1979). Why should the same reinforcement schedules produce different behavior patterns in humans and nonhumans?

One explanation is that the discrepancies between animal and human performance on reinforcement schedules occur because people are capable of both contingency-shaped behavior and **rule-governed behavior**. Skinner (1969) proposed that because people have language, they can be given verbal instructions or rules to follow, and these rules may or may not have anything to do with the prevailing reinforcement contingencies. For example, a mother may tell a child, "Stay out of drafts or you will catch a cold," and the child may follow this rule for a long time, regardless of whether it is truly effective in preventing colds. With respect to laboratory experiments on reinforcement schedules, this theory states that human participants may behave differently from animals because they are following rules about how to respond (e.g., "Press the response button as rapidly as possible," or "Wait for about a minute, and then respond"). They may form these rules on their own, or they may get them from the instructions the experimenter provides before the experiment begins. Once a human participant receives or creates such a rule, the actual reinforcement contingencies may have little or no effect on his or her behavior. For instance, if the experimenter says, "Press the key rapidly to earn the most money," the participant may indeed respond rapidly on an FI schedule even though rapid responding is not necessary on this schedule.

Several types of evidence support the idea that human performance on reinforcement schedules is often rule governed, at least in part. Many studies have shown that the instructions given to participants can have a large effect on their response patterns (e.g., Bentall & Lowe, 1987; Catania, Matthews, & Shimoff, 1982). If participants are given no specific rule to follow, they may form one on their own. Human participants have sometimes been asked, either during an experiment or at the end, to explain why they responded the way they did. In some cases there is a close correspondence between a person's verbal descriptions and his or her actual response patterns (Wearden, 1988). However, there are also cases where human participants asked to explain their behaviors can give no rule, or the rule they give does not describe their actual behavior patterns (Matthews, Catania, & Shimoff, 1985). Therefore, it seems likely that other variables also contribute to the differences between human and nonhuman performance on reinforcement schedules. For instance, a primary reinforcer, food, is usually used with animal subjects, but with humans the reinforcers in many experiments have been conditioned reinforcers (e.g., points that may later be exchanged for small amounts of money). In addition, animals and humans usually come to the laboratory with very different reinforcement histories. It is important to remember that operant behavior is affected by many variables, and this can make the task of analyzing the behavior complex and challenging.

THE EXPERIMENTAL ANALYSIS OF REINFORCEMENT SCHEDULES

Throughout the preceding discussions of reinforcement schedules, the explanations of why particular schedules produce specific response patterns have been casual and intuitive. For example, we noted that it would not "make sense" to have a long postreinforcement pause on a VR schedule or to respond at a very rapid rate on a VI schedule. This level of discussion can make the basic facts about reinforcement schedules easier to learn and remember. However, such imprecise statements are no substitute for a scientific analysis of exactly which independent variables (which characteristics of the reinforcement schedule) control which dependent variables (which aspects of the subject's behavior). This section presents a few examples that show how a scientific analysis can either improve on intuitive explanations of behavior or distinguish among different explanations, all of which seem intuitively reasonable.

PRACTICE QUIZ 1: CHAPTER 6

1. In a cumulative record, fast responding is indicated by a _____, and no responding is indicated by a _____.
2. Responding on an FR schedule typically shows a(n) _____ pattern, and responding on an FI schedule typically shows a(n) _____ pattern.
3. Responding on _____ schedules is usually rapid and steady, and responding on _____ schedules is usually slower and steady.
4. A behavior has a high _____ if it is not affected much by distractions or environmental changes.
5. _____ behavior is controlled by the schedule of reinforcement; _____ behavior is controlled by instructions subjects are given or form on their own.

ANSWERS

1. steep line, horizontal line 2. stop-and-go, accelerating 3. VR, VI 4. behavioral momentum 5. contingency-shaped, rule-governed

Cause of the FR Postreinforcement Pause

Why do animals pause after reinforcement on FR schedules? Several possible explanations seem intuitively reasonable. Perhaps the postreinforcement pause is the result of fatigue: The subject has made many responses and has collected a reinforcer; now it rests to alleviate its fatigue. A second possibility is satiation: Consuming the food causes a slight decrease in the animal's level of hunger, which results in a brief interruption in responding. A third explanation is that on an FR schedule, the animal is farthest from the next reinforcer immediately after receiving the previous reinforcer: Many responses will be required before another reinforcer is delivered. We can call these three explanations of the FR postreinforcement pause the fatigue hypothesis, the satiation hypothesis, and the remaining-responses hypothesis. Each of these hypotheses sounds plausible, but how can we determine which is correct? Several types of evidence help to distinguish among them.

First, there is the finding that postreinforcement pauses become larger as the size of the FR increases. This finding is consistent with both the fatigue and remaining-responses hypotheses, but it contradicts the satiation hypothesis. Because the subject can collect reinforcers at a faster rate on a small FR schedule, its level of hunger should be lower; according to the satiation hypothesis, pauses should be longer on smaller FR schedules, not on larger FR schedules.

Data that help to distinguish between the fatigue and remaining-responses hypotheses are provided by studies that combine two or more different FR schedules into what is called a multiple schedule. In a **multiple schedule**, the subject is presented with two or more different schedules, one at a time, and each schedule is signaled by a different discriminative stimulus. For example, Figure 6.7 illustrates a portion of a session involving a multiple FR 10 FR 100 schedule. When the response key is blue, the schedule is FR 100; when it is red, the schedule is FR 10. The key color remains the same until a reinforcer is earned, at which point there is a 50% chance that the key color (and schedule) will switch.

The behavior shown in Figure 6.7, though hypothetical, is representative of the results from actual studies that used multiple FR schedules (Mintz, Mourer, & Gofseyeff, 1967). Examine the postreinforcement pauses that occurred at points a, b, c, d, e, and f. Notice that sometimes the pause after FR 100 is long (f), but sometimes it is short (a, b). Sometimes the pause after FR 10 is short (b), but sometimes it is long (c, e). The data show that we cannot

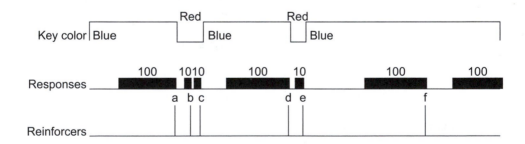

Figure 6.7 A hypothetical but typical pattern of response from a multiple schedule where the blue key color signaled that the schedule was FR 100 and the red key color signaled that the schedule was FR 10.

predict the size of the postreinforcement pause by knowing how many responses the subject has just made. This fact forces us to reject the fatigue hypothesis.

However, it is possible to predict the size of the pause by knowing the size of the upcoming ratio. Notice that the pause is short whenever the key color is red (points a, b, and d), which is the discriminative stimulus for FR 10. The pause is long when the key color is blue (points c, e, and f), the discriminative stimulus for FR 100. This pattern is exactly what would be predicted by the remaining-responses hypothesis: The size of the postreinforcement pause is determined by the upcoming FR requirement. Experiments of this type have shown quite clearly that the size of the postreinforcement pause depends on how much work must be done before the next reinforcer is delivered and that the factors of satiation and fatigue play at most a minor role.

Comparisons of VR and VI Response Rates

Experiments with both humans and animals have shown that if a VR schedule and a VI schedule deliver the same number of reinforcers per hour, subjects usually respond faster on the VR schedule (Baxter & Schlinger, 1990; Matthews, Shimoff, Catania, & Sagvolden, 1977). Why is responding faster on VR schedules than on VI schedules even in cases where the rates of reinforcement are the same for the two schedules?

One theory about this difference in response rates can be classified as a **molecular theory**, which means that it focuses on small-scale events—the moment-by-moment relationships between responses and reinforcers. The other theory is a **molar theory**, one that deals with large-scale measures of behavior and reinforcement. To be more specific, molecular theories usually discuss events that have time spans of less than 1 minute, whereas molar theories discuss relationships measured over at least several minutes and often over the entire length of an experimental session.

To account for the different response rates on VR and VI schedules, a popular molecular theory is the **interresponse time (IRT) reinforcement theory**. IRT is the time between two consecutive responses. In essence, this theory states that response rates are slower on VI schedules than on VR schedules because long IRTs (long pauses between responses) are more frequently reinforced on VI schedules. This theory was first proposed by Skinner (1938) and later supported by others (Anger, 1956; Platt, 1979). Remember that a VI schedule has a timer that sets up each reinforcer, so if there is a long pause in responding (a long IRT), there is a good chance that a reinforcer will be waiting when the next response is finally made. However, if there is a quick and rapid burst of responses (a series of short IRTs), the chances of a reinforcer becoming available during that short period of time are small. Therefore, on a VI schedule, long IRTs are more likely to be followed by a reinforcer. On a VR schedule, however, the delivery of reinforcement depends entirely on the number of responses produced, not on the passage of time. Therefore, there is no selective strengthening of long pauses on VR schedules. However, if the individual makes a burst of rapid responses, there is an increasing chance that one of those will complete the VR requirement and deliver a reinforcer.

To provide evidence for their viewpoint, those who favor IRT reinforcement theory have arranged schedules that reinforce different IRTs with different probabilities. For example, Shimp (1968) set up a schedule in which only IRTs between 1.5 and 2.5 seconds or between

3.5 and 4.5 seconds were reinforced. As the theory of selective IRT reinforcement would predict, IRTs of these two sizes increased in frequency, just as IRT reinforcement theory predicted. In another experiment, Shimp (1973) mimicked the pattern of IRT reinforcement that occurs in a typical VI schedule: He did not use a VI clock but simply reinforced long IRTs with a high probability and short IRTs with a low probability. The result of this "synthetic VI" schedule was a pattern of responding indistinguishable from that of a normal VI schedule—moderate, steady responding with a mixture of long and short IRTs.

A molar theory of the VI–VR difference might be called the **response–reinforcer correlation theory** (Baum, 1973; Green, Kagel, & Battalio, 1987), which focuses on the long-term relation between response rate and reinforcement rate on these two schedules. Figure 6.8 shows the relationship between a subject's average response rate and overall reinforcement rate for a typical VR schedule and a typical VI schedule. On VR 60, as on all ratio schedules, there is a linear relationship between response rate and reinforcement rate. For instance, a response rate of 60 responses per minute will produce 60 reinforcers per hour, and a response rate of 90 responses per minute will produce 90 reinforcers per hour. The relationship on the VI 60-second schedule (as on all VI schedules) is very different. No matter how rapidly the subject responds, it cannot obtain more than the scheduled 60 reinforcers per hour. The reason that the reinforcement rate drops with very low response rates is that the VI clock will sometimes be stopped (having stored a reinforcer), and it will not start again until the subject makes a response and collects a reinforcer. But as long as the subject responds at a modest rate, it will obtain close to 60 reinforcers per hour.

Let us try to understand how the different functions in Figure 6.8 could cause the response rate difference between VI and VR. Suppose that after extensive experience on VR 60, a pigeon's response rate is about 60 responses per minute (where the two functions cross in Figure 6.8), and it is earning about 60 reinforcers per hour. Now suppose the schedule is switched to VI 60 seconds. The same response rate would continue to produce 60 reinforcers per hour. However, the pigeon's response rate is not completely steady: Sometimes

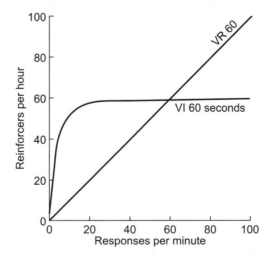

Figure 6.8 The relationship between rate of response and rate of reinforcement on a VR 60 schedule and a VI 60-second schedule.

the pigeon responds slightly slower and sometimes slightly faster, and it eventually learns that slower responding has little effect on reinforcement rate on the VI schedule. The pigeon's behavior may gradually drop to, say, 20 responses per minute without much decrease in the rate of reinforcement. Speaking loosely, we could say that on VI 60 seconds, the pigeon has learned that the extra 40 responses per minute are "not worth it" because they produce only a minor increase in reinforcement rate.

Probably the best way to decide between the molar and molecular theories is to use a schedule in which the molar contingencies favor rapid responding and the molecular contingencies favor slow responding (or vice versa). Experiments with pigeons (Vaughan, 1987) and rats (Cole, 1999) used some complex schedules that had these properties. For instance, one schedule used by Vaughan had the molar features of a VR schedule (faster response rates produced more reinforcers) but the molecular features of a VI schedule (reinforcement was more likely after a long IRT). As predicted by IRT reinforcement theory, the pigeons responded slowly on this schedule (and thereby lost reinforcers in the long run). Conversely, the pigeons responded rapidly on a schedule in which the molecular contingencies favored rapid responding (short IRTs) but the molar contingencies favored slow responding (so once again the pigeons lost reinforcers in the long run). In a similar way, Tanno and Sakagami (2008) used some complex schedules to compare the effects of molar and molecular variables. They found that the long-term correlation between response rates and reinforcement had very little effect on the rats' responding. However, they responded rapidly when short IRTs were selectively reinforced and slowly when long IRTs were selectively reinforced. All of these results support the molecular approach, for they indicate that the animals were sensitive to the short-term consequences of their behavior but not to the long-term consequences.

APPLICATIONS OF OPERANT CONDITIONING

Within the field of behavior modification, operant conditioning principles have been applied to so many different behaviors that they are too numerous to list, let alone describe, in a few pages. Operant conditioning principles have been used to help people who wish to improve themselves by losing weight, smoking or drinking less, or exercising more. They have been applied to a wide range of children's problems, including classroom disruption, poor academic performance, fighting, tantrums, extreme passivity, and hyperactivity. They have been used in attempts to improve the daily functioning of adults and children who have more serious behavior problems and must be institutionalized. These principles have also been applied to problems that affect society as a whole, such as litter and pollution, the waste of energy and resources, workplace accidents, delinquency, shoplifting, and other crimes. Because of the number and diversity of these applications, this section can do no more than describe a few representative examples.

Teaching Language to Children With Autism

Autism is a severe disorder that affects roughly 1 in every 100 children, usually appearing when a child is a few years old. One major symptom of autism is extreme social withdrawal. The child shows little of the normal interest in watching and interacting with other people.

Children with autism do not acquire normal language use: They either remain silent or exhibit echolalia, which is the immediate repetition of any words they hear. These children frequently spend hours engaging in simple repetitive behaviors such as rocking back and forth or spinning a metal pan on the floor. Despite considerable research, the causes of autism are not well understood.

Ivar Lovaas (1967) developed an extensive program based on operant conditioning principles designed to teach children with severe autism to speak, to interact with other people, and in general to behave more normally. Lovaas's methods make use of many of the operant conditioning principles we have already discussed, plus some new ones. At first, a therapist uses some tasty food as a primary reinforcer and starts by reinforcing the child simply for sitting quietly and looking at the experimenter. Next, using shaping, the therapist rewards the child for making any audible sounds, and then for making sounds that more and more closely mimic the word spoken by the therapist. For instance, if the child's name is Billy, the therapist may say the word "Billy" as a discriminative stimulus, after which any verbal response that approximates this word will be reinforced. So as not to rely entirely on food as a reinforcer (which would lose its effectiveness rapidly because of satiation), the therapist establishes other stimuli as conditioned reinforcers. Before presenting the food, the therapist might say "Good!" or give the child a hug—two stimuli that can eventually be used as reinforcers by themselves.

Early in this type of training, the therapist might use her hand to aid the child in his mouth and lip movements. This type of physical guidance is one example of a prompt. A **prompt** is any stimulus that makes a desired response more likely. In this example, the therapist's prompt of moving the child's lips and cheeks into the proper shape makes the production of the appropriate response more likely. Whenever a prompt is used, it is usually withdrawn gradually in a procedure known as **fading**. The therapist may do less and less of the work of moving the child's lips and cheeks into the proper position, then perhaps just touch the child's cheek lightly, then not at all. This type of training demands large amounts of time and patience. It might take several days before the child masters his first word. However, the pace of progress quickens as additional words are introduced, and after a few weeks the child may master several new words each day.

At this stage of training, the child is only imitating words he hears. The next step is to teach him the meanings of these words. Training begins with concrete nouns such as nose, shoe, and leg. The child is taught to identify the correct object in response to the word as a stimulus (e.g., by rewarding an appropriate response to the instruction, "Point to your nose") and to produce the appropriate word when presented with the object (Therapist: "What is this?" Billy: "Shoe"). Later in training, similar painstaking techniques are used to teach the child the meanings of verbs and adjectives, of prepositions such as in and on, and of abstract concepts such as first, last, more, less, same, and different. This program can produce dramatic improvements in the behavior of children who typically show negligible improvement from any other type of therapy. Over the course of several months, Lovaas typically found that a child who was initially aloof and completely silent became friendly and affectionate and learned to use language to answer questions, to make requests, or to tell stories.

How successful is this behavioral treatment in the long run? Lovaas (1987) compared children who had received extensive behavioral treatment for autism (40 hours a week for 2 or more years) with children who had received minimal treatment (10 hours a week or less). At ages 6 or 7, the differences between groups were dramatic: Nearly half of the children from the treatment group had normal IQs and academic performance, as compared to only 2% of the children from the control group. Six years later, the children in the treatment group continued to maintain their advantage over those in the control group. Some performed about as well as average children of the same age on tests of intelligence and adaptive behavior (McEachin, Smith, & Lovaas, 1993). These results are encouraging, for they suggest that if extensive behavioral treatment is given to young children with autism, it can essentially eliminate the autistic symptoms in at least some of them.

To be most effective, behavioral treatment for autism should begin at an early age, and it should be intensive: The child should receive many hours of treatment per week for a period of several years. However, researchers have been testing new behavioral treatments for children on the autism spectrum that are less time-consuming, and some seem promising. For example, a technique called Pivotal Response Training targets important social and communication skills that the child can later use in many different situations, thereby maximizing their impact. In many cases, the child's parents are taught to use this training at home. There is a strong emphasis on keeping motivation high by giving the child choices among tasks and reinforcers (Koegel, Bimbela, & Schreibman, 1996). Although more research on Pivotal Response Training is needed, a number of studies found that it produced substantial improvements in children's verbal and social skills (Lydon, Healy, & Leader, 2011; Ventola et al., 2014).

Token Reinforcement

In behavioral psychology, a *token* is defined as "an object or symbol that is exchanged for goods or services" (Hackenberg, 2009, p. 257). Research with various species of animals suggests that tokens can act as conditioned reinforcers—that is, their delivery can strengthen operant responses. Wolfe (1936) taught chimpanzees to insert poker chips into a vending machine to receive small amounts of food or water. The poker chips could then be used as reinforcers to establish and maintain new behaviors, such as lifting a weighted lever arm. Marbles have been used as tokens for rats (Malagodi, 1967) and illuminated lights as tokens for pigeons (Bullock & Hackenberg, 2006). Tokens can produce response patterns that are very similar to those obtained with primary reinforcers such as food. For instance, Malagodi's rats exhibited stop-and-go responding when marbles were delivered on an FR schedule and slower, steady responding when they were delivered on a VI schedule. Tokens can also serve as discriminative stimuli, signaling the upcoming delivery of a primary reinforcer (Mazur & Biondi, 2013).

In human applications, tokens may be physical objects such as poker chips or gold stars on a bulletin board, or they may simply be points added in a record book. **Token systems** have been used in classrooms, psychiatric institutions, prisons, and homes for juvenile offenders. What all token systems have in common is that each individual can earn tokens by performing any of a number of different desired behaviors and can later exchange these tokens for a variety of "backup" or primary reinforcers.

In the past, token systems have been used in psychiatric hospitals to improve the day-to-day functioning of patients. In one such program, patients received tokens for specific behaviors from three broad categories: personal hygiene, social interaction, and job performance (Schaefer & Martin, 1966). The purpose was to reinforce behaviors would be considered normal and desirable not only within the hospital but also in the outside world. The tokens were used to purchase food items, cigarettes, access to television, and recreational activities. The token program remained in effect for 3 months, and there were substantial increases in the reinforced behaviors. Other studies also found that token systems could produce impressive improvements in psychiatric patients. However, the use of token systems in psychiatric hospitals has declined over the years for several reasons (Glynn, 1990). These systems require a good deal of time and effort and a well-trained staff. In addition, there has been an increasing emphasis on pharmacological treatments for psychiatric patients. Some court rulings have restricted what can legally be done with token systems. For these reasons, it seems unlikely that token systems will be used extensively in psychiatric institutions in the foreseeable future.

Although their use with psychiatric patients has declined, token systems are now very commonly used in classrooms. Tokens may be delivered for good academic performance or for good behavior (Figure 6.9). In one instance, the classroom behavior of special education students was improved by giving them tokens for such behaviors as paying attention, using appropriate language, cooperating with others, and following instructions (Cavalier, Feretti, & Hodges, 1997). Teachers can set up a system in which tokens are exchanged for snacks, small prizes, or access to special activities.

In some cases, token reinforcement can be combined with modern technology to make the process more efficient and convenient. Dallery, Glenn, and Raiff (2007) offered vouchers to smokers for reducing their levels of carbon monoxide (which measures how much they had been smoking). The entire project was conducted over the Internet. Twice a day, participants used a webcam to record themselves taking a breath test for carbon monoxide. Over a 4-week period, they earned vouchers for greater and greater decreases in carbon monoxide levels, and the vouchers could be used to buy items from merchants on the Internet. Figure 6.10 shows the carbon monoxide levels from all 20 participants during the four weeks of the experiment. The individual results were variable, but many participants showed dramatic reductions in smoking as the treatment progressed.

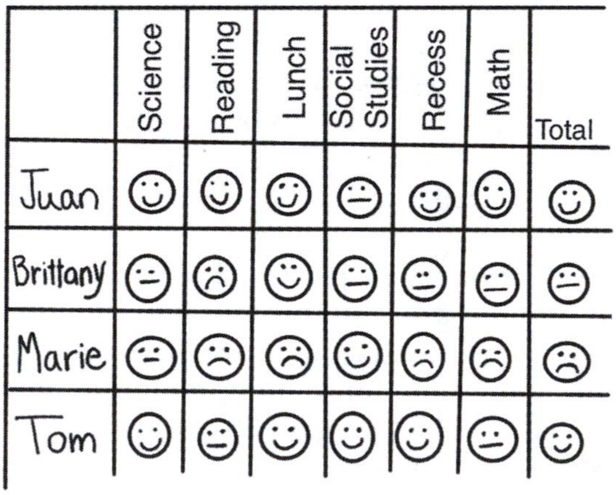

	Science	Reading	Lunch	Social Studies	Recess	Math	Total
Juan	☺	☺	☺	😐	☺	☺	☺
Brittany	😐	☹	☺	😐	😐	😐	😐
Marie	😐	☹	☹	☺	☹	☹	☹
Tom	☺	😐	☺	☺	☺	😐	☺

Figure 6.9 Many teachers use token systems in the classroom, such as these happy, neutral, and sad faces that represent different levels of performance. Students who obtain enough happy faces earn small prizes or special activities.

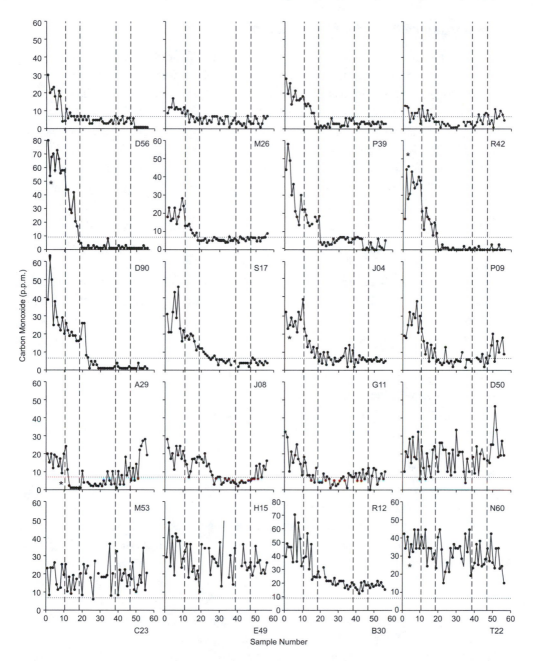

Figure 6.10 Carbon monoxide levels from 20 smokers are shown from a 4–week study in which they earned tokens exchangeable for rewards by smoking less. (From Dallery, J., Glenn, I.M., & Raiff, B.R., 2007, An Internet-based abstinence reinforcement treatment for cigarette smoking, *Drug and Alcohol Dependence, 86,* 230–238. Reprinted by permission of Elsevier.)

BOX 6.2   APPLYING THE RESEARCH

Organizational Behavior Management

An area of applied behavior analysis known as **organizational behavior management** is devoted to using the principles of behavioral psychology to improve human performance in the workplace (Johnson, Redmon, & Mawhinney, 2001). Researchers in this field have addressed such matters as worker productivity, supervisor effectiveness, accident prevention, quality improvement, and customer satisfaction. The idea of organizational behavior management is to apply a scientific approach to workplace behavior.

When behavior analysts serve as consultants for a business organization, the process usually involves several different steps. The organization's leaders must decide on the goals they wish to achieve and describe them in concrete terms (e.g., reducing the number of days per month that the average employee is absent from work). Current practices of the company are then observed, and data are collected on the workers' behaviors. The behavior analysts then make recommendations for changes of two main types—antecedent-based interventions and consequence-based interventions (Wilder, Austin, & Casella, 2009). Antecedent-based interventions focus on events that occur before the work is done, including such matters as providing appropriate worker training, clarifying tasks, and setting goals. Consequence-based interventions focus on the events that occur after the work is done, and they can include the use of praise, monetary rewards, and feedback. Data are collected to evaluate whether the changes are having the desired effects, and further adjustments are made as needed.

An early study by Wallin and Johnson (1976) used a simple VR schedule (a lottery) to reduce employee absenteeism and tardiness in a small electronics company. Workers were allowed to participate in a monthly lottery if their attendance record had been perfect for the past month, and the winner received a $10 prize. In the first 11 months of the lottery system, employee absenteeism was 30% lower than in the previous 11 months. This simple program saved the company thousands of dollars in sick-leave expenditures. But monetary reinforcers are not always necessary. Camden and Ludwig (2013) provided weekly personal and public feedback to nursing assistants in a health care clinic about their absences and the problems they caused (the number of understaffed shifts and the names of coworkers who had to work extra hours to cover their shifts). This simple change produced a decrease in absenteeism by nearly 50%.

Reinforcement procedures have also been used to decrease workplace accidents. Workers in two open-pit mines were given trading stamps (exchangeable for various types of merchandise) in return for accident-free performance. The workers could earn stamps in a variety of ways: by completing a year without a lost-time accident, by following safety standards, and so on. They lost stamps if someone in their group had an accident or damaged equipment. After the adoption of the trading-stamp program, lost-time accidents decreased by more than two thirds. The monetary savings from reduced accident rates were at least 15 times greater than the cost of the trading-stamp program (Fox, Hopkins & Anger, 1987). Quite a few other studies have found that such reinforcement programs can both reduce workplace accidents and save companies substantial amounts of money.

Often the workplace changes include several different components. In a hospital's operating room, behavior analysts used a combination of goal setting, task clarification, and feedback to increase the use of safe methods of passing sharp surgical instruments from one person to another. Baseline measurements showed that surgeons and staff frequently used unsafe techniques that increased the risk of a cut or puncture wound. In a meeting with operating room personnel, a "challenging but realistic" goal for improvement was agreed upon. Task clarification was accomplished by having staff model safe and unsafe techniques so that everyone understood the proper techniques. For feedback, the operating room procedures were observed and recorded, and each week the percentage of safe transfers was reported to the staff. Under this program, the use of safe techniques increased by a factor of two (Cunningham & Austin, 2007).

Organizational behavior management has been used for many different types of companies, both large and small, in many different sectors of the economy, including human services, manufacturing, transportation, and education. Of course, no two companies are exactly alike, but by comparing the results from many different cases, researchers can start to draw general conclusions about what methods of behavior change are the most effective.

Behavior Therapy for Marital Problems

Some therapists have used behavioral principles to aid couples who seek help for marital problems. Jacobson and Follette (1985) recognized that in unhappy married couples, each spouse tends to resort to threats, punishment, and retaliation in an attempt to get what he or she wants from the other. For this reason, the initial phases of therapy are designed to promote more positive interactions between partners. To encourage a reciprocal exchange of reinforcers between spouses, a contingency contract is often used. A **contingency contract** is a written agreement that lists the duties (behaviors) required of each party and the privileges (reinforcers) that will result if the duties are performed. In most cases, both spouses play active roles in creating the contract and indicate their agreement with the terms of the contract by signing it.

A contingency contract can help to encourage the exchange of reinforcers and to let each partner know what behaviors the other desires. For instance, the husband may agree to do the dishes in the evening if and only if the wife took the children to school that morning. Conversely, the wife agrees to take the children to school the next morning if and only if the husband did the dishes the night before. The use of a written contract ensures that both partners understand what is expected of them. This part of behavioral marital therapy is called behavior exchange because each spouse makes an effort to perform specific behaviors that will please the other.

Behavior exchange is just one part of behavioral marital therapy. Another important component is training in communication and problem-solving skills. N. S. Jacobson (1977) observed that unhappy couples often have difficulty communicating, and they find it difficult to solve even the simplest of problems that may arise. As part of their therapy, a couple first reads a book about problem solving in marriage, then they try to solve a very minor problem as the therapist watches. For instance, the wife may complain that she does not like always having to remind the husband to take out the garbage. The couple then tries to find a solution to this small problem that satisfies both spouses. Whenever one spouse responds in an inappropriate way, the therapist interrupts, points out the flaw, and suggests a better alternative. After a little trial and error, the couple usually finds a solution to this minor problem. Over time, they gradually work up to bigger problems, and they are typically given "homework assignments" in which they engage in problem solving on a regular basis between meetings with the therapist.

This general approach is often called *cognitive-behavior therapy* (CBT) because of its emphasis on problem solving and communication between partners. It offers a promising approach to the treatment of marital discord: One review of 17 separate studies concluded that a couple's chances of successfully resolving their marital difficulties more than doubled if the couple received this type of therapy (Halweg & Markman, 1988). Although these techniques do not work for everyone, they can help many unhappy couples improve the quality of their marriages. As with most types of behavior modification, behavioral therapy for couples is not a fixed and unchanging system; it continues to evolve as therapists experiment with new techniques and measure their effectiveness (West, 2013).

Conclusions

The successful application of the principles of reinforcement to a wide array of behavior problems provides one of the strongest pieces of evidence that the research of the operant conditioning laboratory is relevant to real-world behavior. The examples described here are just a small sample of what has been accomplished in the field of applied behavior analysis. Other examples will be presented in later chapters. With further research in this area, psychologists should continue to develop a more complete understanding of how "voluntary" behaviors are affected by their consequences.

PRACTICE QUIZ 2: CHAPTER 6

1. Research results favor the _____ theory of FR postreinforcement pauses over the _____ and _____ theories.
2. IRT reinforcement theory states that longer IRTs are more likely to be reinforced on _____ schedules, but bursts of responding are more likely to be reinforced on _____ schedules.
3. _____ theories deal with long-term relationships between behavior and reinforcement, whereas _____ theories deal with moment-to-moment relationships between behavior and reinforcement.
4. Physically guiding the movements of a learner is an example of a _____; gradually removing this physical guidance is called _____.
5. In behavioral marital therapy, a written agreement between spouses is called a _____.

ANSWERS

1. remaining-responses, fatigue, satiation 2. VI, VR 3. molar, molecular 4. prompt, fading 5. contingency contract

SUMMARY

An FR schedule delivers a reinforcer after a fixed number of responses, and it typically produces a postreinforcement pause followed by rapid responding. A VR schedule delivers a reinforcer after a variable number of responses, and it typically leads to rapid, steady responding. On an FI schedule, the requirement for reinforcement is one response after a fixed amount of time. Subjects often exhibit a postreinforcement pause and then an accelerating response pattern. VI schedules are similar except that the time requirement is variable, and they typically produce moderate, steady responding.

Performance on a reinforcement schedule can be affected by the quality and amount of reinforcement, the response effort, and the individual's level of motivation and past experience. People may also respond according to rules they have been taught or have learned on their own. When reinforcement is discontinued, extinction is usually rapid after CRF, slower after FI or FR, and slowest after VI or VR.

Experimental analysis has shown that the postreinforcement pause on FR schedules occurs primarily because each reinforcer is a signal that many responses must be completed before the next reinforcer. Regarding the question of why VR schedules produce faster responding than VI schedules, IRT reinforcement theory states that long pauses are often reinforced on VI schedules, whereas bursts of rapid responses are more likely to be reinforced on VR schedules. A different theory states that subjects learn that more rapid responding yields more reinforcers on VR schedules but not on VI schedules.

Reinforcement schedules are frequently used in behavior therapy. Children with autism have been taught to speak by using positive reinforcement, shaping, prompting, and fading. Token systems and other reinforcement techniques have been used in some psychiatric hospitals, schools, and businesses. In behavior therapy for couples, contingency contracts help partners increase the exchange of positive reinforcers.

Review Questions

1. For each of the four basic reinforcement schedules, describe the rule for reinforcement, the typical response pattern, and the rate of extinction.

2. From your own experience, describe a situation that resembles one of the four simple reinforcement schedules. How is the reinforcement schedule in your example similar to the laboratory example? Are there any important differences between the two? Is the behavior pattern in real life similar to behavior in the laboratory?

3. What are some factors that can affect performance on a reinforcement schedule? Illustrate using concrete examples.

4. What is the difference between the molecular and molar theories of behavior? Describe a molecular theory and a molar theory of why responding is usually faster on VR schedules than on VI schedules.

5. Give a few examples of how the principles of operant conditioning have been used in behavior therapy. In describing the methods, identify as many different terms and principles of operant conditioning as you can.

REFERENCES

Anger, D. (1956). The dependence of interresponse times upon the relative reinforcement of different interresponse times. *Journal of Experimental Psychology, 52*, 145–161.

Baum, W.M. (1973). The correlation-based law of effect. *Journal of the Experimental Analysis of Behavior, 20*, 137–153.

Baxter, G.A., & Schlinger, H. (1990). Performance of children under a multiple random-ratio random-interval schedule of reinforcement. *Journal of the Experimental Analysis of Behavior, 54*, 263–271.

Bentall, R.P., & Lowe, C.F. (1987). The role of verbal behavior in human learning: III. Instructional effects in children. *Journal of the Experimental Analysis of Behavior, 47*, 177–190.

Blakely, E., & Schlinger, H. (1988). Determinants of pausing under variable-ratio schedules: Reinforcer magnitude, ratio size, and schedule configuration. *Journal of the Experimental Analysis of Behavior, 50*, 65–73.

Bullock, C.E., & Hackenberg, T.D. (2006). Second-order schedules of token reinforcement with pigeons: Implications for unit price. *Journal of the Experimental Analysis of Behavior, 85*, 95–106.

Camden, M.C., & Ludwig, T.D. (2013). Absenteeism in health care: Using interlocking behavioral contingency feedback to increase attendance with certified nursing assistants. *Journal of Organizational Behavior Management, 33*, 165–184.

Capaldi, E.J. (1966). Partial reinforcement: A hypothesis of sequential effects. *Psychological Review, 73*, 459–477.

Catania, A.C., Matthews, B.A., & Shimoff, E. (1982). Instructed versus shaped human verbal behavior: Interactions with nonverbal responding. *Journal of the Experimental Analysis of Behavior, 38*, 233–248.

Cavalier, A.R., Feretti, R.P., & Hodges, A.E. (1997). Self-management within a classroom token economy for students with learning disabilities. *Research in Developmental Disabilities, 18*, 167–178.

Cole, M.R. (1999). Molar and molecular control in variable-interval and variable-ratio schedules. *Journal of the Experimental Analysis of Behavior, 71*, 319–328.

Critchfield, T.S., Haley, R., Sabo, B., Colbert, J., & Macropoulis, G. (2003). A half century of scalloping in the work habits of the United States Congress. *Journal of Applied Behavior Analysis, 36*, 465–486.

Crossman, E.K., Bonem, E.J., & Phelps, B.J. (1987). A comparison of response patterns on fixed-, variable-, and random-ratio schedules. *Journal of the Experimental Analysis of Behavior, 48*, 395–406.

Cunningham, T.R., & Austin, J. (2007). Using goal setting, task clarification, and feedback to increase the use of the hands-free technique by hospital operating room staff. *Journal of Applied Behavior Analysis, 40*, 673–677.

Dallery, J., Glenn, I.M., & Raiff, B.R. (2007). An Internet-based abstinence reinforcement treatment for cigarette smoking. *Drug and Alcohol Dependence, 86*, 230–238.

Ferster, C.B., & Skinner, B.F. (1957). *Schedules of reinforcement.* New York: Appleton-Century-Crofts.

Fox, D.K., Hopkins, B.L., & Anger, W.K. (1987). The long-term effects of a token economy on safety performance in open-pit mining. *Journal of Applied Behavior Analysis, 20*, 215–224.

Glynn, S.M. (1990). Token economy approaches for psychiatric patients: Progress and pitfalls over 25 years. *Behavior Modification, 14*, 383–407.

Green, L., Kagel, J.H., & Battalio, R.C. (1987). Consumption-leisure tradeoffs in pigeons: Effects of changing marginal rates by varying amount of reinforcement. *Journal of the Experimental Analysis of Behavior, 47*, 17–28.

Hackenberg, T.R. (2009). Token reinforcement: A review and analysis. *Journal of the Experimental Analysis of Behavior, 91,* 257–286.

Halweg, K., & Markman, H.J. (1988). The effectiveness of behavioral marriage therapy: Empirical status of behavioral techniques in preventing and alleviating marital distress. *Journal of Consulting and Clinical Psychology, 56,* 440–447.

Horsley, R.R., Osborne, M., Norman, C., & Wells, T. (2012). High-frequency gamblers show increased resistance to extinction following partial reinforcement. *Behavioural Brain Research, 229,* 438–442.

Humphreys, L.G. (1939). The effect of random alternation of reinforcement on the acquisition and extinction of conditioned eyelid reactions. *Journal of Experimental Psychology, 25,* 141–158.

Jacobson, N.S. (1977). Problem solving and contingency contracting in the treatment of marital discord. *Journal of Consulting and Clinical Psychology, 45,* 92–100.

Jacobson, N.S., & Follette, W.C. (1985). Clinical significance of improvement resulting from two behavioral marital therapy components. *Behavior Therapy, 16,* 249–262.

Johnson, C.M., Redmon, W.K., & Mawhinney, T.C. (2001). *Handbook of organizational performance: Behavior analysis and management.* New York: Haworth Press.

Koegel, R.L., Bimbela, A., & Schreibman, L. (1996). Collateral effects of parent training on family interactions. *Journal of Autism and Developmental Disorders, 26,* 347–359.

Leander, J.D., Lippman, L.G., & Meyer, M.E. (1968). Fixed interval performance as related to subject's verbalization of the reinforcement contingency. *Psychological Record, 18,* 469–474.

Lovaas, O.I. (1967). A behavior therapy approach to the treatment of childhood schizophrenia. In J.P. Hill (Ed.), *Minnesota symposium on child psychology* (pp. 108–159). Minneapolis, MN: University of Minnesota Press.

Lovaas, O.I. (1987). Behavioral treatment and normal educational and intellectual functioning in young autistic children. *Journal of Consulting and Clinical Psychology, 55,* 3–9.

Lowe, C.F. (1979). Determinants of human operant behaviour. In M.D. Zeiler & P. Harzem (Eds.), *Advances in the analysis of behaviour: Vol. 1. Reinforcement and the organization of behaviour* (pp. 159–192). Chichester, England: Wiley.

Lydon, H., Healy, O., & Leader, G. (2011). A comparison of Video Modeling and Pivotal Response Training to teach pretend play skills to children with Autism Spectrum Disorder. *Research in Autism Spectrum Disorders, 5,* 872–884.

Macaskill, A.C., & Hackenberg, T.D. (2012). Providing a reinforcement history that reduces the sunk cost effect. *Behavioural Processes, 89,* 212–218.

Malagodi, E.F. (1967). Fixed-ratio schedules of token reinforcement. *Psychonomic Science, 8,* 469–470.

Matthews, B.A., Catania, A.C., & Shimoff, E. (1985). Effects of uninstructed verbal responding on nonverbal responding: Contingency descriptions versus performance descriptions. *Journal of the Experimental Analysis of Behavior, 43,* 155–164.

Matthews, B.A., Shimoff, E., Catania, A.C., & Sagvolden, T. (1977). Uninstructed human responding: Sensitivity to ratio and interval contingencies. *Journal of the Experimental Analysis of Behavior, 27,* 453–467.

Mawhinney, V.T., Bostow, D.E., Laws, D.R., Blumenfeld, G.J., & Hopkins, B.L. (1971). A comparison of students studying-behavior produced by daily, weekly, and three-week testing schedules. *Journal of Applied Behavior Analysis, 4,* 257–264.

Mazur, J.E., & Biondi, D.R. (2013). Pigeons' choices with token stimuli in concurrent variable-interval schedules. *Journal of the Experimental Analysis of Behavior, 99,* 159–178.

McEachin, J.J., Smith, T., & Lovaas, O.I. (1993). Long-term outcome for children with autism who received early intensive behavioral treatment. *American Journal of Mental Retardation, 97,* 359–372.

Milo, J.S., Mace, F.C., & Nevin, J.A. (2010). The effects of constant versus varied reinforcers on preference and resistance to change. *Journal of the Experimental Analysis of Behavior, 93*, 385–394.

Mintz, D.E., Mourer, D.J., & Gofseyeff, M. (1967). Sequential effects in fixed-ratio postreinforcement pause duration. *Psychonomic Science, 9*, 387–388.

Mowrer, O.H., & Jones, H. (1945). Habit strength as a function of the pattern of reinforcement. *Journal of Experimental Psychology, 35*, 293–311.

Nevin, J.A. (1974). Response strength in multiple schedules. *Journal of the Experimental Analysis of Behavior, 21*, 389–408.

Nevin, J.A. (1992). An integrative model for the study of behavioral momentum. *Journal of the Experimental Analysis of Behavior, 57*, 301–316.

Nevin, J.A., & Grace, R.C. (2000). Behavioral momentum and the law of effect. *Behavioral and Brain Sciences, 23*, 73–130.

Platt, J.R. (1979). Interresponse-time shaping by variable-interval-like interresponse-time reinforcement contingencies. *Journal of the Experimental Analysis of Behavior, 31*, 3–14.

Podlesnik, C.A., & Shahan, T.A. (2010). Extinction, relapse, and behavioral momentum. *Behavioural Processes, 84*, 400–410.

Powell, R.W. (1969). The effect of reinforcement magnitude upon responding under fixed-ratio schedules. *Journal of the Experimental Analysis of Behavior, 12*, 605–608.

Richards, J.B., Sabol, K.E., & Seiden, L.S. (1993). DRL interresponse-time distributions: Quantification by peak deviation analysis. *Journal of the Experimental Analysis of Behavior, 60*, 361–385.

Schaefer, H.H., & Martin, P.L. (1966). Behavioral therapy for "apathy" of schizophrenics. *Psychological Reports, 19*, 1147–1158.

Shimp, C.P. (1968). Magnitude and frequency of reinforcement and frequencies of interresponse times. *Journal of the Experimental Analysis of Behavior, 11*, 525–535.

Shimp, C.P. (1973). Synthetic variable-interval schedules of reinforcement. *Journal of the Experimental Analysis of Behavior, 19*, 311–330.

Skinner, B.F. (1938). *The behavior of organisms.* New York: Appleton-Century-Crofts.

Skinner, B.F. (1969). *Contingencies of reinforcement: A theoretical analysis.* Upper Saddle River, NJ: Prentice-Hall.

Tanno, T., & Sakagami, T. (2008). On the primacy of molecular processes in determining response rates under variable-ratio and variable-interval schedules. *Journal of the Experimental Analysis of Behavior, 89*, 5–14.

Vaughan, W. (1987). Dissociation of value and response strength. *Journal of the Experimental Analysis of Behavior, 48*, 367–381.

Ventola, P., Friedman, H.E., Anderson, L.C., Wolf, J.M., Oosting, D., Foss-Feig, J., & . . . Pelphrey, K.A. (2014). Improvements in social and adaptive functioning following short-duration PRT program: A clinical replication. *Journal of Autism and Developmental Disorders, 44*, 2862–2870.

Wallin, J.A., & Johnson, R.D. (1976). The positive reinforcement approach to controlling employee absenteeism. *Personnel Journal, 55*, 390–392.

Wanchisen, B.A., Tatham, T.A., & Mooney, S.E. (1989). Variable-ratio conditioning history produces high- and low-rate fixed-interval performance in rats. *Journal of the Experimental Analysis of Behavior, 52*, 167–179.

Wearden, J.H. (1988). Some neglected problems in the analysis of human behavior. In G. Davey & C. Cullen (Eds.), *Human operant conditioning and behavior modification* (pp. 197–224). Chichester, England: Wiley.

Weiner, H. (1964). Conditioning history and human fixed-interval performance. *Journal of the Experimental Analysis of Behavior, 7*, 383–385.

Weisberg, P., & Waldrop, P.B. (1972). Fixed-interval work habits of Congress. *Journal of Applied Behavior Analysis, 5*, 93–97.

West, C. (2013). Behavioral marital therapy, third wave. In A. Rambo, C. West, A. Schooley, & T.V. Boyd (Eds.), *Family therapy review: Contrasting contemporary models* (pp. 221–226). New York, NY, US: Routledge/Taylor & Francis Group.

Wilder, D.A., Austin, J., & Casella, S. (2009). Applying behavior analysis in organizations: Organizational behavior management. *Psychological Services, 6*, 202–211.

Wolfe, J.B. (1936). Effectiveness of token rewards for chimpanzees. *Comparative Psychology Monographs, 12*, 1–72.

CHAPTER 7

Avoidance and Punishment

Learning Objectives

After reading this chapter, you should be able to

- identify different procedures for increasing or decreasing behavior
- describe three theories of avoidance and explain their strengths and weaknesses
- discuss the phenomenon of learned helplessness as it occurs in animals and in people
- describe factors that determine whether punishment will be effective
- explain the disadvantages of using punishment as a method of controlling behavior
- describe different types of behavior decelerators and how they are used in behavior therapy

Chapters 5 and 6 were devoted to the topic of positive reinforcement, in which a response is followed by a reinforcer and as a result the response is strengthened. However, positive reinforcement is only one of four possible relationships between a behavior and its consequences. Figure 7.1 presents these four possibilities in the form of a two-by-two matrix. First, after a behavior occurs, a stimulus can be presented, or a stimulus can be removed or omitted. In each of these cases, the result could be either an increase or a decrease in the behavior, depending on the nature of the stimulus. Since we have already examined positive reinforcement, this chapter will focus on the other three cases.

We can begin with some definitions. With **negative reinforcement** (cell 3), a behavior increases if some stimulus is removed after the behavior occurs. For example, suppose a

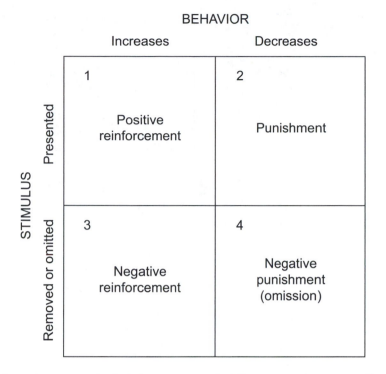

Figure 7.1 A two-by-two matrix depicting two types of reinforcement and two types of punishment.

person with a headache takes some ibuprofen, and the headache promptly goes away. In this case, the individual **escapes** from the pain of the headache by performing some behavior. As a result, this behavior should be strengthened in the future: The next time the person has a headache, he is likely to take ibuprofen again. Another type of negative reinforcement is **avoidance**, in which a response prevents an unpleasant stimulus from occurring in the first place. For example, paying your income tax avoids the unpleasant consequences of failing to do so.

Cell 2 represents the procedure of **punishment,** in which a behavior is followed by an unpleasant stimulus, and the behavior then decreases. Cell 4 represents **negative punishment** (also called **omission**) in which a pleasant stimulus is removed or omitted if a behavior occurs. If a parent refuses to give a child her usual weekly allowance after some bad behavior (such as staying out too late), this is an example of negative punishment. To help you remember these terms, Figure 7.2 gives a pictorial example of each.

The first part of this chapter surveys a number of experiments on negative reinforcement, and it discusses some of the theoretical issues about avoidance that psychologists have debated over the years. Next, we will look at the two types of punishment procedures. Although punishment is, in theory, the opposite of reinforcement, some psychologists have concluded that punishment is not an effective form of behavioral control. We will consider the evidence and attempt to draw some conclusions. Finally, we will examine some of the ways that punishment has been used in behavior modification.

Figure 7.2 Two types of reinforcement and two types of punishment. (1) Rewarding a dog for a new trick is positive reinforcement. (2) Getting burned from touching a hot skillet is punishment. (3) Driving around a pothole is negative reinforcement (avoidance). (4) Time-out for bad behavior is negative punishment (omission).

ESCAPE AND AVOIDANCE

A Representative Experiment

Solomon and Wynne (1953) conducted an experiment that illustrates many of the properties of negative reinforcement. Dogs were tested in a **shuttle box**—a chamber with two rectangular compartments separated by a barrier several inches high. A dog could move from one compartment to the other simply by jumping over the barrier. There were two overhead lights, one for each compartment. Every few minutes, the light above the dog was turned off (but the light in the other compartment remained on). If the dog remained in the dark compartment, after 10 seconds the dog received a shock from the floor of the chamber until it hopped over the barrier to the other compartment. Thus the dog could escape from the shock by jumping over the barrier. However, the dog could also *avoid* the shock completely by jumping over the barrier before the 10 seconds of darkness had elapsed. The next trial was the same, except that the dog had to jump back into the first compartment to escape or avoid the shock.

For the first few trials a typical dog's responses were escape responses—it did not jump over the barrier until the shock had started. After a few trials, a dog would start making avoidance responses—it would jump over the barrier soon after the light went out, and if it jumped in less than 10 seconds it did not receive the shock. After a few dozen trials, a typical dog would almost always jump over the barrier just 2 or 3 seconds after the light went out. Many dogs never again received a shock after their first successful avoidance response because they always jumped in less than 10 seconds after the light went out.

Results such as these had led earlier psychologists (e.g., Mowrer, 1947) to ponder a question that is sometimes called the **avoidance paradox**: How can the nonoccurrence of an event (shock) serve as a reinforcer for the avoidance response? These psychologists had no problem explaining escape responses because there the response produced an obvious stimulus change: The shock stopped when the escape response was made. But with avoidance responses, there was no such change: There was no shock before the avoidance response and no shock after it. Some theorists felt it did not make sense to say that no change in the stimulus conditions (no shock before the jump and no shock after) could act as a reinforcer for jumping. It was this puzzle about avoidance responses that led to the development of an influential theory of avoidance called **two-factor theory**, or two-process theory.

Two-Factor Theory

The two factors, or processes, of this theory are classical conditioning and operant conditioning, and according to the theory both are necessary for avoidance responses to occur. These two factors can be illustrated in the experiment of Solomon and Wynne. An unconditioned response to shock is fear. Through classical conditioning, this fear response is transferred from the unconditioned stimulus (shock) to a conditioned stimulus (the 10 seconds of darkness that preceded each shock). The second factor, based on operant conditioning, is escape from a fear-provoking CS. A dog could escape from a dark compartment to an illuminated compartment by jumping over the barrier. The crucial point is that in two-factor theory, what we have been calling *avoidance* responses is redefined as *escape* responses. The theory says that the reinforcer for jumping is not the avoidance of the shock but rather the escape from a fear-eliciting CS. Removing the fear-evoking CS (darkness) is an observable change in the stimulus environment that could certainly act as a negative reinforcer. This is two-factor theory's solution to the avoidance paradox.

Although two-factor theory became a popular explanation of avoidance behavior, it had some problems. One problem concerned the relation between fear and avoidance responses. If the theory is correct, we should observe an increase in fear when the signal for shock is presented and a decrease in fear once the avoidance response is made. However, observable signs of fear frequently disappear as animals become more experienced in avoidance tasks. Solomon and Wynne (1953) noted that early in their experiment a dog would show various signs of fear (whining, urination, shaking) when the light was turned off. Later, once the dog became proficient in making the avoidance response, these observable signs of emotion disappeared. But according to two-factor theory, fear should be greatest when avoidance responses are the strongest, since fear is supposedly what motivates the avoidance response.

To deal with this problem, some versions of two-factor theory have downplayed the role of fear in avoidance learning. For example, Dinsmoor (2001) has maintained that it is not necessary to assume that the CS in avoidance learning produces fear (as measured by heart rate or other physical signs). We only need to assume that the CS has become aversive (meaning that it has become a stimulus the animal will try to remove).

A second serious problem for two-factor theory is that avoidance responses are often very slow to extinguish. According to the principles of classical conditioning, the CR of fear (or aversion, if we use Dinsmoor's approach) should gradually weaken on every trial without shock. If the CS (lights off in the Solomon and Wynne experiment) no longer elicits fear or aversion, the avoidance response should not occur either. Therefore, two-factor theory predicts that avoidance responding should gradually deteriorate after a series of trials without shock. However, in the experiments of Solomon and Wynne, many dogs responded for several hundred trials without receiving a shock. In addition, their response latencies continued to decrease during these trials even though no shock was received. This suggests that the strength of the avoidance response was increasing, not decreasing, during these shock-free trials.

These findings were troublesome for two-factor theory, and many psychologists viewed the slow extinction of avoidance behavior as a major problem for the theory. To try to deal with these problems, two other theories of avoidance were developed.

One-Factor Theory

To put it simply, **one-factor theory** states that the classical conditioning component of two-factor theory is not necessary. There is no need to assume that escape from a fear-eliciting CS is the reinforcer for an avoidance response because, contrary to the assumptions of two-factor theory, avoidance of a shock can in itself serve as a reinforcer. An experiment by Murray Sidman (1953) illustrates this point.

In the **Sidman avoidance task** (or **free–operant avoidance**), there is no signal preceding shock, but if the subject makes no responses, shocks occur at perfectly regular intervals. For instance, in one condition of Sidman's experiment, a rat would receive a shock every 5 seconds throughout the session if it made no avoidance response (Figure 7.3a). However, if the rat made an avoidance response (pressing a lever), the next shock did not occur until 30 seconds after the response. Each response postponed the next shock for 30 seconds (Figure 7.3b). By responding regularly (say, once every 20 to 25 seconds), a rat could avoid all the shocks. In practice, Sidman's rats did not avoid all the shocks, but they did respond frequently enough to avoid many of them.

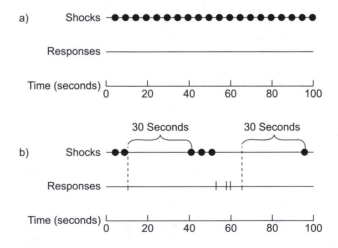

Figure 7.3 The procedure in one condition of Sidman's (1953) avoidance task. (a) If the subject makes no responses, a shock is delivered every 5 seconds. (b) Each response postpones the next shock for 30 seconds.

On the surface, these results seem to pose a problem for two-factor theory because there is no signal before a shock. If there is no fear-eliciting CS, why does an avoidance response occur? Actually, two-factor theorists had a simple answer to this question. Although there was no external CS in Sidman's task, the passage of time might serve as a CS because the shocks occurred at regular intervals. That is, once a rat was familiar with the procedure, its fear might increase as more and more time elapsed without a response. The rat could associate fear with the stimulus "a long time since the last response," and it could remove this stimulus (and the associated fear) by making a response.

To make a better case for one-factor theory, we need an experiment in which neither an external stimulus nor the passage of time could serve as a reliable signal that a shock was approaching. To accomplish this, Herrnstein and Hineline (1966) developed a procedure in which the passage of time was not a reliable signal that a shock was approaching. The basic idea was that by pressing a lever, a rat could switch from a schedule that delivered shocks at a rapid rate to one that delivered shocks at a slower rate. For example, in one condition there was a 30% chance of shock if the rat had not recently pressed the lever but only a 10% chance if the rat had recently pressed the lever. Obviously, to reduce the number of shocks, the animal should remain on the 10% schedule as much as possible. However, the key feature of this procedure was that pressing the lever did not ensure any amount of shock-free time. Sometimes, just by chance, a rat would press the lever and get a shock almost immediately. This is because lever pressing in this procedure only produced a lower rate of shocks on average; it did not guarantee any fixed shock-free time.

Herrnstein and Hineline (1966) found that 17 of their 18 rats eventually acquired the avoidance response. They concluded (1) that animals can learn an avoidance response when neither an external CS nor the passage of time is a reliable signal for shock and (2) that to master this task, animals must be sensitive to the average shock frequencies when they respond and when they do not respond. They reasoned that the fear-conditioning factor in two-factor theory is a needless complication: Why not simply assume that a reduction in shock frequency is the reinforcer for the avoidance response? For this reason, one-factor theory of avoidance is sometimes called the *shock-frequency reduction* theory (Hineline, 2001).

One-factor theory offers a simple explanation for the slow extinction of avoidance responses. We have seen that once an avoidance response is acquired, the animal may avoid every scheduled shock by making the appropriate response. Now suppose that at some point the experimenter turns off the shock generator. From the animal's perspective, the following trials will appear no different from the previous trials: The stimulus comes on, the subject responds, the stimulus goes off, no shock occurs. Since the animal can discriminate no change in the conditions, there is no change in behavior either, according to this reasoning.

Cognitive Theory

Seligman and Johnston (1973) developed a **cognitive theory of avoidance** that they felt was superior to both two-factor and one-factor theories. They proposed that in a typical avoidance task an animal gradually develops two expectations: (1) no shock will occur if it makes an avoidance response and (2) shock will occur if it does not make the response. Because the animal prefers the first option over the second option, it makes the response.

Once these two expectations have been formed, Seligman and Johnston assumed that the animal's behavior will not change until one or both of the expectations are violated. This can explain the slow extinction of avoidance behavior. As long as the animal responds on each extinction trial, all it can observe is that a response is followed by no shock. This observation is consistent with the animal's expectation, so there is no change in its behavior. Presumably, extinction will only begin to occur if the animal eventually fails to make a response on some trial (perhaps by mistake, or because it is distracted, or for some such reason). Only on a trial without an avoidance response can the animal observe an outcome (no response leads to no shock) that is inconsistent with its expectations.

A variation of cognitive theory proposed by Lovibond (2006) maintains that individuals can learn more detailed expectations that include information about the three parts of the three-term contingency (discriminative stimulus, operant response, and consequence). For instance, an individual might learn that in the presence of one warning signal, a specific response will avoid one type of aversive event, but if another warning signal occurs, a different avoidance response is required to avoid a different aversive event. Research with college students has found that they can and do develop these more elaborate three-part expectations in avoidance tasks (Declercq, De Houwer, & Baeyens, 2008).

Biological Constraints in Avoidance Learning

As if the theoretical analysis of avoidance was not confusing enough, the picture is further complicated by evidence that biological constraints can also play an important role in avoidance learning, just as they can in classical conditioning and with the use of positive reinforcement. Robert Bolles (1970) proposed that animals exhibit a type of preparedness in avoidance learning. In this case, the preparedness consists of a propensity to perform certain behaviors in a potentially dangerous situation. Bolles was critical of the traditional theories of avoidance learning. He stated:

> What keeps our little friends alive in the forest has nothing to do with avoidance learning as we ordinarily conceive of it or investigate it in the laboratory. . . . What keeps animals alive in the wild is that they have very effective innate defensive reactions which occur when they encounter any kind of new or sudden stimulus.

(pp. 32–33)

Bolles called these innate behavior patterns **species–specific defense reactions (SSDRs).** As the name implies, SSDRs may be different for different animals, but Bolles suggested that they usually fall into one of three categories: freezing, fleeing, and fighting (adopting an aggressive posture and/or behaviors). In laboratory studies of avoidance, an avoidance response will be quickly learned if it is identical with or at least similar to one of the subject's SSDRs. If the required avoidance response is not similar to an SSDR, the response will be learned slowly or not at all. To support this hypothesis, Bolles noted that rats can learn to avoid a shock by jumping or running out of a compartment in one or only a few trials. The rapid acquisition presumably reflects the fact that for rats, fleeing is a highly probable response to danger. However, it is very difficult to train a rat to avoid shock by pressing a lever, presumably because this response is unlike any of the creature's typical responses to danger (Figure 7.4).

Figure 7.4 Running or fleeing, a species–specific defense reaction for many animals, is obviously incompatible with making an operant response such as pressing a lever. (ziggy_mars/Shutterstock)

The important point here is that the difficulty in learning new responses such as lever pressing depends on the nature of the reinforcer. When the reinforcer is avoidance of shock, lever pressing is a difficult response for rats to acquire, and some rats never learn it. Yet when the reinforcer is food or water, lever pressing is a relatively easy response for rats to learn. As another example, we know it is quite easy to shape a pigeon to peck a key when food is the reinforcer. In comparison, it is very difficult to train a pigeon to peck a key to avoid a shock. The problem is apparently that a pigeon's most usual response to an aversive stimulus is to fly away, a response that has almost nothing in common with standing in place and pecking. Because of examples like this, Fanselow (1997) has argued that the basic principle of negative reinforcement (which states that any response that helps to avoid an aversive event will be strengthened) is not especially useful when SSDRs take over: Even a simple response such as pressing a lever or pecking a key may be difficult for the animal to learn.

A few studies have shown that it is possible to train animals to make an arbitrary operant response in an avoidance situation by somehow making the desired response more compatible with the SSDRs of that species. For example, in response to a mild shock, a pigeon may exhibit SSDRs from the "fighting" category, including flapping its wings. Beginning with this response of wing flapping, Rachlin (1969) trained pigeons to operate a "key" that protruded into the chamber in order to avoid the shock. With rats, Modaresi (1990) found that lever pressing was much easier to train as an avoidance response if the lever was higher on the wall, and especially if lever presses not only avoided the shocks but produced a "safe area" (a platform) on which the rats could stand. Modaresi showed that these two features coincided with the rats' natural tendencies to stretch upward and to seek a safe area when facing a potentially painful stimulus. Both of these studies are consistent with Bolles's claim that the ease of learning an avoidance response depends on the similarity between that response and one of the animal's SSDRs.

Conclusions About the Theories of Avoidance

Over the years, two-factor theory has been a popular theory of avoidance behavior, but it has several problems. Avoidance learning can occur when there is no external signal for shock (Herrnstein & Hineline, 1966). In addition, two-factor theory has difficulty explaining the slowness of extinction in avoidance tasks. Both one-factor theory and cognitive theory avoid these problems by assuming that a fear-eliciting CS is not an indispensable requirement for avoidance behavior. However, we have seen evidence that fear does play a role in some avoidance situations, and for this and other reasons some learning theorists have continued to favor two-factor theory over the other two theories. After several decades of research and debate, the question of which theory of avoidance is best has not been settled to everyone's satisfaction. This may be a sign that each theory is partially correct. Perhaps fear does play an important role in some avoidance situations, but it is not a necessary role; avoidance responding may sometimes occur in the absence of fear, as the one-factor and cognitive theories propose.

BOX 7.1   APPLYING THE RESEARCH

The Procedure of Response Blocking (Flooding)

The slow extinction of avoidance responses is not inevitable: Extinction can be speeded up by using a procedure called **response blocking** (also called **flooding**). As its name suggests, response blocking involves presenting the signal that precedes shock but preventing the subject from making the avoidance response. In one experiment, rats learned to avoid a shock by running from one compartment to another (Page & Hall, 1953). After the response was learned, one group of rats received normal extinction trials. A second group had the extinction trials preceded by five trials in which a rat was retained in the first compartment for 15 seconds, with the door to the second compartment closed. Thus these rats were prevented from making the avoidance response, but unlike in the acquisition phase, they received no shocks in the first compartment. Extinction proceeded much more rapidly in the response-blocking group. There is considerable evidence that response blocking is an effective way to accelerate the extinction of avoidance responses.

This procedure has been adopted by some behavior therapists as a treatment for phobias. The major difference between flooding and systematic desensitization

(Chapter 3) is that the hierarchy of fearful events or stimuli is eliminated. Instead of beginning with a stimulus that elicits only a small amount of fear, a therapist using a flooding procedure starts immediately with a highly feared stimulus and forces the patient to remain in the presence of this stimulus until the patient's external signs of fear subside. For example, an 11-year-old boy with a fear of loud noises was exposed to the noise of many bursting balloons in a small room (with the boy's full consent and that of his parents). He was encouraged by the therapist to break balloons himself, and within two sessions his fear of the noises had disappeared (Yule, Sacks, & Hersov, 1974).

Studies comparing the effectiveness of flooding and systematic desensitization have found that they are about equally effective (Morganstern, 1973), but flooding can sometimes succeed in eliminating a phobia when systematic desensitization has failed. Yule et al. (1974) cautioned that flooding should be used with care and that long-duration sessions are essential: The therapist should first observe the onset of fear, and then continue with the procedure until a definite reduction in fear is seen. If the session is terminated too soon, the patient's phobia might actually increase. Despite these drawbacks, flooding can be an effective form of treatment for phobias when used carefully (Zoellner, Abramowitz, Moore, & Slagle, 2009).

Other behavioral treatments also rely on prolonged stimulus exposure to eliminate unwanted behaviors. For example, patients with obsessive-compulsive disorders (which involve repeatedly and excessively engaging in rituals such as hand washing, checking to make sure doors are locked, etc.) can be treated by exposing them to the stimuli that trigger these reactions while preventing them from performing the ritualistic behaviors (Abramowitz & Foa, 2000). Research has shown that this approach can be effective in reducing compulsive behaviors.

LEARNED HELPLESSNESS

Aversive stimuli can do more than produce fear and avoidance responses. Abundant research with both animals and people has shown that repeated exposure to aversive events that are unpredictable and out of the individual's control can have long-term debilitating effects. Seligman and his colleagues (Maier & Seligman, 1976) have proposed that in such circumstances, both animals and people may develop the expectation that their behavior has little effect on their environment, and this expectation may generalize to a wide range of situations. Seligman calls this general expectation **learned helplessness**. Consider the following experiment. A dog is first placed in a harness where it receives a series inescapable shocks. On the next day, the dog is placed in a shuttle box where it receives escape/avoidance trials similar to those administered by Solomon and Wynne (1953): A 10-second period of darkness is followed by shock unless the dog jumps into the other compartment. Whereas Solomon and Wynne's dogs learned the task within a few trials, about two thirds of Seligman's dogs never learned either to escape or avoid the shock. Seligman concluded that in the initial training with inescapable shock, the dogs developed an expectation that its behavior has no effect on the aversive consequences it experiences, and this expectation of helplessness carried over to the shuttle box.

Similar experiments have been conducted with humans. For instance, in one study (Hiroto & Seligman, 1975) college students were first presented with a series of loud noises that they could not avoid. They were then asked to solve a series of anagrams. These students had much greater difficulty solving the anagrams than students who were not exposed to the unavoidable noises. A typical control participant solved all the anagrams and got faster and faster as the trials proceeded. A typical participant in the noise group would fail on most of the problems, apparently giving up on a problem before the allotted time had expired. Seligman's explanation was the same for both the animal and human cases: Early experience with uncontrollable aversive events produces a sense of helplessness that carries over into other situations, leading to learning and performance deficits.

Many psychologists believe that learned helplessness can contribute to the severe and prolonged periods of depression that some people experience. Hundreds of studies have been published on learned helplessness in humans, and this research has branched in many directions. Psychologists have applied the concept of learned helplessness to women who have been the victims of domestic violence (Walker, 2009), to the ability of the elderly to cope with their problems (Flannery, 2002), to new employees who experience failures in the workplace (Boichuk et al., 2014), and to many other situations where people might feel that they have little control over important events in their lives.

Seligman suggested that learned helplessness can be prevented through what he called *immunization*. If an animal's first exposure to shock is one where it can control the shock, later exposure to uncontrollable shocks is less likely to produce learned helplessness. At the human level, Seligman suggested that feelings of helplessness in a classroom environment may be prevented by making sure that a child's earliest classroom experiences are ones where the child succeeds (ones where the child demonstrates a mastery over the task at hand). McKean (1994) has made similar suggestions for helping college students who exhibit signs of helplessness in academic settings. Such students tend to view course work as uncontrollable, aversive, and inescapable. They assume that they are going to do poorly and give up easily whenever they experience difficulty with course assignments or other setbacks. To assist such students, McKean suggests that professors should make their courses as predictable and controllable as possible (e.g., by clearly listing all course requirements on the syllabus, by explaining the skills students will need to succeed in the course, and by suggesting how to develop these skills). Initial course assignments should be ones that students are likely to complete successfully, so they gain confidence that they have the ability to master the requirements of the course.

Seligman (2006) has also proposed that a method for combating learned helplessness and depression is to train people in **learned optimism**. The training involves a type of cognitive therapy in which people practice thinking about potentially bad situations in more positive ways. For instance, a middle-aged woman taking a college course might be disappointed with her exam grade and think, "I am too old for this. I bet everyone else did better than I did. It was a mistake for me to return to college now." Seligman proposes that this type of helpless thinking can be changed if a person learns to recognize and dispute such negative thoughts. For instance, the woman could think, "A grade of B– is not that bad. I am working full time and did not have as much time to prepare as I would like. Now that I know what to expect, I will do better on the next exam." Seligman argues that by regularly practicing the technique of disputing one's thoughts of helplessness and dejection, a person can learn to avoid them. Some writers have questioned the effectiveness of Seligman's techniques to teach optimism (e.g., Kelley, 2004), but others have found that they can be beneficial (Gilboy, 2005). Perhaps it should not be too surprising that just as learned helplessness can result from experiences with uncontrollable aversive events, there may be other learning experiences that can result in learned optimism.

PRACTICE QUIZ 1: CHAPTER 7

1. Two types of negative reinforcement are _____ and _____.
2. According to the two-factor theory of avoidance, a _____ develops to an initially neutral stimulus that precedes an aversive event.
3. Extinguishing an avoidance response by physically preventing the individual from making the response is called _____.
4. _____ are behaviors such as fleeing, freezing, or fighting that animals tend to make in dangerous situations.
5. According to Seligman, teaching people to think about potentially bad situations in more positive ways can lead to _____.

ANSWERS

1. escape, avoidance 2. fear response 3. response blocking or flooding 4. SSDRs 5. learned optimism

---

RESEARCH ON PUNISHMENT

Is Punishment the Opposite of Reinforcement?

According to Figure 7.1, punishment should have the opposite effect on behavior as positive reinforcement: Reinforcement should increase behavior, and punishment should decrease behavior. Whether this is actually the case is an empirical question, however, and such illustrious psychologists as Thorndike and Skinner concluded that it was not. Based his own research, Skinner concluded that punishment produces only a "temporary suppression" of behavior.

Are the effects of punishment merely temporary? In some cases they can be, and animals can habituate to a relatively mild punisher. In an experiment by Azrin (1960), pigeons were responding steadily for food on a VI schedule, and then punishment was introduced—each response produced a mild shock. Response rates decreased immediately, but over the course of several sessions, they returned to their preshock levels. However, when Azrin used more intense shocks, there was little or no recovery in responding over the course of the experiment. Based on these and other similar results, there is no doubt that suitably intense punishment can produce a permanent decrease or disappearance of the punished behavior.

Although Skinner did not define suppression, later writers took it to mean a general decrease in behavior that is not limited to the particular behavior that is being punished.

Does the use of punishment lead to a general reduction in all behavior, or does only the punished behavior decrease? An experiment by Schuster and Rachlin (1968) investigated this question. Pigeons could sometimes peck at the left key in a test chamber, and at other times they could peck at the right key. Both keys offered identical VI schedules of food reinforcement, but then different schedules of shock were introduced on the two keys. When the left key was lit (signaling that the VI schedule was available on this key), some of the pigeon's key pecks were followed by shock. However, when the right key was lit, shocks were presented regardless of whether the pigeon pecked at the key. Under these conditions, responding on the left key decreased markedly, but there was little change in response rate on the right key.

Studies like this have established that punishment does more than simply cause a general decrease in activity. When a particular behavior is punished, that behavior will exhibit a large decrease in frequency while other, unpunished behaviors usually show no substantial change. To summarize, contrary to the predictions of Thorndike and Skinner, research results suggest that the effects of punishment are directly opposite to those of reinforcement: Reinforcement produces an increase in whatever specific behavior is followed by the hedonically positive stimulus, and punishment produces a decrease in the specific behavior that is followed by the aversive stimulus. In both cases, we can expect these changes in behavior to persist as long as the reinforcement or punishment contingency remains in effect.

Factors Influencing the Effectiveness of Punishment

Many years ago, Azrin and Holz (1966) examined a number of variables that determine what effects a punishment contingency will have. To their credit, all of their major points appear as valid now as when their findings were published. Several of their points are described in this section.

Manner of Introduction

If one's goal is to obtain a large, permanent decrease in some behavior, then Azrin and Holz (1966) recommended that the punisher be immediately introduced at its full intensity. We have already seen that subjects can habituate to a mild punisher. The end result is that a given intensity of punishment may completely eliminate a behavior if it is introduced suddenly, but it may have little or no effect on behavior if it is approached gradually. Azrin, Holz, and Hake (1963) reported that a shock of 80 volts following each response completely stopped pigeons' key-peck responses if the 80-volt intensity was used from the outset. However, if the punishment began at lower intensities and then slowly increased, the pigeons continued to respond even when the intensity was raised to as much as 130 volts. Since the goal when using punishment is to eliminate an undesirable behavior, not to shape a tolerance of the aversive stimulus, the punisher should be at its maximum intensity the first time it is presented.

Immediacy of Punishment

Just as the most effective reinforcer is one that is delivered immediately after the operant response, a punisher that immediately follows a response is most effective in decreasing the frequency of the response. The importance of delivering punishment immediately may explain why many common forms of punishment are ineffective. For example, the mother who tries to decrease a child's misbehavior with the warning, "Just wait until your father gets home," is describing a very long delay between a behavior and its punishment. It would not be surprising if this contingency had little effect on the child's behavior. The same principle applies in the classroom where a scolding from the teacher is most effective if the teacher scolds a child immediately after the child has misbehaved, not after some time has passed (Abramowitz & O'Leary, 1990). It has also been suggested that one reason some people engage in crimes even though they are likely to get caught eventually is that they receive the rewards immediately but the punishment is delayed. A large-scale study of adolescents in the United States concluded that those who were involved in crimes such as burglary or car theft tended to be less sensitive to delayed consequences than those who never engaged in these criminal activities (Nagin & Pogarsky, 2004).

Schedule of Punishment

Like positive reinforcers, punishers need not be delivered after every occurrence of a behavior. Azrin and Holz concluded, however, that the most effective way to eliminate a behavior is to punish every response rather than to use some intermittent schedule of punishment. In an experiment with rats where lever pressing for food also produced shocks on an FR schedule, the effects of this punishment decreased as the size of the FR increased (Azrin et al., 1963). The same general rule applies to human behavior: The most powerful way to reduce behavior is to punish every occurrence (Hare, 2006). The schedule of punishment can also affect the response patterns over time, and they are often the opposite of those obtained with positive reinforcement. For example, whereas an FI schedule of reinforcement produces an accelerating pattern of responding, an FI schedule can produce a deceleration—declining response rates as the next punisher approaches (Azrin, 1956). FR schedules of reinforcement produce a pause-then-respond pattern, but FR schedules of punishment produce a respond-then-pause pattern (Hendry & Van-Toller, 1964). These and other studies on schedules of punishment strengthen the view that punishment is the opposite of reinforcement in its effects on behavior.

Motivation to Respond

Azrin and Holz noted that the effectiveness of a punishment procedure is inversely related to the intensity of the individual's motivation to respond. Azrin et al. (1963) demonstrated this point by observing the effects of punishment on pigeons' food-reinforced responses when the birds were maintained at different levels of food deprivation. Punishment had little effect on response rates when the pigeons were very hungry, but when these animals were only slightly food deprived, the same intensity of punishment produced a complete cessation of responding. This finding is not surprising, and its implications for human behavior should be clear: If a behavior is highly motivated (e.g., parents stealing food because their children are starving), the threat of punishment is not likely to have much effect.

Reinforcement of Alternative Behaviors

Based on their research with animals, Azrin and Holz concluded that punishment is much more effective when the individual is provided with an alternative way to obtain the reinforcer. For instance, it is much easier to use punishment to stop a pigeon from pecking at a response key that delivers food if another key is available that also produces food (without punishment). For this reason, when behavior therapists decide that it is necessary to use punishment to eliminate some unwanted behavior (e.g., fighting among children), they almost always pair this punishment with reinforcement for an alternative behavior that is incompatible with the unwanted behavior (e.g., cooperative play). A study with four children who engaged in frequent self-injurious behaviors (hitting themselves, head banging) showed how the mere availability of an alternative source of reinforcement can increase the effectiveness of a punishment procedure (Thompson, Iwata, Conners, & Roscoe, 1999). Before treatment began, a suitable reinforcer was found for each child, such as a toy, a game, or a string of beads. During treatment, every instance of a self-injurious behavior was followed by mild punishment (such as brief physical restraint, or a reprimand—"Don't do that!"). On some days, the alternative reinforcer preferred by each child was available, whereas on other days the alternative reinforcer was not available. Figure 7.5 shows that for each child, the punishment was more effective in reducing self-injurious behavior when the alternative reinforcer was available.

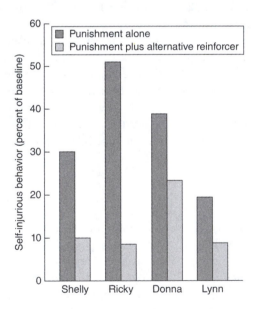

Figure 7.5 Frequency of self-injurious behavior (plotted as a percentage of the frequency before treatment began) is shown for four children under conditions with punishment alone and with punishment plus the availability of an alternative reinforcer. (Based on Thompson et al., 1999)

Punishment as a Discriminative Stimulus

Imagine an experiment in which a pigeon's responses go unpunished during some portions of the session but are followed by shock during other parts of the session. Each time the shock begins, the pigeon's response rate increases! This behavior seems paradoxical until we learn that the pigeon can obtain food only during those periods when its responses are punished; an extinction schedule is in effect during the periods when responses are not shocked (Holz & Azrin, 1961). In other words, the shocks following responses served as discriminative stimuli for the availability of food reinforcement because they were the only stimuli that differentiated between the periods of reinforcement and extinction. Azrin and Holz suggested that similar explanations may account for some instances of self-injurious behaviors that appear equally paradoxical at first glance. Because self-injurious behaviors often bring to the individual the reinforcers of sympathy and attention, the aversive aspects of this type of behavior (pain) may serve as discriminative stimuli that reinforcement is imminent.

Disadvantages of Using Punishment

Although Azrin and Holz (1966) concluded that punishment can be a method of behavior change that is at least as effective as reinforcement, they warned that it can produce a number of undesirable side effects. First, they noted that punishment can elicit several emotional effects, such as fear and anger, which are generally disruptive of learning and performance. A study on guard dogs that had been trained through the use of a shock collar found that these dogs exhibited signs of fear and stress whenever their owner was present, even when they were not in the training situation (Schilder & van der Borg, 2004). Similarly, many studies have found that the children of parents who use corporal punishment have a higher risk of developing anxiety disorders (Graham & Weems, 2015).

Second, punishment can sometimes lead to a general suppression of all behaviors, not only the behavior being punished. Imagine that a child in a classroom raised his hand, asked a question, and the teacher replied, "Well, that's a very stupid question." The teacher's remark might be intended to try to reduce the number of stupid questions that children ask, but the likely result would be a decrease in all questions, good or bad, both from that child and from everyone else in the class.

A third disadvantage is that in real-world situations the use of punishment demands the continual monitoring of the individual's behavior. In contrast, use of reinforcement does not necessarily demand such monitoring because it is in the individual's interest to point out instances of a behavior that is followed by a reinforcer. If a child receives a reinforcer for cleaning up her room, she will probably make sure her parents see the room after it is cleaned. On the other hand, if the child is punished for a messy room, she is unlikely to call her parents to see the messy room so that she can be punished.

Along the same lines, a practical problem with the use of punishment is that individuals may try to circumvent the rules or escape from the situation entirely. Azrin and Holz (1966) described the behavior of a clever rat that was scheduled to receive shocks for some of its lever presses while working for food reinforcement. The rat learned to avoid the shocks by lying on its back while pressing the lever, thereby using its fur as insulation from the shocks delivered via the metal floor of the chamber. We might expect people to be even more ingenious in their tricks to circumvent a punishment contingency. If a teacher's primary method of behavioral control in the classroom is punishment, the children will surely try to hide evidence of any misbehavior. They may also try to avoid school altogether by pretending to be sick or by playing hooky.

Another problem with using punishment is that it can lead to aggression against either the punisher or whoever happens to be around. The constant risk of bodily harm faced by prison guards (and by prisoners) attests to this fact. Aggression as a response to aversive stimulation is not unique to humans. Ulrich and Azrin (1962) reported a study in which two rats were placed in an experimental chamber. The animals behaved peaceably until they began to receive shocks, at which point they began to fight. Similar results have been obtained with pigeons, mice, hamsters, cats, and monkeys.

A final problem with using punishment is that in institutional settings, the people who must actually implement a behavior modification program may be reluctant to use punishment. Various studies have examined the attitudes of personnel who work with institutionalized patients, such as individuals with a developmental handicap. The staff in such institutions preferred other techniques for changing behavior, such as instruction, modeling, and reinforcement, over punishment (Davis & Russell, 1990). Perhaps these individuals have learned, through their daily work experiences, about some of the disadvantages of punishment described in the preceding paragraphs.

Given the numerous disadvantages of punishment, Azrin and Holz suggested that it should be used reluctantly and with great care. However, they pointed out that punishment will always be a part of our environment. It might be possible to legislate punishment out of existence in institutions such as prisons, schools, and psychiatric hospitals. It would be much more difficult, however, to eliminate punishment in everyday interpersonal interactions (between parent and child, between spouses, etc.). Finally, the physical environment is full of potential punishers that are impossible to eliminate. Just think of the possible punishing consequences that might follow the wrong behavior while one is driving a car, walking through a forest, swimming, skiing, cooking, or performing almost any behavior. As Vollmer (2002, p. 469) put it, "Punishment happens." Since punishment cannot be eliminated from our environment, it is important for behavioral psychologists to continue to study this phenomenon in order to increase our understanding of how it influences behavior.

Negative Punishment (Omission)

Cell 4 in Figure 7.1 represents the procedure of negative punishment or omission in which some stimulus is removed if a response occurs, resulting in a decrease in responding. The possibility of losing a reinforcer can have strong effects on behavior. In one study, college students played a game in which they could win or lose money by clicking on moving targets on a computer screen. Whenever money could be lost by choosing a particular target, the students showed a strong tendency to avoid that target. Based on a quantitative analysis of the students' choices, the researchers estimated that the punishing effect of losing money was about three times as powerful as the reinforcing effect of winning the same amount of money (Rasmussen & Newland, 2008). Omission procedures are most effective if the omission occurs immediately after the undesired behavior, every time the behavior occurs. In one case, therapists used time-outs to discourage an adult with developmental disabilities from putting his hands in his mouth (which caused his hands to become red and swollen). Time-outs reduced hand-mouthing action to near-zero levels if they occurred on a schedule of continuous punishment, but the time-outs had much less effect if they were delivered on FI schedules (Lerman, Iwata, Shore, & DeLeon, 1997). With both positive and negative punishment, immediacy and consistency are important.

BEHAVIOR DECELERATORS IN BEHAVIOR THERAPY

The term **behavior decelerator** is sometimes used to refer to any technique that can lead to a slowing, reduction, or elimination of unwanted behaviors. Punishment and omission are two of the most obvious methods for reducing undesired behaviors, but they are by no means the only ones. Behavior therapists have developed a variety of other useful behavior deceleration techniques, and we will examine some of the most common ones.

Punishment

Wherever possible, behavior therapists avoid using punishment because the comfort and happiness of the patient is one of their major concerns. However, if a behavior is dangerous or otherwise undesirable, and if other techniques are impractical or unsuccessful, the use of punishment may be deemed preferable to doing nothing at all.

One nonphysical form of punishment that is frequently used by parents and teachers is scolding or reprimanding a child for bad behavior. This tactic can certainly influence a child's behavior, but not always in the way the adult wants. The problem is that a reprimand is a form of attention, and we have already seen that attention can be a powerful reinforcer. O'Leary, Kaufman, Kass, and Drabman (1970) found that the manner in which a reprimand is given is a major factor determining its effectiveness. Most teachers use loud or public reprimands that are heard not only by the child involved but by all others in the classroom. However, when second-grade teachers were instructed to use "soft" or private reprimands wherever possible (i.e., to walk up to the child and speak quietly, so that no other children could hear), they observed a 50% decrease in disruptive behavior.

Stronger forms of punishment are sometimes necessary when a child's behavior is a more serious problem than a mere classroom disturbance. For example, some children with autism or developmental disabilities engage in self-injurious behaviors such as repeatedly slapping themselves in the face, biting deep into their skin, or banging their heads against any solid object. Because of the risk of severe injury, these children are sometimes kept in physical restraints around the clock, except when a therapist is in the immediate vicinity. Prochaska, Smith, Marzilli, Colby, and Donovan (1974) described the treatment of a 9-year-old girl who would hit her nose and chin with her fist at a rate of about 200 blows per hour if she was not restrained. After nonaversive procedures were tried unsuccessfully, the therapists decided to use a shock to her leg as a punisher for head banging. After receiving several half-second shocks, the girl's head banging stopped completely, and there was an overall improvement in her behavior. The use of shock as a punisher with children is a controversial matter (see Box 7.2), but to be fair, the aversive features of this procedure must be weighed against the consequences of doing nothing.

One promising development in the treatment of self-injurious behaviors is the finding that sometimes relatively mild punishers can be effective. For example, Fehr and Beckwith (1989) found that head hitting by a 10-year-old boy with a handicap could be reduced by spraying a water mist in the child's face. This treatment was especially effective when used in combination with reinforcement for other, better behavior. Water mist has also been successfully used to reduce aggression and other unwanted behaviors (Matson & Duncan, 1997).

BOX 7.2   IN THE MEDIA

Punishment Can Be Effective, but Should It Be Used in Therapy?

Showing that punishment *can* be used successfully is not the same as showing that it *should* be used as a technique of behavioral control. In recent years, the controversy over whether behavior therapists should be allowed to use aversive stimuli to control the behavior of their patients has intensified. Much of the controversy has focused on the treatment of children or adults with severe developmental and behavioral disorders. With these individuals, aversive stimuli are sometimes used to eliminate self-destructive or other dangerous behaviors.

One line of argument against the use of aversive stimuli is based on legal principles. In the United States, an important principle is the "right to refuse treatment." This principle states that even if a treatment is known to be effective, and even if the treatment is clearly in the best interests of the individual, that individual has the right to refuse the treatment. For example, a person could refuse to have an infected tooth extracted even if failure to remove the tooth could cause a life-threatening spread of the infection. It is easy to imagine a person refusing a behavioral treatment that involved aversive stimuli, even if the treatment would be beneficial in the long run. In the case of people with developmental disabilities, the issue is even more complicated because these people are usually classified as "incompetent" to make their own decisions, and treatment decisions must be made by their legal guardians.

Those who work with the developmentally disabled are divided on this issue. Some therapists are against the use of aversive stimuli under any circumstances for ethical reasons, while others argue that it would be unethical to restrict the use of the most effective treatments available, even if they involve aversives. Psychologists also disagree about the effectiveness of aversive treatments and how they compare to nonaversive procedures. Some claim that nonaversive alternatives (e.g., reinforcement of alternative behaviors, shaping, extinction, etc.) can be just as effective, but others disagree, arguing that the data have not yet shown that nonaversive techniques can be equally effective for severe behavior problems.

No one advocates the unrestricted and indiscriminate use of aversive stimuli as a means of behavior control. The debate is about whether aversive procedures should only be used as a last resort or whether they should never be used at all (Vollmer, Peters, & Slocum, 2015). Perhaps, as time passes, a combination of ethical debate, court decisions, and more data about the effectiveness of alternative techniques will help to settle this issue. For now, the future of aversive stimuli in behavioral treatments remains unclear.

Negative Punishment: Response Cost and Time-Out

It is easy to incorporate a negative punishment contingency in any token system: Whereas tokens can be earned by performing desirable behaviors, some tokens are lost if the individual performs an undesirable behavior. The loss of tokens, money, or other conditioned reinforcers following the occurrence of undesirable behaviors is called **response cost**. Behavioral interventions that include a response-cost arrangement have been used with children, people with developmental disabilities, prison inmates, and patients in psychiatric hospitals (Maffei-Almodovar & Sturmey, 2013). A study with a group of disruptive first graders used response cost as part of a token system in which they could earn tokens (simple check marks on a sheet of paper) for on-task behavior and lose tokens for disruptive or inappropriate behaviors. The tokens could later be exchanged for small snacks. The response cost contingency was effective in reducing disruptive behaviors, and for many of the children they dropped to zero (Donaldson, DeLeon, Fisher, & Kahng, 2014).

Probably the most common form of negative punishment is the **time-out**, in which one or more desirable stimuli are temporarily removed if the individual performs some unwanted behavior. In one case study, time-out was combined with reinforcement for alternative behaviors to eliminate the hoarding behavior of a patient in a psychiatric hospital (Lane, Wesolowski, & Burke, 1989). This case study illustrates what researchers call an **ABAB design**. Each "A" phase is a baseline phase in which the patient's behavior is recorded, but no treatment is given. Each "B" phase is a treatment phase. Stan was an adult with a brain injury, and he frequently hoarded such items as cigarette butts, pieces of dust and paper, food, and small stones by hiding them in his pockets, socks, or underwear. In the initial 5-day baseline phase, the researchers observed an average of about 10 hoarding episodes per day. This was followed by a treatment phase (Days 6 through 15) in which Stan was rewarded for two alternative behaviors—collecting baseball cards and picking up trash and throwing it away properly. During this phase, any episodes of hoarding were punished with a time-out period in which Stan was taken to a quiet area for 10 seconds. The number of hoarding episodes decreased during this treatment phase (see Figure 7.6). In the second baseline phase,

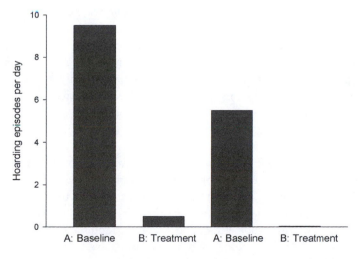

Figure 7.6 Number of hoarding episodes by a man with brain injury in the last two days of four phases: two baseline phases and two treatment phases in which hoarding was punished with time-outs and alternative behaviors were reinforced. (Based on Lane et al., 1989)

the treatment was discontinued, and during this phase Stan's hoarding behavior increased. Finally, in the second treatment phase, the time-outs and reinforcement for alternative behaviors resumed, and Stan's hoarding gradually declined and eventually stopped completely. In a follow-up 1 year later, no hoarding was observed. This ABAB design demonstrated the effectiveness of the treatment procedures because Stan's hoarding occurred frequently in the two baseline phases and decreased dramatically in the two treatment phases.

Time-outs are often used with children, as when a parent tells a child to go to his or her room for misbehaving, and this can be a simple but effective means of reducing behavior problems. In classroom situations, time-outs in which a child is sent to an isolated room can reduce aggressive or disruptive behaviors. Time-outs can also be effective if teachers simply remove a child from some ongoing activity. For example, because fourth-grade children in one elementary school were constantly unruly and disruptive during gym class, their teachers set up a time-out contingency. Any child who behaved in a disruptive way was immediately told to stop playing and to go sit on the side of the room, where he or she had to remain until all the sand had flowed through a large hourglass (which took about 3 minutes). Children who repeatedly misbehaved also lost free play time and other desirable activities (a response cost contingency). This omission procedure was very effective, and disruptive behavior during gym class soon dropped by 95% (White & Bailey, 1990). Using time-out techniques is not always easy, however. They can be difficult to implement for a teacher who also has a room full of other children to teach (Warzak, Floress, Kellen, Kazmerski, & Chopko, 2012). Nevertheless, both time-out and response cost deserve consideration as methods of behavior deceleration because they can reduce unwanted behaviors without presenting any aversive stimulus.

Overcorrection

In some cases, if an individual performs an undesired behavior, the parent, therapist, or teacher requires several repetitions of an alternate, more desirable behavior. This technique is called **overcorrection**, and it often involves two elements: restitution (making up for the wrongdoing) and positive practice (practicing a better behavior). The corrective behavior is usually designed to require more time and effort than the original bad behavior. For example, Adams and Kelley (1992) taught parents how to use an overcorrection procedure to reduce aggression against siblings. After an instance of physical or verbal aggression against a sibling, restitution might consist of an apology, and the positive practice might involve sharing a toy, touching the sibling gently, or saying something nice. This positive practice was repeated several times. If the child did not practice these behaviors appropriately, the practice trials started over from the beginning. This procedure produced a significant reduction in aggression between siblings.

Overcorrection has frequently been used with individuals who have mental disabilities to reduce aggression and other undesirable behaviors. For example, Sisson, Hersen, and Van Hasselt (1993) used overcorrection as part of a treatment package to teach adolescents with profound disabilities to package items and sort them by zip code. Maladaptive behaviors included stereotyped motions such as flapping hands, rocking back and forth, and twirling and flipping the items. After each occurrence of such a behavior, the therapist guided the patient through three repetitions of the correct sequence of behaviors.

Overcorrection meets the technical definition of a punishment procedure because a sequence of events (the correction procedure) is contingent on the occurrence of an undesired behavior, and the behavior decreases as a result. A difference from other punishment techniques, however, is that during the corrective exercises, the learner is given repeated practice performing a more desirable behavior. This may be the most beneficial component of the overcorrection procedure because providing the learner with a more desirable alternative behavior is an important ingredient in many behavior reduction treatments.

Extinction

If an undesired behavior occurs because it is followed by some positive reinforcer, and if it is possible to remove that reinforcer, the behavior should eventually disappear through simple extinction. One of the most common reinforcers to maintain unwanted behaviors is attention. In the home, the classroom, or the psychiatric hospital, disruptive or maladaptive behavior may occur because of the attention it attracts from parents, peers, teachers, or hospital staff. These behaviors will sometimes disappear if they are ignored by those who previously provided their attention. For example, a woman had a skin rash that did not go away because she continually scratched herself in the infected areas. The therapist suspected that this scratching behavior was maintained by the attention the woman received concerning her rash from her family and fiancé (who applied skin cream to the rash for her). The therapist asked her family and fiancé to avoid all discussion of the rash and not to help her treat it. The scratching behavior soon extinguished and the rash disappeared (Walton, 1960).

Extinction is sometimes slow, especially if the unwanted behavior has been intermittently reinforced in the past. In addition, the unwanted behaviors sometimes increase rather than decrease at the beginning of the extinction process. (Parents who decide to ignore tantrums in an effort to extinguish them may initially witness one of the worst tantrums they have ever seen.) As with any extinguished behavior, episodes of spontaneous recovery may occur. Nevertheless, when used properly, extinction can be a very useful method of eliminating unwanted behaviors. One of the most effective ways to use extinction is to combine it with the reinforcement of other, more desirable behaviors.

Escape Extinction

This procedure can be used when an undesired behavior is maintained by escape from some situation the individual does not like. For instance, some children with developmental disabilities exhibit food refusal: They will not eat, nor will they swallow food put in their mouths. Of course, the longer this behavior continues, the greater the risks to the child's health. Why this behavior occurs is not clear, but researchers have observed that food refusal often leads to escape from the situation—the caregiver does not force the child to eat, and the attempt to feed the child eventually ends. In **escape extinction**, the caregiver does not allow the child to escape from the situation until the child eats. This may involve keeping a spoonful of food in the child's mouth until the child swallows the food. Although some might question such a forceful technique, keep in mind how serious a problem refusing to eat can be. This method is very effective in reducing food refusal behaviors (Tarbox, Schiff, & Najdowski, 2010).

As another example, therapists at one institution found that a few children with developmental disabilities would engage in self-injurious behavior (head banging, hand biting, etc.) whenever they were instructed to work on educational tasks, and by doing so they escaped from their lessons. The therapists therefore began an extinction procedure in which the child's tutor would ignore the self-injurious behavior, tell the child to continue with the lesson, and manually guide the child through the task if necessary. In this way, the reinforcer (escape from the lesson) was eliminated, and episodes of self-injurious behavior decreased dramatically (Pace, Iwata, Cowdery, Andree, & McIntyre, 1993).

Response Blocking

For behaviors that are too dangerous or destructive to wait for extinction to occur, an alternative is response blocking, which is physically restraining the individual to prevent the inappropriate behavior. Most parents of young children probably use response blocking quite often to prevent their youngsters from doing something that would be harmful to themselves or to others (Figure 7.7). Behavior therapists have used response blocking to reduce or eliminate such behaviors as self-injury, aggression, and destruction of property by children or adults with developmental disabilities (Smith, Russo, & Le, 1999).

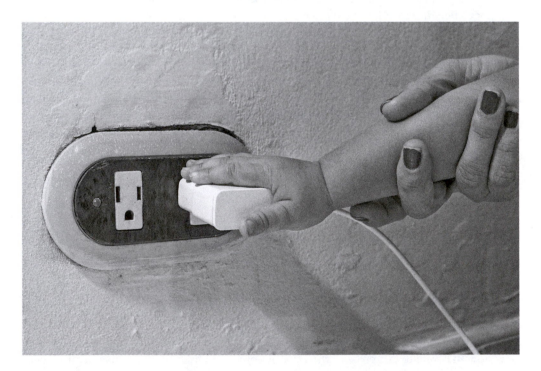

Figure 7.7 Sometimes the best and fastest way to deal with a dangerous behavior is response blocking—physically preventing the behavior. (Luis Echeverri Urrea/Shutterstock.com)

Response blocking can have both short-term and long-term benefits. First, by preventing the unwanted behavior, immediate damage or injury can be avoided. Second, as the individual learns that the behavior will be blocked, attempts to initiate this behavior usually decline. For example, to prevent a girl with developmental disabilities from poking her fingers in her eyes, Lalli, Livezey, and Kates (1996) had the girl wear safety goggles. Unlike cases of response blocking in which the therapist manually restrains the patient, this use of goggles had the advantage of blocking the unwanted behaviors even when the girl was alone. After she stopped trying to poke at her eyes, the goggles were gradually replaced with her normal eyeglasses, and her eye-poking behavior did not reappear.

Differential Reinforcement of Alternative Behavior

A classic study by Ayllon and Haughton (1964) offers a good illustration of how extinction of inappropriate behaviors can be combined with reinforcement of more appropriate behaviors—a procedure known as **differential reinforcement of alternative behavior (DRA)**. Ayllon and Haughton worked with patients in a psychiatric hospital who engaged in psychotic or delusional speech. They found that this inappropriate speech was often reinforced by the psychiatric nurses through their attention, sympathy, and conversation. Ayllon and Haughton conducted a two-part study. In the first part, the nurses were explicitly instructed to reinforce psychotic speech with attention and tangible items (gum, candy, etc.). Psychotic speech increased steadily during this part of the study. In the second phase, the nurses were told to ignore psychotic speech, but to reinforce normal speech (e.g., conversations about the weather, ward activities, or other everyday topics). This study demonstrated both the power of attention as a reinforcer and how attention can be withheld from inappropriate behaviors and delivered for more desirable alternative behaviors.

This chapter has already mentioned several other cases in which reinforcement of alternative behaviors has been successfully combined with other behavior deceleration techniques. In modern behavior therapy, DRA is a common part of treatment packages for behavior reduction. Petscher, Rey, and Bailey (2009) reviewed over 100 studies in which DRA was used with successful results. It has been used effectively for such problems as food refusal, aggression, disruptive classroom behavior, and self-injurious behavior. The logic is that most behavior reduction techniques teach a person what not to do, but they do not teach the patient what to do. DRA remedies this deficiency, and it provides more acceptable behaviors to fill the "behavioral vacuum" that is created when one behavior is reduced.

Stimulus Satiation

If it is not feasible to remove the reinforcer that is maintaining an undesired behavior, it is sometimes possible to present so much of the reinforcer that it loses its effectiveness due to **stimulus satiation**. Ayllon (1963) described a female psychiatric patient who hoarded towels in her room. Despite the nurses' efforts to remove them, she usually had more than 20 towels in the room. A program of stimulus satiation was begun in which the nurses brought her many towels each day. At first, the woman seemed to enjoy touching, folding, and stacking them, but soon she started to complain that she had enough and that the towels were in her way. Once the number of towels in her room reached about 600, she started removing them on her own. The nurses then stopped bringing her towels, and afterward, no further instances of hoarding were observed.

One unusual example of stimulus satiation involved no physical objects at all. A psychiatric patient who complained of hearing voices was given ample time to listen to these voices. For 85 half-hour sessions, the patient was instructed to sit in a quiet place and record when the voices were heard, what they said, and how demanding the tone of voice was. By the end of these sessions, the rate of these hallucinations was close to zero (Glaister, 1985). This version of stimulus satiation has also been used to treat obsessive thoughts.

PRACTICE QUIZ 2: CHAPTER 7

1. To minimize the chance that the learner will habituate to a punishing stimulus, it should be introduced _____.
2. In terms of timing, the most effective punisher is one that is delivered _____.
3. In practice, it is always best to couple punishment of an undesired behavior with reinforcement of _____.
4. In an ABAB design, each "A" represents a _____ period, and each "B" represents a _____ period.
5. If an undesired behavior is being maintained by the attention it receives, it can usually be decreased by using _____.

ANSWERS

1. at full intensity 2. immediately 3. an alternative behavior, or a more desirable behavior 4. baseline, treatment 5. extinction

SUMMARY

In negative reinforcement, an aversive stimulus is removed or eliminated if a response occurs. Two variations of negative reinforcement are escape and avoidance. The two-factor theory of avoidance states that avoidance involves (1) learning to fear a previously neutral stimulus and (2) responding to escape from this stimulus. A number of studies have supported the two-factor theory, but some findings pose problems for the theory: Well-practiced subjects continue to make avoidance responses while showing no measurable signs of fear, and extinction of avoidance responses is very slow.

The one-factor theory of avoidance states that removing a fear-provoking CS is not necessary for avoidance responding and that avoidance of the aversive event is in itself the reinforcer. Studies supporting one-factor theory have shown that animals can learn avoidance responses when there is no CS to signal an upcoming shock. The cognitive theory of avoidance states that subjects learn to expect that (1) if they respond, no aversive event will occur and (2) if they do not respond, an aversive event will occur. To teach a subject that the second expectation is no longer correct, response blocking (or flooding) can be used.

Seligman showed that if animals are presented with aversive stimuli that they cannot avoid, they may develop learned helplessness. He suggested that unavoidable aversive events can lead to helplessness and depression in people, and this theory has been applied to many aspects of human behavior.

In punishment, an aversive stimulus is presented if a response occurs, and the response is weakened. Many factors influence the effectiveness of punishment, including its intensity, immediacy, and schedule of presentation, and the availability of alternative behaviors. There are disadvantages to using punishment: It requires continual monitoring of the subject, and it can lead to undesirable side effects, such as aggression, a decrease in other behaviors, or attempts to escape from the situation.

Behavior therapists usually do not use punishment unless there is no feasible alternative; nevertheless, punishment can be an effective way of reducing a variety of unwanted behaviors in both children and adults. Other methods for reducing unwanted behaviors include response cost, time-out, overcorrection, extinction, escape extinction, response blocking, reinforcement of alternative behavior, and stimulus satiation.

Review Questions

1. What factors comprise the two-factor theory of avoidance? What types of evidence pose problems for the theory?
2. Considering the research on how learned helplessness develops, explain what types of experiences could lead to learned helplessness in (a) a freshman in college, (b) a baseball pitcher traded to a new team, or (c) an elderly resident in a nursing home.
3. Name several factors that determine the effectiveness of a punishment procedure. Give a concrete example to illustrate each factor. What are some potential disadvantages of using punishment?
4. Imagine a toddler who has developed the habit of disrupting any games his older brothers and sisters are playing. Describe at least two different techniques of behavior deceleration that a parent might use in this situation.
5. Describe some examples of how punishment has been successfully used in behavior therapy, and discuss some details that probably helped ensure the success of the procedures.

REFERENCES

Abramowitz, A. J., & O'Leary, S.G. (1990). Effectiveness of delayed punishment in an applied setting. *Behavior Therapy, 21,* 231–239.

Abramowitz, J.S., & Foa, E.B. (2000). Does major depressive disorder influence outcome of exposure and response prevention for OCD? *Behavior Therapy, 31,* 795–800.

Adams, C.D., & Kelley, M.L. (1992). Managing sibling aggression: Overcorrection as an alternative to time-out. *Behavior Therapy, 23,* 707–717.

Ayllon, T. (1963). Intensive treatment of psychotic behavior by stimulus satiation and food reinforcement. *Behaviour Research and Therapy, 1,* 53–62.

Ayllon, T., & Haughton, E. (1964). Modification of symptomatic verbal behavior of mental patients. *Behaviour Research and Therapy, 2*, 87–97.

Azrin, N.H. (1956). Effects of two intermittent schedules of immediate and nonimmediate punishment. *Journal of Psychology, 42*, 3–21.

Azrin, N.H. (1960). Effects of punishment intensity during variable-interval reinforcement. *Journal of the Experimental Analysis of Behavior, 3*, 123–142.

Azrin, N.H., & Holz, W.C. (1966). Punishment. In W.K. Honig (Ed.), *Operant behavior: Areas of research and application* (pp. 380–447). Upper Saddle River, NJ: Prentice Hall.

Azrin, N.H., Holz, W.C., & Hake, D.F. (1963). Fixed–ratio punishment. *Journal of the Experimental Analysis of Behavior, 6*, 141–148.

Boichuk, J.P., Bolander, W., Hall, Z.R., Ahearne, M., Zahn, W.J., & Nieves, M. (2014). Learned helplessness among newly hired salespeople and the influence of leadership. *Journal of Marketing, 78*, 95–111.

Bolles, R.C. (1970). Species-specific defense reactions and avoidance learning. *Psychological Review, 77*, 32–48.

Davis, J.R., & Russell, R.H. (1990). Behavioral staff management: An analogue study of acceptability and its behavioral correlates. *Behavioral Residential Treatment, 5*, 259–270.

Declercq, M., De Houwer, J., & Baeyens, F. (2008). Evidence for an expectancy-based theory of avoidance behaviour. *Quarterly Journal of Experimental Psychology, 61*, 1803–1812.

Dinsmoor, J.A. (2001). Stimuli inevitably generated by behavior that avoids electric shock are inherently reinforcing. *Journal of the Experimental Analysis of Behavior, 75*, 311–333.

Donaldson, J.M., DeLeon, I.G., Fisher, A.B., & Kahng, S.W. (2014). Effects of and preference for conditions of token earn versus token loss. *Journal of Applied Behavior Analysis, 47*, 537–548.

Fanselow, M.S. (1997). Species-specific defense reactions: Retrospect and prospect. In M.E. Bouton & M.S. Fanselow (Eds.), *Learning, motivation, and cognition: The functional behaviorism of Robert C. Bolles* (pp. 321–341). Washington, DC: American Psychological Association.

Fehr, A., & Beckwith, B.E. (1989). Water misting: Treating self-injurious behavior in a multiply handicapped, visually impaired child. *Journal of Visual Impairment and Blindness, 83*, 245–248.

Flannery, R.B. (2002). Treating learned helplessness in the elderly dementia patient: Preliminary inquiry. *American Journal of Alzheimer's Disease and Other Dementias, 17*, 345–349.

Gilboy, S. (2005). Students' optimistic attitudes and resiliency program: Empirical validation of a prevention program developing hope and optimism. *Dissertation Abstracts International, 66*(6-B), 3434.

Glaister, B. (1985). A case of auditory hallucination treated by satiation. *Behaviour Research and Therapy, 23*, 213–215.

Graham, R.A., & Weems, C.F. (2015). Identifying moderators of the link between parent and child anxiety sensitivity: The roles of gender, positive parenting, and corporal punishment. *Journal of Abnormal Child Psychology, 43*, 885–893.

Hare, R.D. (2006). The effects of delay and schedule of punishment on avoidance of a verbal response class. *Dissertation Abstracts International: Section B. The Sciences and Engineering, 67*, 581.

Hendry, D.P., & Van-Toller, C. (1964). Fixed-ratio punishment with continuous reinforcement. *Journal of the Experimental Analysis of Behavior, 7*, 293–300.

Herrnstein, R.J., & Hineline, P.N. (1966). Negative reinforcement as shock-frequency reduction. *Journal of the Experimental Analysis of Behavior, 9*, 421–430.

Hineline, P.N. (2001). Beyond the molar-molecular distinction: We need multiscaled analyses. *Journal of the Experimental Analysis of Behavior, 75*, 342–347.

Hiroto, D.S., & Seligman, M.E.P. (1975). Generality of learned helplessness in man. *Journal of Personality and Social Psychology, 31*, 311–327.

Holz, W.C., & Azrin, N.H. (1961). Discriminative properties of punishment. *Journal of the Experimental Analysis of Behavior, 4*, 225–232.

Kelley, T.M. (2004). Positive psychology and adolescent mental health: False promise or true break-through? *Adolescence, 39*, 257–278.

Lalli, J.S., Livezey, K., & Kates, K. (1996). Functional analysis and treatment of eye poking with response blocking. *Journal of Applied Behavior Analysis, 29*, 129–132.

Lane, I.M., Wesolowski, M.D., & Burke, W.H. (1989). Teaching socially appropriate behavior to eliminate hoarding in a brain-injured adult. *Journal of Behavior Therapy and Experimental Psychiatry, 20*, 79–82.

Lerman, D.C., Iwata, B.A., Shore, B.A., & DeLeon, I.G. (1997). Effects of intermittent punishment on self-injurious behavior: An evaluation of schedule thinning. *Journal of Applied Behavior Analysis, 30*, 198–201.

Lovibond, P.F. (2006). Fear and avoidance: An integrated expectancy model. In M.G. Craske, D. Hermans, & D. Vansteewegen (Eds.), *Fear and learning: Basic science to clinical application* (pp. 117–132). Washington, DC: American Psychological Association.

Maffei-Almodovar, L., & Sturmey, P. (2013). Evidence-based practice and crisis intervention. In D.D. Reed, F.D. DiGennaro Reed, & J.K. Luiselli (Eds.), *Handbook of crisis intervention and developmental disabilities* (pp. 49–69). New York, NY, US: Springer Science + Business Media.

Maier, S.F., & Seligman, M.E.P. (1976). Learned helplessness: Theory and evidence. *Journal of Experimental Psychology: General, 105*, 3–46.

Matson, J.L., & Duncan, D. (1997). Aggression. In N.N. Singh (Ed.), *Prevention and treatment of severe behavior problems: Models and methods in developmental disabilities* (pp. 217–236). Pacific Grove, CA: Brooks/Cole.

McKean, K.J. (1994). Academic helplessness: Applying learned helplessness theory to undergraduates who give up when faced with academic setbacks. *College Student Journal, 28*, 456–462.

Modaresi, H.A. (1990). The avoidance barpress problem: Effects of enhanced reinforcement and an SSDR-congruent lever. *Learning and Motivation, 21*, 199–220.

Morganstern, K.P. (1973). Implosive therapy and flooding procedures: A critical review. *Psychological Bulletin, 79*, 318–334.

Mowrer, O.H. (1947). On the dual nature of learning—a reinterpretation of "conditioning" and "problem solving." *Harvard Educational Review, 17*, 102–148.

Nagin, D.S., & Pogarsky, G. (2004). Time and punishment: Delayed consequences and criminal behavior. *Journal of Quantitative Criminology, 20*, 295–317.

O'Leary, K.D., Kaufman, K.F., Kass, R.E., & Drabman, R.S. (1970). The effects of loud and soft reprimands on the behavior of disruptive students. *Exceptional Children, 37*, 145–155.

Pace, G.M., Iwata, B.A., Cowdery, G.E., Andree, P.J., & McIntyre, T. (1993). Stimulus (instructional) fading during extinction of self-injurious escape behavior. *Journal of Applied Behavior Analysis, 26*, 205–212.

Page, H.A., & Hall, J.F. (1953). Experimental extinction as a function of the prevention of a response. *Journal of Comparative and Physiological Psychology, 46*, 33–34.

Petscher, E.S., Rey, C., & Bailey, J.S. (2009). A review of empirical support for differential reinforcement of alternative behavior. *Research in Developmental Disabilities, 30*, 409–425.

Prochaska, J., Smith, N., Marzilli, R., Colby, J., & Donovan, W. (1974). Remote-control aversive stimulation in the treatment of head-banging in a retarded child. *Journal of Behavior Therapy and Experimental Psychiatry, 5*, 285–289.

Rachlin, H. (1969). Autoshaping of key pecking in pigeons with negative reinforcement. *Journal of the Experimental Analysis of Behavior, 12*, 521–531.

Rasmussen, E.B., & Newland, M.C. (2008). Asymmetry of reinforcement and punishment in human choice. *Journal of the Experimental Analysis of Behavior, 89*, 157–167.

Schilder, M.B.H., & van der Borg, J.A.M. (2004). Training dogs with help of the shock collar: Short and long term behavioural effects. *Applied Animal Behaviour Science, 85*, 319–334.

Schuster, R., & Rachlin, H. (1968). Indifference between punishment and free shock: Evidence for the negative law of effect. *Journal of the Experimental Analysis of Behavior, 11*, 777–786.

Seligman, M.E.P. (2006). *Learned optimism: How to change your mind and your life.* New York: Vintage Books.

Seligman, M.E.P., & Johnston, J.C. (1973). A cognitive theory of avoidance learning. In F.J. McGuigan & D.B. Lumsden (Eds.), *Contemporary approaches to conditioning and learning* (pp. 69–110). Washington, DC: Winston-Wiley.

Sidman, M. (1953). Two temporal parameters of the maintenance of avoidance behavior by the white rat. *Journal of Comparative and Physiological Psychology, 46*, 253–261.

Sisson, L.A., Hersen, M., & Van Hasselt, V.B. (1993). Improving the performance of youth with dual sensory impairment: Analyses and social validation of procedures to reduce maladaptive responding in vocational and leisure settings. *Behavior Therapy, 24*, 553–571.

Smith, R.G., Russo, L., & Le, D.D. (1999). Distinguishing between extinction and punishment effects of response blocking: A replication. *Journal of Applied Behavior Analysis, 32*, 367–370.

Solomon, R.L., & Wynne, L.C. (1953). Traumatic avoidance learning: Acquisition in normal dogs. *Psychological Monographs, 67*, 354.

Tarbox, J., Schiff, A., & Najdowski, A.C. (2010). Parent-implemented procedural modification of escape extinction in the treatment of food selectivity in a young child with autism. *Education and Treatment of Children, 33*, 223–234.

Thompson, R.H., Iwata, B.A., Conners, J., & Roscoe, E.M. (1999). Effects of reinforcement for alternative behavior during punishment of self-injury. *Journal of Applied Behavior Analysis, 32*, 317–328.

Ulrich, R.E., & Azrin, N.H. (1962). Reflexive fighting in response to aversive stimulation. *Journal of the Experimental Analysis of Behavior, 5*, 511–520.

Vollmer, T.R. (2002). Punishment happens: Some comments on Lerman and Vorndran's review. *Journal of Applied Behavior Analysis, 35*, 469–473.

Vollmer, T.R., Peters, K.P., & Slocum, S.K. (2015). Treatment of severe behavior disorders. In H.S. Roane, J.E. Ringdahl, T.S. Falcomata, H.S. Roane, J.E. Ringdahl, & T.S. Falcomata (Eds.), *Clinical and organizational applications of applied behavior analysis* (pp. 47–67). San Diego, CA, US: Elsevier.

Walker, L.E.A. (2009). *The battered woman syndrome* (3rd ed.). New York: Springer.

Walton, D. (1960). The application of learning theory to the treatment of a case of neurodermatitis. In H.J. Eysenck (Ed.), *Behavior therapy and the neuroses* (pp. 272–274). Oxford: Pergamon Press.

Warzak, W.J., Floress, M.T., Kellen, M., Kazmerski, J.S., & Chopko, S. (2012). Trends in time-out research: Are we focusing our efforts where our efforts are needed? *The Behavior Therapist, 35*, 30–33.

White, A.G., & Bailey, J.S. (1990). Reducing disruptive behaviors of elementary physical education students with sit and watch. *Journal of Applied Behavior Analysis, 23*, 353–359.

Yule, W., Sacks, B., & Hersov, L. (1974). Successful flooding treatment of a noise phobia in an eleven-year-old. *Journal of Behavior Therapy and Experimental Psychiatry, 5*, 209–211.

Zoellner, L.A., Abramowitz, J., Moore, S.A., & Slagle, D.M. (2009). Flooding. In W.T. O'Donohue & J.E. Fisher (Eds.), *General principles and empirically supported techniques of cognitive behavior therapy* (pp. 300–308). Hoboken, NJ: Wiley.

CHAPTER 8

Theories and Research on Operant Conditioning

Learning Objectives

After reading this chapter, you should be able to

- discuss whether performing a response and receiving a reinforcer are essential in the learning and in the performance of a new behavior
- describe studies on how reinforcement can be used to control visceral responses, and explain how these techniques have been used in biofeedback
- list five different theories about how we can predict what will serve as a reinforcer, and discuss their strengths and weaknesses
- explain how a functional analysis of reinforcers can be used to determine the causes of unusual or puzzling behaviors
- give examples of how the field of behavioral economics has been applied to animal and human behaviors

---

The theoretical issues examined in this chapter are very broad, and they deal with matters of importance to the entire field of learning. They concern such basic issues as what ingredients, if any, are essential for learning to take place and under what conditions a supposed reinforcer will strengthen the behavior it follows. The topics can be divided into four general categories. First, we will consider whether both the performance of a response and the reinforcement of that response are necessary for learning to take place. Second, we will examine attempts to use reinforcement to control "visceral" responses—responses of the body's glands and organs that usually occur without our awareness. Third, we will trace the history of attempts to develop a method for predicting which stimuli will be effective reinforcers for a given individual and which will not. Being able to predict what will be a reinforcer is clearly important in applied behavior analysis, and we will see that it is also important from a scientific standpoint. Finally, we will survey recent efforts to link principles from behavioral psychology with those of economists in a growing field of research known as behavioral economics.

THE ROLE OF THE RESPONSE

Operant conditioning might be described as "learning by doing": An animal performs some response and experiences the consequences, and the future likelihood of that response is changed. For Thorndike, the performance of the response was a necessary part of the learning process. After all, if a response does not occur, how can it be strengthened by reinforcement? Convinced that a pairing of response and reinforcer is essential for learning, Thorndike (1946) proposed the following experiment:

> Put the rat, in a little wire car, in the entrance chamber of a maze, run it through the correct path of a simple maze and into the food compartment. Release it there and let it eat the morsel provided. Repeat 10 to 100 times according to the difficulty of the maze under ordinary conditions. . . . Then put it in the entrance chamber free to go wherever it is inclined and observe what it does. Compare the behavior of such rats with that of rats run in the customary manner.
>
> (p. 278)

Thorndike predicted that a rat that was pulled passively through a maze would perform like a naive subject in the later test since the animal had no opportunity to perform a response. On this and other issues, Thorndike's position was challenged by Edward C. Tolman (1932), who might be characterized as an early cognitive psychologist. According to Tolman, operant conditioning involves not the simple strengthening of a response but the formation of an expectation. In a maze, for example, a rat develops an expectation that a reinforcer will be available in the goal box. In addition, Tolman proposed that the rat acquires a **cognitive map** of the maze—a general understanding of the spatial layout of the maze. Tolman proposed that both of these types of learning could be acquired by passive observation as well as by active responding, so that animals should be able to learn something in the type of experiment Thorndike described.

One study fashioned according to Thorndike's specifications was conducted by McNamara, Long, and Wike (1956), who used two groups of rats in an elevated T-maze. Rats in the control group ran through the maze in the usual fashion, and a correct turn at the choice point brought the animal to some food. Control rats received 16 trials in the maze, and by the end of training they made the correct turn on 95% of the trials. Rats in the experimental group received 16 trials in which they were transported through the maze in a wire basket. Each experimental rat was paired with a control rat: It was transported to the correct or incorrect arm of the maze in exactly the same sequence of turns that its counterpart in the control group happened to choose. This training was followed by a series of extinction trials in which all rats ran through the maze, but no food was available. During these extinction tests, the experimental animals performed just as well as the control group even though they had never been reinforced for running through the maze.

Similar findings of learning without the opportunity to practice the operant response have been obtained in other studies (Dodwell & Bessant, 1960; Keith & McVety, 1988). Dodwell and Bessant found that rats benefited substantially from riding in a cart through a water maze with eight choice points. This shows that animals can learn not only a single response but also a complex chain of responses without practice. These studies make it clear that, contrary to Thorndike's prediction, active responding is not essential for the acquisition of an operant response.

THE ROLE OF THE REINFORCER

Is Reinforcement Necessary for Operant Conditioning?

From a literal point of view, the answer to this question is obviously yes since by definition operant conditioning consists of presenting a reinforcer after some response. But we have seen that, loosely speaking, operant conditioning can be called a procedure for the learning of new "voluntary," or nonreflexive, behaviors. A better way to phrase this question might be "Is reinforcement necessary for the learning of all new voluntary behaviors?" Thorndike and other early behaviorists believed that it was, but again Tolman took the opposite position. A famous experiment by Tolman and Honzik (1930), called the **latent learning** experiment, provided evidence on this issue.

In the Tolman and Honzik experiment, rats received 17 trials in a maze with 14 choice points, one trial per day. The rats were divided into three groups. Group 1 was never fed in the maze; when the rats reached the goal box, they were simply removed from the maze. Rats in Group 2 received a food reinforcer in the goal box on every trial. In Group 3, the conditions were switched on Day 11: For the first 10 trials there was no food in the goal box, but on Trials 11 through 17 food was available.

Figure 8.1 shows the average number of errors (wrong turns) from each group. Rats in Group 2 (consistently reinforced) displayed a typical learning curve, with the number of errors decreasing to about three per trial by the end of the experiment. Rats in Group 1 (never reinforced) showed much poorer performance. Their error rate dropped slightly but leveled off at about seven errors per trial. The results from Group 3 are the most interesting. On the first 11 trials, their results resembled those of Group 1. On Trial 12, however (right after the first trial with food), the performance of Group 3 improved dramatically, and they actually made slightly fewer errors than Group 2 for the remainder of the experiment. In other words, as soon as rats in Group 3 learned that food was available in the goal box, their performance became equal to that of rats that had been consistently reinforced since the beginning of the experiment.

Tolman and Honzik concluded that although the rats in Group 3 received no food on Trials 1 to 10, they learned just as much about the maze as rats in Group 2. However, because at first they received no food in the maze, Group 3 rats were not motivated to display what they had learned. Only after food was available did the rats in Group 3 translate their learning into performance. These findings tell us that reinforcement is not necessary for the *learning* of a new response, but it is necessary for the *performance* of that response. Several dozen experiments on latent learning were conducted between the 1920s and 1950s, and most of them found evidence that learning can occur when the experimenter provides no

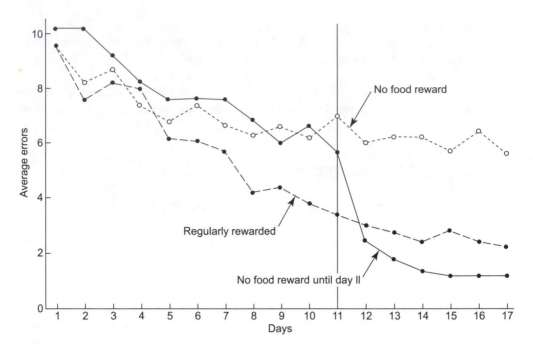

Figure 8.1 Mean number of errors on each trial for the three groups in the Tolman and Honzik (1930) experiment on latent learning.

obvious reinforcer such as food (MacCorquodale & Meehl, 1954). All learning theorists are now acutely aware of the distinction between learning and performance, largely because of Tolman's influential work.

Can Reinforcement Control Visceral Responses?

In a theoretical debate that began before theories of avoidance learning were developed (Chapter 7), two–factor theorists were those who believed that classical conditioning and operant conditioning are two distinctly different types of learning. Konorski and Miller (1937), who favored two–factor theory, proposed that although operant responses are clearly controlled by their consequences, classically conditioned responses are not. They hypothesized that reinforcement can control the behavior of the skeletal muscles (those involved in movement of the limbs) but not visceral responses (the behavior of the glands, organs, and the smooth muscles of the stomach and intestines). On the other hand, one-factor theorists believed that reinforcement and punishment are universal principles of learning that can be used to control all types of behavior, including the responses of an individual's glands, organs, and smooth muscles.

For many years it was impossible to perform a meaningful experiment about this matter because scientists had no way to separate skeletal and visceral responses. Suppose a misguided one-factor theorist offered to deliver a reinforcer, a $20 bill, if you increased your heart rate by at least 10 beats per minute. You could easily accomplish this by running up a flight of stairs or by doing a few push-ups. This demonstration of the control of heart rate through reinforcement would not convince any two-factor theorist, who would simply point out that what the reinforcer increased was the activity of the skeletal muscles, and the increase in heart rate was an automatic, unlearned response to the body's increase in activity. That is, the increase in heart rate was not a direct result of the reinforcement; rather, it was a by-product of skeletal activity. To perform a convincing study, it is necessary to eliminate any possible influence of the body's skeletal muscles.

During the 1960s, Neal Miller and his colleagues devised a procedure that met this requirement. Rats were given an injection of the drug *curare*, which causes a temporary paralysis of all skeletal muscles. However, the normal activity of the glands and organs is not affected by curare, so it might be possible to observe the direct control of visceral responses by reinforcement. But what could serve as an effective reinforcer for a para-lyzed rat? To solve this problem, Miller made use of a finding by Olds and Milner (1954) that a mild, pulsating electrical current delivered via an electrode to certain structures in the brain acts as a powerful reinforcer. Rats will press a lever at high rates for many hours if this type of electrical stimulation of the brain (ESB) is made contingent on this response.

In one set of experiments, Miller and DiCara (1967) attempted to increase or decrease the heart rates of different rats, using ESB as reinforcement. After measuring a rat's baseline heart rate (which averaged about 400 beats per minute), the experimenters began a shap-ing procedure. If the goal was an increase in heart rate, reinforcement would be provided for some small (e.g., 2%) increase. The criterion for reinforcement was then gradually raised. With other rats, Miller and DiCara used a similar procedure to try to shape decreases in heart rate. They obtained substantial changes in heart rate in both directions: By the end of a session, the average heart rate was over 500 beats per minute for subjects reinforced for a rapid heart rate and about 330 beats per minute for subjects reinforced for a slow heart rate.

Miller's research group also found that reinforcement could control many visceral responses besides heart rate (DiCara, 1970). They found that curarized rats could either dilate or constrict the blood vessels of the skin, increase or decrease the activity of the intestines, and increase or decrease the rate of urine production by the kidneys. The speci-ficity of some of these responses was quite impressive. Unfortunately, later studies by both Miller and others had difficulties in replicating the early results on the control of heart rate by ESB reinforcement. Sometimes such control was demonstrated, but often it was not, and there was no obvious pattern in the successes and failures (Miller & Dworkin, 1974). If we must try to draw some conclusions from these conflicting data, it seems that reinforcement can exert direct control over some visceral responses when the activity of the skeletal muscles has been eliminated, but this control is not as easy to obtain as the early studies seemed to suggest.

From a practical standpoint, however, an important question is whether reinforcement techniques can be used to control internal bodily processes *under any circumstances*, not just in the extreme case where the body is temporarily paralyzed by a drug. If people can learn to control such bodily processes as heart rate, blood pressure, muscle tension, intestinal activ-ity, etc., there could be substantial medical benefits. The next section describes some attempts to train people to control their internal bodily processes to obtain health benefits.

Biofeedback

Some psychologists have speculated that one reason we have so little control over many of our bodily functions is that feedback from our organs and glands is weak or nonexistent. The term **biofeedback** refers to any procedure designed to supply the individual with amplified feedback about some bodily process. The reasoning is that improved feedback may lead to the possibility of better control.

The procedures of biofeedback can be illustrated by examining one study on the control of muscle tension in the forehead. Excessive tension in the forehead muscles is the cause of muscle-contraction headaches, which some people experience at a high frequency. Budzyn-ski, Stoyva, Adler, and Mullaney (1973) attempted to train adults who suffered from frequent muscle-contraction headaches to relax these muscles. During therapy sessions, each patient received electromyogram (EMG) biofeedback: Electrodes attached to the patient's forehead monitored muscle tension, and the level of tension was translated into a continuous train of clicks the patient could hear. The patient was instructed to slow down the rate of clicking, thereby decreasing the tension in these muscles. Patients learned to accomplish this task almost immediately, and their average muscle tension levels were about 50% lower in the first biofeedback session than in the preceding baseline sessions. After biofeedback training, patients could produce low-forehead tension without the biofeedback equipment, and they were instructed to practice this muscle relaxation at home. There was a marked reduction in headaches for about 75% of the patients, and these improvements were maintained in a 3-month follow-up. On average, patients reported a decrease of about 80% in the frequency and severity of their headaches, and many were able to decrease or eliminate medication they had been taking. A review of over 100 studies concluded that biofeedback can be quite effective for tension and migraine headaches both in the short term and in follow-ups of a year or more (Nestoriuc, Martin, Rief, & Andrasik, 2008).

Using EMG biofeedback in the opposite way—to increase muscle tension—can also have therapeutic benefits. Johnson and Garton (1973) used biofeedback to treat 10 patients with hemiplegia (paralysis on one side of the body) who had failed to improve with traditional muscular-rehabilitation training. With electrodes connected to the paralyzed muscles of the leg, a patient received auditory feedback on the level of muscle tension (which was initially very low, of course). Any increase in muscle tension would produce a louder sound, and a patient's task was to increase the loudness of the signal. All patients rapidly learned how to do this, and after a number of sessions, all showed some improvement in muscle functioning. Five improved to the point where they could walk without a leg brace. This study and others have demonstrated quite convincingly that EMG biofeedback can be a useful supplement to traditional rehabilitation therapy for certain muscular disorders, producing improvements that would not be obtained without the biofeedback.

Feedback from an EMG device is only one of many types of biofeedback; some other examples include feedback on heart rate, cardiac irregularities, blood pressure, skin tempera-ture, electrical activity of the brain, stomach acidity, and intestinal activity. Biofeedback has been tried as a treatment for many different problems with varying degrees of success. For instance, training patients to increase the temperature of their hands has been found to be an effective treatment for migraine headaches in both children and adults (Nestoriuc & Martin, 2007; Scharff, Marcus, & Masek, 2002). In one study, a combination of skin tem-perature biofeedback and training in other skills (including progressive relaxation techniques) produced substantial improvement in patients suffering from irritable bowel syndrome, a disorder with symptoms that include frequent intestinal pain, gas, and diarrhea (Schwartz, Taylor, Scharff, & Blanchard, 1990). In treating patients who complained of shortness of breath and other breathing difficulties during panic attacks, therapists found that these symptoms could be reduced by providing respiratory biofeedback, including feedback on the depth and regularity of their breathing (Meuret, Wilhelm, & Roth, 2004).

Not all attempts to treat medical problems with biofeedback have been successful. For instance, some attempts to use biofeedback as a treatment for high blood pressure have not obtained good results, whereas others have found substantial decreases in blood pressure levels in most patients (Nakao, Nomura, Shimosawa, Fujita, & Kuboki, 2000). As with other treatments for medical problems, there are often large individual differences in how well patients respond to biofeedback. There has been some modest progress in predicting which individuals will benefit from biofeedback treatments and which will not (Weber, Köberl, Frank, & Doppelmayr, 2011).

Research on biofeedback has grown substantially over the years, and biofeedback techniques have been applied to an increasingly diverse array of medical disorders. The effectiveness of biofeedback must be judged on a problem-by-problem basis. For some medical problems, biofeedback may be ineffective. For other problems, it may be only as effective as other, less expensive treatments. For still others, it may produce health improvements that are superior to those of any other known treatment.

BOX 8.1   APPLYING THE RESEARCH

Neurofeedback: Controlling Your Brain Waves

Neurofeedback is a type of biofeedback designed to help people control the electrical activity of their brains. It has been used in attempts to treat a variety of medical problems, including epilepsy, chronic pain, anxiety, depression, and addictions (Jensen et al., 2013; Sterman & Thompson, 2014). One area where neurofeedback has been extensively studied is in the treatment of children diagnosed with attention-deficit hyperactivity disorder (ADHD). For example, in one study (Linden, Habib, & Radojevic, 1996) children with ADHD were given 40 sessions of neurofeedback in which each child received feedback on the electrical activity of his or her brain. The purpose of the training was to increase a particular brain wave pattern called beta waves, which are thought to be associated with an attentive and alert mental state. A child received feedback whenever beta waves were present in the electroencephalogram (EEG) recording. After their training sessions were completed, these children obtained higher scores on an IQ test and exhibited greater attentiveness.

Many other studies have examined neurofeedback for ADHD in both children and young adults. Some have found significant benefits from this treatment, but others have not. As a result, there is still a debate among practitioners about what role neurofeed-back should play in the treatment of ADHD. Some maintain that it can be an effective alternative to medication. Others have included neurofeedback as one part of a larger treatment package for ADHD (Little, Lubar, & Cannon, 2010).

Another area where neurofeedback shows promise is in the treatment of epilepsy. Because epileptic seizures are caused by abnormal brain activity, it seems reasonable to suggest that controlling brain waves might help to prevent seizure episodes. There is evidence that training patients to produce specific types of brain wave patterns can reduce the frequency of seizures. One study found that the reductions in seizures continued 10 years after neurofeedback treatment (Strehl, Birkle, Wörz, & Kotchoubey, 2014).

Other psychologists have examined whether neurofeedback can be used to enhance the cognitive performance of normal adults. Zoefel, Huster, and Herrmann (2011) gave college students five sessions of neurofeedback training to increase alpha waves—brain waves that have a distinct cyclical pattern occurring at a frequency of about 10 cycles per second. By the fifth session, their EEGs showed a clear increase in alpha waves (Figure 8.2). As a measure of cognitive functioning, the students were given a mental rotation test (in which they had to decide which of two objects presented in different orientations in a visual display were identical). Their performance on this task was better than before the neurofeedback training and better than that of a control group that did not receive the training. There are also some intriguing studies showing that neurofeedback training can enhance the artistic, musical, and creative performances of healthy adults (Gruzelier, 2014). These are preliminary findings, but they suggest that learning to control one's brain waves may be beneficial in a variety of different ways.

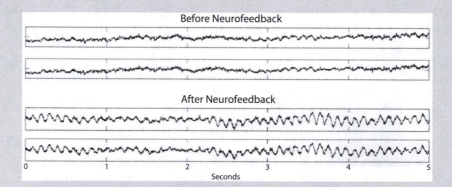

Figure 8.2 Sample brain wave patterns from a college student before and after five sessions of neurofeedback training for alpha waves. (From Zoefel, B., Huster, R. J., & Herrmann, C.S., 2011, Neurofeedback training of the upper alpha frequency band in EEG improves cognitive performance, *NeuroImage, 54,* 1427–1431. Adapted by permission of Elsevier.)

HOW CAN WE PREDICT WHAT WILL BE A REINFORCER?

The past several chapters should leave no doubt that the principle of reinforcement is one of the most central concepts in the behavioral approach to learning. However, critics of the behavioral approach have argued that the definition of reinforcement is circular and, therefore, that the concept is not scientifically valid. This is a serious criticism, so we need to take a look at what the term *circular* means and whether it applies to the concept of reinforcement.

A simple definition of a reinforcer is "a stimulus that increases a behavior that it follows." As a concrete example, suppose a mother has found that she can get her son to wash the dishes every evening (which he would normally try to avoid) if she lets him watch television only after the dishes are done. If asked, "Why did the boy wash the dishes?" a behavioral psychologist might say, "Because television is a reinforcer." If asked, "How do you know television is a reinforcer?" the reply might be "Because it increased the behavior of doing the dishes." The circularity in this sort of reasoning should be clear: A stimulus is called a reinforcer because it increases some behavior, and it is said to increase the behavior because it is a reinforcer (Figure 8.3). As stated, this simple definition of a reinforcer makes

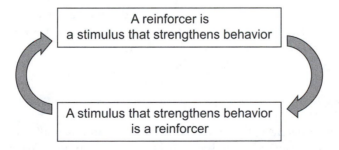

Figure 8.3 Critics have said that the concept of reinforcement is circular. The circularity can be avoided by finding an independent way to predict in advance what will serve as a reinforcer.

no specific predictions whatsoever. If the boy did not do the dishes, this would not be a problem for the behavioral psychologist, who could simply conclude, "Television is not a reinforcer for this boy."

If there were nothing more to the concept of a reinforcer than this, then critics would be correct in saying that the term is circular and not predictive. To deal with this issue, behavioral psychologists have tried to find a way to predict which stimuli will be reinforcers and which will not. The problem boils down to finding some rule that will tell us in advance whether a stimulus will act as a reinforcer. If we can find such a rule, one that makes new, testable predictions, then the circularity of the term *reinforcer* will be broken. Several attempts to develop this sort of rule are described below.

Need Reduction

Clark Hull (1943) proposed that all primary reinforcers are stimuli that reduce some biological need and that all stimuli that reduce a biological need will act as reinforcers. The simplicity of this **needreduction theory** is appealing, and it is certainly true that many primary reinforcers serve important biological functions. We know that food, water, warmth, and avoidance of pain are all primary reinforcers, and each also plays an important role in the continued survival of an organism. Unfortunately, it does not take much thought to come up with exceptions to this rule. For example, sexual stimulation is a powerful reinforcer, but despite what you may hear some people claim, no one will die if deprived of sex indefinitely. Another example of a reinforcer that serves no biological function is saccharin (or any other artificial sweetener). Saccharin has no nutritional value, but because of its sweet taste it is a reinforcer for both humans and nonhumans. People purchase saccharin and add it to their coffee or tea, and rats choose to drink water flavored with saccharin over plain water.

Besides reinforcers that satisfy no biological needs, there are also examples of biological necessities for which there is no corresponding reinforcer. One such example is vitamin B1 (thiamine). Although intake of thiamine is essential for maintaining good health, animals such as rats apparently cannot detect the presence or absence of thiamine in their food by smell or taste. As a result, rats suffering from a thiamine deficiency will not immediately select a food that contains thiamine over one that does not.

It makes sense that most biological necessities will function as reinforcers because a creature could not survive if it were not strongly motivated to obtain these reinforcers. As a predictor of reinforcing capacity, however, the need-reduction hypothesis is inadequate because there are many exceptions to this principle—reinforcers that satisfy no biological needs and biological needs that are not translated into reinforcers.

Drive Reduction

Recognizing the problems with the need-reduction hypothesis, Hull and his student Neal Miller (1948, 1951) proposed the **drive-reduction theory** of reinforcement. This theory states that strong stimulation of any sort is aversive to an organism, and any reduction in this stimulation acts as a reinforcer for the immediately preceding behavior. The term *drive* *reduction* was chosen because many of the strong stimuli an animal experiences are frequently called drives (the hunger drive, the sex drive, etc.). In addition, the theory asserts that other strong stimuli (e.g., loud noise, intense heat, fear) will also provide reinforcement when their intensity is reduced. A reduction in stimulation of any sort should serve as a reinforcer.

There are at least two major problems with the drive-reduction theory. First, if we measure the intensity of stimulation using an objective, physical scale of measurement, not all reductions in stimulation act as reinforcers. For example, reducing the room temperature from 100°F to 75°F (which is the reduction of a stimulus, heat) would probably serve as a reinforcer for most animals, but reducing the room temperature from 25°F to 0°F (an equally large reduction in heat) would not. Common sense tells us that 100°F is "too hot" and 0°F is "too cold," but that is beside the point; one reduction in heat serves as a reinforcer and the other does not.

Second, there are many examples of reinforcers that either produce no decrease in stimulation or actually produce an increase in stimulation. Sheffield, Wulff, and Backer (1951) found that male rats would repeatedly run down an alley when the reinforcer was a female rat in heat. This reinforcer produced no decrease in the male's sex drive because the rats were always separated before they could have sex, yet the male rat's high speed of running continued trial after trial. Similarly, we know that sexual foreplay is reinforcing for human beings even when it does not culminate in intercourse. The popularity of pornographic magazines, movies, and Internet sites provides further evidence on this point.

There are countless examples, from many different species, where an increase in stimulation acts as a primary reinforcer. Human infants, kittens, and other young animals spend long periods of time playing with toys and other objects that produce ever-changing visual, auditory, and tactile stimulation. The opportunity to run in a running wheel can serve as a reinforcer for rats (Belke & Pierce, 2009). Photographs presented as a slide show can serve as reinforcers for monkeys, and motion pictures are even stronger reinforcers (Blatter & Schultz, 2006). A great variety of stimuli and activities that increase sensory stimulation can serve as reinforcers for adult humans: music, engaging in sports and exercise, mountain climbing, skydiving, horror films, and the like. There seems to be no way to reconcile these facts with the drive-reduction hypothesis.

Trans-Situationality

Because of the problems with the need-reduction and drive-reduction theories, Paul Meehl (1950) adopted a more modest theoretical position, but one that still offered the possibility of making new predictions and thereby avoiding the circularity of the term *reinforcer*. Meehl invoked the concept of **trans-situationality**, which simply means that a stimulus that acts as a reinforcer in one situation will also be a reinforcer in other situations. For example, suppose that through a simple experiment we determine that water sweetened with saccharin can reinforce wheel running by a mouse: Running in the activity wheel increases if every few revolutions of the wheel are followed by access to the saccharin solution. Having established that saccharin is a reinforcer for wheel running, the principle of trans-situationality states that we can make new predictions. For instance,

Mother's observation:

Pizza is a reinforcer for doing homework.

Trans-situationality predictions:

Pizza will be a reinforcer for:
    doing the dishes
    cleaning room
    mowing the lawn
    coming home on time
    etc.

Figure 8.4 The principle of trans-situationality can be used to predict what will be an effective reinforcer in new situations.

we should be able to use saccharin as a reinforcer for lever pressing, climbing a ladder, learning the correct sequence of turns in a maze, and so on. In the same way, a mother can use the principle of trans-situationality to predict what will be a reinforcer for her child (Figure 8.4).

In reality, the principle of trans-situationality works quite well in many cases. Parents and teachers know that reinforcers such as snacks, beverages, toys, games, recess, and so on can be used to strengthen a multitude of different behaviors. There is, however, one problem with this principle: In some cases, a reinforcer in one situation does not act as a reinforcer in another situation. The first person to document clear exceptions to the principle of trans-situationality was David Premack, whose influential experiments and writings changed the way many psychologists think about reinforcement.

Premack's Principle

The procedure of reinforcement can be described as a contingency between a behavior (the operant response) and a stimulus (the reinforcer). This description suggests that when using reinforcement, we are dealing with two distinct classes of events: reinforceable behaviors on one hand and reinforcing stimuli on the other. One of Premack's contributions was to show that there is no clear boundary between these two classes of events and that it may be counterproductive to talk about two separate classes at all. He pointed out that nearly all reinforcers involve both a stimulus (such as food) and a behavior (such as eating), and it may be the latter that actually strengthens the operant response. Is it water or the act of drinking that is a reinforcer for a thirsty animal? Is a toy a reinforcer for a child or is it the behavior of playing with the toy? Is a window with a view a reinforcer for a monkey or is it the behavior of looking? Premack proposed that it is more accurate to characterize the reinforcement procedure as a contingency between one behavior and another than as a contingency between a behavior and a stimulus. For example, he would state that in many operant conditioning experiments with rats, the contingency is between the behavior of lever pressing and the behavior of eating—eating can occur if and only if a lever press occurs.

How does Premack's idea about behaviors as reinforcers relate to the principle of trans-situationality? If trans-situationality is correct, then there must be one subset of behaviors that we might call *reinforcing behaviors* (e.g., eating, drinking, playing) and another subset of behaviors that are *reinforceable behaviors* (e.g., doing homework, house-cleaning, going to work). According to the principle of trans-situationality, any behavior selected from the first subset should serve as a reinforcer for any behavior in the second subset. However, Premack's experiments showed several ways in which trans-situationality can be violated.

To replace the principle of trans-situationality, Premack (1959, 1965) proposed an alternative theory, now called **Premack's principle**, which provides a straightforward method for determining whether one behavior will act as a reinforcer for another. The key is to measure the durations of the behaviors in a baseline situation, where all behaviors can occur at any time without restriction. Premack's principle states that *more probable behaviors will reinforce less probable behaviors*. "More probable" simply means the behavior that the individual spends more time doing when there are no restrictions on what the individual can do. Premack suggested that instead of talking about two categories of behaviors—reinforceable behaviors and reinforcing behaviors—we should rank behaviors on a scale of probability that ranges from behaviors of high probability to those of zero probability. Behaviors higher on the probability scale will serve as reinforcers for behaviors that are lower on the probability scale.

A study Premack (1963) conducted with Cebus monkeys highlights the advantages of Premack's principle and the weaknesses of the trans-situationality principle. These monkeys are inquisitive animals that will explore and manipulate any objects placed in their environment. Premack allowed the monkeys to play with different mechanical objects. Figure 8.5 shows that for one monkey, Chicko, operating a lever had the highest probability, operating a plunger had the lowest, and opening a small door had an inter-mediate probability.

Later, Premack arranged different contingencies in which one item served as the "operant response" and the other as the potential "reinforcer"—the reinforcer was locked and could not be operated until the monkey first played with the other object. In six different phases, every possible combination of operant response and reinforcer was tested, and Figure 8.5 shows the results. The lever served as a reinforcer for both door opening and plunger pulling. Door opening reinforced plunger pulling but it did not reinforce lever pressing. Plunger pulling did not reinforce either of the other behaviors. You should see that each of these six results is in agreement with the principle that more probable behaviors will reinforce less probable behaviors.

Notice that door opening, the behavior of intermediate probability, violated the prin-ciple of trans-situationality. When it was contingent on plunger pulling, door opening was a reinforcer. When it led to the availability of lever pressing, it played the role of a reinforceable response. Which was door opening, then, a reinforcer or a reinforceable response? Premack's answer is that it can be either, depending on the behavior's relative position on the scale of probabilities. A behavior will act as a reinforcer for behaviors that are lower on the probability scale, and it will be a reinforceable response for behaviors

L = Lever Pressing
D = Door Opening
P = Plunger Pulling

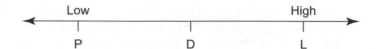

Contingency Conditions	Result	Conclusion
1. D ⟶ L	D Increases	L Reinforces D
2. P ⟶ L	P Increases	L Reinforces P
3. L ⟶ D	L Does Not Increase	D Does Not Reinforce L
4. P ⟶ D	P Increases	D Reinforces P
5. L ⟶ P	L Does Not Increase	P Does Not Reinforce L
6. D ⟶ P	D Does Not Increase	P Does Not Reinforce D

Figure 8.5 The procedure used in Premack's (1963) experiment and the results from one monkey, Chicko. The notation D→L means that Chicko was required to open the door before being allowed to operate the lever.

higher on the probability scale. For this reason, Premack's principle is sometimes called a principle of reinforcement relativity: There are no absolute categories of reinforcers and reinforceable responses, and which role a behavior plays depends on its relative location on the probability scale.

Premack (1971) also proposed a principle of punishment that is complementary to his reinforcement principle: *Less probable behaviors will punish more probable behaviors.* Since an individual may not perform a low-probability behavior if given a choice, the experimenter can arrange a **reciprocal contingency**, which requires that two behaviors occur in a fixed proportion. For example, in one condition of an experiment I conducted (Mazur, 1975), rats were required to engage in 15 seconds of wheel running for every 5 seconds of drinking. The results from one typical rat show how this experiment simultaneously verified Premack's reinforcement and punishment rules. In baseline sessions, this rat spent about 17% of the session drinking and about 10% of the session running (Figure 8.6). But

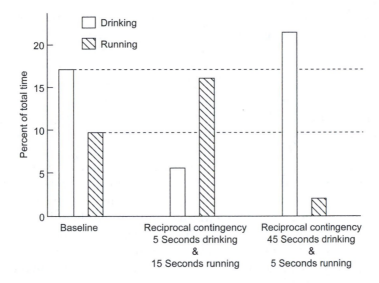

Figure 8.6 The performance of one rat in Mazur's (1975) experiment. In the first reciprocal contingency, running time increased and drinking time decreased compared to their baseline levels. In the second reciprocal contingency, running time decreased and drinking time increased compared to their baseline levels.

when the rat was required to spend 15 seconds running for every 5 seconds of drinking, the percentage of time spent running increased compared to baseline, while drinking time decreased compared to baseline. In other words, the higher probability behavior, drinking, reinforced running, and at the same time, the running requirement punished drinking. All the other rats in this experiment showed similar results. Other studies have also found support for Premack's rules (Amari, Grace, & Fisher, 1995; Hanley, Iwata, Roscoe, Thompson, & Lindberg, 2003).

Premack's Principle in Behavior Modification

Although we have focused on the theoretical implications of Premack's principle, it has had a large impact on the applied field of behavior modification in several ways. First, it has stressed that behaviors themselves can serve as reinforcers, thereby encouraging behavior therapists to use such reinforcers in their work. Therapists now frequently instruct clients to use "Premackian reinforcers," such as reading, playing cards, phoning a friend, or watching television, as reinforcers for desired behaviors such as exercising, studying, or avoiding smoking. Premackian reinforcers have also been widely adopted in classroom settings. Imagine the difficulties teachers would face in setting up a token system if they relied only on tangible reinforcers such as snacks, beverages, toys, and prizes. The costs of using such items as reinforcers would be prohibitive, and problems of satiation would be commonplace. However, by making certain activities contingent on good behavior, teachers gain access to a wide variety of inexpensive reinforcers.

Premack's principle was used by the parents of a 7-year-old boy who refused to eat all but a few very specific foods and who would become aggressive if they tried to feed him anything else. His parents were concerned about his health on such a restricted diet, so behavior therapists devised the following plan. At mealtimes, the parents would tell the boy that if he ate a small amount of a new food, he could then eat one of his favorite foods. If he refused to eat the new food, he would not be allowed to eat his favorite food (but he was given a less preferred food so he would not go hungry). As a result of this simple strategy, the boy gradually began to eat a wider variety of foods, and he was calmer when presented with new foods (Brown, Spencer, & Swift, 2002).

Homme, deBaca, Devine, Steinhorst, and Rickert (1963) used Premack's principle to control the behavior of a class of nursery-school children. Among the most probable behaviors of these children were running around the room, screaming, pushing chairs about, and so on. A program was then established in which these high-probability behaviors were made contingent on low-probability behaviors, such as sitting quietly and listening to the teacher. After a few minutes of such a low-probability behavior, the teacher would ring a bell and give the instructions "run and scream," at which point the children could perform these high-probability behaviors for a few minutes. Then the bell would ring again and the teacher would give instructions for another behavior, which might be one of high or low probability. After a few days, the children's obedience of the teacher's instructions was nearly perfect.

A similar procedure was used by Azrin, Vinas, and Ehle (2007) with two 13-year-old boys diagnosed with ADHD. They were so active and disruptive in the classroom that it was a problem for the whole class. The researchers observed that when they were allowed in the school's recreation room, the boys spent most of their time engaged in vigorous physical activity with the play equipment. This high-probability behavior was therefore used as a reinforcer for sitting quietly and attentively during class. After several minutes of appropriate behavior, the teacher would say, "You can now play because you have been so calm and attentive," and the boys were allowed to play in the recreation room for a few minutes. Under this arrangement, the boys' behaviors during class improved dramatically.

These examples illustrate just a few of the many ways that Premack's principle has been used in applied settings. Although the next section shows that the principle has limitations, it has proven to be a successful rule of thumb for deciding which events will be reinforcers and which will not.

Response Deprivation Theory

Research has shown that Premack's principle usually makes very good predictions about what will serve as reinforcers or punishers. There are, however, certain cases where, contrary to Premack's principle, a low-probability behavior can actually be used as a reinforcer for a behavior of higher probability. My experiment with rats running and drinking (Mazur, 1975) illustrates how this can happen. Recall that one rat spent about 17% of the time drinking and 10% running in baseline sessions (Figure 8.6). This animal's ratio of drinking time to running time was therefore about 1.7 to 1. In one of the reciprocal contingencies, 45 seconds of drinking were required for every 5 seconds of running. This is a 9:1 ratio of drinking to running, which is higher than the rat exhibited in baseline. Figure 8.6 shows that in this reciprocal contingency, running time decreased to about 2% of the session time while drinking time actually increased to 21%. Therefore, contrary to Premack's principle, in this case a low-probability behavior actually reinforced a high-probability behavior.

To handle results of this type, Timberlake and Allison (1974; Allison, 1993) proposed the **response deprivation theory** of reinforcement, which is actually a refinement of Premack's principle. The essence of this theory is that whenever a contingency restricts an individual's access to some behavior compared to baseline (when there are no restrictions on any behavior), the restricted behavior will serve as a reinforcer, regardless of whether it is a high-probability or a low-probability behavior. To understand how this theory works, imagine that a man typically spends 30 minutes a day working out with his home exercise equipment, and he spends 60 minutes a day studying for a difficult graduate course. He decides that he should be spending more time on this course, but he has trouble making himself study any longer. To use response deprivation theory, the man makes an agreement with his wife (who will act to enforce the rule) that for every 20 minutes he spends studying, he earns 5 minutes of exercise time (see Figure 8.7). Notice that if the man continued to study just 60 minutes a day, he would earn only 15 minutes of exercise time, so this would deprive him of the 30 minutes of exercise that he used to have. Therefore, according to response deprivation theory, this contingency produces a relative deprivation of exercise. Because of this, the theory predicts that the man will strike some compromise between studying and exercising—for example, he might increase his studying to 100 minutes a day and earn 25 minutes of exercise time (which is closer to his baseline level of 30 minutes). Seeing this increase in studying compared to baseline, we would say that exercising (the lower-probability behavior) has served as a reinforcer for studying.

In summary, response deprivation theory states that in any schedule where the proportion of two behaviors is controlled, the more restricted behavior will act as a reinforcer for the less restricted behavior, regardless of whether it is the high- or low-probability

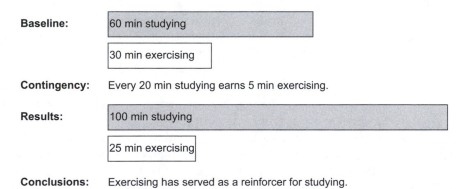

Figure 8.7 A hypothetical example of response deprivation theory. Because the contingency deprives the man of his usual amount of exercise time, exercising should serve as a reinforcer for studying.

behavior. Although it may be a little more difficult to understand than Premack's principle, response deprivation theory is the most reliable predictor of reinforcer effectiveness of all the theories we have examined. It allows us to predict whether an activity will serve as a reinforcer by observing the probability of that behavior (and of the behavior to be reinforced) in a baseline situation. This theory has been tested both in laboratory experiments with animals and in applied settings with people, and it has proven to be an accurate rule for predicting when a contingency will produce an increase in a desired behavior and when it will not (Klatt & Morris, 2001). For example, Konarski (1987) set up different contingencies between two behaviors in a population of adults with developmental disabilities, and this allowed him to make a direct comparison of the predictions of Premack's principle and response deprivation theory. The predictions of Premack's principle succeeded in some cases and failed in others, but the predictions of response deprivation theory proved to be correct almost 100% of the time. Because response deprivation theory allows us to predict in advance what will serve as a reinforcer, the definition of a reinforcer is no longer circular.

The Functional Analysis of Behaviors and Reinforcers

Response deprivation theory offers a good way to predict when an activity will serve as an effective reinforcer. However, a different problem that often challenges behavior therapists is to determine what reinforcer is maintaining some undesired behavior. Those who work with children or adults who have autism or developmental disabilities often see bizarre or inappropriate behaviors that seem to occur for no obvious reasons. Examples include the destruction of toys or other objects, aggression against peers or caregivers, screaming, self-injurious behaviors (SIBs), and chewing on inedible objects. One useful first step toward eliminating these behaviors is to conduct a **functional analysis**, which is a method that allows the therapist to determine what reinforcer is maintaining the unwanted behavior.

These maladaptive behaviors may occur for many possible reasons. An aggressive act may allow a child to seize a desired toy (a positive reinforcer). Destroying objects may lead to attention from the caregiver (another positive reinforcer). Screaming or disruptive behavior may produce an interruption in an unwanted lesson or activity (a negative reinforcer). In addition, some behaviors (e.g., chewing on inedible objects, repetitive motions, or SIBs) may produce what is called **automatic reinforcement**; that is, sensory stimulation from the behavior may serve as its own reinforcer (Fisher, Adelinis, Thompson, Worsdell, & Zarcone, 1998).

How can the cause of a particular maladaptive behavior be determined? Using the method of functional analysis, the patient's environment is systematically changed in ways that allow the therapist to test different explanations of the inappropriate behavior. For example, Watson, Ray, Turner, and Logan (1999) used functional analysis to evaluate the SIB of a 10-year-old boy who had a mental disability. In his classroom, the boy would frequently bang his head on the table, slap his face, and scratch at his face with his fingernails. On different days, the boy's teacher reacted to episodes of SIB in different ways. On some days, the teacher immediately said, "Don't do that" after each instance of SIB to see if the behavior was being reinforced by the teacher's attention. On other days, the boy was given a toy or other item

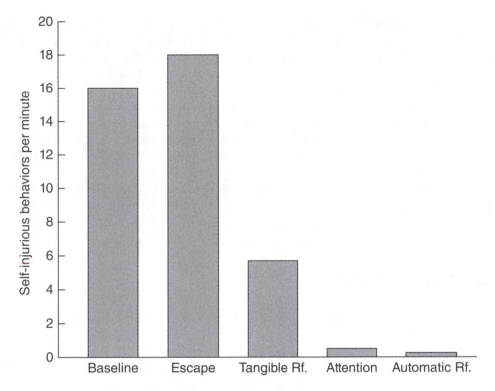

Figure 8.8 An example of functional analysis (Watson et al., 1999). The rates of SIB exhibited by a boy with a mental disability are shown for five different experimental conditions.

after each instance of SIB to see if tangible reinforcers might be strengthening this behavior. To assess the possibility that the SIB might be producing automatic reinforcement, the boy was sometimes placed in a room by himself, where he could receive no attention or tangible reinforcers if he engaged in SIB. Finally, on some days, whatever task the boy was working on was terminated after an instance of SIB to determine whether the behavior might be reinforced by escape from unpleasant tasks.

Figure 8.8 shows the results from these tests. Look at these results, and try to decide what was causing the SIB. Compared to the normal classroom situation (labeled "Baseline"), the rate of SIB was much lower in the situations testing the effects of attention, tangible reinforcers, and automatic reinforcement, but it was higher when it allowed the boy to escape from the ongoing task. The researchers therefore concluded that the SIB was actually escape behavior. As a treatment, they instructed the boy's teacher to allow him to end a nonpreferred task and switch to a more preferred task if he completed it without any instance of SIB. After this approach was adopted, the boy's SIB virtually disappeared.

Functional analysis must be done on a case-by-case basis because the same behaviors may occur for different reasons for different people. In one survey of more than 100 individuals who engaged in SIB, functional analysis found that for about a third of them, the behavior was being maintained by attention from the caregiver. For these individuals, the SIB was greatly reduced by having the caregiver ignore instances of SIB but give the patients attention when they were engaged in other behaviors (Fischer, Iwata, & Worsdell, 1997). In another example of functional analysis, researchers found that finger sucking by two children was being maintained not by attention or by escape from unpleasant tasks but by automatic reinforcement (the sensory stimulation of the fingers). When bandages or rubber gloves were put on the children's fingers, their finger sucking decreased (Ellingson et al., 2000). Functional analysis can also be used for adults with psychological disorders who display unusual or disturbing behaviors (Strohmeier, Pace, & Luiselli, 2014).

The power of functional analysis is that the therapist need not simply watch helplessly and wonder why a maladaptive behavior is occurring. By the appropriate manipulation of the environment, possible sources of reinforcement can be evaluated, and based on this information, an appropriate treatment plan can be tailored to the needs of each individual.

BEHAVIORAL ECONOMICS

This chapter has described several different theories about reinforcement. To achieve a better understanding of how reinforcement works in everyday settings, some psychologists have turned to theories from the field of economics. Microeconomics, which is concerned with the behavior of individual consumers, and the study of operant conditioning, which is concerned with the behavior of individual organisms, have several common features. Both disciplines examine how the individual works to obtain relatively scarce and precious commodities (consumer goods in economics, reinforcers in operant conditioning). In both cases the resources of the individual (money in economics, time or behavior in operant conditioning) are limited. Both disciplines attempt to predict how individuals will allocate their limited resources to obtain scarce commodities. Because of these common interests, some psychologists and economists have begun to share theoretical ideas and research techniques. The field of **behavioral economics** is a product of these cooperative efforts. This section describes a few of the ways in which economic concepts have been applied to human and animal behaviors, both inside and outside the laboratory.

Optimization: Theory and Research

A basic question for microeconomists is how individual consumers will distribute their incomes among all the possible ways it can be spent, saved, or invested. Suppose a woman brings home $800 a week after taxes. How much of this will she spend on food, on rent, on household items, on clothing, on entertainment, on charitable contributions, and so on? **Optimization theory** provides a straightforward and reasonable answer: She will distribute her income in whatever way maximizes her "subjective value" (or loosely speaking, in whatever way gives her the most satisfaction). Although this principle is easy to state, putting it into practice can be extremely difficult. How can we know whether buying a new pair of shoes or giving that same amount of money to a worthy charity will give the woman greater satisfaction? For that matter, how does the woman know? Despite these difficulties, optimization theory maintains that people can and do make such judgments and then distribute their income accordingly.

Because the "subjective value" of any reinforcer will vary from one person to another, testing the principle of optimization in a rigorous way is not easy. Nevertheless, by making some reasonable assumptions about which reinforcers have greater or lesser value, researchers have been able to obtain concrete evidence that supports optimization theory. As shown in the next section, some of this evidence has come from studies with nonhuman subjects.

Optimization and Behavioral Ecology

Behavioral ecologists study the behaviors of animals in their natural habitats or in semi-naturalistic settings, and they attempt to determine how the behavior patterns of different species are shaped by environmental factors and the pressures of survival. It is easy to see why the concept of optimization is appealing to behavioral ecologists, with their interest in the relationship between evolution and behavior: Animals whose behaviors are more nearly optimal should increase their chances of surviving and of breeding offspring that will have similar behavioral tendencies. Behavioral ecologists have documented many cases where an animal's behaviors are close to optimal; these cases involve such varied pursuits as foraging for food, searching for a mate, and choosing group size (Krebs & Davies, 1978).

Here is one example of how the principle of optimization can be applied to animal behavior. When searching for its prey, any predator must make decisions. If a large prey is encountered, it should of course be captured. On the other hand, if a small prey is encountered, the predator's decision is trickier. If a long time is required to chase, capture, and eat the small prey, it may not be worthwhile to go after it because during this time the predator will miss the opportunity to capture any larger prey that might come along. A general rule is that if the density of large prey is low (so that encounters with large prey are rare), the predator should go after any prey, large or small. If the density of large prey is high, however, the predator should ignore small prey because in chasing them it would lose valuable time during which a large prey might come along.

Werner and Hall (1974) tested these predictions by placing 10 bluegill sunfish in a large aquarium with three sizes of prey (smaller fish). When prey density was low (20 of each type), the sunfish ate all three types of prey as often as they were encountered. When prey density was high (350 of each type), the sunfish ate only the largest prey. When prey density was intermediate (200 of each type), the sunfish ate only the two largest prey types. By measuring the time the sunfish required to capture and eat prey of each type, Werner and Hall were able to calculate that the behaviors of the sunfish were exactly what optimization theory predicted for all three situations.

This example shows how scientists have applied optimization theory to the behaviors of animals in naturalistic settings. Operant conditioning experiments have also provided some support for the theory (Silberberg, Bauman, & Hursh, 1993). In the psychological laboratory, optimization theory can be put to a more rigorous test, and its predictions can be compared to those of alternative theories. Some of this research will be described in Chapter 12.

Elasticity and Inelasticity of Demand

In operant research, many studies have been done to see how behavior changes as the requirements of a reinforcement schedule become more severe, such as when a ratio requirement is increased from FR 10 to FR 100. This question is similar to the economic question of how the demand for a commodity changes as its price increases. Economists use the term **elastic demand** if the amount of a commodity purchased decreases markedly when its price increases. Demand is typically elastic when close substitutes for the product are readily available. For example, the demand for a specific brand of cola would probably drop dramatically if its price increased by 50% because people would switch to other brands that taste about the same. Conversely, the term **inelastic demand** means changes in price of a product have relatively little effect on the amount purchased. This is generally the case for products with no close substitutes. In modern society, the demand for gasoline is fairly inelastic because many people have no alternative to driving their cars to work, school, shopping centers, and so on.

One way behavioral economists can measure demand with people is simply by using a questionnaire format. In one study, college students were asked to estimate how much alcohol they would consume during an evening at a bar, depending on the prices of the drinks (which ranged from free drinks to $9 per drink). Figure 8.9 shows that the students' answers conformed to a typical **demand curve**—they estimated that they would drink a lot if the drinks were free or inexpensive, but their estimated consumption decreased steadily as the prices of the drinks increased (Murphy, MacKillop, Skidmore, & Pederson, 2009).

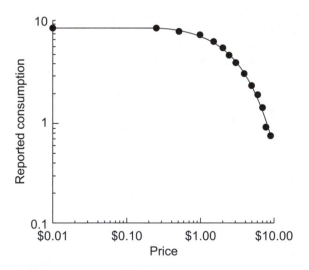

Figure 8.9 A demand curve obtained by asking college students about how much alcohol they would consume in an evening at different prices per drink. (From Murphy, J.G., MacKillop, J., Skidmore, J.R., Pederson, A.A., 2009, Reliability and validity of a demand curve measure of alcohol reinforcement. *Experimental and Clinical Psychopharmacology, 17,* 396–404. © American Psychological Association. Reprinted with permission.)

Demand curves can be obtained from animals by measuring how much they respond for a particular type of reinforcer while increasing the "price" by requiring more and more responses per reinforcer. For example, Madden, Smethells, Ewan, and Hursh (2007) had rats press a lever for food pellets on schedules that ranged from FR 1 to FR 200 or higher. The food pellets were formulated to satisfy all the rats' dietary needs. The data are shown as triangles in Figure 8.10. As the size of the FR schedule increased, the rats' demand for food decreased, but only slightly. In another phase of this experiment, the researchers used the same procedure to obtain demand curves when the reinforcer was fat (a liquid consisting of corn oil mixed in water, which provided calories but was not a complete diet). As shown by the open circles in Figure 8.10, the demand for fat was more elastic than for food pellets—as the size of the FR schedules increased, the rats' consumption of fat decreased much more sharply.

Besides providing examples of two reinforcers with different elasticities of demand, this experiment shows that deciding which of two reinforcers is "stronger" is a complex question with no simple answer. Notice that with very small FR schedules, the rats earned more fat reinforcers than food pellets, but with larger FR schedules, they earned more food pellets than fat reinforcers. Which, then, is the more effective reinforcer? One possible answer to this question is to determine which reinforcer has the higher peak output (the reinforcement schedule at which the individual makes the most total responses, which can be calculated by multiplying the number of reinforcers earned times the size of the ratio schedule). In Figure 8.10, these points are marked by the vertical lines, and they show that food pellets had a higher peak output than fat. However, other researchers have proposed other ways to compare the strengths of two different reinforcers, such as by measuring which is preferred in a choice situation, which can sustain the highest response ratio before an animal stops responding, and other measures (Hursh & Silberberg, 2008). Unfortunately, these different measures of reinforcer strength do not always agree. At least for now, a seemingly simple question, "Which of two reinforcers is stronger?" does not appear to have a simple answer.

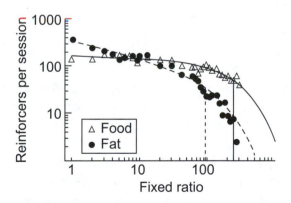

Figure 8.10 Demand curves for food pellets and for fat, obtained by having rats work for these two reinforcers on different FR schedules. (From Madden, G. J., Smethells, J.R., Ewan, E.E., & Hursh, S.R., Tests of behavioral-economic assessments of relative reinforcer efficacy: Economic substitutes. *Journal of the Experimental Analysis of Behavior, 87,* 219–240. Copyright 2007 by the Society for the Experimental Analysis of Behavior.)

BOX 8.2   APPLYING THE RESEARCH

Behavioral Economics and Drug Abuse

Animal experiments can often provide valuable information about matters that are of great importance to human behavior. One such area involves the effects of addictive drugs on an individual's behavior. Many laboratory experiments have examined how animals respond when given the opportunity to work to obtain drugs such as alcohol, heroin, or cocaine. These drugs can serve as powerful reinforcers for animals ranging from rats to monkeys, and economic concepts can be used to analyze the effects of a drug more precisely. For example, some studies have used animal subjects to measure the elasticity of different drugs. Animals may be allowed to work for drugs on FR schedules of different sizes to determine how the "price" of the drug affects consumption. Surprisingly, some drugs considered to be highly addictive have relatively elastic demand. One experiment with rats found that demand for cocaine was much more elastic than demand for food (Christensen, Silberberg, Hursh, Huntsberry, & Riley, 2008).

Research with animals has also found that other factors besides price can affect demand for a drug, such as the availability of substitutes and competition from other reinforcers. In one study, baboons had to choose between food and intravenous injections of heroin. When both were plentiful (a choice was available every 2 minutes), the baboons chose the two alternatives about equally often, and as a result they consumed a good deal of heroin. But when the two reinforcers were less plentiful (a choice was available only every 12 minutes), the baboons chose food most of the time, and their consumption of heroin decreased dramatically (Elsmore, Fletcher, Conrad, & Sodetz, 1980). Studies like this show that even addictive drugs conform to standard economic principles of supply and demand and that drug consumption will decrease if the cost gets high enough. Furthermore, it does not always take a manipulation as extreme as decreasing the availability of food to reduce drug consumption. Carroll (1993) showed that rhesus monkeys' demand for the drug PCP could be substantially reduced simply by giving them access to saccharin as an alternative reinforcer. Similar results have been obtained with other addictive drugs.

Research using the behavioral economic approach to drug addiction has also been conducted with human participants, involving such drugs as nicotine, caffeine, alcohol, and heroin. As with the animal studies, this research has shown that economic principles can be applied to drugs just as well as to other commodities (Bickel, Johnson, Koffarnus, MacKillop, & Murphy, 2014). For instance, as the price of a drug increases, or as substitute reinforcers become more available, drug consumption declines (Bickel, DeGrandpre, & Higgins, 1995). This research can help to analyze the effectiveness of different treatments for drug addictions. Consider the strategy of treating heroin addicts by giving them methadone as a substitute. In economic terms, methadone is an imperfect substitute for heroin because it delivers some but not all of the reinforcing properties of heroin. More specifically, methadone prevents the withdrawal symptoms associated with heroin abstinence, but it does not provide the euphoria, or "high," that heroin does. In addition, for a drug user, the clinical setting in which methadone is administered may not be as reinforcing as the social environment in which heroin is typically used (Hursh, 1991). For these reasons, it would be a mistake to expect the availability of methadone treatment to eliminate heroin use, even if the treatment were freely and easily available to all those who currently use heroin.

Vuchinich (1999) has argued that to reduce drug abuse in our society, a multifaceted approach is best. First, the cost of using drugs should be increased through stricter drug enforcement policies that reduce the supply. Second, the community must make sure that reinforcers are available for other, nondrug activities. For young people who may be tempted to experiment with drugs, sports and recreational programs that require participants to avoid drugs may be effective. For recovering addicts, the alternative reinforcers can be provided by supportive family and friends and a job that demands a drug-free employee. Third, Vuchinich emphasizes that the reinforcers for nondrug activities should be ones that can be delivered promptly because delayed reinforcers are notoriously ineffective.

Other Applications

Behavioral economic principles have been applied to other behavior problems, including smoking, overeating, and compulsive gambling (Buscemi, Murphy, Berlin, & Raynor, 2014; Cherukupalli, 2010). One important theme of the behavioral economic approach is that although it can sometimes be difficult to change such behaviors, it is not impossible. Behavioral economists and psychologists argue that these problem behaviors should not be viewed as incurable diseases but rather as economic behaviors that follow the same principles as do other behaviors (Heyman, 2009). Whether one uses the terminology of economics (supply, demand, elasticity) or of learning theory (reinforcement, punishment, stimulus control), these behaviors can be changed by appropriate modifications in the individual's environment.

As the field of behavioral economics has grown, researchers have examined an

PRACTICE QUIZ 2: CHAPTER 8

1. The fact that such things as sex and artificial sweeteners are reinforcers is a problem for _____ theory.
2. The fact that visual stimulation, exercise, and horror films can be reinforcers is a problem for _____ theory.
3. According to Premack's principle, _____ behaviors will reinforce _____ behaviors.
4. The procedure of using a series of test conditions to determine what is maintaining a person's maladaptive behavior is called _____.
5. If the demand for a product decreases sharply when its price increases, demand for the product is called _____.

ANSWERS

1. need-reduction 2. drive-reduction 3. more probable, less probable 4. functional analysis 5. elastic

increasing variety of topics, such as how much time supermarket shoppers take to make decisions on high-priced versus low-priced items (Oliveira-Castro, 2003), when customers do and do not use a maximization strategy when choosing between different brands of products (Foxall & Schrezenmaier, 2003), and what factors affect how much money employees save for retirement (Howard & Yazdipour, 2014). Combining principles from psychology and from economics has become a fruitful way to analyze a wide range of consumer behaviors.

SUMMARY

Thorndike predicted that an individual must actively respond for learning to occur, but experiments in which animals were passively transported through mazes showed that they learned without active responding. In the latent learning experiment of Tolman and Honzik, rats showed immediate improvement in their performance once food was presented at the end of a maze. Tolman and Honzik concluded that the rats had learned the maze without reinforcement but that reinforcement was necessary before they would perform the correct responses.

Studies with animals found that reinforcement can control visceral responses such as heart rate and stomach activity, but some of these findings have been difficult to replicate. Nevertheless, research with human patients has found many useful medical applications of biofeedback, in which a person is given continuous feedback about some bodily process and attempts to control it. Biofeedback has been used successfully for headaches, some types of muscular paralysis, stomach and intestinal disorders, and a variety of other ailments.

How can we predict what will be a reinforcer? The need-reduction and drive-reduction theories have obvious shortcomings. The principle of trans-situationality states that a reinforcer in one situation will be a reinforcer in other situations. Premack's principle states that more probable behaviors will reinforce less probable behaviors. But the best general rule for predicting what will be a reinforcer seems to be response deprivation theory, which states that whenever a contingency is arranged between two behaviors, the more restricted behavior should act as a reinforcer for the less restricted behavior.

The field of behavioral economics combines the techniques of operant research and the principles of economics. Optimization theory, which states that individuals will distribute their money, time, or responses in a way that optimizes subjective value, has been applied to many cases of animal behavior in natural settings. Other research has tested economic principles about supply and demand, elasticity, and substitutability among reinforcers using animals and humans in controlled environments.

Review Questions

1. How were the three different groups of rats treated in Tolman and Honzik's classic experiment on latent learning? How did each of the three groups perform, and what did Tolman and Honzik conclude?
2. Describe one biofeedback procedure used to treat a medical problem. What type of feedback is given, how do subjects respond, and how effective is the treatment in the long run?
3. What are need-reduction theory, drive-reduction theory, and the principle of trans-situationality? What are their weaknesses? How do Premack's principle and response deprivation theory predict what will serve as a reinforcer?
4. What are some reasons why children with psychological problems may exhibit bizarre behaviors? How can a functional analysis determine the cause of such behaviors?
5. How can economic concepts such as price, elasticity, and substitutability be applied to drug abuse? How do addictive drugs compare to other reinforcers?

REFERENCES

Allison, J. (1993). Response deprivation, reinforcement, and economics. *Journal of the Experimental Analysis of Behavior, 60*, 129–140.

Amari, A., Grace, N.C., & Fisher, W.W. (1995). Achieving and maintaining compliance with the ketogenic diet. *Journal of Applied Behavior Analysis, 28*, 341–342.

Azrin, N.H., Vinas, V., & Ehle, C.T. (2007). Physical activity as reinforcement for classroom calmness of ADHD children: A preliminary study. *Child & Family Behavior Therapy, 29*, 1–8.

Belke, T.W., & Pierce, W.D. (2009). Body weight manipulation, reinforcement value and choice between sucrose and wheel running: A behavioral economic analysis. *Behavioural Processes, 80*, 147–156.

Bickel, W.K., DeGrandpre, R.J., & Higgins, S.T. (1995). The behavioral economics of concurrent drug reinforcers: A review and reanalysis of drug self-administration research. *Psychopharmacology, 118*, 250–259.

Bickel, W.K., Johnson, M.W., Koffarnus, M.N., MacKillop, J., & Murphy, J.G. (2014). The behavioral economics of substance use disorders: Reinforcement pathologies and their repair. *Annual Review of Clinical Psychology, 10*, 641–677.

Blatter, K., & Schultz, W. (2006). Rewarding properties of visual stimuli. *Experimental Brain Research, 168*, 541–546.

Brown, J.F., Spencer, K., & Swift, S. (2002). A parent training programme for chronic food refusal: A case study. *British Journal of Learning Disabilities, 30*, 118–121.

Budzynski, T.H., Stoyva, J.M., Adler, C.S., & Mullaney, M.A. (1973). EMG biofeedback and tension headache: A controlled outcome study. In L. Birk (Ed.), *Biofeedback: Behavioral medicine* (pp. 37–50). New York: Grune & Stratton.

Buscemi, J., Murphy, J.G., Berlin, K.S., & Raynor, H.A. (2014). A behavioral economic analysis of changes in food-related and food-free reinforcement during weight loss treatment. *Journal of Consulting and Clinical Psychology, 82*, 659–669.

Carroll, M.E. (1993). The economic context of drug and non-drug reinforcers affects acquisition and maintenance of drug-reinforced behavior and withdrawal effects. *Drug and Alcohol Dependence, 33*, 201–210.

Cherukupalli, R. (2010). A behavioral economics perspective on tobacco taxation. *American Journal of Public Health, 100*, 609–615.

Christensen, C.J., Silberberg, A., Hursh, S.R., Huntsberry, M.E., & Riley, A.L. (2008). Essential value of cocaine and food in rats: Tests of the exponential model of demand. *Psychopharmacology, 198*, 221–229.

DiCara, L.V. (1970). Learning in the autonomic nervous system. *Scientific American, 222*, 30–39.

Dodwell, P.C., & Bessant, D.E. (1960). Learning without swimming in a water maze. *Journal of Comparative and Physiological Psychology, 53*, 422–425.

Ellingson, S.A., Miltenberger, R.G., Stricker, J.M., Garlinghouse, M.A., Roberts, J., Galensky, T.L., & Rapp, J.T. (2000). Analysis and treatment of finger sucking. *Journal of Applied Behavior Analysis, 33*, 41–52.

Elsmore, T.F., Fletcher, G.V., Conrad, D.G., & Sodetz, F.J. (1980). Reduction of heroin intake in baboons by an economic constraint. *Pharmacology, Biochemistry and Behavior, 13*, 729–731.

Fischer, S.M., Iwata, B.A., & Worsdell, A.S. (1997). Attention as an establishing operation and as reinforcement during functional analyses. *Journal of Applied Behavior Analysis, 30*, 335–338.

Fisher, W.W., Adelinis, J.D., Thompson, R.H., Worsdell, A.S., & Zarcone, J.R. (1998). Functional analysis and treatment of destructive behavior maintained by termination of "don't" (and symmetrical "do") requests. *Journal of Applied Behavior Analysis, 31*, 339–356.

Foxall, G.R., & Schrezenmaier, T.C. (2003). The behavioral economics of consumer brand choice: Establishing a methodology. *Journal of Economic Psychology, 24*, 675–695.

Gruzelier, J.H. (2014). EEG-neurofeedback for optimising performance II: Creativity, the performing arts and ecological validity. *Neuroscience and Biobehavioral Reviews, 44*, 142–158.

Hanley, G.P., Iwata, B.A., Roscoe, E.M., Thompson, R.H., & Lindberg, J.S. (2003). Response-restriction analysis II: Alteration of activity preferences. *Journal of Applied Behavior Analysis, 36*, 59–76.

Heyman, G.M. (2009). *Addiction: A disorder of choice.* Cambridge, MA: Harvard University Press.

Homme, L.E., deBaca, P.C., Devine, J.V., Steinhorst, R., & Rickert, E.J. (1963). Use of the Premack principle in controlling the behavior of nursery school children. *Journal of the Experimental Analysis of Behavior, 6*, 544.

Howard, J.A., & Yazdipour, R. (2014). Retirement planning: Contributions from the field of behavioral finance and economics. In H.K. Baker & V. Ricciardi (Eds.), *Investor behavior: The psychology of financial planning and investing* (pp. 285–305). Hoboken, NJ, US: John Wiley & Sons Inc.

Hull, C.L. (1943). *Principles of behavior.* New York: Appleton-Century-Crofts.

Hursh, S.R. (1991). Behavioral economics of drug self-administration and drug abuse policy. *Journal of the Experimental Analysis of Behavior, 56*, 377–393.

Hursh, S.R., & Silberberg, A. (2008). Economic demand and essential value. *Psychological Review, 115*, 186–198.

Jensen, M.P., Gertz, K.J., Kupper, A.E., Braden, A.L., Howe, J.D., Hakimian, S., & Sherlin, L.H. (2013). Steps toward developing an EEG biofeedback treatment for chronic pain. *Applied Psychophysiology and Biofeedback, 38*, 101–108.

Johnson, H.E., & Garton, W.H. (1973). Muscle reeducation in hemiplegia by use of electromyographic device. *Archives of Physiological and Medical Rehabilitation, 54*, 320–325.

Keith, J.R., & McVety, K.M. (1988). Latent place learning in a novel environment and the influences of prior training in rats. *Psychobiology, 16*, 146–151.

Klatt, K.P., & Morris, E.K. (2001). The Premack principle, response deprivation, and establishing operations. *The Behavior Analyst, 24*, 173–180.

Konarski, E.A. (1987). Effects of response deprivation on the instrumental performance of mentally retarded persons. *American Journal of Mental Deficiency, 91*, 537–542.

Konorski, J., & Miller, S. (1937). On two types of conditioned reflex. *Journal of Genetic Psychology, 16*, 264–272.

Krebs, J.R., & Davies, N.B. (Eds.). (1978). *Behavioral ecology: An evolutionary approach*. Sunderland, MA: Sinauer.

Linden, M., Habib, T., & Radojevic, V. (1996). A controlled study of the effects of EEG biofeedback on cognition and behavior of children with attention deficit disorder and learning disabilities. *Biofeedback and Self-Regulation, 21*, 35–49.

Little, K.D., Lubar, J.F., & Cannon, R. (2010). Neurofeedback: Research-based treatment for ADHD. In R.A. Carlstedt & R.A. Carlstedt (Eds.), *Handbook of integrative clinical psychology, psychiatry, and behavioral medicine: Perspectives, practices, and research* (pp. 807–821). New York: Springer.

MacCorquodale, K., & Meehl, P.E. (1954). Edward C. Tolman. In W.K. Estes, S. Koch, K. Mac-Corquodale, P. Meehl, C.G. Mueller, Jr., W.N. Schoenfeld, & W.S. Verplanck (Eds.), *Modern learning theory* (pp. 177–266). New York: Appleton-Century-Crofts.

Madden, G.J., Smethells, J.R., Ewan, E.E., & Hursh, S.R. (2007). Tests of behavioral-economic assessments of relative reinforcer efficacy: Economic substitutes. *Journal of the Experimental Analysis of Behavior, 87*, 219–240.

Mazur, J.E. (1975). The matching law and quantifications related to Premack's principle. *Journal of Experimental Psychology: Animal Behavior Processes, 1*, 374–386.

McNamara, H.J., Long, J.B., & Wike, E.L. (1956). Learning without response under two conditions of external cues. *Journal of Comparative and Physiological Psychology, 49*, 477–480.

Meehl, P.E. (1950). On the circularity of the law of effect. *Psychological Bulletin, 47*, 52–75.

Meuret, A.E., Wilhelm, F.H., & Roth, W.T. (2004). Respiratory feedback for treating panic disorder. *Journal of Clinical Psychology, 60*, 197–207.

Miller, N.E. (1948). Studies of fear as an acquirable drive I: Fear as motivation and fear-reduction as reinforcement in the learning of new responses. *Journal of Experimental Psychology, 38*, 89–101.

Miller, N.E. (1951). Learnable drives and rewards. In S.S. Stevens (Ed.), *Handbook of experimental psychology* (pp. 435–472). New York: Wiley.

Miller, N.E., & DiCara, L. (1967). Instrumental learning of heart rate changes in curarized rats: Shaping, and specificity to discriminative stimulus. *Journal of Comparative and Physiological Psychology, 63*, 12–19.

Miller, N.E., & Dworkin, B.R. (1974). Visceral learning: Recent difficulties with curarized rats and significant problems for human research. In P.A. Obrist, A.H. Black, J. Brener, & L.V. DiCara (Eds.), *Cardiovascular psychophysiology* (pp. 312–331). Chicago, IL: Aldine.

Murphy, J.G., MacKillop, J., Skidmore, J.R., & Pederson, A.A. (2009). Reliability and validity of a demand curve measure of alcohol reinforcement. *Experimental and Clinical Psychopharmacology, 17*, 396–404.

Nakao, M., Nomura, S., Shimosawa, T., Fujita, T., & Kuboki, T. (2000). Blood pressure biofeedback treatment of white-coat hypertension. *Journal of Psychosomatic Research, 48*, 161–169.

Nestoriuc, Y., & Martin, A. (2007). Efficacy of biofeedback for migraine: A meta-analysis. *Pain, 128*, 111–127.

Nestoriuc, Y., Martin, A., Rief, W., & Andrasik, F. (2008). Biofeedback treatment for headache disorders: A comprehensive efficacy review. *Applied Psychophysiology and Biofeedback, 33*, 125–140.

Olds, J., & Milner, P. (1954). Positive reinforcement produced by electrical stimulation of septal area and other regions of rat brain. *Journal of Comparative and Physiological Psychology, 47*, 419–427.

Oliveira-Castro, J.M. (2003). Effects of base price upon search behavior of consumers in a supermarket: An operant analysis. *Journal of Economic Psychology, 24*, 637–652.

Premack, D. (1959). Toward empirical behavioral laws I: Positive reinforcement. *Psychological Review, 66*, 219–233.

Premack, D. (1963). Rate differential reinforcement in monkey manipulation. *Journal of the Experimental Analysis of Behavior, 6*, 81–89.

Premack, D. (1965). Reinforcement theory. In D. Levine (Ed.), *Nebraska symposium on motivation* (pp. 123–180). Lincoln, NE: University of Nebraska Press.

Premack, D. (1971). Catching up with common sense or two sides of a generalization: Reinforcement and punishment. In R. Glaser (Ed.), *The nature of reinforcement* (pp. 121–150). New York: Academic Press.

Scharff, L., Marcus, D.A., & Masek, B.J. (2002). A controlled study of minimal-contact thermal biofeedback treatment in children with migraine. *Journal of Pediatric Psychology, 27*, 109–119.

Schwartz, S.P., Taylor, A.E., Scharff, L., & Blanchard, E.B. (1990). Behaviorally treated irritable bowel syndrome patients: A four-year follow-up. *Behavioral Research and Therapy, 28*, 331–335.

Sheffield, F.D., Wulff, J.J., & Backer, R. (1951). Reward value of copulation without sex drive reduction. *Journal of Comparative and Physiological Psychology, 44*, 3–8.

Silberberg, A., Bauman, R., & Hursh, S. (1993). Stock optimizing: Maximizing reinforcers per session on a variable-interval schedule. *Journal of the Experimental Analysis of Behavior, 59*, 389–399.

Sterman, M.B., & Thompson, L.M. (2014). Neurofeedback for seizure disorders: Origins, mechanisms and best practices. In D.S. Cantor & J.R. Evans (Eds.), *Clinical neurotherapy: Application of techniques for treatment* (pp. 301–319). San Diego, CA, US: Elsevier.

Strehl, U., Birkle, S.M., Wörz, S., & Kotchoubey, B. (2014). Sustained reduction of seizures in patients with intractable epilepsy after self-regulation training of slow cortical potentials—10 years after. *Frontiers in Human Neuroscience, 8*, ArtID 604.

Strohmeier, C., Pace, G.M., & Luiselli, J.K. (2014). Brief (test-control) functional analysis and treatment evaluation of aggressive behavior evoked by divided attention. *Behavioral Interventions, 29*, 331–338.

Thorndike, E.L. (1946). Expectation. *Psychological Review, 53*, 277–281.

Timberlake, W., & Allison, J. (1974). Response deprivation: An empirical approach to instrumental performance. *Psychological Review, 81*, 146–164.

Tolman, E.C. (1932). *Purposive behavior in animals and men.* New York: Appleton-Century Crofts.

Tolman, E.C., & Honzik, C.H. (1930). Introduction and removal of reward, and maze performance in rats. *University of California Publications in Psychology, 4*, 257–275.

Vuchinich, R.E. (1999). Behavioral economics as a framework for organizing the expanded range of substance abuse interventions. In J.A. Tucker, D.M. Donovan, & G.A. Marlatt (Eds.), *Changing addictive behavior: Bridging clinical and public health strategies* (pp. 191–218). New York: Guilford Press.

Watson, T.S., Ray, K.P., Turner, H.S., & Logan, P. (1999). Teacher-implemented functional analysis and treatment: A method for linking assessment to intervention. *School Psychology Review, 28*, 292–302.

Weber, E., Köberl, A., Frank, S., & Doppelmayr, M. (2011). Predicting successful learning of SMR neurofeedback in healthy participants: Methodological considerations. *Applied Psychophysiology and Biofeedback, 36*, 37–45.

Werner, G.E., & Hall, D.J. (1974). Optimal foraging and size selection of prey by the bluegill sunfish (*Lepomis macrochirus*). *Ecology, 55*, 1042–1052.

Zoefel, B., Huster, R.J., & Herrmann, C.S. (2011). Neurofeedback training of the upper alpha frequency band in EEG improves cognitive performance. *NeuroImage, 54*, 1427–1431.

CHAPTER 9

Stimulus Control and Concept Learning

Learning Objectives

After reading this chapter, you should be able to

- discuss the debate over whether generalization gradients are innate or learned, and evaluate the evidence for each position
- discuss the debate over whether stimulus control is absolute or relational, and evaluate the evidence for each position
- define behavioral contrast and discuss different theories of why it occurs
- define errorless discrimination learning and give examples of its use in behavior modification
- explain what is known about the structure of natural concepts, and describe the research on natural concept learning by animals
- describe some of the ways that stimulus control techniques are used in behavior modification

The relationship between stimuli and the behaviors that follow them is the topic of this chapter, a topic called **stimulus control**. As we have seen throughout this book, predicting what response will occur in the presence of a given stimulus is a challenging task, even when the same stimulus is presented again and again in a controlled laboratory environment. But in the real world, all creatures are repeatedly confronted with stimuli and events they have never experienced before, and their survival may depend on an adaptive response. The topic of stimulus control includes research on how creatures respond to such novel stimuli. In previous chapters we used the term *generalization* to describe the transfer of responding from trained to untrained stimuli. In this chapter, we will examine the process of generalization more closely. We will also explore the topic of concept learning, which involves the classification of different objects into a single category (e.g., "trees"), even though their visual appearances may sometimes have little in common.

GENERALIZATION GRADIENTS

Measuring Generalization Gradients

Suppose that we have trained a pigeon to peck at a yellow key by reinforcing pecks with food on a VI schedule. Now we want to determine how much generalization there will be to other colors, such as blue, green, orange, and red. How can we collect this information? One way is to use *probe trials*, in which the other colors are briefly presented to measure the pigeon's responding but no reinforcer is given. The probe trials are occasionally inserted among reinforced trials with the training stimulus. For instance, 90% of the trials might involve the yellow key light and the VI schedule, but 10% of the trials would include the other colors and an extinction schedule. Another method for obtaining generalization gradients is to follow training with the yellow light with a continuous set of extinction trials with both the yellow light and other colors. In this method, the trick is to obtain enough trials with each stimulus before responding extinguishes. Often this can be accomplished by keeping the durations of the extinction trials short.

With human subjects, other techniques for measuring generalization are available. For example, Droit-Volet (2002) first asked young children to listen to several presentations of a 4-second tone. The children were then given test trials with tones of different durations; they were told to respond by saying "yes" if it was the same 4-second tone and "no" if the tone was longer or shorter in duration. As Figure 9.1 shows, Droit-Volet obtained a fairly symmetrical generalization gradient, with the most "yes" responses to the 4-second tone and fewer "yes" responses to shorter or longer tones.

What Causes Generalization Gradients?

Why should reinforcement of a behavior in the presence of one stimulus cause this behavior to occur to similar stimuli that have never been used in training? Pavlov's (1927) answer was that generalization is an automatic by-product of the conditioning process. His basic idea was that the effects of conditioning somehow spread across to nearby neurons in the cerebral cortex. Although the neural details of Pavlov's theory are not accurate, his more general view that generalization is an inherent property of the nervous system seems quite sensible.

A very different hypothesis was proposed by Lashley and Wade (1946). They theorized that some explicit discrimination training along the dimension in question (such as wavelength of light or frequency of tone) is necessary before the typical peaked generalization gradient is obtained. For instance, if the dimension of interest is color, they would claim that

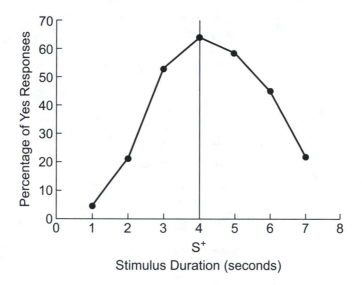

Figure 9.1 A generalization gradient obtained when children were trained to identify a 4-second tone and then were tested with tones of longer and shorter durations. (From Droit-Volet, 2002, Scalar timing in temporal generalization in children with short and long stimulus durations, *Quarterly Journal of Experimental Psychology, 55A,* 1193–1209. Copyright The Experimental Psychology Society, reprinted by permission of Taylor & Francis Ltd, www.tandfonline.com on behalf of the Experimental Psychology Society.)

the learner must receive experience in which reinforcers are delivered when a particular color is present but not when the color is absent. Without such discrimination training, Lashley and Wade proposed that the generalization gradient would be flat; that is, the individual would respond just as strongly to all colors—there would be no discrimination among them. In short, whereas Pavlov proposed that generalization gradients are innate, Lashley and Wade proposed that they depend on learning experiences.

How Experience Affects the Shape of Generalization Gradients

A nice set of experiments by Jenkins and Harrison (1960, 1962) provided support for the position of Lashley and Wade by showing that an animal's experience can have a major effect on the shape of its generalization gradient. Three groups of pigeons responded on a VI schedule for food reinforcement in the presence of a 1,000-Hz tone. One group received *nondifferential training*, in which every trial was the same—the key light was lit, the 1,000-Hz tone was on, and the VI schedule was in effect. Once the pigeons were responding steadily, they received a series of extinction trials with different tone frequencies, and some trials had no tone at all. The results are presented in the top panel of Figure 9.2. As Lashley and Wade predicted, the pigeons in this group produced generalization gradients that were basically flat: Response rates were roughly the same at all tone frequencies!

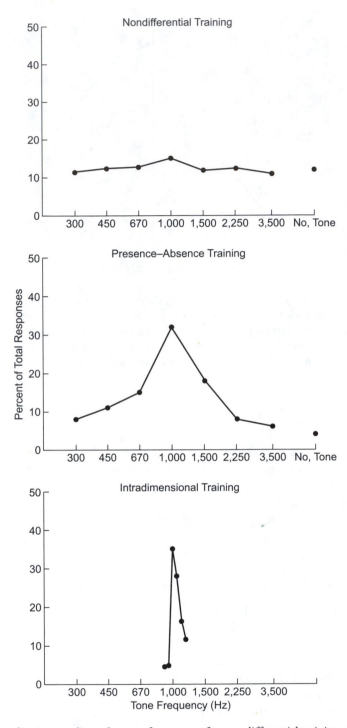

Figure 9.2 Generalization gradients for tone frequency after nondifferential training with a 1,000-Hz tone (top panel), presence–absence training with a 1,000-Hz tone (center panel), and intradimensional training with a 1,000-Hz tone as S+ and a 950-Hz tone as S− (bottom panel). (Based on data from Jenkins & Harrison, 1960, 1962)

Pigeons in the second group received *presence–absence training*, which included two types of trials: (1) trials with the 1,000-Hz tone and the VI schedule for food, exactly as in the first group, and (2) trials without the tone, during which the key light was lit as usual but no food was ever delivered. The 1,000-Hz tone would be called an S+ (a discriminative stimulus for reinforcement) and the absence of the tone would be called an S– (a discriminative stimulus for the absence of reinforcement). When these pigeons were later tested with other tone frequencies, they produced typical generalization gradients with sharp peaks at 1,000 Hz, as shown in the center panel in Figure 9.2. Notice that in this condition, the tone was the only stimulus reliably correlated with reinforcement (because the key light and the other sights and smells of the chamber were present both on reinforced trials and on extinction trials). Because it was the best signal for the availability of reinforcement, the tone came to exert control over the pigeons' responding, as can be seen in the declines in response rate that occurred when the tone's frequency was changed.

A third group tested by Jenkins and Harrison (1962) received discrimination training in which the 1,000-Hz tone was the S+ and a 950-Hz tone was an S–. In other words, food was available on trials with the 1,000-Hz tone but not on trials with the 950-Hz tone. This type of training is called *intradimensional training* because S+ and S– came from the same stimulus dimension (tone frequency). When tested with different tones in extinction, these pigeons produced much narrower generalization gradients, as shown in the bottom panel of Figure 9.2. These very sharply peaked gradients showed that an animal's experience can have major effects on the shape of its generalization gradients. In summary, these experiments support Lashley and Wade's hypothesis that the shapes of generalization gradients depend on an individual's experience.

The story is not so simple, however. Other studies have shown that peaked generalization gradients can sometimes be obtained with nondifferential training. For example, Guttman and Kalish (1956) found peaked gradients with different key colors after pigeons received nondifferential training with a yellow key light. These results seem to support Pavlov's theory that no special training is necessary for generalization gradients to appear. In defense of their theory, Lashley and Wade suggested that although animals might receive only nondifferential training within an experiment, they may have learned from their everyday experiences prior to the experiment that different stimuli along the dimension in question can signal different consequences. The pigeons in the Guttman and Kalish experiment might have learned from their everyday experiences that color is frequently an informative characteristic of a stimulus; as a result, they were predisposed to "pay attention" to the color of the key in the experimental chamber.

How Sensory Deprivation Affects the Shape of Generalization Gradients

Once the possibility of preexperiment learning is entertained, the Lashley and Wade theory becomes quite difficult to test. It becomes necessary to prevent the possibility of discrimination learning along the dimension in question from the moment an animal is born. Rudolph, Honig, and Gerry (1969) conducted such an experiment by raising chickens and quail in an environment that was illuminated with a monochromatic green light of 530 nanometers (nm). Because this special light emitted only a single wavelength, all objects appeared green regardless of their actual color in white light. (Imagine watching a black-and-white movie while wearing green-tinted glasses: Everything on the screen would appear as a mixture of green and black.) The birds were also trained to peck a green key for food. When tested with other key colors, the birds displayed typical generalization gradients, with peaks at 530 nm. Other experiments of this type found similar results. These results clearly contradict the theory of Lashley and Wade, because normal generalization gradients were found with birds that had absolutely no prior experience with different colors.

To summarize, the research on the relationship between experience and generalization has shown that Pavlov's theory and Lashley and Wade's theory are both partially right and partially wrong. The experiments of Jenkins and Harrison found flat generalization gradients for the pigeons that had no discrimination training, and the type of training the pigeons received had major effects on the shapes of their gradients. In contrast, the experiments on sensory deprivation showed that peaked generalization gradients can sometimes be observed even when animals have no prior experience with a particular stimulus dimension. The results suggest a compromise position: In some cases, discrimination learning may be necessary before stimulus control is obtained; in other cases, no experience may be necessary. The evidence that, for birds, such experience is necessary for tones but not for colors is consistent with the idea that vision is a dominant sensory modality for these creatures. Perhaps we might say that birds are "prepared" to associate the color of a stimulus with the consequences that follow, but they are not prepared to associate the pitch of a tone with subsequent events.

IS STIMULUS CONTROL ABSOLUTE OR RELATIONAL?

Imagine a simple experiment on discrimination learning in which a chicken is presented with two discriminative stimuli, a medium gray card and a dark gray card. Approaching the medium gray card is reinforced, but approaching the dark gray card is not. With enough training, the chicken will learn to choose the medium gray card. But exactly what has the animal learned? According to the **absolute theory of stimulus control**, the animal has simply learned about the two stimuli separately: It has learned that choosing the medium gray color produces food and choosing the dark gray color produces no food.

On the other hand, according to the **relational theory of stimulus control**, the animal has learned something about the relationship between the two stimuli: It has learned that the *lighter gray* is associated with food. The absolute position assumes that the animal responds to each stimulus without reference to the other; the relational position assumes that the animal responds to the relationship between the two. C. Lloyd Morgan (1894), an early writer on animal behavior, favored the absolute position because he believed that nonhumans are simply not capable of understanding relationships such as *lighter*, *darker*, *larger*, or *redder*. These relationships are abstract concepts that are not part of any single stimulus, and he felt that animals do not have the capacity to form such abstractions. An early advocate of the relational position was the German psychologist Wolfgang Kohler (1939). The question of whether animals can learn about relationships continues to intrigue modern psychologists (Wright & Lickteig, 2010). Let us look at the evidence on both sides of this debate and attempt to come to some resolution.

Transposition and Peak Shift

In support of the relational position, Kohler (1939) presented evidence for a phenomenon called **transposition**. After training several chickens on the task just described, Kohler gave them several trials on which the two stimuli were (1) the medium gray card that had previously served as the S+ and (2) a card with a lighter gray. Which stimulus would the chickens choose? If the absolute theory is correct, the chickens should choose the medium gray, because choosing that particular shade of gray had been reinforced in the past. However, if the chickens had learned to respond to the relation between the two training stimuli (choosing the lighter gray), they should choose the novel, light gray card. Across several extinction trials, all of the chickens showed a preference for the light gray card over the previously reinforced medium gray card, supporting the relational theory (Figure 9.3). The term *transposition* is meant to convey the idea that the animal has transferred the relational rule ("Choose the lighter gray") to a new pair of stimuli.

Kohler also found evidence for transposition with chimpanzees, and similar results have been obtained with several other species, including human children (Alberts & Ehrenfreund, 1951), penguins (Manabe, Murata, Kawashima, Asahina, & Okutsu, 2009), and even turtles (Leighty, Grand, Pittman Courte, Maloney, & Bettinger, 2013). These results constitute one important piece of evidence for the relational theory.

In research on generalization gradients, Hanson (1959) discovered a phenomenon called **peak shift** that is in some ways similar to transposition. Pigeons in a control group received several sessions of training in which pecking at a 550-nm key light occasionally produced food, and they had no training with any other key color. In an experimental group, pigeons received intradimensional training with the 550-nm key light as S+ and a 555-nm key light

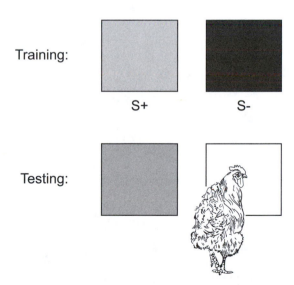

Figure 9.3 In Kohler's (1939) experiment on transposition, chickens were first rewarded for approaching the medium gray card (S+). In the test phase, they tended to approach the lighter of the two cards, not the S+ used in training.

as S–. After this training, Hanson measured the birds' responses to a range of different key colors during extinction so as to obtain generalization gradients.

As shown in Figure 9.4, the control group produced a typical generalization gradient with a peak at 550 nm, as expected. However, the experimental group produced a peak around 530 to 540 nm rather than at the previously reinforced wavelength of 550 nm. The term *peak shift* refers to this shift in the generalization gradient in a direction away from the S–. Peak shift has been observed with many other stimuli besides colors and with many different species, including humans (Derenne, 2010).

The absolute position would seem to predict a peak at 550 nm for both groups, since this was the S+. However, the relational position can account for this peak shift as follows. Lights of both 550 and 555 nm are greenish yellow, but the shorter wavelength is a bit greener. The pigeons that received intradimensional training might have learned that the *greener* of the two stimuli was a signal for reinforcement. This would explain why they responded more to the 530- and 540-nm stimuli, which are greener still.

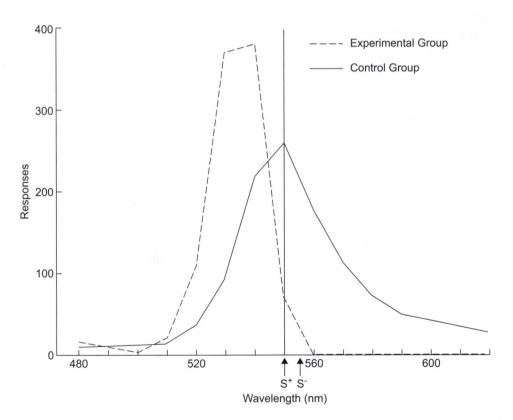

Figure 9.4 Generalization gradients for wavelength of light. The control group was trained only with a 550-nm key light at S+. The experimental group shows a peak shift to the left after training with a 550-nm key light as S+ and a 555-nm key light as S–. (From Hanson, H.M., 1959, Effects of discrimination training on stimulus generalization, *Journal of Experimental Psychology, 58,* 321–334. © American Psychological Association. Reprinted with permission.)

Spence's Theory of Excitatory and Inhibitory Gradients

Although the findings on transposition and peak shift seem to favor the relational theory, a clever version of the absolute theory developed by Kenneth Spence (1937) can account quite nicely for both of these phenomena. Spence proposed that in intradimensional training, an excitatory generalization gradient develops around the S+ and an inhibitory gradient develops around the S−. Here is how this reasoning might apply to Hanson's experiment. Figure 9.5a depicts an excitatory generalization gradient around 550 nm and an inhibitory gradient centered around 555 nm. The term *associative strength* refers to the ability of each stimulus to elicit a response. Spence proposed that the net associative strength of any stimulus can be determined by subtracting its inhibitory strength from its excitatory strength. For each wavelength, the result of this subtraction is shown in Figure 9.5b.

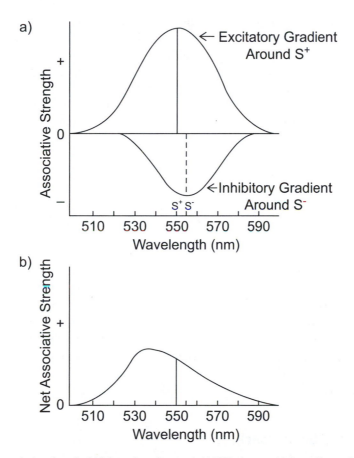

Figure 9.5 An analysis of peak shift based on Spence's (1937) theory. (a) Intradimensional training is assumed to produce an excitatory gradient around S+ (550 nm) and an inhibitory gradient around S− (555 nm). (b) The net associative strength of each wavelength equals the difference between its excitatory strength and inhibitory strength. Because of the inhibitory gradient around S−, the peak of this gradient is shifted from S+ in a direction away from S−.

Notice that the S+, at 550 nm, has the highest excitatory strength, but it also has a good deal of inhibitory strength because of its proximity to the S−. On the other hand, a stimulus in the vicinity of 530 to 540 nm has considerable excitatory strength but relatively little inhibitory strength (because it is farther away from the S−). The result is that stimuli around 530 to 540 nm actually have a higher net associative strength than the S+ of 550 nm. By comparing Figures 9.4 and 9.5, you can see that Spence's theory predicts the type of peak shift that Hanson actually obtained. His theory does a very good job of accounting for peak shift, and it can also account for transposition using the same type of reasoning about excitatory and inhibitory gradients.

The Intermediate-Size Problem

Although Spence's theory offers a reasonable explanation of both transposition and peak shift, it does not predict the results on a test called the **intermediate-size problem**. Gonzalez, Gentry, and Bitterman (1954) conducted an experiment on the intermediate-size problem with chimpanzees. Their stimuli were nine squares of different sizes. Their smallest square (Square 1) had an area of 9 square inches, and their largest square (Square 9) had an area of about 27 square inches. During training, the chimpanzees were always presented with Squares 1, 5, and 9, and they were reinforced if they chose the intermediate square, Square 5. (Of course, the left-to-right locations of the squares varied randomly from trial to trial so that the chimps could not use position as a discriminative stimulus.)

On test trials, the chimpanzees were presented with different sets of three squares, and they were reinforced no matter which square they chose. For example, suppose the three squares were Squares 4, 7, and 9. The predictions of the relational position are straightforward: If the chimps had learned to choose the square of intermediate size, they should choose Square 7. Figure 9.6 helps to explain the predictions of Spence's theory. The initial training should have produced an excitatory gradient around Square 5 and inhibitory gradients around Squares 1 and 9. Because Square 5 is flanked on each side by an inhibitory gradient, there is no peak shift in this case; instead, the inhibitory gradients simply sharpen the gradient of net associative strength around Square 5. Therefore, a chimpanzee should choose whichever stimulus is closer to Square 5 (Square 4 in this example). The actual results supported the relational theory and contradicted Spence's theory: The chimps usually chose the square of intermediate size on test trials regardless of which three squares were presented. They behaved as though they were responding to the relationships among the stimuli, not their absolute sizes.

Other Data, and Some Conclusions

Lazareva and her colleagues conducted a careful series of experiments with pigeons to reexamine the debate over absolute versus relational stimulus control (Lazareva, Wasserman, & Young, 2005; Lazareva, Young, & Wasserman, 2014). Figure 9.7 gives one example of the type of procedure they used. On some trials, the pigeons were trained with Circle 1 as S− and Circle 2 as S+. On other trials, they were trained with Circle 5 as S− and

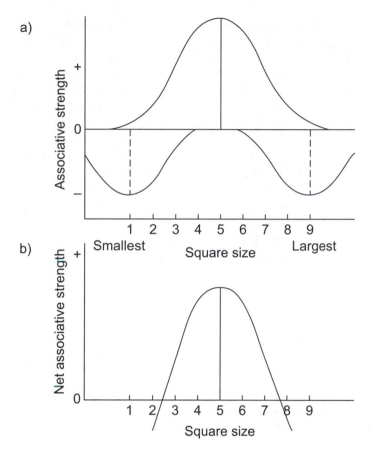

Figure 9.6 An application of Spence's (1937) theory to the intermediate-size problem. (a) In initial training, an excitatory gradient develops around S+ (Square 5) and inhibitory gradients develop around the two S–s (Squares 1 and 9). (b) Because of the two symmetrical inhibitory gradients, there is no peak shift in the gradient of net associative strength.

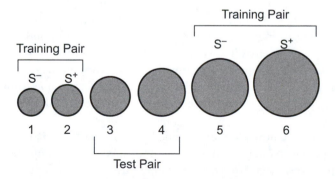

Figure 9.7 Examples of the types of stimuli and tests used by Lazareva and colleagues to compare the absolute and relational theories of stimulus control. After discrimination training with Circle 1 versus Circle 2, and training with Circle 5 versus Circle 6, pigeons were tested with a new pair of stimuli— Circle 3 versus Circle 4.

Circle 6 as S+. Therefore, in both cases, a choice of the larger circle was reinforced. Then the pigeons were given a choice between two new stimuli, Circles 3 and 4. Notice that Circle 3 is similar in size to Circle 2 (an S+) and Circle 4 is similar to Circle 5 (an S–). Therefore, Spence's theory predicts that through the process of generalization, the pigeons should choose Circle 3 over Circle 4. However, if the pigeons learned the relational rule of always picking the larger circle, they should choose Circle 4. The pigeons did show a preference for Circle 4 over Circle 3, which supported the prediction of the relational theory.

Lazareva and her colleagues concluded that although there may be some situations where animals respond to the absolute properties of stimuli as Spence theorized, most of the evidence now favors the relational approach to stimulus control. They also found that relational responding was stronger when their animals were trained with more examples (e.g., four different pairs of circles, with the larger circle serving as S+ in every pair). It makes sense that giving animals more examples, all of them consistent with the same relational rule, should help them learn the rule better. They concluded that there is "strong support for the idea that animals are indeed capable of relational responding" (Lazareva et al., 2005, p. 43).

BEHAVIORAL CONTRAST

Phenomena such as peak shift and transposition show that it is often impossible to predict how one stimulus will affect an individual's behavior unless we also take into account other stimuli—either those currently present or encountered in the past. The phenomenon of **behavioral contrast** (Reynolds, 1961) also shows that stimuli cannot be judged in isolation.

An experiment by Gutman (1977) provides a good example of behavioral contrast. Pigeons responded on a key in a chamber where there were two discriminative stimuli, a noise and a light, which alternated every 3 minutes throughout a session (in what is called a **multiple schedule**). In Phase 1, a VI 30-second schedule was in effect when the noise was on, and a separate VI 30-second schedule was in effect when the light was on. Not surprisingly, response rates during the noise and light were about the same in this condition (Figure 9.8). In Phase 2, the schedule operating during the noise was switched to extinction. Figure 9.8 shows that, as expected, responding became slower and slower during the noise. What was more surprising, however, was that response rates increased dramatically in the presence of the light, even though the reinforcement schedule for the light was not changed. This change in responding to one stimulus that occurs after a change in the reinforcement schedule for another stimulus is called behavioral contrast.

To be more specific, Gutman's study provided an example of **positive contrast**, because there was an *increase* in responding during the unchanged light component. The opposite effect has also been observed. For example, suppose that instead of extinction the schedule for the noise delivered three times as many reinforcers in Phase 2. The likely result would be an increase in responding during the noise and a decrease in responding during the light. This decrease in responding during the unchanged light component would be called **negative contrast**.

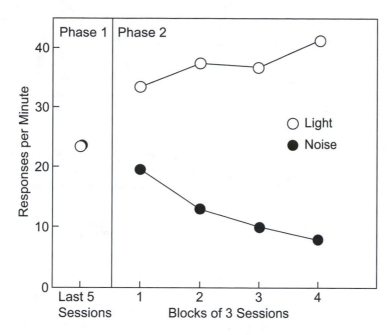

Figure 9.8 Results from Gutman's (1977) experiment on behavioral contrasts in rats. When both the light and the noise signaled VI 30-second schedules (Phase 1), response rates were about the same for both stimuli. When the noise signaled a period extinction (Phase 2), response rates declined toward zero when the noise was present but increased substantially above those of Phase 1 when the light was present.

Behavioral contrast has been observed with many different types of reinforcers and with many different species, from bumblebees to humans. There are several different theories about why it occurs. According to the *behavioral reallocation hypothesis*, faster responding in the unchanged component (positive contrast) is possible because of the slower responding that occurs in the component that is changed to extinction. The slower responding in the extinction component might allow the subject to recover from fatigue, so the "well-rested" animal can respond faster in the unchanged component (Dougan, McSweeney, & Farmer-Dougan, 1986).

Another theory of behavioral contrast is the *reinforcer habituation/satiation hypothesis* (McSweeney & Weatherly, 1998). The basic idea behind this theory is the well-established finding that the more frequently a reinforcer is presented over a short period of time, the less effective it becomes because of habituation, satiation, or both. In Gutman's experiment, less food was delivered in Phase 2, so there was probably less habituation and satiation to the food, which could explain why there was faster responding in the light component than in Phase 1.

A third theory of behavioral contrast focuses on a comparison of the two reinforcement rates (Herrnstein, 1970). According to this theory, rate of response in one component of a multiple schedule depends not only on the reinforcement available during that component but also on the rate of reinforcement in the other component. To speak loosely, it is as though the animal judges the value of one component by comparing it to its neighbors.

In the first phase of Gutman's experiment, the schedule during the light component was "nothing special" since the same schedule was available during the noise component. The light therefore produced only a moderate rate of response. During the second phase of the experiment, the light component was quite attractive compared to the extinction schedule of the noise component, so the light produced a high response rate.

In a review of the many experiments and theories about behavioral contrast, Williams (2002) concluded that it is caused by several different factors, and no single theory can account for all of the data. Habituation and satiation probably contribute to the effect, as does the sort of comparison process proposed by Herrnstein (1970). Williams also presented evidence that behavioral contrast is largely based on anticipation of the upcoming component, rather than a reaction to the preceding component. For example, if a multiple schedule includes three components—A, B, and C—that are repeatedly presented in this order, responding in component B is mostly affected by the schedule in component C. More recently, however, Killeen (2014) showed that the schedule in component A also has a short-lived effect on responding in component B, and he developed a mathematical model that takes into account the effects of both the preceding and upcoming components.

Although the phenomenon of behavioral contrast is easy to describe, explaining why it occurs has turned out to be much harder, and it appears to be produced by several different factors. Although its causes are complex, behavioral contrast demonstrates that it can be dangerous to study reinforcement schedules as though they were isolated entities. An individual's behavior on one reinforcement schedule may be greatly influenced by events occurring before and after the schedule is in effect.

PRACTICE QUIZ 1: CHAPTER 9

1. Lashley and Wade proposed that generalization gradients were the result of experience, and without discrimination training, animals would show _____ generalization gradients.
2. In _____ training, one stimulus serves as a S+ and another stimulus on the same dimension serves as S–.
3. In the phenomenon of peak shift, the peak of the generalization shifts from the S+ in the direction _____ the S–.
4. Results from the intermediate-size problem favor the _____ theory of stimulus control.
5. Suppose that responding during either blue or yellow stimuli is reinforced, but then the schedule for the yellow stimulus switches to extinction. Responding during the blue stimulus should _____, which is called _____ behavioral contrast.

ANSWERS

1. flat 2. intradimensional 3. away from 4. relational 5. increase, positive

---

ERRORLESS DISCRIMINATION LEARNING

Suppose that as a laboratory exercise for a course on learning, your assignment is to teach a pigeon a strong discrimination between red and green key colors. The red key will signal a VI 1-minute schedule, and you would like moderate, steady responding to this key color.

The green key will signal extinction, so you would like no responding when the key is green. You could begin by using food to shape pecking at the red key. At first, you would reinforce every response and then gradually shift to longer and longer VI schedules. After several sessions with a VI 1-minute schedule on the red key, the pigeon would probably respond steadily throughout the session, and you could then introduce the green key color and its extinction schedule. From now on, sessions might alternate between 3-minute red components and 3-minute green components. At first, we would expect the pigeon to respond when the key was green because of generalization, but eventually responses to green should decrease to a low level.

This might sound like a sensible plan for developing a good red/green discrimination, but Terrace (1966) listed several reasons why it is not ideal. This method takes a long time, and along the way the animal makes many "errors" (unreinforced responses on the green key). Because the training must continue for several sessions before a good discrimination is achieved, there are likely to be many setbacks owing to the spontaneous recovery of responding on the green key at the start of each session. It also appears that this type of discrimination training is aversive for the animal. The pigeon may exhibit aggressive behavior, such as wing flapping. If another pigeon is present in an adjacent compartment, the pigeon may engage in an aggressive display and eventually attack the other animal. Such attacks typically occur soon after the transition from S+ to S−. A final problem with this procedure is that even after months of training, the animal's performance is usually not perfect—there are occasional bursts of responding to the S−.

Terrace (1963) showed that there is a better method of discrimination training, which he called **errorless discrimination learning** because the learner typically makes few or no responses to the S−. The errorless discrimination procedure differs from the traditional procedure in two main ways. First, rather than waiting for strong, steady responding to the S+, the experimenter introduces the S− early in the training procedure. Terrace introduced the S− within 30 seconds of the pigeon's first peck at the red key. Second, a fading procedure is used to make it unlikely that the learner will respond to the S−. At first, the S− was presented for only 5 seconds at a time, which gave the pigeon little chance to respond in its presence. In addition, Terrace knew that pigeons usually do not peck at a dark key, so at the beginning of training, the S− was not an illuminated green key but a dark key. The S− was then gradually changed from a dark key to a dimly lit green key, and over trials the intensity of the green light was increased. In summary, in Terrace's procedure the S− was introduced early in training, it was presented very briefly at first, and it was initially a stimulus that was unlikely to elicit responding.

Terrace's errorless discrimination procedure proved to be an effective way to decrease the number of responses to the S− and improve the learner's long-term performance. In one experiment, pigeons trained with a conventional discrimination procedure made an average of more than 3,000 responses to the S− during 28 sessions, but those trained with the errorless procedure averaged only about 25 responses to the S−. Terrace also reported that other disadvantages of the traditional discrimination training were reduced—there were no setbacks at the beginning of a new session and no signs that the training was aversive for the animals.

BOX 9.1   APPLYING THE RESEARCH

Errorless Learning in Education

B. F. Skinner (1958) maintained that classroom curricula should be designed so that the student almost never makes a mistake. His reasoning is that if we do not want children to avoid learning experiences, and if making an incorrect response (and thereby failing to receive reinforcement) is aversive, then we should try to eliminate these aversive episodes as much as possible. Because errorless discrimination training can accomplish this and produce good learning in a minimum amount of time, variations of Terrace's techniques have been used in many educational settings.

In one example, Duffy and Wishart (1987) used a fading procedure to teach children with Down syndrome to identify basic shapes such as ovals and rectangles. Some of the children were taught using a conventional trial-and-error method using cards with three shapes, such as the right-hand card in Figure 9.9. A child would be asked to "point to the rectangle" and would be praised if he or she made a correct response. If the child made an error (which happened frequently in the conventional procedure), the teacher would say, "No, that is not right. Try again the next time." The errorless learning procedure was exactly the same, except that at first the cards had only the correct shape and two blank spaces, as on the left-hand card in Figure 9.9. Not surprisingly, the children had little problem pointing to the correct shape. Then, very small incorrect shapes were added, as on the center card in Figure 9.9; over trials, the sizes of the incorrect shapes were gradually increased until they were the same size as the correct shape. Duffy and Wishart found that with the errorless procedure, the children made very few mistakes during training, and their performance remained slightly better at the end of training. They also reported that the children's attitudes toward the learning situation seemed to be better with the errorless procedure, perhaps because they did not suffer many failures.

Because of these benefits, errorless learning procedures, along with other techniques that gradually increase the difficulty of the discriminations, have frequently been incorporated in teaching procedures for children with developmental disabilities (Mueller & Palkovic, 2007). However, there can be both advantages and disadvantages to using errorless discrimination procedures. After errorless training, the children may have difficulty learning discrimination reversals, in which the roles of S+ and S– are reversed (McIlvane, Kledaras, Iennaco, McDonald, & Stoddard, 1995). They may also have difficulty generalizing and maintaining their discrimination skills in new situations (Jones & Eayrs, 1992). Educators must therefore carefully consider both the benefits and limitations when deciding whether to use errorless discrimination training or alternative techniques.

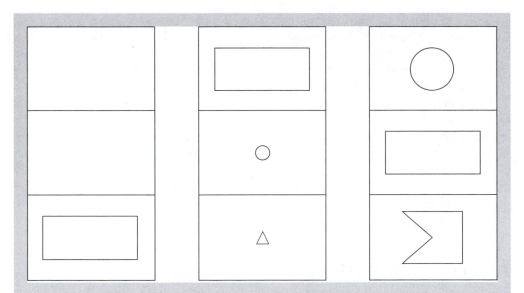

Figure 9.9 Examples of the types of cards used by Duffy and Wishart (1987) to teach children with Down syndrome the names of shapes. Errorless learning started with only the correct shape (left), then small incorrect shapes were added (center), and the incorrect shapes gradually became larger until they were the same size as the correct shape (right).

Adult learners can also benefit from errorless discrimination training. For example, it has been widely used to reteach adults information they have lost as a result of Alzheimer's disease or other brain disorders. In one study, 12 patients in the early stages of Alzheimer's disease were given errorless training to help them relearn names of people they had forgotten. As a result of this training, the patients were significantly better at remembering the names of these people when they saw their faces, and the improvement in the memories persisted 6 months later. The improvement, however, was specific to those names and faces they had studied; when trying to remember the names of other people, they were no better than before. In other words, the errorless training techniques helped these patients relearn specific information they had lost; it did not produce overall improvement in their memory functioning (Clare, Wilson, Carter, Roth, & Hodges, 2002). As is the case with children, research with adults has shown that errorless procedures can be beneficial for some types of learning but that making errors can be advantageous in other learning tasks (Cyr & Anderson, 2015).

CONCEPT LEARNING

Many of the discrimination tasks described in this chapter might seem quite artificial for three reasons: (1) The stimuli were simple, idealized images that an animal would be unlikely to encounter in the natural environment (e.g., a perfect square, uniformly red, on a plain white background); (2) only a small number of stimuli were used (sometimes just two stimuli, S+ and S–); and (3) the difference between positive and negative instances was well defined and unambiguous. For instance, the S+ might be a red square and the S– a green square, and the animal would not be presented with any other shapes nor with any squares that were a mixture of red and green.

In research on the topic of *concept learning*, or *categorization*, all three of these restrictions are removed. This research is designed to resemble more closely the types of discriminations an individual must learn in the natural environment. For example, when an animal learns to discriminate between predators and nonpredators or between edible plants and poisonous plants, (1) the stimuli will generally not be simple, idealized forms, (2) there may be countless examples from each category, and (3) the distinction between positive and negative instances may not be large or obvious. Research on concept learning has explored how both animals and people learn to make such complex discriminations.

The Structure of Natural Categories

Eleanor Rosch (1973, 1975) conducted a series of experiments on how people respond to different members of "natural" categories—categories of objects found in the real world, such as birds, vegetables, or vehicles. Two of her most important conclusions were that the boundaries of these categories are not distinct and that people tend to judge some members of a category as "good" or "typical" examples of the category and others as "bad" or "atypical" examples. Rosch used the terms **central instances** and **peripheral instances** to refer to typical and atypical examples, respectively.

In one experiment, Rosch (1973) simply asked people to estimate the typicality of different examples of various categories on a 7-point rating scale, with 1 signifying a very typical instance and 7 a very atypical example. Her participants found this an easy task, and different instances received very different rankings. For example, in the category of birds, robin received a mean ranking of 1.1, chicken a mean ranking of 3.8, and bat a mean ranking of 5.8. Thus, robins were judged to be typical birds, chickens were rated as much less typical, and bats were treated as very marginal examples of birds. The example of bats illustrates how the boundaries of a natural category may be indistinct. Bats are not really birds at all, but many people probably do not know this, and they may consider bats as (atypical) members of the bird category. Conversely, whereas an olive is a fruit, many people do not classify it as such, and in Rosch's study it received a mean rating of 6.2.

Rosch described three important characteristics of natural categories. First, people tend to agree about which examples are central and which are peripheral. Second, if people are asked to list the members of various categories, they list central instances more frequently. For instance, when Battig and Montague (1969) asked adults to make lists of birds, robin was listed by 377 people, chicken by 40 people, and bat by only 3 people. Third, in reaction-time tests, people take longer to decide that peripheral examples are members of the category.

It is interesting to speculate about how children learn to identify members and nonmembers of various natural categories. Language might play an important role: A parent may point to a robin and say, "That is a bird." Later, the parent may tell the child that it is a robin, and that robins are one type of bird. Yet language alone cannot explain why natural categories have the structure they do (with central instances, peripheral instances, and ambiguous boundaries). Although a child may be taught "A robin is a bird" and "A chicken is a bird," the child will still judge the chicken to be an atypical bird and will be a bit slower to agree that a chicken is a bird. Why does this happen?

Cognitive psychologists have proposed many different theories of human concept learning, including exemplar theories, prototype theories, and feature theories. According to **exemplar theories** (e.g., Jäkel, Schölkopf, & Wichmann, 2008), a category such as bird consists of the memory of many individual examples of birds the person has seen. If a newly encountered instance is similar to the examples in memory, it will be judged to be a member of the bird category. According to **prototype theories** (e.g., Hampton, 2006), through experience with many birds a person develops a prototype—an idea of what an ideal or typical bird is like. If a new instance is very similar to the prototype, it will be considered a central instance of a bird. If it is only moderately similar to the prototype, it will be considered a peripheral instance. If it is very unlike the prototype, it will not be considered a member of the bird category. According to **feature theories**, a person judges whether a given instance is a member of a category by checking for specific features (e.g., Spalding & Ross, 2000). Members of the bird category might include the following features, among others: It has wings, feathers, a beak, and two legs, it sings, it flies, it perches in trees. A robin has all of these features, so it is judged to be a typical bird; a chicken does not, so it is judged to be less typical. There has been extensive debate about which theory of concept learning is best.

Regardless of how people manage to classify natural objects, the task is a complex one. Consider the natural concept of tree. For many people, the ideal tree might be something like a full-grown maple tree, with a sturdy brown trunk and a full canopy of large green leaves. Yet people can correctly identify objects as trees even when they have none of the characteristics of this ideal tree (e.g., a small sapling with no leaves, half buried in snow). Recognizing the impressive concept-learning abilities that people possess, some psychologists wondered whether any other animals have the ability to learn natural concepts.

Animal Studies on Natural Concept Learning

Quite a few experiments have examined natural concept learning by animals. Herrnstein and his colleagues had pigeons view slides of everyday objects or scenes. In one experiment, Herrnstein (1979) used the natural concept of tree: If a slide contained one tree, several trees, or any portion of a tree (e.g., a branch, a part of the trunk), it was a positive instance, and pecking at the response key was reinforced on a VI schedule. If the slide did not contain a tree or any portion of a tree, it was a negative instance—pecking produced no food, and the slide remained on the screen until 2 seconds elapsed without a peck.

In each session, a pigeon saw 80 different slides, half positive instances and half negative. At first, the same 80 slides were presented each session. The pigeons quickly learned to discriminate between positive and negative instances, and after only a few sessions they were responding substantially faster to the positive slides than to negative slides. You might think

Figure 9.10 People have no difficulty classifying objects as "trees" even though they vary greatly in their appearance, and neither do pigeons.

that the pigeons did not learn anything about the general category of tree, but simply learned about the 80 slides individually. However, when presented with slides they had never seen before, the pigeons responded about as rapidly to the positive slides and about as slowly to the negative slides as they did to old positive and negative slides, respectively. In other words, they were able to classify new slides as trees or nontrees about as well as the old slides (Figure 9.10).

Similar concept-formation experiments with pigeons have used many other categories besides trees. Among the concepts that pigeons have successfully learned are people (Herrnstein & Loveland, 1964), water (Herrnstein, Loveland, & Cable, 1976), fish (Herrnstein & de Villiers, 1980), and artificial objects (Lubow, 1974). They have also been trained to distinguish among the different letters of the alphabet (Blough, 1982). The ability to learn natural concepts has also been found in many other species, including monkeys, orangutans, dogs, and mynahs.

One question that arises from this research is whether animals recognize that the two-dimensional slides or pictures that they view are actually images of three-dimensional objects. This is a difficult question to answer, but some research suggests that they can. Delius (1992) presented pigeons with actual three-dimensional objects that were either spherical (marbles, peas, ball bearings, etc.) or nonspherical (dice, buttons, nuts, flowers, etc.), and each choice of a spherical object was reinforced with food. The pigeons quickly learned to choose the spherical objects. They were then tested with photographs or black-and-white drawings of spherical and nonspherical objects, and they chose the pictures of spherical objects with a high level of accuracy. In a related study, Honig and Stewart (1988) found that pigeons responded to photographs taken at two distinctive locations in ways that suggested they had formed concepts of the actual physical locations represented in the photographs. These studies show that, at least under certain conditions, animals can learn the correspondence between pictures and three-dimensional objects.

In a clever experiment by Watanabe, Sakamoto, and Wakita (1995), pigeons were taught to discriminate between the paintings of two artists, the impressionist Monet and the abstract painter Picasso. After they learned this discrimination with one set of paintings for each artist, they were able to correctly categorize new paintings by Monet and Picasso that they had not seen before. Furthermore, without additional training, they were also able to distinguish between the works of other impressionist painters (Renoir and Cezanne) and other abstract painters (Matisse and Braque). The experimenters also tested the birds with some familiar paintings that were presented upside down or reversed left to right. With the abstract paintings of Picasso, this had little effect on the birds' accuracy. However, with Monet's paintings, which depict more realistic three-dimensional objects to the human eye, the birds made more errors with the upside-down or reversed images. This finding provides a bit more evidence that pigeons can respond to two-dimensional images as representations of three-dimensional objects.

Possibly the most basic question about animal concept learning is the same one that is asked about human concept learning: How do they do it? The three classes of theories developed for human concept learning (prototype theories, exemplar theories, and feature theories) have also been applied to animal concept learning, and as with human concept learning, there is no agreement about which type of theory is best. However, there are some interesting similarities between human and animal concept learning. Like people, animals differentiate between central and peripheral instances of a category. For example, they respond more slowly to instances that contain only a few features of the positive category than instances that contain more positive features (Jitsumori, 2006). In some cases, they may display a stronger response to a prototypical example they have never seen before than to less central examples that they have seen before (Pearce, 1989).

Another characteristic of concept learning that is shared by people and animals is flexibility—animals can learn to classify stimuli according to a variety of different criteria, depending on what the task demands. They can classify instances as positive or negative either on the basis of the overall characteristics of the image or on small details. For instance, pigeons in one experiment had to categorize computer-modified pictures of human faces as male or female. The pigeons could successfully use small textural details (the smoothness of the face) or large-scale features (the overall shape of the face), whichever was relevant for the particular set of slides with which they were trained (Troje, Huber, Loidolt, Aust, & Fieder, 1999).

As more evidence of flexibility, animals can also learn concepts that vary in their level of generality. Vonk and MacDonald (2004) tested orangutans' abilities to learn three classification tasks. The first and most concrete task was to distinguish between orangutans and other primates. The second task, which involved more general categories, was to distinguish between primates and other animals. The third task, involving the broadest and most general categories, was to distinguish between animals and nonanimals. Notice that in the most concrete task, the positive instances (pictures of different orangutans) would have many perceptual similarities, whereas in the most general task, the positive instances (pictures of different animals) were perceptually much more varied. Nevertheless, the orangutans were able to learn all three tasks quite well.

Others animals, including pigeons and monkeys, have also been able to learn more general concepts similar to those used with the orangutans, with varying degrees of success (Roberts & Mazmanian, 1988). Taken as a whole, the animal research has shown that even though they do not have language to help them, animals have some impressive abilities when it comes to concept learning. Whether animals can learn even more challenging and more abstract concepts, such as analogies, will be examined in Chapter 10.

BOX 9.2   SPOTLIGHT ON RESEARCH

Stimulus Equivalence Training

One important ability of humans (and possibly other animals, though this is uncertain) is that they can learn to categorize stimuli together even if the stimuli have nothing in common. This ability is crucial in learning language, in learning to read, and for other intellectual skills. Written and spoken words are arbitrary stimuli that refer to objects or events in the world. For example, a child in elementary school must learn that the spoken word "six," the written word "six," the number "6," and the Roman numeral "VI" all refer to the same quantity. Behavioral psychologists sometimes refer to this phenomenon as **stimulus equivalence**: The different stimuli can be used interchangeably by a person who understands spoken and written English.

Psychologists have conducted numerous experiments in laboratory settings to investigate how and when people can learn such stimulus equivalence (e.g., Sidman & Tailby, 1982; Zinn, Newland, & Ritchie, 2015). These laboratory procedures are now being used in a variety of applied settings. In some cases, stimulus equivalence training can assist children who are having difficulty learning to read. For example, one group of children was given practice in (1) matching written words to spoken words and (2) writing printed words by copying them. After this practice, the children were able to read the written words (which they could not do before), even though the practice did not involve reading the written words out loud. Evidently, this training helped the children learn equivalences between (1) hearing a spoken word, (2) seeing the written word, and (3) reading the word out loud. Besides learning to read the words they had practiced, the children were also able to read other words that used the same syllables in different combinations (Melchiori, de Souza, & de Rose, 2000).

Similar procedures have been used to teach children with visual disabilities the braille alphabet by training equivalence relations among printed letters, braille letters, and spoken letters (Toussaint & Tiger, 2010). Stimulus equivalence training can also be used for more advanced academic skills. In one study, equivalence-based training was given to college students in introductory psychology in an attempt to teach them a difficult topic (the concept of a statistical interaction). On a post-test, students who were given the training obtained an average score of 92%, compared to 57% in a control group that did not receive the training (Fields et al., 2009). If stimulus equivalence training continues to produce encouraging results such as these, it will surely be used in more clinical and educational settings in the future.

STIMULUS CONTROL IN BEHAVIOR MODIFICATION

Almost every instance of behavior modification involves stimulus control in one way or another. For instance, treatments of phobias are designed to eliminate a response (a fear reaction) that is under the control of a certain class of stimuli (the phobic objects or situations). What is special about the following examples, however, is that one of the main features of the behavioral treatment is the development of appropriate stimulus control.

Study Habits and Health Habits

There are many different reasons why some students do poorly in school. One frequent problem among students who do poorly is that no matter where they are, studying is a low-probability behavior. The problem is that there are no stimuli that reliably elicit study behavior. A student may go to her room after dinner, planning to study, but may turn on the television or stereo instead. She may go to the library with her reading assignments but may find herself socializing with friends or taking a nap instead of reading.

Recognizing that poor study habits are frequently the result of ineffective stimulus control, Fox (1962) devised the following program for a group of college students who were having difficulty. The students were assigned a specific hour of the day, and they were instructed to spend at least a part of this hour, every day, studying their most difficult course. This studying was to be done in the same place every day (usually in a small room of a library or a classroom building). The student was told to take only materials related to the course into that room and not to use that room on other occasions. A student was not necessarily expected to spend the entire hour in that room: If the student began to daydream or became bored or restless, he was to read one more page and then leave immediately. The purpose of this procedure was to establish a particular time and place as a strong stimulus for studying a particular subject by repeatedly pairing this time and place with nothing but study behavior (Figure 9.11). At first, the students found it difficult to study for long in this new setting, and they would leave the room well before the hour was over. Gradually, however, their study periods grew longer, and eventually they could spend the entire hour in productive study. At this point, the therapist chose the student's second-most difficult course, and the stimulus control procedure was

Figure 9.11 An effective strategy of stimulus control is to have a specific time and place for studying where there are few opportunities for competing behaviors. (www.BillionPhotos.com/Shutterstock.com)

repeated. Before long, each student was studying each of his courses for 1 hour a day at a specific time and place.

All of Fox's students exhibited substantial improvement in their grades. It is not certain how much of this improvement was due to better stimulus control because the students were also given training in other techniques, including the SQ3R method (survey, question, read, recite, and review). However, setting a time and place for studying is at least an important first step. Other evidence suggests that combining stimulus control techniques with other behavioral methods such as self-reinforcement can lead to improved academic performance (Richards, 1981).

Stimulus control techniques have also been used to promote healthier lifestyles and combat obesity. Some of the techniques are designed to reduce overeating. For instance, because people often eat excessively while watching television, a simple but helpful strategy is never to allow yourself to eat snacks in front of the television (Gore, Foster, DeiLillo, Kirk, & West, 2003). Other techniques are aimed at increasing physical activity and reducing sedentary behaviors such as watching television and using computers. One group of researchers worked with obese children and their parents to try to reduce sedentary behaviors. The methods included having the children keep logs to record the amount of time they engaged in sedentary behaviors, posting signs around the house encouraging more physical activity, and limiting the number of hours the television was on (a technique known as **narrowing** because the opportunities to engage in an undesirable activity are restricted). These methods proved effective—the children's levels of daily physical activity increased, and they lost weight (Epstein, Paluch, Kilanowski, & Raynor, 2004).

Insomnia

Most people have experienced occasional insomnia, but persistent, severe insomnia can be a serious problem. A person who lies in bed awake most of the night is unlikely to function well the next day. Although some cases of chronic insomnia are due to medical problems, many are the result of inappropriate stimulus control. That is, the stimulus of one's bed does not reliably produce the behavior of sleeping. The role of stimulus control becomes apparent if we compare the behavior of insomniacs with those of people without sleeping problems. A normal person exhibits one sort of stimulus control: She is able to sleep well in her own bed, but she may have some difficulty falling asleep in a different place, such as on a couch or in a hotel room. An insomniac may exhibit exactly the opposite pattern: He may have difficulty falling asleep in his own bed, but he may fall asleep on a couch, in front of the television, or in a different bed. This pattern shows that insomnia is often not a general inability to fall asleep but a failure to fall asleep in the presence of a particular stimulus, one's own bed.

The reason a person's own bed may fail to serve as a stimulus for sleeping is fairly clear: The bed may become associated with many activities that are incompatible with sleeping, including reading, watching television, eating, and thinking about the day's events or one's problems. To make one's bed a more effective stimulus for sleeping, some behavior therapists recommend that the client never do anything but sleep there. Bootzin (1972) described the case of a man who would lie in bed for several hours each night worrying about everyday problems before falling asleep with the television on. The man was instructed to go to bed each night when he felt sleepy but not to watch television or do anything else in bed. If he could not get to sleep after a few minutes, he was to get out of bed and go into another room. He could then do whatever he liked, and he was not to go back to bed until he felt sleepy. Each time he went to bed, the same instructions were to be followed: Get up and leave the room if you do not fall asleep within a few minutes. At first, he had to get up many times each night before falling asleep, but after a few weeks he would usually fall asleep within a few minutes the first time he got in bed.

The techniques first devised by Bootzin have been used with many insomniac patients with good results (Taylor & Roane, 2010). The procedure is effective for at least two reasons. First, since the clients are instructed to remain out of bed when they cannot sleep, their need for sleep increases early in the program, when they spend a large part of the night out of bed. Therefore, when they go to bed, their chances of falling asleep are greater. Second, since the bed is used only for sleeping, its associations with other behaviors gradually decrease and at the same time its association with sleep increases.

This type of behavioral intervention can now be delivered more precisely with the assistance of modern computer technology. Riley, Mihm, Behar, and Morin (2010) gave adults with insomnia small hand-held computers that recorded their sleeping and waking patterns.

The computers provided the patients with customized instructions and prompts about when to go to bed, when to get out of bed if they were still awake, and so on. This technology is still being tested and refined, but preliminary results suggest that it can improve the sleep quality of people with chronic insomnia.

The usefulness of these procedures for training stimulus control may hinge on the reduction of incompatible behaviors. The student in a quiet room of the library will have little to do but study. In addition, those few behaviors other than studying that can occur (such as daydreaming) are prevented because the student is instructed to leave the room immediately if he or she stops studying. Similarly, the therapy for insomnia involves preventing the client from engaging in any behavior other than sleeping in one's bed. In a sense, then, these stimulus control techniques are the opposite of the procedure of reinforcing incompatible behaviors so as to eliminate an undesirable behavior. In the former, incompatible behaviors are prevented, and in the latter, they are reinforced.

SUMMARY

Pavlov proposed that generalization is an automatic by-product of the conditioning process, whereas Lashley and Wade proposed that experience is necessary for typical gradients to occur. Each theory seems to be correct in some cases and wrong in others. Some experiments found that discrimination training was necessary before typical generalization gradients appeared. However, experiments on sensory deprivation supported Pavlov's position by finding generalization gradients for color with birds that were raised in an environment with only one color.

Another question is whether stimulus control is absolute or relational. Spence's theory of absolute stimulus control can account for peak shifts in generalization gradients by assuming that an excitatory gradient develops around the S+ and an inhibitory gradient develops around the S−. However, this theory cannot explain results from the intermediate-size problem, which supports the position that animals can respond to relationships between stimuli. Other evidence also suggests that animals are capable of learning relational rules.

Terrace developed an errorless discrimination training procedure, in which the S− is introduced very early in training but under conditions in which the subject is not likely to respond to this stimulus. Errorless discrimination training has been successfully used in a variety of educational settings with both children and adults.

Concept learning occurs when individuals learn to treat one class of stimuli as positive and another class as negative. For natural categories, people tend to differentiate between central instances (typical examples) and peripheral instances (atypical examples). There are several different theories of how concept learning takes place, including exemplar theories, prototype theories, and feature theories. Studies with pigeons and other animals show that they can readily learn such natural categories as tree, water, and people.

Stimulus control techniques are used in behavior modification when a desired response seldom occurs in the presence of the appropriate stimulus. For students who have difficulty studying, a special location can be trained as a strong discriminate stimulus for study behavior. If a person's insomnia is due to poor stimulus control, the person's bed can be trained as a strong discriminative stimulus for sleeping.

Review Questions

1. What was Pavlov's theory about the cause of generalization gradients? What is another theory about them? What do experiments on discrimination training and on sensory deprivation tell us about this issue?

2. Describe the difference between the absolute and relational theories of stimulus control. What do studies on transposition, peak shift, and the intermediate-size problem indicate about these theories?

3. What is errorless discrimination learning? Describe how this technique could be used to teach young children the names of different types of flowers.

4. Describe some findings about natural categories in humans and some findings about natural category learning by pigeons. What do these studies demonstrate about concept formation by animals?

5. Give one or two examples of how stimulus control techniques have been used in behavior-modification programs. Describe some specific procedures that the client must practice in order for the treatment to work.

REFERENCES

Alberts, E., & Ehrenfreund, D. (1951). Transposition in children as a function of age. *Journal of Experimental Psychology, 41*, 30–38.

Battig, W.F., & Montague, W.E. (1969). Category norms for verbal items in 56 categories: A replication and extension of the Connecticut category norms. *Journal of Experimental Psychology Monograph, 3*, Pt. 2.

Blough, D.S. (1982). Pigeon perception of letters of the alphabet. *Science, 218*, 397–398.

Bootzin, R.R. (1972). Stimulus control treatment for insomnia. *Proceedings of the 80th Annual Convention of the American Psychological Association, 7*, 395–396.

Clare, L., Wilson, B.A., Carter, G., Roth, I., & Hodges, J.R. (2002). Relearning face-name associations in early Alzheimer's disease. *Neuropsychology, 16*, 538–547.

Cyr, A., & Anderson, N.D. (2015). Mistakes as stepping stones: Effects of errors on episodic memory among younger and older adults. *Journal of Experimental Psychology: Learning, Memory, and Cognition, 41*, 841-850.

Delius, J.D. (1992). Categorical discrimination of objects and pictures by pigeons. *Animal Learning and Behavior, 20*, 301–311.

Derenne, A. (2010). Shifts in postdiscrimination gradients with a stimulus dimension based on bilateral facial symmetry. *Journal of the Experimental Analysis of Behavior, 93*, 485–494.

Dougan, J.D., McSweeney, F.K., & Farmer-Dougan, V.A. (1986). Behavioral contrast in competitive and noncompetitive environments. *Journal of the Experimental Analysis of Behavior, 46*, 185–197.

Droit-Volet, S. (2002). Scalar timing in temporal generalization in children with short and long stimulus durations. *Quarterly Journal of Experimental Psychology, 55A*, 1193–1209.

Duffy, L., & Wishart, J.G. (1987). A comparison of two procedures for teaching discrimination skills to Down's syndrome and non-handicapped children. *British Journal of Educational Psychology, 57*, 265–278.

Epstein, L.H., Paluch, R.A., Kilanowski, C.K., & Raynor, H.A. (2004). The effect of reinforcement or stimulus control to reduce sedentary behavior in the treatment of obesity. *Health Psychology, 4*, 371–380.

Fields, L., Travis, R., Roy, D., Yadlovker, E., De Aguiar-Rocha, L., & Sturmey, P. (2009). Equivalence class formation: A method for teaching statistical interactions. *Journal of Applied Behavior Analysis, 42*, 575–593.

Fox, L. (1962). Effecting the use of efficient study habits. *Journal of Mathletics, 1*, 75–86.

Gonzalez, R.C., Gentry, G.V., & Bitterman, M.E. (1954). Relational discrimination of intermediate size in the chimpanzee. *Journal of Comparative and Physiological Psychology, 47*, 385–388.

Gore, S.A., Foster, J.A., DeiLillo, V.G., Kirk, K., & West, D.S. (2003). Television viewing and snacking. *Eating Behaviors, 4*, 399–405.

Gutman, A. (1977). Positive contrast, negative induction, and inhibitory stimulus control in the rat. *Journal of the Experimental Analysis of Behavior, 27*, 219–233.

Guttman, N., & Kalish, H.I. (1956). Discriminability and stimulus generalization. *Journal of Experimental Psychology, 51*, 79–88.

Hampton, J.A. (2006). Concepts as prototypes. In B.H. Ross (Ed.), *The psychology of learning and motivation: Advances in research and theory* (Vol. 46, pp. 79–113). San Diego, CA: Elsevier.

Herrnstein, R.J. (1970). On the law of effect. *Journal of the Experimental Analysis of Behavior, 13*, 243–266.

Herrnstein, R.J. (1979). Acquisition, generalization, and reversal of a natural concept. *Journal of Experimental Psychology: Animal Behavior Processes, 5*, 116–129.

Herrnstein, R.J., & de Villiers, P.A. (1980). Fish as a natural category for people and pigeons. In G.H. Bower (Ed.), *The psychology of learning and motivation* (Vol. 14, pp. 59–95). New York: Academic Press.

Herrnstein, R.J., & Loveland, D.H. (1964). Complex visual concept in the pigeon. *Science, 146*, 549–551.

Herrnstein, R.J., Loveland, D.H., & Cable, C. (1976). Natural concepts in pigeons. *Journal of Experimental Psychology: Animal Behavior Processes, 2*, 285–302.

Honig, W.K., & Stewart, K.E. (1988). Pigeons can discriminate locations presented in pictures. *Journal of the Experimental Analysis of Behavior, 50*, 541–551.

Jäkel, F., Schölkopf, B., & Wichmann, F.A. (2008). Generalization and similarity in exemplar models of categorization: Insights from machine learning. *Psychonomic Bulletin & Review, 15*, 256–271.

Jenkins, H.M., & Harrison, R.H. (1960). Effects of discrimination training on auditory generalization. *Journal of Experimental Psychology, 59*, 246–253.

Jenkins, H.M., & Harrison, R.H. (1962). Generalization gradients of inhibition following auditory discrimination learning. *Journal of the Experimental Analysis of Behavior, 5*, 435–441.

Jitsumori, M. (2006). Category structure and typicality effects. In E.A. Wasserman & T.R. Zentall (Eds.), *Comparative cognition: Experimental explorations of animal intelligence* (pp. 343–362). New York: Oxford University Press.

Jones, R.S., & Eayrs, C.B. (1992). The use of errorless learning procedures in teaching people with a learning disability: A critical review. *Mental Handicap Research, 5*, 204–214.

Killeen, P.R. (2014). A theory of behavioral contrast. *Journal of the Experimental Analysis of Behavior, 102*, 363–390.

Kohler, W. (1939). Simple structural function in the chimpanzee and the chicken. In W.D. Ellis (Ed.), *A source book of gestalt psychology* (pp. 217–227). New York: Harcourt Brace.

Lashley, K.S., & Wade, M. (1946). The Pavlovian theory of generalization. *Psychological Review, 53*, 72–87.

Lazareva, O.F., Wasserman, E.A., & Young, M.E. (2005). Transposition in pigeons: Reassessing Spence (1937) with multiple discrimination training. *Learning & Behavior, 33*, 22–46.

Lazareva, O.F., Young, M.E., & Wasserman, E.A. (2014). A three-component model of relational responding in the transposition paradigm. *Journal of Experimental Psychology: Animal Learning and Cognition, 40*, 63–80.

Leighty, K.A., Grand, A.P., Pittman Courte, V.L., Maloney, M.A., & Bettinger, T.L. (2013). Relational responding by eastern box turtles (*Terrapene carolina*) in a series of color discrimination tasks. *Journal of Comparative Psychology, 127*, 256–264.

Lubow, R.E. (1974). High-order concept formation in the pigeon. *Journal of the Experimental Analysis of Behavior, 21*, 475–483.

Manabe, K., Murata, M., Kawashima, T., Asahina, K., & Okutsu, K. (2009). Transposition of line-length discrimination in African penguins (*Spheniscus demersus*). *Japanese Psychological Research, 51*, 115–121.

McIlvane, W.J., Kledaras, J.B., Iennaco, F.M., McDonald, S.J., & Stoddard, L.T. (1995). Some possible limits on errorless discrimination reversals in individuals with severe mental retardation. *American Journal of Mental Retardation, 99*, 430–436.

McSweeney, F.K., & Weatherly, J.N. (1998). Habituation to the reinforcer may contribute to multiple-schedule behavioral contrast. *Journal of the Experimental Analysis of Behavior, 69*, 199–221.

Melchiori, L.E., de Souza, D.G., & de Rose, J.C. (2000). Reading, equivalence, and recombination of units: A replication with students with different learning histories. *Journal of Applied Behavior Analysis, 33*, 97–100.

Morgan, C.L. (1894). *An introduction to comparative psychology*. London: W. Scott.

Mueller, M.M., & Palkovic, C.M. (2007). Errorless learning: Review and practical application for teaching children with pervasive developmental disorders. *Psychology in the Schools, 44*, 691–700.

Pavlov, I.P. (1927). *Conditioned reflexes*. Oxford: Oxford University Press.

Pearce, J.M. (1989). The acquisition of an artificial category by pigeons. *Quarterly Journal of Experimental Psychology, 41B*, 381–406.

Reynolds, G.S. (1961). An analysis of interactions in a multiple schedule. *Journal of the Experimental Analysis of Behavior, 4*, 107–117.

Richards, C.S. (1981). Improving college students' study behaviors through self-control techniques: A brief review. *Behavioral Counseling Quarterly, 1*, 159–175.

Riley, W.T., Mihm, P., Behar, A., & Morin, C.M. (2010). A computer device to deliver behavioral interventions for insomnia. *Behavioral Sleep Medicine, 8*, 2–15.

Roberts, W.A., & Mazmanian, D.S. (1988). Concept learning at different levels of abstraction by pigeons, monkeys, and people. *Journal of Experimental Psychology: Animal Behavior Processes, 14*, 247–260.

Rosch, E. (1973). On the internal structure of perceptual and semantic categories. In T.E. Moore (Ed.), *Cognitive development and the acquisition of language* (pp. 111–144). New York: Academic Press.

Rosch, E. (1975). Cognitive representations of semantic categories. *Journal of Experimental Psychology: General, 104*, 192–233.

Rudolph, R.L., Honig, W.K., & Gerry, J.E. (1969). Effects of monochromatic rearing on the acquisition of stimulus control. *Journal of Comparative and Physiological Psychology, 67*, 50–57.

Sidman, M., & Tailby, W. (1982). Conditional discrimination versus matching to sample: An extension of the testing paradigm. *Journal of the Experimental Analysis of Behavior, 37*, 5–22.

Skinner, B.F. (1958). Teaching machines. *Science, 128*, 969–977.

Spalding, T. L., & Ross, B. H. (2000). Concept learning and feature interpretation. *Memory & Cognition, 28*, 439–451.

Spence, K.W. (1937). The differential response in animals to stimuli varying within a single dimension. *Psychological Review, 44*, 430–444.

Taylor, D.J., & Roane, B.M. (2010). Treatment of insomnia in adults and children: A practice-friendly review of research. *Journal of Clinical Psychology, 66*, 1137–1147.

Terrace, H.S. (1963). Errorless transfer of a discrimination across two continua. *Journal of the Experimental Analysis of Behavior, 6*, 223–232.

Terrace, H.S. (1966). Stimulus control. In W.K. Honig (Ed.), *Operant conditioning: Areas of research and application* (pp. 271–344). Upper Saddle River, NJ: Prentice Hall.

Toussaint, K.A., & Tiger, J.H. (2010). Teaching early braille literacy skills within a stimulus equivalence paradigm to children with degenerative visual impairments. *Journal of Applied Behavior Analysis, 43*, 181–194.

Troje, N.F., Huber, L., Loidolt, M., Aust, U., & Fieder, M. (1999). Categorical learning in pigeons: The role of texture and shape in complex static stimuli. *Vision Research, 39*, 353–366.

Vonk, J., & MacDonald, S.E. (2004). Levels of abstraction in orangutan (*Pongo abelii*) categorization. *Journal of Comparative Psychology, 118*, 3–13.

Watanabe, S., Sakamoto, J., & Wakita, M. (1995). Pigeons' discrimination of paintings by Monet and Picasso. *Journal of the Experimental Analysis of Behavior, 63*, 165–174.

Williams, B.A. (2002). Behavioral contrast redux. *Animal Learning and Behavior, 30*, 1–20.

Wright, A.A., & Lickteig, M.T. (2010). What is learned when concept learning fails?—a theory of restricted-domain relational learning. *Learning and Motivation, 41*, 273–286.

Zinn, T.E., Newland, M.C., & Ritchie, K.E. (2015). The efficiency and efficacy of equivalence-based learning: A randomized controlled trial. *Journal of Applied Behavior Analysis, 48*, 865–882.

CHAPTER 10

Comparative Cognition

Learning Objectives

After reading this chapter, you should be able to

- describe how short-term memory and rehearsal have been studied with animals
- describe how long-term memory has been studied with animals
- explain what is known about animals' abilities to measure time, to count, and to learn serial patterns
- discuss different attempts to teach language to animals and evaluate their success
- describe research on animals' abilities in the areas of object permanence, analogies, and metacognition

In recent years there has been increasing interest in applying concepts from cognitive psychology (which previously focused almost exclusively on people) to animals. Through this interest a new field has emerged called **animal cognition** or **comparative cognition**. A major purpose of this field is to compare the cognitive processes of different species, including humans. By making such comparisons, researchers hope to find commonalities in the ways different species receive, process, store, and use information about their world. The comparative approach can give us a better perspective on those abilities that we have in common with other species, and it can also help us understand what makes the human species unique. This chapter will survey some of the major topics of traditional cognitive psychology, including memory, problem solving, reasoning, and language. We will try to determine how animals' abilities in each of these domains compare to those of people.

MEMORY AND REHEARSAL

A prevalent view about human memory is that it is important to distinguish between **long-term memory**, which can retain information for months or years, and **short-term memory**, which can only hold information for a matter of seconds. The facts in your long-term memory include such items as your birthday, the names of your friends, the fact that 4 + 5 = 9, the meaning of the word rectangle, and thousands of other pieces of information. An example of an item in short-term memory is a phone number you have just looked up for the first time. If someone distracts you for a few seconds after you looked up the number, you will probably forget the number and have to look it up again. The following sections will survey animal research on both types of memory as well as rehearsal, a process that is important for both types of memory.

Short-Term Memory, or Working Memory

Besides being short-lived, short-term memory is also said to have a very limited capacity compared to the large capacity of long-term memory. Although your short-term memory is large enough to hold a seven-digit phone number long enough to dial it, you would probably have great difficulty remembering two new phone numbers at once.

In both human and animal research, the term **working memory** is now frequently used instead of short-term memory (Baddeley, 2010). This change in terminology reflects the view that the information in working memory is used to guide whatever tasks the individual is currently performing. For example, suppose you are working on a series of simple addition problems, without the aid of a calculator. At any given moment, your working memory would contain several different pieces of information: that you are adding the hundreds column, that the total so far is 26, that the next number to be added is 8, and so on. Notice that the information must continually be updated: Your answers would be incorrect if you remembered the previous total rather than the present one or if you failed to add the hundreds column because you confused it with the hundreds column of the previous problem. In many tasks like this, people need to remember important details about their current task and to ignore similar details from already completed tasks. In a similar way, a butterfly searching for nectar may need to remember which patches of flowers it has already visited today, and it must not confuse today's visits with yesterday's.

Research with animals has examined different properties of working memory, such as its duration, its capacity, and factors that affect accuracy of performance. The following sections describe two techniques that are frequently used to study working memory in animals.

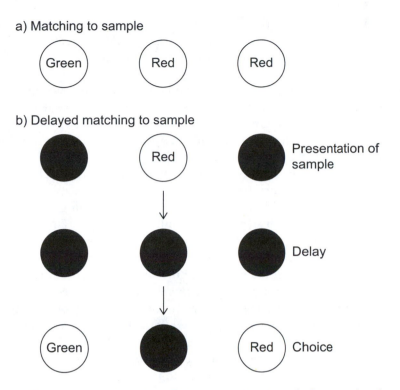

a) Matching to sample

Green   Red   Red

b) Delayed matching to sample

⬤   Red   ⬤   Presentation of sample

⬤   ⬤   ⬤   Delay

Green   ⬤   Red   Choice

Figure 10.1 (a) The procedure of simple matching to sample: The right key matches the center key, so a peck at the right key is the correct response. (b) The procedure of delayed matching to sample: A peck at the right key is again the correct response, but now the pigeon must remember the sample color through the delay interval.

Delayed Matching to Sample

As an introduction to delayed matching to sample, Figure 10.1a diagrams the simpler task of *matching to sample* as it might be used with pigeons in a chamber with three response keys. Before each trial, the center key is lit with one of two colors (e.g., red or green). This color is called the *sample stimulus*. Typically, the pigeon must peck at this key to light the two side keys: The left key will then become green and the right key red, or vice versa. These two colors are called the *comparison stimuli*. The pigeon's task is to peck at the side key that has the same color as the center key. A correct response produces a food reinforcer; an incorrect response produces no food. Matching to sample is an easy task for pigeons and other animals, and once they learn the task they can perform with nearly 100% accuracy.

Figure 10.1b diagrams the more complex procedure of **delayed matching to sample (DMTS)**. In this case, the sample is presented for a certain period of time, then there is a delay during which the keys are dark, and finally the two side keys are lit. Once again, the correct response is a peck at the comparison stimulus that matches the sample, but because the sample is no longer present, the pigeon must remember its color through the delay if it is to perform better than chance. Since one of the two keys is correct, chance performance is 50%. If the animal is correct more than 50% of the time, this means it has remembered something about the sample through the delay interval.

By using delays of different durations in the DMTS procedure, we can measure how long information about the sample is retained in working memory. The answer is different for different species. For example, the circles in the upper panel of Figure 10.2 show the accuracy of pigeons in an experiment by Grant (1975). The average percentage of correct choices decreased steadily with longer delays, and with the 10-second delay, the pigeons made the correct choice about 66% of the time. The results from a similar study with monkeys and 4-year-old children are shown in the bottom panel of Figure 10.2. The monkeys did better on this task than the young children. However, by age 5 the children outperformed the monkeys, and their DMTS performance steadily improved up to at least age 14.

Performance on this task can be affected by many factors, such as the presence of other stimuli that can interfere with the memory of the sample. In human memory tasks, two types of interference have long been recognized: retroactive interference and proactive interference. **Retroactive interference** occurs when the presentation of some new material interferes with the memory of something that was learned earlier. For example, suppose that in a list-learning task like the one used by Ebbinghaus (1885; see Chapter 1), a person memorizes List A, then List B, and then is tested on List A. The memorization of List B will impair the person's memory of List A and lead to poorer performance than if the person never had to learn List B. **Proactive interference** occurs when previously learned material impairs the learning of new material. For example, it might be easy to memorize one list, List D, in isolation, but this list may be much harder to learn if it is preceded by the memorization of Lists A, B, and C.

Both types of interference have been found with animals in DMTS. Retroactive interference can be demonstrated by presenting various sorts of stimuli during the delay interval. Not surprisingly, when the sample and comparison stimuli are different colors, matching performance is impaired if colored lights are presented during the delay interval (Jarvik, Goldfarb, & Carley, 1969). In fact, any sort of surprising or unexpected stimulus presented during the delay interval is likely to impair performance on the matching task.

To demonstrate the existence of proactive interference in DMTS, studies have shown that stimuli presented before the sample can impair performance (White, Parkinson, Brown, & Wixted, 2004). Proactive interference can occur if a series of trials are presented in rapid succession because the memory of the preceding trials can interfere with performance on later trials. For example, the triangles in the upper panel of Figure 10.2 show the results from a condition in which each DMTS trial was immediately preceded by one or more interference trials in which the opposite color was correct. As can be seen, performance was considerably worse when these interference trials were added.

Variations of the DMTS task have also been used with humans. A participant may be presented with one or more sample stimuli, such as nonsense syllables or unfamiliar shapes. After a delay, a comparison stimulus is presented and the person must decide if it was one of the sample stimuli. Using the DMTS task along with brain recording techniques such as

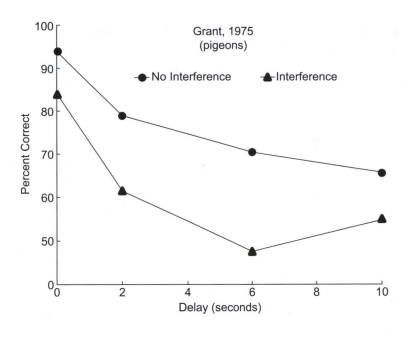

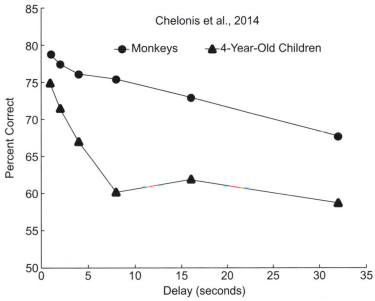

Figure 10.2 The upper panel shows the performance of pigeons in a delayed matching-to-sample task, where the delay between sample and choice stimuli was varied. The lower panel shows the performance of monkeys and 4-year-old children on a similar task. Note that the scale on the x-axis is different in the two panels. (Top: From Grant, D.S., 1975, Proactive interference in pigeon short-term memory, *Journal of Experimental Psychology: Animal Behavior and Processes, 1,* 207–220. © American Psychological Association. Adapted with permission Bottom: Adapted from *Behavioural Processes,* Vol. 103, Chelonis, J.J., Cox, A.R., Karr, M.J., Prunty, P.K., Baldwin, R.L., & Paule, M.G., Comparison of delayed matching-to-sample performance in monkeys and children, 261–268. Copyright 2014, with permission from Elsevier.)

functional magnetic resonance imaging, researchers can identify which parts of the brain are involved in working memory, and this research can help to understand various brain disorders. For instance, individuals with schizophrenia perform worse than normal adults on the DMTS task, and they also show different patterns of brain activity when they perform this task (Koychev, El-Deredy, Haenschel, & Deakin, 2010).

The Radial-Arm Maze

An apparatus frequently used in memory research with rodents is the **radial-arm maze**, which simulates a situation in which an animal explores a territory in search of food. Figure 10.3 shows the floor plan of a typical eight-arm maze used for rats. The entire maze is a platform that rests a few feet above the floor; the maze has no walls, so the rat can see any objects that may be in the room (windows, doors, desks, etc.). At the end of each arm is a cup in which a bit of food can be stored. In a typical experiment, some food is deposited at the end of each arm. The rat is placed in the center area to start a trial and is given time to explore the maze and collect whatever food it can find. Once the rat collects the food in one arm, it will find no more food in that arm if it returns later during the same trial. The most efficient strategy for obtaining food is therefore to visit each arm once and only once.

An easy way for a rat to perform this task would be simply to start at one arm and then go around the maze in a clockwise (or counter-clockwise) pattern, but rats do not follow

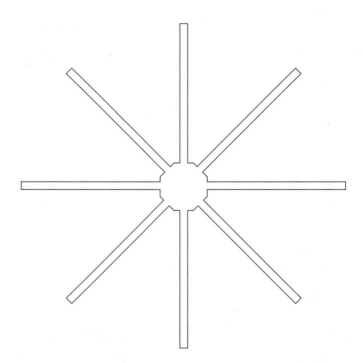

Figure 10.3 The floor plan of an eight-arm maze for rats.

this type of strategy. Instead, they seem to select successive arms in a haphazard manner. What they do use to orient their travels within the maze are visual landmarks in the room surrounding the maze. The landmarks help the animals identify individual arms and keep track of which ones they have already visited (Babb & Crystal, 2003; Mazmanian & Roberts, 1983).

Perhaps the most remarkable feature of an average rat's performance on this task is its accuracy. The first visit to any arm is considered a correct response, and any repeat visit is an error because there will be no food. If a trial is ended after the rat visits eight arms (including any repeat visits), it will usually make seven or eight correct responses (Olton, 1978). This performance means that the rat is very skillful at avoiding the arms that it has already visited on the current trial. With larger, 17-arm mazes, rats still average about 15 correct responses out of 17 visits (Olton, Collison, & Werz, 1977), and similar performance has been obtained from gerbils (Wilkie & Slobin, 1983). It is commonly said that human working memory can retain only about seven unrelated items at once (e.g., seven words or seven random digits). With this number as a point of comparison, the nearly flawless performance of rats in a 17-arm maze is especially impressive. Equally impressive are the time intervals over which rats can remember which arms they have visited. Beatty and Shavalia (1980) allowed rats to visit four arms of an eight-arm maze, after which they were removed from the maze. If they were returned to the maze as much as 4 hours later, the rats were almost perfect in their selection of the four arms they had not previously visited. This finding shows why working memory is probably a more appropriate term than short-term memory. In research with people, short-term memory has generally referred to information that is lost in a matter of seconds, but a rat's memory for its travels in the radial-arm maze can last 100 times longer. Compared to the very rapid forgetting typically found in DMTS, this research also shows that how long information remains in working memory can vary greatly depending on the nature of the task.

Rehearsal

The concept of **rehearsal** is easy to understand when thinking about human learning. We can rehearse a speech by reading it aloud or by reading it silently. It seems natural to think of rehearsal as overt or silent speech in which we repeatedly recite whatever we wish to remember. Theories of human memory state that rehearsal can keep information active in short-term memory (which is called **maintenance rehearsal**), and it can also promote the transfer of this information into long-term memory (sometimes called **associative rehearsal**).

Because we tend to equate rehearsal with speech, it may surprise you to learn that psychologists have found good evidence for rehearsal in animals. Since animals do not use language, what does it mean to say that they can engage in rehearsal? With animals, rehearsal is more difficult to define, but it refers to an active processing of stimuli or events after they have occurred. Rehearsal cannot be observed directly; its existence can only be inferred from an animal's performance on tasks that make use of short- or long-term memory. The available data suggest that rehearsal seems to serve the same functions for animals as it does for people.

Maintenance Rehearsal

Evidence for maintenance rehearsal in animals comes from a technique called **directed forgetting**. When this technique is used with human participants, items such as pictures or words are presented, and after each item the person is instructed either to remember it or to forget it. The typical finding is that people recall more of the items they were instructed to remember, presumably because they rehearsed them (e.g., Quinlan, Taylor, & Fawcett, 2010). To examine directed forgetting with animals, a variation of DMTS can be used. On each trial, first a sample stimulus is presented, and then either a "remember cue" or a "forget cue" is presented during the delay that follows the sample stimulus. The remember cue tells the animal that it is important to remember the sample because a test is coming up (i.e., the comparison stimuli will soon follow). The forget cue tells the animal that it is safe to forget the sample because there will be no test on this trial (Figure 10.4). Therefore, the animal is "directed" either to remember or to forget the sample. If an animal can choose whether to engage in rehearsal, it should eventually learn to follow the directions and rehearse the sample when it sees the remember cue but not when it sees the forget cue. Once an animal is well trained on this task, occasional probe trials are included—the forget cue is presented, but then (in what should be a surprise to the animal) the comparison stimuli are presented, and a correct choice is reinforced. The idea is that if the animals had learned not to bother rehearsing on trials with the forget cue, they should perform poorly on these occasional surprise quizzes. In one study with pigeons,

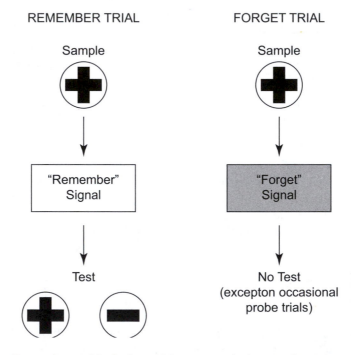

Figure 10.4 On "remember trials" of a directed forgetting task, the animal is given a signal to remember the sample stimulus and then receives a reinforcer if it makes the correct choice. On "forget trials" there is no test except on occasional probe trials.

this is exactly what was found: On probe trials that followed the forget cues, the pigeons averaged about 70% correct choices, compared to about 90% on trials with the remember cue (Maki & Hegvik, 1980).

Evidence for directed forgetting has been obtained with other species, including monkeys and rats (Miller & Armus, 1999; Tu & Hampton, 2014). In another experiment with pigeons, Milmine, Watanabe, and Colombo (2008) recorded the activity of individual neurons in the prefrontal cortex (a part of the brain associated with working memory), and they found significantly greater activity during the delay intervals after remember cues than after forget cues. Taken together, these studies on directed forgetting make a strong case that, like people, nonhuman animals can choose whether to rehearse information they have recently received.

Associative Rehearsal

Research on human memory has shown that rehearsal increases the strength of long-term memory. If people are given a list of items to remember and then given a distraction-free period (in which they presumably recite or rehearse the material in some way), their ability to recall the list items at a later time will be improved. In a clever series of experiments, Wagner, Rudy, and Whitlow (1973) demonstrated that rehearsal also contributes to the strength of long-term learning in classical conditioning with rabbits. They demonstrated that the acquisition of a CR proceeds more slowly if some *posttrial episode (PTE)* that "distracts" the animal occurs shortly after each conditioning trial. They also showed that surprising PTEs are more distracting (interfere more with learning) than expected PTEs. Expected PTEs were sequences of stimuli that the rabbits had seen many times, whereas surprising PTEs were arrangements of stimuli that the animals had not seen before. During classical conditioning, the rabbits received a series of trials on which a CS was paired with a US (an electrical pulse in the vicinity of the eye, which produced an eyeblink). For all rabbits, a PTE occurred 10 seconds after each conditioning trial. However, for half of the rabbits, the PTE was an expected sequence of stimuli, and for the other half, it was a surprising sequence of stimuli. The eyeblink conditioning to the CS developed much more slowly in the rabbits that received surprising PTEs.

The researchers reasoned that in order for a long-term CS–US association to develop, an animal needs a distraction-free period after each conditioning trial during which rehearsal takes place. The surprising PTEs distracted the rabbits and interrupted their rehearsal of the events that had just occurred, so the rate of conditioning was slowed. The expected PTEs caused less disruption of rehearsal because the rabbits had seen these PTEs before, so they had more time to rehearse, and they learned faster.

If this reasoning is correct, then the sooner a surprising PTE occurs after the conditioning trial, the greater should be the disruption of conditioning. To test this prediction, Wagner, Rudy, and Whitlow varied the time between the trial and the surprising PTE from 3 to 300 seconds for different groups of subjects. Figure 10.5 shows the median percentages of CRs to the new CS over the first 10 conditioning trials. As can be seen, the PTEs had their greatest disruptive effects when they closely followed each conditioning trial and thereby kept rehearsal to a minimum.

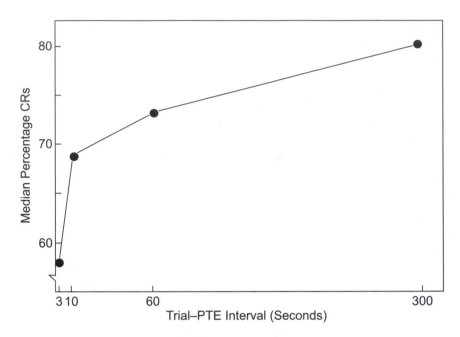

Figure 10.5 The percentage of conditioned eyeblink responses in four different groups of rabbits in the Wagner et al. (1973) experiment. For each group, the x-axis shows the amount of time that elapsed between each conditioning trial and a surprising PTE. (From Wagner, A.R., Rudy, J.W., Whitlow, J.W., 1973, Rehearsal in animal conditioning, *Journal of Experimental Psychology, 97,* 407–426, © American Psychological Association. Reprinted with permission.)

Long-Term Memory, Retrieval, and Forgetting

In contrast to the very limited size of short-term memory, the storage capacity of long-term memory is very large. It is probably safe to say that no one has yet found a way to measure and quantify this capacity for either animals or people, but some studies have demonstrated impressive feats of learning and remembering. Vaughan and Greene (1983, 1984) trained pigeons to classify slides of everyday scenes as either "positive" (responses to these slides were reinforced with food) or "negative" (responses to these slides were never reinforced). Each slide was randomly assigned to the positive or negative category, so the only way to know which was which was to remember each individual slide. They started with 40 positive slides and 40 negative slides. After about 10 daily sessions, the pigeons were discriminating between positive and negative slides with better than 90% accuracy. They were then trained with more slides, and with 320 slides their accuracy was still above 90%. Taking this method further, Cook, Levison, Gillett, and Blaisdell (2005) trained pigeons with over 1,600 slides, and they found accuracy levels above 75%. Equally impressive memory for pictures has been found with humans (Shepard, 1967).

Studies with other species of birds have demonstrated similar feats of memory, often involving memory for caches—sites where the birds have stored food. For example, a bird known as Clark's nutcracker gathers more than 20,000 pine seeds each fall and stores them in the ground in several thousand different locations. To survive the winter, the bird must recover a large portion of these seeds. Field observations and laboratory experiments have shown that nutcrackers do not use random searching or olfactory cues in recovering their caches. Although they may use certain characteristics of cache sites to aid their searches (e.g., the appearance of the soil above a cache), the birds' memories of specific visual landmarks and spatial cues are much more important (Kelly, Kamil, & Cheng, 2010; Vander Wall, 1982).

Other studies with animals have investigated the time course of forgetting from long-term memory, just as Ebbinghaus (1885) tested his recall of nonsense syllables after different intervals to construct a forgetting curve (see Chapter 1). The general shape of forgetting curves for animals is similar to the pattern in Figure 1.3: Forgetting is rapid at first, with a substantial loss during the first 24 hours, but subsequent forgetting proceeds at a much slower rate (Gleitman, 1971).

What causes the forgetting of information in long-term memory? For humans, a prevalent view is that interference from other stimuli and events, to which we are constantly exposed in daily life, is a major cause of forgetting (Wixted, 2004), and this view has substantial empirical support. Both proactive and retroactive interference have been observed in studies of animal long-term memory (Amundson & Miller, 2008; Engelmann, 2009). As an example of proactive interference, suppose that a pigeon receives several days of training on a discrimination task in which S+ is blue and S− is green. Then the roles of S+ and S− are reversed for one session, and the bird learns to respond to the green stimulus. If the bird is then tested on the following day, the early training with blue as the S+ is likely to interfere with the bird's memory of the more recent training, and it may respond more to blue and less to green. This is an instance of proactive interference because the memory of the early training impairs the memory of the later training.

If an individual forgets something that was learned long ago, is this because the memory has been lost forever, or is the problem one of retrieval failure (the memory is still there but it is difficult to find)? In research on human memory, there is evidence that many instances of forgetting are really cases of retrieval failure. Although you may not be able to recall some information on your first attempt (e.g., the Democratic candidate elected president of the United States in 1980), you may succeed if you are given a hint (e.g., peanuts).

One phenomenon that supports the concept of retrieval failure is the **context–shift effect**: if you learn some new information in one context (such as a particular room), your recall of the information will be better if you are tested in the same context than in a new context (a different room). The context-shift effect has been found with both humans and animals (Millin & Riccio, 2004; Smith & Vela, 2001), and it shows how specific cues can help one remember things that would otherwise be forgotten.

Based on the idea that forgetting is often a problem of retrieval failure, many experiments with animals have shown that "forgotten" memories can be recovered if the animal is given an appropriate clue or reminder. For example, Gordon, Smith, and Katz (1979) trained rats on an avoidance task in which a rat had to go from a white room to a black room to avoid a shock. Three days after training, rats in one group were given a reminder of their previous avoidance learning: They were simply confined in the white compartment for 15 seconds, with no shock. Rats in a control group were not returned to the test chamber. Twenty-four hours later, both groups were tested in extinction to see how quickly they would move into the black chamber. The rats that had received the reminder treatment entered the black room significantly faster, presumably because the reminder served to revive their memories of their earlier avoidance training. The general conclusion from this line of research is that any stimulus that is present during a learning experience (including the room or chamber in which the learning takes place) can later serve as a reminder and make it more likely that the experience will be remembered.

BOX 10.1   SPOTLIGHT ON RESEARCH

Chunking of Information by Animals

Many experiments with humans have shown that memorizing is easier if a long list of information is divided into portions of more manageable size called **chunks** (Miller, 1956). For example, the telephone number 711–2468 consists of seven digits, which is about all that human short-term memory can hold at once. However, the burden on memory is lightened if "711" reminds you of the name of a chain of convenience stores, and if you remember "2468" as the first four even numbers. In this way, the problem of remembering seven pieces of information is reduced to remembering two chunks of information.

Experiments have shown that animals can also use chunking to help them learn and remember a long list. In one experiment (Terrace, 1991), five stimuli were presented in random locations on a translucent screen, and pigeons had to peck the five stimuli in the correct order to obtain food (see Figure 10.6a). Some of the stimuli were different colors and others were white shapes on a black background. Terrace wanted to see whether pigeons could learn the list of five stimuli faster if it were divided into two chunks, with only colors in one chunk and only shapes in the other. Five groups of pigeons learned a different list of colors and/or shapes. As Figure 10.6b shows, the list for Group II was nicely divided into two chunks: The first three stimuli were colors and the last two were shapes. The list for Group IV was divided into one large chunk of four colors, followed by the diamond shape. The lists for the other three groups were not organized into chunks. As Terrace expected, the two groups that had lists divided into chunks required significantly less practice to learn the correct pecking sequence. As more evidence that the pigeons in these two groups were using chunks, Terrace found that the longest hesitation between pecks occurred at the switch between colors and shapes. For instance, in Group II, the pigeons would peck the three colors quickly, then hesitate briefly, and then peck the two shapes in rapid succession.

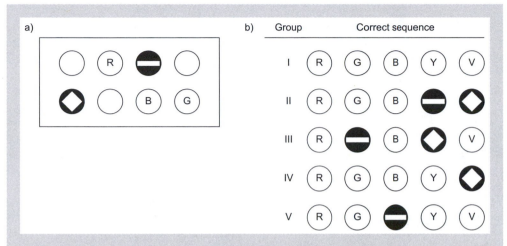

Figure 10.6 (a) In Terrace's (1991) experiment, five visual stimuli were arranged randomly in any of eight locations on a rectangular screen, and a pigeon received food only if it pecked the stimuli in exactly the correct sequence. (b) For the five groups of pigeons, the correct sequence is shown (R = red, G = green, B = blue, Y = yellow, V = violet).

If a set of stimuli is not already organized into chunks, animals may develop their own chunks. Dallal and Meck (1990) found evidence for chunking by rats in a 12-arm radial maze. Four arms (in different parts of the maze) had sunflower seeds at the end, four had food pellets, and four had rice puffs. For one group of rats, the locations of the different types of food were the same trial after trial. With practice, they tended to select the arms in chunks based on the different food types. For example, a rat might first go to the arms with sunflower seeds, then those with food pellets, and finally those with rice puffs. A typical rat's performance was usually not so perfectly organized, but there was a strong tendency to group the arms by food type. As a result, their accuracy (i.e., not going down the same arm twice) was better than for rats in a second group where the food locations were changed every trial (so they could not use a chunking strategy). Dallal and Meck concluded that by chunking on the basis of food type, the rats were able to decrease the burdens on their working memories and thereby perform more accurately.

Some animals may use chunking as a learning strategy in their natural environments. Suge and Okanoya (2010) found that when Bengalese finches listen to the songs of others of their species, they perceive them as chunks, not as individual notes. Williams and Staples (1992) studied how young male zebra finches learned songs up to 15 notes long from older male finches. They found that the older finches tended to divide their songs into chunks of about three notes; the younger finches would copy these chunks, and eventually they could put the chunks together into a complete song.

Human beings are much better at learning lists than the animals in these experiments. For instance, a child can memorize a list of five items without much effort, but the pigeons in Terrace's experiment needed over 100 sessions to do so. Still, the research on chunking demonstrates more similarities between human and animal memory: If a list is already organized into chunks, both animals and people can learn the list faster. If a set of items is not already organized, both animals and people may group similar items together, and this will help to improve memory and avoid mistakes.

TIMING AND COUNTING

Experiments on an "Internal Clock"

Try to imagine what would happen in the following experiment. A rat is first trained on an FI 40-second schedule. A light is turned on to signal the start of each 40-second interval, and after the reinforcer, the light is turned off during an intertrial interval, and then the next trial begins. Training on this schedule continues until the animal's response rate in each interval consistently shows the accelerating pattern that is typical of FI performance. Now the procedure is changed so that on occasional trials no reinforcer is delivered—the light remains on for about 80 seconds, and then the trial ends in darkness. With further training, the animal will learn that a reinforcer is available after 40 seconds on some trials but not on others. How do you think the animal will respond on nonreinforced trials?

PRACTICE QUIZ 1: CHAPTER 10

1. DMTS is a procedure used to study _____ memory.
2. When the presentation of new material interferes with the memory of something learned earlier, this is called _____.
3. _____ rehearsal serves to keep information in short-term memory.
4. If a surprising event occurs soon after a classical conditioning trial, this will result in _____ conditioning than would have occurred without the surprising event.
5. If an animal seems to have forgotten some new learning, it is sometimes possible for the animal to recover the learning if given a _____.

ANSWERS

1. short-term or working 2. retroactive interference 3. maintenance 4. less 5. reminder or clue

Figure 10.7 presents the results from an experiment like the one just described (Roberts, 1981). The open circles show that on trials without reinforcement, response rates started low, increased for a while, reached a maximum at about 40 seconds, and then declined. The location of the peak indicates that the rats were able to estimate the passage of time fairly accurately since they responded the fastest at just about the time a response might be reinforced (around 40 seconds). On other trials, a tone was presented instead of the light, and the tone usually meant that a reinforcer was available on an FI

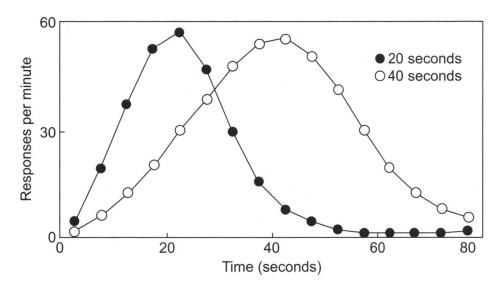

Figure 10.7 Rats' response rates in an experiment using the peak procedure. The filled circles show the results from trials with a tone that usually signaled an FI 20-second schedule. The open circles show the results from trials with a light that usually signaled an FI 40-second schedule. (From Roberts, S., 1981, Isolation of an internal clock, *Journal of Experimental Psychology: Animal Behavior Processes, 7,* 1242–1268. ©American Psychological Association. Adapted with permission.)

20-second schedule. The filled circles in Figure 10.7 show the results from nonreinforced test trials with the tone. Again, response rates first increased and then decreased, but on these trials the peak response rate occurred at about 20 seconds. These results show that the rats had learned that the tone signaled a 20-second interval and the light signaled a 40-second interval, and in both cases they could estimate these intervals fairly well. This procedure for studying animal timing abilities is called the **peak procedure** because the peak of the response-rate function tells us how accurately the animals could time the intervals.

How accurately can animals distinguish between two events that have different durations? Suppose a rat receives food for pressing the left lever after a 5-second tone and for pressing the right lever after an 8-second tone. Experiments using this type of procedure with both rats and pigeons have shown that they can discriminate between two stimuli if their durations differ by roughly 25% (Church, Getty, & Lerner, 1976; Stubbs, 1968). This finding illustrates a principle of perception called **Weber's law**, which says that the amount a stimulus must be changed before the change is detectable is proportional to the size of the stimulus. Weber's law was first applied to human perception, but it applies equally well to animals. Thus, an animal may be able to discriminate between a 4-second tone and a 5-second tone (which differ by 25%), but not between a 10-second tone and an 11-second tone (which differ by only 10%), even though there is a 1-second difference in both cases.

This research shows that animals are fairly good at judging durations, but it does not tell us exactly how they measure the passage of time. Some psychologists have proposed that every animal has an "internal clock" that it can use to time the duration of events in its environment. Church (1984) and Roberts (1982) claimed that in some respects an animal's internal clock is analogous to a stopwatch. Like a stopwatch, the internal clock can be used to time different types of stimuli. Roberts trained rats to press one lever after a 1-second tone and another after a 4-second tone. When the stimuli were then changed to 1- and 4-second lights, the rats continued to choose correctly without additional training. Like a stopwatch, the internal clock can be stopped and then restarted (e.g., if a stimulus light is turned off for 5 or 10 seconds and then turned back on).

Other theories of animal timing have been developed over the years, including the *behavioral theory of timing* (Killeen & Fetterman, 1988) and the *learning-to-time theory* (Machado & Arantes, 2006). The details of these theories are complex, but in essence they state that animals can use their own behaviors to measure durations. For example, if a reinforcement schedule requires that the animal wait for 5 seconds and then make a response (a DRL schedule, as described in Chapter 6), the animal might walk to all four corners of the experimental chamber and then make the operant response. In this way, the animal could time the 5-second interval with reasonable accuracy.

The research on this topic has shown that animals have fairly versatile timing abilities. They can discriminate between stimuli of slightly different durations, and they can transfer this skill from a visual stimulus to an auditory stimulus. They can time the total duration of a stimulus that is temporarily interrupted. They can time the total duration of a compound stimulus that begins as a light and then changes to a tone. An animal's ability to time events is certainly far less accurate than an ordinary wristwatch, but then so is a person's.

Counting

Many of the techniques used to study animals' counting abilities are similar to those used to study timing, and the results are similar as well. Mechner (1958) used a variation of a FR schedule in which a rat had to switch from one lever to another after completing the ratio requirement. For example, if 16 responses were required, on half of the trials, the 16th consecutive response on lever A was reinforced. On the other half of the trials, the rat had to make 16 or more consecutive responses on lever A and then 1 response on lever B to collect the reinforcer. If the rat switched too early (say, after 14 responses), there was no reinforcer, and the rat had to start from the beginning and make another 16 responses on key A before a reinforcer was available. In four different conditions, either 4, 8, 12, or 16 consecutive responses were required. For these four conditions, Figure 10.8 shows one rat's probability of switching to lever B after different run lengths (where a run is a string of consecutive responses on lever A). We can see that as the ratio requirement increased, the average run length also increased in a systematic way. When 4 responses were required, the most common run length was 5; when 16 responses were required, the most common run length was 18. Producing run lengths that were, on the average, slightly longer than required was a sensible strategy because the penalty for switching too early was severe. More recent studies with pigeons, using procedures similar to Mechner's, obtained very similar results, and they

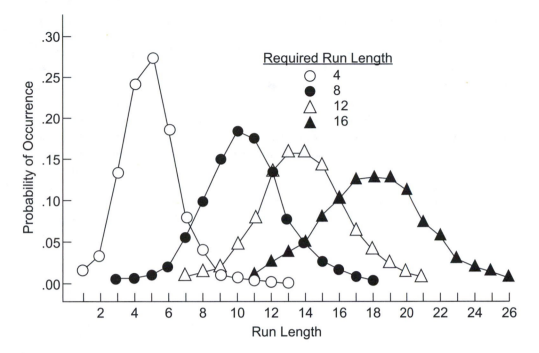

Figure 10.8 One rat's probability of switching from lever A to lever B after different run lengths in Mechner's (1958) experiment. The required run length is the number of consecutive responses required on lever A before a switch to lever B would be reinforced. (Adapted from Mechner, F., Probability relations within response sequences under ratio reinforcement, *Journal of the Experimental Analysis of Behavior, 1,* 109–121. Copyright 1958 by the Society for the Experimental Analysis of Behavior, Inc.)

provided further evidence that number discrimination by animals follows Weber's law (Fetterman & Killeen, 2010).

The counting abilities displayed by the rats and pigeons in these experiments were not exact: On some trials they switched too early, and on others they made more responses than necessary. This is actually quite similar to what human adults or children do when they do not have the time or interest in getting an exact total—they estimate, using what has been called an *approximate number system* (Bonny & Lourenco, 2013). Of course, when it is necessary, humans can also count objects to get an exact number. Can animals learn to count objects in an exact rather than an approximate way? A few studies suggest that they can, at least with small numbers. In one experiment, rats were able to learn a discrimination in which three bursts of noise served as the S+ and either two or four bursts served as S− (Davis & Albert, 1986). Capaldi and Miller (1988) found evidence that the rats learned abstract concepts of number that could transfer from one type of stimulus to another. Some writers have proposed that counting is a skill that animals can learn only with difficulty, but Capaldi and Miller concluded just the opposite, stating that "rats assign abstract number tags to reinforcers readily, easily, and under most, if not all, circumstances" (1988, p. 16).

Another study found evidence of a rudimentary counting ability in domestic dogs (West & Young, 2002).

Other evidence for an exact counting ability was presented by Pepperberg (1987), who trained a parrot, Alex, to respond to any number of objects from two through six by actually saying the appropriate number. In training, a number of objects (e.g., keys, small pieces of paper or wood, corks) would be placed on a tray, and Alex was reinforced if he said the correct number. For instance, the experimenter might present three corks and ask, "What's this?" The correct response would be "Three corks." Different objects were used on different trials so that Alex would not simply learn to say "three" whenever he saw corks. After a few months of training, Alex was responding correctly on about 80% of the trials. To show that Alex's counting ability was not limited to the training stimuli, new objects were presented on test trials. In some cases, Alex did not even know the names of the objects (e.g., wooden beads or small bottles), but he was able to give the correct number of objects on about 75% of the test trials with new stimuli. Pepperberg found that Alex could count up to six objects, whether familiar or novel, with a high degree of accuracy.

Matsuzawa (1985) has reported a similar counting skill in a chimpanzee by having the chimp press response keys with the numbers 1 through 6 on them. Brannon and Terrace (2000) taught macaques to point to arrays of abstract shapes in order of increasing number: To receive a reward, the monkey had to first point to the array with one shape, then to the arrays with two, three, and four shapes. After learning this task, the monkeys were able to transfer this ability to arrays with between five and nine shapes, even though they had received no training with these larger numbers. These studies, along with Pepperberg's research with Alex, provide the best evidence available for accurate counting by animals.

ANIMAL LANGUAGE

Communicating through language is one of the most impressive behaviors that people can perform. Some scientists and philosophers have claimed that the ability to use language is one skill that only human beings possess (e.g., Chomsky, 1972). For this reason, attempts to teach language to chimpanzees and other animals have received tremendous attention. This section describes some of the most important studies on this topic and examines what the animals have been able to accomplish.

Research With Chimpanzees

In early attempts to teach language to chimpanzees, some researchers tried to get the animals to speak (e.g., Kellogg & Kellogg, 1933). These studies were unsuccessful, mainly because a chimpanzee's vocal apparatus does not permit it to make many human speech sounds. To avoid this problem, Gardner and Gardner (1969) decided to try to teach a chimpanzee, Washoe, to use American Sign Language (ASL). Using a mixture of modeling, manual guidance, and a good deal of patience, they were able to teach Washoe to produce signs for quite a few different words, including nouns (e.g., *flower, toothbrush, hat*), verbs (*go, listen, tickle*), adjectives (*sweet, funny, more*), pronouns (*you, me*), and prepositions (*in, out*). After 4 years, Washoe had learned about 130 signs. This was quite an impressive vocabulary (though still small compared to that of the average 4-year-old child, who knows several thousand words).

After being taught a sign in a few contexts, Washoe sometimes used it in a new situation without further training. For instance, she was taught the sign for *more* in combination with a few different signs (including *more tickle* and *more swinging*), and she later began to use the sign to ask for more food and for more of other activities. Although she frequently used signs in various combinations, the order in which she used the signs in a "sentence" was quite inconsistent. For example, she might sign the phrase *food eat* on some occasions and *eat food* on others, with no apparent reason for the different word orders. In contrast, both children and adults tend to use consistent word orders whether they are using spoken or sign language. In short, Washoe had a good vocabulary but poor (perhaps nonexistent) grammar.

Instead of using ASL, David Premack (1971, 1983) constructed a language consisting of different shapes that represented different words. Sentences were created by placing the shapes on a magnetic board in a specific order. Premack's pupil, a 6-year-old chimpanzee named Sarah, learned to respond appropriately to many different configurations of these symbols. The order of symbols was a critical part of the language Sarah learned, and she demonstrated an impressive ability to respond on the basis of symbol order. For instance, after Sarah learned the symbols for different colors and for the word *on*, she was taught to respond appropriately to the sequences *green on red* versus *red on green*: In the first case she would put a green card on top of a red card, and in the second case she would do the opposite. This shows that her responses were controlled by the order of the symbols, not just by the symbols themselves. Having succeeded at this task, Sarah was then able to respond correctly to new symbol strings such as *blue on yellow* with no further training. Sarah had learned not only that the order of symbols was important but that this same order could be applied to other symbols as well. This example demonstrates an understanding of a grammatical rule, that is, an abstract rule about sentence structure that applies to entire classes of words.

Sarah was able to learn many grammatical forms and concepts, including plurals, yes–no questions, and quantifiers (*all, some, none,* and *several*). One disappointing feature of her performance, however, was that she seldom initiated a conversation. Her use of the symbol language was almost exclusively confined to answering questions posed by the experimenters. Furthermore, if one of her trainers placed a question on the board and then left the room, Sarah would usually give either an incorrect response or none at all. This behavior contrasts quite starkly with that of young children, who spontaneously practice and use the words they have learned, even when no one is listening.

One researcher who came to pessimistic conclusions about chimp language learning was Herbert Terrace (1979), who taught ASL to a chimpanzee named Nim Chimpsky. Nim learned about 125 signs for nouns, verbs, adjectives, pronouns, and prepositions. He frequently used these signs in combinations of two or more, but like Washoe, Nim showed very little consistency of word order. Based on his analyses of the behaviors of

Nim, Washoe, Sarah, and other chimps, Terrace concluded that they had learned only the most primitive grammatical rules, and that frequently they would just string together signs in a random order. They relied heavily on imitation and on prompting by their trainers; they showed little spontaneous use of language. The complexity and length of their sentences did not increase with additional training. Terrace (1979) concluded that what these chimps had learned lacked many of the essential characteristics of human language.

Research With Other Species

One of the most accomplished animal language learners to date has been Kanzi, a bonobo trained by Savage-Rumbaugh and her associates (Savage-Rumbaugh, 1986; Segerdahl, Fields, & Savage-Rumbaugh, 2005). Kanzi was taught to use lexigrams—pictorial symbols that represent words. He learned over 300 lexigrams and used them in a relatively consistent order (e.g., referring first to an action and then an object), which is evidence of a basic grammar. He exhibited an understanding of many spoken English words in addition to the lexigrams. He discriminated among different word orders in spoken sentences and responded appropriately. Language studies have also been conducted with other primates, including gorillas and orangutans (e.g., Bonvillian & Patterson, 1999; Miles, 1999). ASL has been used in some cases and pictorial symbols in others. In many of these studies, the animals were able to learn well over 100 signs.

There have also been some studies with nonprimates. Herman, Richards, and Wolz (1984) trained two bottle-nosed dolphins to respond to about two dozen manual gestures by engaging in the appropriate activities. For example, a trainer might make the gestures for *frisbee fetch basket*, and the dolphin would then find the frisbee and put it in the basket. The dolphins could also answer questions about whether a particular object was or was not present in the tank (Herman & Forestell, 1985). Similar work has been done with sea lions (Schusterman & Krieger, 1984). And the parrot Alex, whose counting abilities have already been described, learned to say about 50 English words and use them appropriately to make requests ("Gimme tickle") and answer questions (Trainer: "What's this?" Alex: "Clothespin"). Alex could also answer questions about the physical properties of objects, describing either an object's shape or color depending on what question his trainer asked (Pepperberg, 2010).

Some studies have looked at dogs' abilities to understand spoken language. Kaminski, Call, and Fischer (2004) tested a pet collie that was trained by its owners to retrieve different objects and found that it had learned the names of about 200 different objects. In addition, if the collie was asked to retrieve an object with a name it had not learned, the dog would go into the room with the objects, bypass familiar objects, and return with the unfamiliar object. The dog seemed to be able to infer the names of new objects using a process of elimination. With another collie, Pilley (2013) found that after extensive training, the dog could respond to the grammatical structure of three-word sentences in much the same way that this ability has been demonstrated with dolphins and sea lions.

Some Conclusions

Terrace was almost surely correct in saying that the linguistic capacities that animals have exhibited are quite limited compared to those of humans. On the positive side, however, this research has shown that animals have at least some measure of language ability. They have demonstrated many of the characteristics of human language:

1. Use of Abstract Symbols
   Possibly the most fundamental characteristic of language is that any arbitrary symbol can be used to represent an object or concept. It is also the characteristic that has been most thoroughly demonstrated in animals. As we have seen, animals of several species have shown the ability to use words, signs, or symbols to represent objects, actions, and descriptions.

2. Productivity
   Much of the power of language stems from the ability to take a finite set of words and combine them in new ways so that one can communicate and understand new ideas. The ability to use words and symbols in new combinations has been observed in the language of chimpanzees and other primates. The studies with dolphins and with the parrot Alex have demonstrated an ability to understand new symbol combinations that they heard or saw for the very first time.

3. Grammar
   The early work by Premack showed that the chimpanzee Sarah could respond not just to individual symbols but to the order in which the symbols were presented. This was also found by Herman in his work with dolphins. In terms of language production, the evidence is not impressive. Chimps and bonobos have shown some degree of regularity in word order, but their sentences are short, and the word order they use is not always consistent. There is evidence that other species (pygmy chimpanzees, dolphins, dogs, and parrots) can learn at least some basic principles of grammar. Nevertheless, even those who are typically enthusiastic about animal language abilities admit that the grammatical skills of nonhumans seem quite limited (Givón & Rumbaugh, 2009).

4. Displacement
   The ability to use language to talk about the past or the future and about objects and events not currently present is called *displacement*. Some studies found that chimpanzees can use their signs to describe behaviors they have just performed or are about to perform (Premack, 1986). In one case, researchers found that two pygmy chimpanzees could use lexigrams to refer to objects and events not present (Savage-Rumbaugh, McDonald, Sevcik, Hopkins, & Rubert, 1986). However, there is considerable debate about this matter. One experiment found that whereas 12-month-old human infants could gesture to communicate about a desired object that was not present, chimpanzees did not do so. The researchers concluded that this may be a uniquely human ability (Liszkowski, Schäfer, Carpenter, & Tomasello, 2009).

5. Use in Communication
   For people, the purpose of language is to communicate with others. Terrace (1979) claimed that the language-trained chimps used their language only to obtain reinforcers,

not to communicate information. However, later findings suggested that animals do use their signs to communicate with other animals or with people. Fouts, Fouts, and Schoenfield (1984) reported that five chimpanzees that had been taught ASL signs would use these signs to communicate with one another, even when no human beings were present to prompt or reinforce these behaviors. Greenfield and Savage-Rumbaugh (1993) found that two different species of chimpanzees used the symbols they were taught by humans to express a variety of different functions, such as agreement, requests, and promises. These chimpanzees often displayed the sort of turn taking in the use of symbols that is typical of human conversations.

In summary, some of the main characteristics of human language have been found, at least at a rudimentary level, in other species. Future research will probably uncover other linguistic abilities in animals. Although no other species has shown the level of language capabilities that people have, it is not quite accurate to say that language is a uniquely human ability.

REASONING BY ANIMALS

Besides language, many other advanced cognitive skills have been studied in animals, including abstract reasoning, problem solving, and the manufacture and use of tools. This section reviews a few of the findings.

Object Permanence

Object permanence is an understanding that objects continue to exist even when they are not visible. The developmental psychologist Jean Piaget (1926) proposed that during the first 2 years of life, human infants proceed through six different stages in which their understanding of object permanence becomes more and more complete. Piaget developed a series of tests to determine which of the six stages an infant has reached, and these tests can be adapted quite easily for use with animals. Research with different species, including cats and dogs, has shown that they follow more or less the same sequence of stages as human infants, eventually reaching stage six, in which they will correctly search for an object after an "invisible displacement" (Dore & Dumas, 1987). For example, Figure 10.9 shows the procedure used by Miller, Rayburn-Reeves, and Zentall (2009). A dog watches as a person places a snack in one of the two containers. The bar with the containers is rotated 90 degrees (an "invisible displacement" because the snack cannot be seen), the room is darkened for a few seconds, and then the dog is allowed to choose one container. Most dogs were successful at this task as long as the period of darkness was not too long. This level of competence has been found in several species of primates (Albiach-Serrano, Call, & Barth, 2010) and birds (Pepperberg & Funk, 1990). However, not all species perform equally well on these tasks. A study with dolphins found that they were successful with visible object displacements but not invisible displacements (Jaakkola, Guarino, Rodriguez, Erb, & Trone, 2010).

Figure 10.9 In this test of object permanence, a dog watches as a person puts a treat in one of the two containers (which are aligned as in the left panel). The bar with the containers is rotated 90 degrees (right panel), the room is darkened for a few seconds, and then the dog is allowed to choose one container. (Reprinted from *Behavioural Processes,* Vol. 81, Miller, H.C., Rayburn-Reeves, R., & Zentall, T., What do dogs know about hidden objects? 439–446. Copyright 2009, with permission from Elsevier.)

Analogies

An **analogy** is a statement of the form "A is to B as C is to D." To test someone's ability to understand analogies, we can give the person two or more choices for D and ask which is correct. For example, consider the analogy, "Lock is to key as can is to _____." Is *paintbrush* or *can opener* a more appropriate answer? On this type of problem, the ability to make judgments about physical similarity is usually not enough. In physical terms, a can opener is not especially similar to a key, a lock, or a can. To solve this analogy, one must understand (1) the relation between lock and key, (2) the relation between can opener and can, and (3) the similarity of the two relations (i.e., that the second item of each pair is used to open the first). In other words, to understand an analogy one must be able to understand a relation (similarity) between two relations.

Gillan, Premack, and Woodruff (1981) tested Sarah, the language-trained chimpanzee, with analogies that involved either perceptual relations or functional relations between objects. The analogy in the previous paragraph involves functional relations because it requires an understanding of the functions the different objects serve, and it was one of the analogies given to Sarah (Figure 10.10). An example of a perceptual analogy is the following: "Large yellow triangle is to small yellow triangle as large red crescent is to (small red crescent or small yellow crescent)?" This analogy also requires an understanding of the relations between objects, but in this case the relations pertain only to the perceptual properties of the objects (their relative sizes).

Sarah was fairly good at solving both types of analogies. There has not been much research on this ability with other species, but one study found that baboons could successfully solve perceptual analogies (Fagot & Parron, 2010).

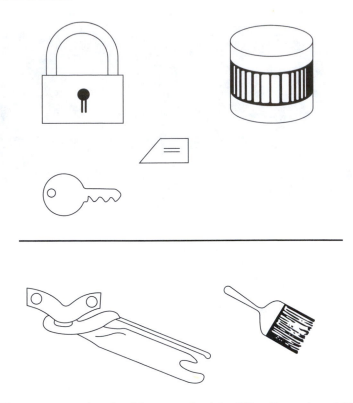

Figure 10.10 Pictures presented to the chimpanzee Sarah by Gillan, Premack, and Woodruff (1981). The pictures represent the analogy, "Lock is to key as can is to what?" Two possible answers, can opener and paintbrush, were presented below the line, and Sarah chose the correct answer. (From Gillan, D. J., Premack, D., & Woodruff, G., 1981, Reasoning in the chimpanzee: I. Analogical reasoning. *Journal of Experimental Psychology: Animal Behavior Processes, 7,* 1–17. © American Psychological Association. Reprinted with permission.)

Transitive Inference

If Adam is shorter than Bill, and if Bill is shorter than Carl, then it follows that Adam is shorter than Carl. This conclusion is justified because inequalities of size are *transitive*; that is, they conform to the following general rule: if A < B and B < C, then A < C. If we draw the correct conclusion about the heights of Adam and Carl without ever having seen them side by side, we are displaying the capacity for **transitive inference**.

Gillan (1981) tested whether chimpanzees were capable of transitive inference by first training them with containers of different colors that had food in some situations but not others. For instance, one chimp was taught that blue was better than black, black was better than red, and so on. In the test for transitive inference, a chimp had to choose between two containers that had never been paired before. For instance, when given a choice between blue and red, would the chimp choose blue? Gillan found that the chimps were capable of making such inferences. Later studies have shown that transitive inference can be found in numerous species, including rats (Davis, 1992), mice (DeVito, Kanter, & Eichenbaum, 2010), and pigeons (von Fersen, Wynne, Delius, & Staddon, 1991).

Tool Use and Manufacture

You might think that only human beings are capable of making and using tools, but this is not so. Several different species are known to use tools of various types (Figure 10.11). For example, sea otters hold rocks against their chests while floating in the water and use them to crack open the shells of mollusks. Several birds, including the woodpecker finch and the crow, use sticks or branches to fish out larvae or insects from holes where their beaks will not reach. Examples of tool use among primates are numerous. For instance, chimpanzees use leaves as towels to wipe themselves or as umbrellas in the rain, and they use sticks and rocks as weapons to defend themselves against predators.

Even more impressive than examples of tool use are the rare instances in which animals have been observed to make a tool and then use it for some specific purpose. One example is a chimpanzee that was taught how to hit one stone against another to make a cutting tool and then to use the tool to cut a cord. Later, the chimp made such cutting tools on his own, learning by trial and error how to smash the stones effectively to get

Figure 10.11 Many animals, like this gorilla, use sticks as tools to extract insects from logs or trees. (dean bertoncelj/Shutterstock.com)

sharp cutting edges (Toth, Schich, Savage-Rumbaugh, Sevcik, & Rumbaugh, 1993). This chimp first learned the skill through observation, but other animals have learned to manufacture tools by themselves. Weir, Chappell, and Kacelnik (2002) found that a female crow learned to bend a straight piece of wire into a hook and then use the hook to pull a container of food out of a vertical pipe. The crow used her beak and foot to bend the wire, and it was not an accidental behavior: Of 10 trials in which the crow was given a straight piece of wire, she bent the wire and successfully retrieved the food container 9 times. These examples of tool making have generated a great deal of interest because they suggest that the animals may have some basic understanding of the cause-and-effect relation between modifying an object and then using that object to accomplish some task.

BOX 10.2   SPOTLIGHT ON RESEARCH

Metacognition: Do Animals Know What They Know?

Stated simply, **metacognition** is thinking about one's thinking. To be more specific, it is the ability to reflect on one's memories and thought processes and make judgments about them. For instance, people can state how sure they are about something they remember or about whether they know a particular piece of information. I may tell you that I am positive I know the name of a particular actor, even though I can't think of it at the moment. I may say I think I remember that Sam was at last summer's department picnic but that I am not really sure. People have the ability to make judgments about the accuracy of their own memories (along with other abilities that would also be classified as metacognition).

In recent years, there have been many studies examining whether animals are also capable of metacognition (Kornell, 2009). Different techniques have been used to test for such abilities, and many of them have obtained positive results. For example, to determine whether rhesus monkeys could judge the accuracy of their memories, they were given a delayed matching-to-sample task in which they had the option of choosing an "uncertainty response," which allowed them to skip a trial and move on to the next one. The monkeys frequently made the uncertainty response when the trial was a difficult one, but they seldom made the uncertainty response on easy trials. This shows that they could accurately judge when they were likely to make mistakes (Hampton, 2001). One study found that apes would seek more information when on trials where they were uncertain but not when they already knew the correct choice (Call, 2010). When rhesus monkeys performed a discrimination task with easy and difficult trials, they chose to take larger risks to obtain greater rewards on the easy trials, which suggests that they knew they would make the correct choice (Shields, Smith, Guttmannova, & Washburn, 2005).

The topic of animal metacognition has received a great deal of attention from behavioral and cognitive psychologists because metacognition has been considered to be a sophisticated human capability. Some psychologists are still skeptical about whether these results are convincing demonstrations of metacognition. However, the evidence for animal metacognition is growing, and it may provide a compelling example of continuity between humans and other animals and offer insights into the evolution of human mental abilities (Smith, Couchman, & Beran, 2014).

CONCLUSIONS

Human beings cannot boast that they are the only species on earth capable of abstract thinking. Many lines of evidence suggest that other animals can learn a variety of tasks that involve abstract reasoning. It seems likely that more examples of abstract reasoning will be found in other species in future research. Perhaps the moral is that it is always risky to claim, "Here is a problem in abstract reasoning that only humans (or only primates) can solve." The danger is that some clever researcher will find a way to teach a bird or rodent to solve exactly that problem. Although no one would seriously question the vast differences between human and nonhuman intellectual abilities, some of the apparent limitations of animals' reasoning abilities might be due to limitations in our current training or testing procedures, not to the animals.

SUMMARY

Practice Quiz 2: Chapter 10

1. In the peak procedure, if an animal's responses are sometimes reinforced 20 seconds after the start of a trial, the rate of responding peaks at about _____ from the start of the trial.
2. Two species that have demonstrated the ability to count by using words or symbols to represent numbers are the _____ and the _____.
3. Grouping similar objects together as a strategy for improving memory is called _____.
4. When the chimpanzee Washoe was taught sign language, she learned the signs for many words, but she showed little ability to use _____.
5. _____ is the understanding that objects continue to exist when they are not visible.

Answers

1. 20 seconds 2. parrot, chimpanzee 3. chunking 4. grammar or consistent word order 5. object permanence

Two procedures used to study short-term memory in animals are DMTS and the radial-arm maze. In DMTS, performance accuracy declines quickly as the delay between sample and comparison stimuli increases. Studies using radial-arm mazes have shown that rats can generally avoid repeat visits to arms of a maze where they have already collected food, even when a maze has as many as 17 arms. Other studies have found evidence for maintenance rehearsal, associative rehearsal, and chunking in animals. Experiments on long-term memory have shown that pigeons can remember several hundred pictures with a high degree of accuracy.

Other studies have demonstrated that long-term memory can be improved if an animal is given an appropriate stimulus as a reminder of a previous learning experience.

Various experiments on timing have demonstrated that the duration of a stimulus can control an animal's behavior with reasonable accuracy and so can the number of stimuli. When researchers have tried to teach language to animals, the responses resemble human language abilities in some respects but not in others. Some chimpanzees have learned to use more than 100 signs or symbols for words, but they seldom use any consistent word order or grammar. However, Premack's research with a chimpanzee and some studies with dolphins showed that the animals could learn the importance of word order. Other studies have found that several species (gorillas, parrots, dogs) can learn the meanings of gestures, symbols, or spoken words.

Animals of various species have exhibited various types of abstract reasoning. For instance, rats, mice, and pigeons can solve problems of transitive inference. Cats, dogs, and birds can perform tasks involving object permanence. Baboons and chimpanzees have successfully solved tests of analogical reasoning. There is also some evidence that nonhuman primates have the capacity for metacognition.

Review Questions

1. Describe how DMTS and the radial-arm maze can be used to study animal short-term memory. Discuss some of the main findings that have been obtained with these procedures.
2. What are maintenance rehearsal and associative rehearsal? Describe one experiment that appears to demonstrate each type of rehearsal in animals.
3. Describe two pieces of evidence that animals can use chunking as an aid to memory.
4. Discuss the strengths and the limitations of the language abilities of chimpanzees trained to use ASL. What other techniques have been used to teach language to animals, what other species have been used, and what has been found?
5. Describe some tasks that have been used to test animals' reasoning abilities. Give examples of reasoning abilities that are found in many species and of abilities that have been found in just a few species.

REFERENCES

Albiach-Serrano, A., Call, J., & Barth, J. (2010). Great apes track hidden objects after changes in the objects' position and in subject's orientation. *American Journal of Primatology, 72,* 349–359.

Amundson, J.C., & Miller, R.R. (2008). Associative interference in Pavlovian conditioning: A function of similarity between the interfering and target associative structures. *Quarterly Journal of Experimental Psychology, 61,* 1340–1355.

Babb, S. J., & Crystal, J.D. (2003). Spatial navigation on the radial maze with trial-unique intramaze cues and restricted extramaze cues. *Behavioural Processes, 64*, 103–111.

Baddeley, A. (2010). Long-term and working memory: How do they interact? In L. Bäckman & L. Nyberg (Eds.), *Memory, aging and the brain: A Festschrift in honour of Lars-Göran Nilsson* (pp. 7–23). New York: Psychology Press.

Beatty, W.W., & Shavalia, D.A. (1980). Rat spatial memory: Resistance to retroactive interference at long retention intervals. *Animal Learning and Behavior, 8*, 550–552.

Bonny, J.W., & Lourenco, S.F. (2013). The approximate number system and its relation to early math achievement: Evidence from the preschool years. *Journal of Experimental Child Psychology, 114*, 375–388.

Bonvillian, J.D., & Patterson, F.P. (1999). Early sign-language acquisition: Comparisons between children and gorillas. In S. Parker, R.W. Mitchell, & H. Miles (Eds.), *The mentalities of gorillas and orangutans: Comparative perspectives* (pp. 240–264). New York: Cambridge University Press.

Brannon, E.M., & Terrace, H.S. (2000). Representation of the numerosities 1–9 by Rhesus Macaques (*Macaca mulata*). *Journal of Experimental Psychology: Animal Behavior Processes, 26*, 31–49.

Call, J. (2010). Do apes know that they could be wrong? *Animal Cognition, 13*, 689–700.

Capaldi, E. J., & Miller, D. J. (1988). Counting in rats: Its functional significance and the independent cognitive processes which comprise it. *Journal of Experimental Psychology: Animal Behavior Processes, 14*, 3–17.

Chelonis, J. J., Cox, A.R., Karr, M. J., Prunty, P.K., Baldwin, R.L., & Paule, M.G. (2014). Comparison of delayed matching-to-sample performance in monkeys and children. *Behavioural Processes, 103*, 261–268.

Chomsky, N. (1972). *Language and the mind*. New York: Harcourt Brace Jovanovich.

Church, R.M. (1984). Properties of the internal clock. In J. Gibbon & L. Allen (Eds.), *Timing and time perception* (Vol. 438, pp. 566–582). New York: Annals of the New York Academy of Sciences.

Church, R.M., Getty, D. J., & Lerner, N.D. (1976). Duration discrimination by rats. *Journal of Experimental Psychology: Animal Behavior Processes, 4*, 303–312.

Cook, R.G., Levison, D.G., Gillett, S.R., & Blaisdell, A.P. (2005). Capacity and limits of associative memory in pigeons. *Psychonomic Bulletin & Review, 12*, 350–358.

Dallal, N.L., & Meck, W.H. (1990). Hierarchical structures: Chunking by food type facilitates spatial memory. *Journal of Experimental Psychology: Animal Behavior Processes, 16*, 69–84.

Davis, H. (1992). Transitive inference in rats (*Rattus norvegicus*). *Journal of Comparative Psychology, 106*, 342–349.

Davis, H., & Albert, M. (1986). Numerical discrimination by rats using sequential auditory stimuli. *Animal Learning and Behavior, 14*, 57–59.

DeVito, L.M., Kanter, B.R., & Eichenbaum, H. (2010). The hippocampus contributes to memory expression during transitive inference in mice. *Hippocampus, 20*, 208–217.

Dore, F.Y., & Dumas, C. (1987). Psychology of animal cognition: Piagetian studies. *Psychological Bulletin, 102*, 219–233.

Ebbinghaus, H. (1885). *Memory*. Leipzig, Germany: Duncker.

Engelmann, M. (2009). Competition between two memory traces for long-term recognition memory. Neurobiology of Learning and Memory, 91, 58–65.

Fagot, J., & Parron, C. (2010). Relational matching in baboons (*Papio papio*) with reduced grouping requirements. *Journal of Experimental Psychology: Animal Behavior Processes, 36*, 184–193.

Fetterman, J.G., & Killeen, P.R. (2010). Categorical counting. *Behavioural Processes, 85*, 28–35.

Fouts, R., Fouts, D., & Schoenfield, D. (1984). Sign language conversation interaction between chimpanzees. *Sign Language Studies, 42*, 1–12.

Gardner, R.A., & Gardner, B.T. (1969). Teaching sign language to a chimpanzee. *Science, 165*, 664–672.

Gillan, D.J. (1981). Reasoning in the chimpanzee: II. Transitive inference. *Journal of Experimental Psychology: Animal Behavior Processes, 7*, 150–164.

Gillan, D.J., Premack, D., & Woodruff, G. (1981). Reasoning in the chimpanzee: I. Analogical reasoning. *Journal of Experimental Psychology: Animal Behavior Processes, 7,* 1–17.

Givón, T.T., & Rumbaugh, S. (2009). Can apes learn grammar? A short detour into language evolution. In J. Guo, E. Lieven, N. Budwig, S. Ervin-Tripp, K. Nakamura, & Ş. Özçalişkan (Eds.), *Crosslinguistic approaches to the psychology of language: Research in the tradition of Dan Isaac Slobin* (pp. 299–309). New York: Psychology Press.

Gleitman, H. (1971). Forgetting of long-term memories in animals. In W.K. Honig & P.H.R. James (Eds.), *Animal memory* (pp. 1–44). New York: Academic Press.

Gordon, W.C., Smith, G.J., & Katz, D.S. (1979). Dual effects of response blocking following avoidance learning. *Behavior Research and Therapy, 17,* 479–487.

Grant, D.S. (1975). Proactive interference in pigeon short-term memory. *Journal of Experimental Psychology: Animal Behavior Processes, 1,* 207–220.

Greenfield, P.M., & Savage-Rumbaugh, E.S. (1993). Comparing communicative competence in child and chimp: The pragmatics of repetition. *Journal of Child Language, 20,* 1–26.

Hampton, R. (2001). Rhesus monkeys know when they remember. *Proceedings of the National Academy of Sciences of the United States of America, 98,* 5359–5362.

Herman, L.M., & Forestell, P.H. (1985). Reporting presence or absence of named objects by a language-trained dolphin. *Neuroscience & Biobehavioral Reviews, 9,* 667–681.

Herman, L.M., Richards, D.G., & Wolz, J.P. (1984). Comprehension of sentences by bottlenosed dolphins. Cognition, 16, 1–90.

Jaakkola, K., Guarino, E., Rodriguez, M., Erb, L., & Trone, M. (2010). What do dolphins (*Tursiops truncatus*) understand about hidden objects? *Animal Cognition, 13,* 103–120.

Jarvik, M.E., Goldfarb, T.L., & Carley, J.L. (1969). Influence of interference on delayed matching in monkeys. *Journal of Experimental Psychology, 81,* 1–6.

Kaminski, J., Call, J., & Fischer, J. (2004). Word learning in a domestic dog: Evidence for "fast mapping". *Science, 304,* 1682–1683.

Kellogg, W.N., & Kellogg, L.A. (1933). *The ape and the child: A study of environmental influence upon early behavior.* New York: McGraw-Hill.

Kelly, D.M., Kamil, A.C., & Cheng, K. (2010). Landmark use by Clark's nutcrackers (*Nucifraga Columbiana*): Influence of disorientation and cue rotation on distance and direction estimates. *Animal Cognition, 13,* 175–188.

Killeen, P.R., & Fetterman, J.G. (1988). A behavioral theory of timing. *Psychological Review, 95,* 274–295.

Kornell, N. (2009). Metacognition in humans and animals. *Current Directions in Psychological Science, 18,* 11–15.

Koychev, I., El-Deredy, W., Haenschel, C., & Deakin, J.F.W. (2010). Visual information processing deficits as biomarkers of vulnerability to schizophrenia: An event-related potential study in schizotypy. *Neuropsychologia, 48,* 2205–2214.

Liszkowski, U., Schäfer, M., Carpenter, M., & Tomasello, M. (2009). Prelinguistic infants, but not chimpanzees, communicate about absent entities. *Psychological Science, 20,* 654–660.

Machado, A., & Arantes, J. (2006). Further tests of the Scalar Expectancy Theory (SET) and the Learning-to-Time (LeT) model in a temporal bisection task. *Behavioural Processes, 72,* 195–206.

Maki, W.S., & Hegvik, D.K. (1980). Directed forgetting in pigeons. *Animal Learning and Behavior, 8,* 567–574.

Matsuzawa, T. (1985). Use of numbers by a chimpanzee. *Nature, 315,* 57–59.

Mazmanian, D.S., & Roberts, W.A. (1983). Spatial memory in rats under restricted viewing conditions. *Learning and Motivation, 14,* 123–139.

Mechner, F. (1958). Probability relations within response sequences under ratio reinforcement. *Journal of the Experimental Analysis of Behavior, 1,* 109–121.

Miles, H.L. (1999). Symbolic communication with and by great apes. In S. Parker, R.W. Mitchell, & H.L. Miles (Eds.), The mentalities of gorillas and orangutans: Comparative perspectives (pp. 197–210). New York: Cambridge University Press.

Miller, G.A. (1956). The magical number seven, plus or minus two. *Psychological Review, 63,* 81–97.

Miller, H.C., Rayburn-Reeves, R., & Zentall, T.R. (2009). What do dogs know about hidden objects? *Behavioural Processes, 81,* 439–446.

Miller, W.S., & Armus, H.L. (1999). Directed forgetting: Short-term memory or conditioned response? *Psychological Record, 49,* 211–220.

Millin, P.M., & Riccio, D.C. (2004). Is the context shift effect a case of retrieval failure? The effects of retrieval enhancing treatments on forgetting under altered stimulus conditions in rats. *Journal of Experimental Psychology: Animal Behavior Processes, 30,* 325–334.

Milmine, M., Watanabe, A., & Colombo, M. (2008). Neural correlates of directed forgetting in the avian prefrontal cortex. *Behavioral Neuroscience, 122,* 199–209.

Olton, D.S. (1978). Characteristics of spatial memory. In S.H. Hulse, H. Fowler, & W.K. Honig (Eds.), *Cognitive processes in animal behavior* (pp. 341–373). Hillsdale, NJ: Erlbaum.

Olton, D.S., Collison, C., & Werz, W.A. (1977). Spatial memory and radial arm maze performance by rats. *Learning and Motivation, 8,* 289–314.

Pepperberg, I.M. (1987). Evidence for conceptual quantitative abilities in the African parrot: Labeling of cardinal sets. *Ethology, 75,* 37–61.

Pepperberg, I.M. (2010). Vocal learning in Grey parrots: A brief review of perception, production, and cross-species comparisons. *Brain and Language, 115,* 81–91.

Pepperberg, I.M., & Funk, M.S. (1990). Object permanence in four species of psittacine birds: An African Grey parrot (*Psittacus erithacus*), an Illiger mini macaw (*Ara maracana*), a parakeet (*Melopsittacus undulatus*), and a cockatiel (*Nymphicus hollandicus*). *Animal Learning and Behavior, 18,* 97–108.

Piaget, J. (1926). *The language and thought of the child* (M. Gabain, Trans.). London: Routledge and Kegan Paul.

Pilley, J.W. (2013). Border collie comprehends sentences containing a prepositional object, verb, and direct object. *Learning and Motivation, 44,* 229–240.

Premack, D. (1971). Language in chimpanzee. *Science, 172,* 808–822.

Premack, D. (1983). The codes of man and beasts. *Behavioral and Brain Sciences, 6,* 125–167.

Premack, D. (1986). *Gavagai!* Cambridge, MA: MIT Press.

Quinlan, C.K., Taylor, T.L., & Fawcett, J.M. (2010). Directed forgetting: Comparing pictures and words. *Canadian Journal of Experimental Psychology/Revue canadienne de psychologie expérimentale, 64,* 41–46.

Roberts, S. (1981). Isolation of an internal clock. *Journal of Experimental Psychology: Animal Behavior Processes, 7,* 242–268.

Roberts, S. (1982). Cross modal use of an internal clock. *Journal of Experimental Psychology: Animal Behavior Processes, 8,* 2–22.

Savage-Rumbaugh, E.S. (1986). *Ape language: From conditioned response to symbol* (pp. 291–310). New York: Columbia University Press.

Savage-Rumbaugh, E.S., McDonald, K., Sevcik, R.A., Hopkins, W.D., & Rubert, E. (1986). Spontaneous symbol acquisition and communicative use by pygmy chimpanzees (*Pan paniscus*). *Journal of Experimental Psychology: General, 115,* 211–235.

Schusterman, R.J., & Krieger, K. (1984). California sea lions are capable of semantic comprehension. *Psychological Record, 34,* 3–23.

Segerdahl, P., Fields, W., & Savage-Rumbaugh, S. (Eds.). (2005). *Kanzi's primal language: The cultural initiation of primates into language.* New York: Palgrave.

Shepard, R.N. (1967). Recognition memory for words, sentences, and pictures. *Journal of Verbal Learning and Verbal Behavior, 6,* 156–163.

Shields, W.E., Smith, J., Guttmannova, K., & Washburn, D.A. (2005). Confidence judgments by humans and rhesus monkeys. *Journal of General Psychology, 132*, 165–186.

Smith, J.D., Couchman, J.J., & Beran, M.J. (2014). Animal metacognition: A tale of two comparative psychologies. *Journal of Comparative Psychology, 128*, 115–131.

Smith, S.M., & Vela, E. (2001). Environmental context-dependent memory: A review and meta-analysis. *Psychonomic Bulletin & Review, 8*, 203–220.

Stubbs, A. (1968). The discrimination of stimulus duration by pigeons. *Journal of the Experimental Analysis of Behavior, 11*, 223–238.

Suge, R., & Okanoya, K. (2010). Perceptual chunking in the self-produced songs of Bengalese finches (*Lonchura striata var. domestica*). *Animal Cognition, 13*, 515–523.

Terrace, H.S. (1979). *Nim*. New York: Knopf.

Terrace, H.S. (1991). Chunking during serial learning by a pigeon: I. Basic evidence. *Journal of Experimental Psychology: Animal Behavior Processes, 17*, 81–93.

Toth, N., Schich, K.D., Savage-Rumbaugh, E.S., Sevcik, R.A., & Rumbaugh, D.M. (1993). Pan the tool-maker: Investigations into the stone toolmaking and tool-using capabilities of a Bonobo (*Pan paniscus*). *Journal of Archaeological Science, 20*, 81–91.

Tu, H.W., & Hampton, R.R. (2014). Control of working memory in rhesus monkeys (*Macaca mulatta*). *Journal of Experimental Psychology: Animal Learning and Cognition, 40*, 467–476.

Vander Wall, S.B. (1982). An experimental analysis of cache recovery by Clark's nutcracker. Animal Behaviour, 30, 84–94.

Vaughan, W., & Greene, S.L. (1983). Acquisition of absolute discriminations in pigeons. In M.L. Commons, A.R. Wagner, & R.J. Herrnstein (Eds.), *Quantitative analyses of behavior: Vol. 4. Discrimination processes* (pp. 231–238). Cambridge, MA: Ballinger.

Vaughan, W., & Greene, S.L. (1984). Pigeon visual memory capacity. *Journal of Experimental Psychology: Animal Behavior Processes, 10*, 256–271.

von Fersen, L., Wynne, C.D., Delius, J.D., & Staddon, J.E.R. (1991). Transitive inference formation in pigeons. *Journal of Experimental Psychology: Animal Behavior Processes, 17*, 334–341.

Wagner, A.R., Rudy, J.W., & Whitlow, J.W. (1973). Rehearsal in animal conditioning. *Journal of Experimental Psychology, 97*, 407–426.

Weir, A.A.S., Chappell, J., & Kacelnik, A. (2002). Shaping of hooks in New Caledonian crows. *Science, 297*, 981.

West, R.E., & Young, R.J. (2002). Do domestic dogs show any evidence of being able to count? *Animal Cognition, 5*, 183–186.

White, K.G., Parkinson, A.E., Brown, G.S., & Wixted, J.T. (2004). Local proactive interference in delayed matching to sample: The role of reinforcement. *Journal of Experimental Psychology: Animal Behavior Processes, 30*, 83–95.

Wilkie, D.M., & Slobin, P. (1983). Gerbils in space: Performance on the 17-arm radial maze. *Journal of the Experimental Analysis of Behavior, 40*, 301–312.

Williams, H., & Staples, K. (1992). Syllable chunking in zebra finch (*Taeniopygia guttata*) song. *Journal of Comparative Psychology, 106*, 278–286.

Wixted, J. (2004). The psychology and neuroscience of forgetting. *Annual Review of Psychology, 55*, 235–269.

CHAPTER 11

Observational Learning and Motor Skills

Learning Objectives

After reading this chapter, you should be able to

- describe several different theories of imitation and discuss their strengths and weaknesses
- explain Bandura's theory about the four factors necessary for successful imitation
- describe several ways in which modeling has been used in behavior therapy
- discuss the roles of reinforcement, knowledge of results, and knowledge of performance in motor-skill learning
- describe Adams's two-stage theory and Schmidt's schema theory and explain how they differ
- compare the response chain approach and the concept of motor programs, and present evidence for the existence of motor programs

---

Let there be no mistake about it: A large proportion of human learning occurs not through classical conditioning or as a result of reinforcement or punishment but through observation. In their classic book, *Social Learning and Personality Development* (1963), Bandura and Walters argued that traditional learning theory was grossly incomplete because it neglected the role of observational learning. As we have seen, traditional learning theory emphasizes the importance of individual experience: An individual performs some behavior and experiences the consequences that follow. The point of Bandura and Walters was that a good deal of learning occurs through vicarious rather than personal experience: We observe the behavior of others, we observe the consequences, and later we may imitate their behavior. In the first part of this chapter, we will survey different theories about how observational learning takes place, and we will examine the importance of observational learning in everyday life and in behavior therapy.

Another topic that has been largely neglected by traditional learning theorists is motor-skill learning. Many everyday behaviors are examples of learned motor skills—walking, driving, writing, typing, playing a musical instrument, playing sports, etc. The second half of this chapter will examine some of the factors that affect our ability to learn and perform motor skills and some of the most popular theories about how motor skills are learned.

THEORIES OF IMITATION

Imitation as an Instinct

Evidence that imitation may be an innate tendency comes from research on both human infants and animals. Meltzoff and Moore (1977) sought to determine whether 12- to 21-day-old infants would imitate any of four gestures made by an adult tester: lip protrusion, mouth opening, tongue protrusion, and sequential finger movement. Meltzoff and Moore found a reliable tendency for the infants to imitate the specific behavior that they had just seen. Because of the young ages of these infants, it seems very unlikely that such imitative behaviors were the result of prior learning.

Although these results are fascinating, the ability of newborns to imitate may be limited to just a few special behaviors. Other research has found little evidence for a general ability to imitate in young children. Children of ages 1 to 2 years were taught to imitate an adult in performing a specific set of gestures (the "baseline matching relations" in Figure 11.1). Once they learned to imitate these gestures, they were tested to see if they would imitate a new set of gestures (the "target matching relations" in Figure 11.1). The children showed very little tendency to imitate the new gestures (Horne & Erjavec, 2007). The researchers concluded that these young children were not yet capable of imitating arbitrary new behaviors, only those that they had been specifically trained to imitate. These findings suggest that a general ability to imitate new behaviors does not appear until later in childhood.

When it comes to imitation by animals, hundreds of experiments have been conducted with such diverse subjects as primates, cats, dogs, rodents, birds, and fish (Robert, 1990). In some cases, animals may simply copy the behaviors of others that are nearby, as when one deer is startled and starts to run and other deer start running as well. This is imitation in its most primitive sense because nothing new is learned: The animals are simply imitating behaviors they already knew how to perform. A more advanced type of social learning, **true imitation**, occurs when an animal imitates a behavior that it has never performed before and probably would not learn on its own. While observing a troop of monkeys living on an island, Kawai (1965) reported several examples of true imitation—novel behaviors that spread quickly through the troop as a result of observational learning. These included

Figure 11.1 In a test of generalized imitation, 1- to 2-year-old children who were first taught to imitate an adult making the gestures in the top set later showed little imitation of the new gestures in the bottom set. (From Horne, P. J., & M. Erjavec, M., Do infants show generalized imitation of gestures? *Journal of the Experimental Analysis of Behavior, 87,* 63–87. Copyright 2007 by the Society for the Experimental Analysis of Behavior, Inc. Reprinted with permission.)

washing the sand off sweet potatoes and bathing in the ocean (which the monkeys had never done until one pioneer took up this activity). Examples of true imitation have also been seen in gorillas and orangutans. Orangutans in captivity have imitated many complex behaviors of their human caretakers, such as "sweeping and weeding paths, mixing ingredients for pancakes, tying up hammocks and riding in them, and washing dishes or laundry" (Byrne & Russon, 1998, p. 678). Researchers have reported examples of true imitation in rats, quail, and other species.

In summary, the ability to learn through observation can be observed in many species, and this lends credence to the view that the tendency to imitate is instinctive. The problem with this account, however, is that it tells us nothing about when imitation will occur and when it will not. Other theories of imitation have tried to answer this question.

Imitation as an Operant Response

In an influential book, *Social Learning and Imitation*, Miller and Dollard (1941) claimed that observational learning is simply a special case of operant conditioning where the discriminative stimulus is the behavior of another person, and the appropriate response is a similar behavior on the part of the observer. One of their many experiments will illustrate their approach. First-grade children participated in this experiment in pairs, with one child being the "leader" and the other the "learner." On each of several trials, the two children would enter a room in which there were two chairs with a large box on top of each. The leader was instructed in advance to go to one of the two boxes, where there might be a piece of candy. The learner could see where the leader went, but not whether the leader obtained any candy. Next, it was the learner's turn to go to one of the two boxes, where he or she might or might not find a piece of candy. Half of the learners were in an imitation group—they were reinforced for making the same choice as the leader. The other learners were in the nonimitation group—they obtained reinforcement if their choice was opposite that of the leader.

The result of this simple experiment was not surprising: After a few trials, children in the imitation group always copied the response of the leader, and those in the nonimitation group always made the opposite response. Miller and Dollard concluded that, like any other operant response, imitation will occur if imitation is reinforced, and nonimitation will occur if nonimitation is reinforced. In both cases, the behavior of another person is the discriminative stimulus that indicates what response is appropriate. According to Miller and Dollard, then, imitative learning fits nicely into the three-term contingency of discriminative stimulus, response, and reinforcement. There is no need to claim that observational learning is a separate class of learning that is different from operant conditioning.

Imitation as a Generalized Operant Response

As Bandura (1969) pointed out, Miller and Dollard's analysis of imitation applies only to those cases where a learner (1) observes the behavior of a model, (2) immediately copies the response, and (3) receives reinforcement. Many everyday examples of imitation do not follow this pattern. Suppose a little girl watches her mother make herself a bowl of cereal: The mother takes a bowl out of the cabinet, pours in the cereal, and then adds milk and sugar. The next day, alone in the kitchen, the girl may decide to make herself a bowl of cereal, and she may do so successfully. Here we have an example of learning by observation, but if the girl had never done this before, obviously these behaviors could not have been reinforced. This is a case of learning without prior practice of the response and without prior reinforcement.

The principle of reinforcement can account for such novel behavior if we include the concept of generalization, however. If the young girl had been previously reinforced for imitating the behaviors of her parents, her imitation of the behaviors involved in making a bowl of cereal might be simply an example of generalization. This explanation seems plausible because most parents frequently reinforce imitation by their children (Figure 11.2). Imitating a parent's behavior of speaking a word or phrase, of solving a puzzle, of holding a spoon correctly, etc., may be reinforced with smiles, hugs, and praise. It would not be surprising if this history of reinforcement led to imitation in new situations—**generalized imitation**.

Generalized imitation has been demonstrated in a various experiments. For example, children with severe developmental disabilities were reinforced for imitating a variety of behaviors performed by the teacher (standing up, nodding yes, opening a door). After establishing imitative responses (which required several sessions), the teacher occasionally performed various new behaviors, and the children would also imitate these behaviors although they never received

Figure 11.2 Children frequently imitate the behaviors of their parents and are rewarded for doing so. (Brenda Delany/Shutterstock)

reinforcers for doing so (Baer, Peterson, & Sherman, 1967). Many other studies have also found generalized imitative behavior in children (e.g., Camòes-Costa, Erjavec, & Horne, 2011).

Bandura's Theory of Imitation

Bandura maintained that the theory of generalized imitation, like the other theories of imitation, is inadequate. His reasons can be illustrated by considering a famous experiment on the imitation of aggressive behaviors by 4-year-olds (Bandura, 1965). Each child first watched a short film in which an adult performed four distinctive aggressive behaviors against an inflated Bobo doll. Some of the children then saw the adult model being reinforced by another adult: She was given a soft drink, candies, and other snacks and was called a "strong champion." Other children saw the model being punished for his aggressive behavior: The model was scolded for "picking on that clown," was spanked, and was warned not to act that way again. For children in a third group, the film contained no consequences for the model's aggressive behavior.

Immediately after viewing the film, a child was brought into a room that contained a Bobo doll and many other toys. The child was encouraged to play with the toys and was left alone in the room but was observed through a one-way mirror. Many instances of aggressive behaviors against the Bobo doll were recorded, and most of these resembled those of the adult model in the film (Figure 11.3).

Figure 11.3 The top row shows frames from a film in which an adult model exhibits a number of different aggressive behaviors toward a Bobo doll. The two bottom rows show children imitating the model after having watched the film. (From Bandura, et al., Imitation of film-mediated aggressive models, Journal of Abnormal Psychology, 66, 1963, 3–11, © American Psychological Association. Reprinted with permission.)

Bandura claimed that two specific findings from this experiment cannot be explained by the theory of generalized imitation. First, the consequences to the model made a difference: Children who saw the model being punished displayed less imitation than children in the other two groups. Second, in the final phase of the study, the experimenter offered to reward the child if he or she would imitate the behavior of the model in the film. With this incentive, children in all three groups produced large and equal amounts of aggressive behavior. Bandura argued that the theory of generalized imitation cannot explain (1) why consequences *to the model* affect the behaviors of the *learner* or (2) why some children did not imitate until they were offered a reward for doing so. We can evaluate the validity of these two points later, but first let us examine the theory Bandura developed as an alternative.

Bandura's theory of imitation (1969) can definitely be classified as a cognitive theory, for it proposes several processes that cannot be observed in an individual's behavior. It states that four factors determine whether imitative behavior will occur:

1. Attentional Processes

   The learner must pay attention to the appropriate features of the model's behavior if imitation is to occur. A young girl may watch her mother make a bowl of cereal, but if she did not pay attention to where the sugar came from and how much to put in, she may be quite unsuccessful in her attempt at imitation.

2. Retentional Processes

   The learner must retain some of the information that is gained through observation if imitation is to occur at a later time. Bandura states that rehearsal can be important here. Thus the little girl may say to herself, "First the cereal, then the milk, then the sugar." Notice that this information is stated in a fairly abstract way, and Bandura assumes that some abstraction of this type is all that is remembered. Thus the child may not remember exactly where in the refrigerator the milk was or exactly where on the table her mother placed the bowl, but such specific information is not usually necessary for successful imitation.

3. Motor Reproductive Processes

   The learner must have the appropriate motor skills in order to imitate a model. In other words, the learner must be able to translate general knowledge ("Put a bowl on the table"; "Pour in some cereal") into a coordinated pattern of muscle movements. In the examples of children making cereal or hitting a Bobo doll, this translation of knowledge into action poses no problem because the children already possessed the required motor skills (handling objects, pouring, kicking, punching, etc.). In other cases of observational learning, however, motor abilities cannot be taken for granted. For example, a model may demonstrate slowly and in a step-by-step manner the sequence of movements involved in juggling three balls, and the learner may retain this information in an abstract form (i.e., he or she may be able to recite the necessary sequences), but the learner may still be unable to produce the appropriate movements without extensive practice. Similarly, imitating behaviors such as doing a cartwheel, landing an airplane, or smoothly plastering a wall may be impossible because the observer lacks the necessary motor skills.

4. Incentive and Motivational Processes
    According to Bandura, the first three processes are all that are necessary for the learning of a new behavior, but the learner will not actually perform the behavior without an appropriate incentive. The learner must have an expectation that performing the new behavior will produce some type of reinforcement. Bandura's (1965) Bobo doll study is a good example. Children who saw the model being punished for aggressive play with the Bobo doll presumably developed the expectation that such behavior would lead to unpleasant consequences, so they were less likely to imitate the model. However, when the experimenter changed the children's expectations by offering rewards for imitating the model, these children exhibited just as much imitation as the other two groups.

Generalized Imitation Versus Bandura's Theory

Not everyone agrees with Bandura's claims that the theory of generalized imitation is inadequate. Kymissis and Poulson (1990) claimed that the theory can account for all types of imitative behaviors using only well-established principles of operant conditioning. Based on what we know about generalization, it seems reasonable to make the following, specific predictions: Imitation will most likely occur in situations that are similar to those where imitation was reinforced in the past. Conversely, imitation will be least likely occur in situations that are similar to those where imitation was punished in the past.

We can apply these two principles to Bandura's (1965) experiment. Why did children frequently fail to imitate the adult model who was punished? According to the theory of generalized imitation, this is because the children had learned from past experience that it is not a good idea to imitate someone who has just been punished. Why did children in all groups display large amounts of imitation when they were offered rewards for doing so? This result is similar to the latent learning experiments in which rats displayed their ability to run through a maze without errors only after food became available in the goal box (as described in Chapter 8). Behavioral psychologists have long recognized the distinction between learning and performance, and most have concluded that reinforcement is not essential for learning, but it is essential for the performance of learned behaviors.

In summary, both the theory of generalized imitation and Bandura's theory can account for these results, but they do so in slightly different ways. Whereas Bandura's theory uses concepts such as attention, retention, and expectation of reward, the theory of generalized imitation relies on behavioral principles such as stimulus discrimination, generalization, and the learning/performance distinction. As in other debates between the cognitive and behavioral approaches, the debate over explanations of imitative behavior is partly about terminology and partly about how much we should speculate about processes that we cannot observe directly.

Mirror Neurons and Imitation

The discovery of **mirror neurons** in the early 1990s added a new dimension to the discussion about whether observational learning is a unique and special type of learning, different from operant learning. What makes mirror neurons unique is that they fire both when an animal makes a certain movement and when the animal observes someone else make that movement. They were discovered by accident while researchers were recording from individual neurons in a monkey's premotor cortex, an area of the brain involved in hand movement and grasping (Di Pellegrino, Fadiga, Gallese, & Rizzolatti, 1992). They found neurons that would fire when a monkey reached for a piece food but also when the experimenter reached for the food (Figure 11.4). Studies using brain-imaging techniques then identified areas of the human brain that act in a similar way—they become active both when the person makes a movement and when the person observes someone else make the same movement (Rizzolatti, Craighero, & Fadiga, 2002). Later, individual motor neurons were found in human patients during the course of brain surgery (Keysers & Gazzola, 2010).

Brain researchers have speculated that mirror neurons could be involved in a number of important human capabilities. Because they respond both when we act and when we see others act, they may help us to understand the actions, intentions, and feelings of other people. Therefore, they may be important for normal social interactions and communication. Research on people with autism spectrum disorders or with schizophrenia has found evidence that their mirror neurons may not function in the same ways as those of normal individuals (Bernier & Dawson, 2009; Mehta et al., 2014). The evidence is preliminary and incomplete, but if it is corroborated it could help to explain why people with these

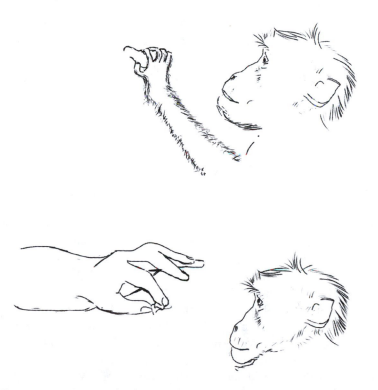

Figure 11.4 Mirror neurons in a monkey's premotor cortex will fire both when it reaches for a peanut and when it watches a person reach for a peanut.

disorders often have difficulties in communication and in understanding the intentions of others.

Not surprisingly, it has also been suggested that mirror neurons are important for observational learning and imitation—they may help to make the connection between seeing someone else perform some action and then being able to perform it ourselves. If so, then the species of animals that are most capable of observational learning should be those that have well-developed mirror neuron systems. It will be interesting to see if future research with other species supports this hypothesis. So far, almost all the research on mirror neurons has been conducted with humans and other primates. However, one study with sparrows found neurons in their brains that responded both when the birds sang a specific song and when they heard it (Prather, Peters, Nowicki, & Mooney, 2008).

EFFECTS OF THE MASS MEDIA

In the modern world, the opportunities for observational learning are not limited to direct personal contact. We are exposed to potential models through TV, radio, movies, the Internet, video games, popular music, and so on. How these cultural influences affect people's behavior is a vast topic. Here, we will take a brief look at just a few effects of the media.

There is substantial evidence that TV viewing can affect the attitudes and behavior of both children and adults. Many studies with children and adolescents have found a positive correlation between the amount of TV they watch and their level of aggressiveness in everyday life (Murray, 2008). However, a problem with correlational evidence is that it is difficult to sort out cause and effect—is TV viewing the cause and aggressive tendencies the effect or vice versa? To address this question, one strategy is to conduct a *longitudinal study* in which the relevant variables are measured at different points in time. For example, Eron, Huesmann, Lefkowitz, and Walder (1972) examined the TV viewing habits and aggressive tendencies of more than 200 third-grade boys; then they reexamined these same boys 10 years later. They found a moderate correlation between preference for violent TV in the third grade and aggressiveness 10 years later. Conversely, they found no correlation between aggressiveness in third grade and preference for violent TV 10 years later. This pattern of results suggests that watching violent TV can lead to later aggressiveness, not the reverse. Other longitudinal studies have corroborated these findings (Anderson & Bushman, 2002). Furthermore, the effects of TV violence are not limited to young children. One longitudinal study found a substantial correlation between the amount of TV exposure at age 22 and assaults and fighting at age 30 (Johnson, Cohen, Smailes, Kasen, & Brook, 2002).

Another research strategy has been to conduct controlled experiments in which participants are randomly assigned to an experimental group that observes aggressive behavior or to a control group that does not. Studies of this type have generally found increases in aggression after children watch violent TV programs (Christensen & Wood, 2007). Some researchers have conducted field experiments in which the TV viewing and the measurement of aggressive behaviors occur in more realistic settings. For example, children have been exposed to either violent or nonviolent TV programs over a period of several weeks, and their aggressiveness has been assessed in normal activities, such as free-play time at school. In general, field experiments have shown a modest effect of TV violence on aggressive behavior (Friedrich-Cofer & Huston, 1986).

Watching TV can, of course, affect children in many other ways as well. Children who sit and watch TV for many hours each day are using up time that might be spent more productively. One extensive correlational study found much lower reading comprehension scores in children who watched more than 4 hours of TV a day (Neuman, 1988). A longitudinal study found that young children who watched more violence on TV were later more likely to show antisocial behaviors, emotional problems, and poor academic performance (Fitzpatrick, Barnett, & Pagani, 2012). However, some types of TV viewing can be beneficial. Educational programs such as *Sesame Street* can give young children valuable information about letters and words, numbers, and social skills. Some longitudinal research has found that children who were regular viewers of *Sesame Street* between the ages of 3 and 5 had higher vocabulary skills 2 years later than those who did not watch this program as often (Fisch & Truglio, 2001). Watching other shows, such as *Arthur* and *Dora the Explorer*, has been correlated with increased vocabulary and language expressive skills in young children (Linebarger & Walker, 2005).

It should come as no surprise that TV can have many different effects on the viewer. As with most examples of modern technology, it is not the device itself but how it is used that determines whether the effects will be desirable or undesirable.

BOX 11.1   IN THE MEDIA

The Effects of Video Games and Popular Music

Many parents are concerned about how their children may be affected by playing video games that include violent actions and by music with violent themes and lyrics. Many popular video games portray graphic acts of violence, such as engaging in hand-to-hand combat or shooting and killing realistic human figures. Of course, children know that what takes place in a video game is not real; still, aggression in game playing might lead to a tendency to be more aggressive in real life. Some studies have found that playing violent video games can increase aggressive behaviors in children, particularly when the games are most realistic (Krcmar, Farrar, & McGloin, 2011). In fact, playing violent video games may have a greater effect on aggressive behavior in children than watching violence on TV because video games involve active participation. One study found that boys who actually played a violent video game were later more aggressive than boys who simply watched another child playing the game (Polman, de Castro, & van Aken, 2008). However, this issue is a complex one, and some researchers have questioned whether the results from correlational and laboratory studies can be related to real-world violence. One recent study found no positive correlation between video game use and the rates of violent crimes in the United States (Markey, Markey, & French, 2014). For now, it is difficult to draw any firm conclusions about the effects of violent video games (Figure 11.5).

Figure 11.5 Playing video games can have both positive and negative effects on children's behavior. (marcogarrincha/Shutterstock)

As with TV viewing, playing video games can also have some positive effects. Regular playing of video games with fast action can lead to improved attention and perceptual skills (Donohue, Woldorff, & Mitroff, 2010). Video games designed for health education and physical education in children have had some success, and those that require physical activity to play the game may help promote physical fitness. With elderly adults, one study found that playing video games that involve physical activity led to less depression (Rosenberg et al., 2010).

There has also been some research on music lyrics and music videos with violent content. Determining the short-term and long-term effects of exposure to such music is a difficult task. However, there is some evidence that listening to music with violent lyrics can increase aggressive thoughts and behaviors in adolescents (Anderson, Carnagey, & Eubanks, 2003; Mast & McAndrew, 2011). Not all studies on this topic have found statistically significant effects, but overall the findings suggest that music with violent and antisocial lyrics can have undesirable effects on the attitudes, emotions, and behaviors of children and teenagers.

MODELING IN BEHAVIOR THERAPY

Bandura and Walters (1963) suggested that a model can influence an observer's behavior in three main ways. First, a model's behavior can facilitate responses the observer already knows how to perform. Second, an observer may learn how to produce totally new behaviors. Third, undesired responses, such as fear reactions to harmless objects or situations (phobias), can be reduced or eliminated.

Facilitation of Low-Probability Behaviors

Modeling has been used in assertiveness training for people who are overly submissive in certain situations and want to develop the ability to stand up for their rights. For example, some wives (or husbands) may do whatever their spouses decide is best, regardless of what they think about a decision. Some young adults may be bullied by their parents into occupations or lifestyles they do not really like. Some people have difficulty refusing unreasonable requests made by friends, employers, coworkers, relatives, or strangers. The goal of assertiveness training is to help people deal with these situations more effectively. Frequently the training consists of a combination of modeling, role playing, and behavior rehearsal, in which the therapist describes a hypothetical situation, models an appropriate response, asks the client to imitate this response, and evaluates the client's performance. A few sessions of such assertiveness training can have long-term benefits (Zhou, Hou, & Bai, 2008).

In another example, O'Connor (1969) used filmed models to increase the sociability of nursery-school children who were socially withdrawn. In a classroom setting, these children would keep to themselves and rarely interact with other children or adults. These children watched a short film that progressed through more involved and energetic social interactions, eventually ending with a scene with six children throwing toys around the room with obvious enjoyment. This method of progressing from simple to more demanding behaviors is called **graduated modeling**, and it is a frequent component in many modeling programs. After the children watched the film, there was a fivefold increase in the number of social interactions.

Acquisition of New Behaviors

A good example of the teaching of new behaviors through modeling is the work of Lovaas and others who have taught children with autism to speak, as described in Chapter 6. This therapy used many behavioral techniques, such as shaping, prompting, fading, and discrimination training, but the teacher's modeling of speech is indispensable at every stage of therapy. The teacher repeatedly models the desired words and the child is rewarded for successful imitation. Modeling (along with other behavioral techniques) has been used to teach children with autism social skills, personal hygiene, and basic reading skills (Marcus & Wilder, 2009).

Modeling has been used for many different purposes, ranging from training computer skills to teaching parents how to handle their children's tantrums and aggressive behaviors. In a technique known as **behavioral skills training**, modeling is used as a part of a larger program that may include verbal instruction, prompting, guided practice, and feedback. Gunby, Carr, and Leblanc (2010) used behavior skills training to teach abduction-prevention skills to three boys with autism. As part of the instruction component, the boys were taught to recite three simple rules about what to do if a stranger asks them to come with him: Say "no," run, tell (i.e., refuse the stranger's request, run to a safe place, and tell a familiar adult what happened). The modeling of these behaviors was done both with a video and with live models. They were later tested in realistic settings to be certain that they had learned the appropriate behaviors. Other applications of behavior skills training have included teaching staff the correct way to give physical assistance to children with physical disabilities (Nabeyama & Sturmey, 2010) and teaching children to avoid playing with firearms (Jostad, Miltenberger, Kelso, & Knudson, 2008).

Elimination of Fears and Unwanted Behaviors

Bandura and his colleagues conducted some of the earliest experiments on modeling as a treatment for phobias. Bandura, Grusec, and Menlove (1967) attempted to reduce excessive fears of dogs in young children. The children were divided into four groups. The first group received graduated modeling in which they observed another child engage in more and more demanding interactions with a friendly dog. The modeling sequences took place in a party context to reduce anxiety. A second group of children observed the same modeling sequences without the party context. A third group experienced the party context with the dog present but with no model (to control for exposure to the dog). A fourth group experienced the party context but without the dog and the model. All children then received two tests in which they were asked to imitate the model, one immediately and a second a month later. Figure 11.6 shows the results. Both groups with the model later showed less fear of a dog than the two groups without a model, and these improvements remained essentially unchanged a month later. Modeling has been successfully used to treat other phobias, such as fears of spiders, birds, needles, or dentists, and in some instances a single treatment session is all that is needed to produce long-lasting benefits (Davis, Ollendick, & Öst, 2009).

Modeling can also be used to reduce other unwanted behaviors. Middleton and Cartledge (1995) used modeling in combination with other behavioral techniques, including reinforcement of incompatible behaviors, to reduce aggressive behaviors in young boys. Meichenbaum and Goodman (1971) used modeling to improve the academic performance of first-grade children with hyperactivity by having models demonstrate how to use self-instructions to avoid reckless and error-prone behaviors. Other studies have found that modeling and self-instruction, often used in combination with other techniques, can be effective in reducing hyperactivity, aggression, and generalized anxiety in children (Gosch, Flannery-Schroeder, Mauro, & Compton, 2006).

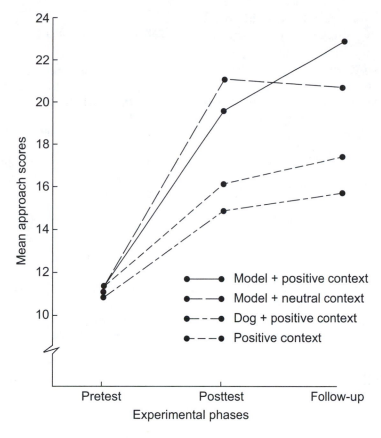

Figure 11.6 Results from the four groups in the Bandura et al. (1967) study on the use of modeling in the treatment of children's fear of dogs. Children who observed a model were more likely to approach and interact with a dog. (From Bandura, A., Grusec, J.E., Menlove, F.L., 1967, Vicarious extinction of avoidance behavior, *Journal of Personality and Social Psychology, 5,* 16–23. © American Psychological Association. Reprinted with permission.)

Video Self-Modeling

The goal of **video self–modeling** is to increase desired behaviors by having people watch themselves correctly perform these behaviors in a video. Dowrick and Raeburn (1995) used this technique with children with severe physical disabilities, such as cerebral palsy or muscular dystrophy. First, each child was asked to perform some practical skill that needed improvement, such as maintaining a good posture, walking, balancing, writing, or dressing. This behavior was video-recorded, and a therapist would give the child instructions, encouragement, and, when necessary, assistance in completing the task. Next, each child's video was edited to remove all examples of errors and inappropriate behaviors, as well as all segments in which the therapist gave the child assistance. What remained, therefore, was a video in which the child was seen performing the behavior correctly, with no help from anyone else. This is important, because the goal is to teach only correct, unassisted behaviors. After the editing, the children watched themselves on the videos, which were shown to them six times over a 2-week period. The researchers found substantial improvement in most of the children on the self-modeled tasks.

Video self-modeling has been used to teach better social and communication skills to children with autism spectrum disorders (Shukla-Mehta, Miller, & Callahan, 2010), to decrease stuttering in adults (Cream, O'Brian, Onslow, Packman, & Menzies, 2009), and to teach simple cooking skills to people with traumatic brain injuries (McGraw-Hunter, Faw, & Davis, 2006). It is becoming an increasing common technique for teaching a variety of skills to both children and adults.

LEARNING MOTOR SKILLS

Motor skills are an essential ingredient for all types of learned behaviors, but people often take for granted their abilities to perform complex movements. The bicyclist seldom marvels at her ability to remain upright on two thin wheels. When typing on a keyboard, we seldom wonder about

---

PRACTICE QUIZ 1: CHAPTER 11

1. According to the theory of _____ imitation, learners will imitate a behavior if they have been reinforced for imitation in similar situations in the past.
2. Besides attentional and retentional processes, Bandura's theory states that _____ processes and _____ processes are necessary for successful imitation.
3. Studies have shown that there is a positive correlation between how much violence children watch and their levels of _____ behavior.
4. Modeling has been used in _____, in which shy or passive individuals learn to avoid letting others take advantage of them by making unreasonable demands or requests.
5. In _____ modeling, the model demonstrates progressively more demanding behaviors as the treatment proceeds.

ANSWERS

1. generalized 2. motor reproductive, incentive and motivational 3. aggressive 4. assertiveness training 5. graduated

---

how we can coordinate 10 fingers to produce several keystrokes a second. Likewise, in previous chapters we have generally taken for granted a learner's ability to make the required response. Now we will examine this ability in some detail. We will start with some variables that can affect how quickly a motor skill is learned and how adroitly it is performed.

Variables Affecting Motor Learning and Performance

Reinforcement and Knowledge of Results

E. L. Thorndike (1927), who is best known for his experiments with the puzzle box (Chapter 5), also conducted some of the earliest research on human motor learning. In one experiment, participants were blindfolded and their goal was to draw a line exactly 3 inches long. One group received reinforcement for each line whose length was within 1/8 inch of 3 inches, plus or minus: Immediately after a participant drew such a line, the experimenter said, "Right," and Thorndike thought of this as reinforcement for making a correct response.

If the line did not meet this criterion, the experimenter said, "Wrong." Participants in the second group received no consequences for accurate or inaccurate lines. They had no way of knowing which lines were close to 3 inches and which were not. These participants showed no improvement over trials. However, participants in the reinforcement group showed a substantial increase in accuracy over trials. Thorndike's conclusion was that the Law of Effect is just as important in human motor learning as it was for his animals in the puzzle box. In both cases, reinforcement "stamps in" or strengthens the correct response, so this response is more likely to be repeated in the future.

Trowbridge and Cason (1932) challenged Thorndike's conclusion that reinforcement is the crucial variable in the acquisition of a motor skill. They argued that, although saying "Right" after a response could sometimes be a reinforcer, in Thorndike's experiment it was important because it gave the participant information or feedback about the accuracy of each response. In the literature on motor-skill learning, this type of feedback is usually called **knowledge of results (KR)**. In short, Trowbridge and Cason proposed that the information provided by the words "Right" and "Wrong" produced the improved accuracy, not the reinforcing and punishing aspects of the words. To test their hypothesis, they repeated Thorndike's experiment, but they used four groups. Two of their groups were the same as Thorndike's: The group that received practice only was called the *No KR Group*, and the group that was told "Right" or "Wrong" was called the *Qualitative KR Group* (because participants received no quantitative feedback on the size of their errors). In addition, Trowbridge and Cason included a *Quantitative KR Group* in which participants were told the direction and magnitude of each error to the nearest eighth of an inch. For instance, if a line was 7/8 inch longer than 3 inches, the experimenter would say, "Plus seven." If a line was 5/8 inch shorter than 3 inches, the experimenter would say, "Minus five." Trowbridge and Cason reasoned that the Quantitative KR Group received more information than the Qualitative KR Group but not more reinforcement. Finally, a fourth group, the *Irrelevant KR Group*, received useless "feedback" after each trial—a meaningless nonsense syllable.

Each group received 100 trials, and the results from the last 10 trials are shown in Figure 11.7. The errors in both the No KR and Irrelevant KR groups were large, and there was no improvement over trials. In the Qualitative KR Group, there was clear improvement over trials, and at the end of the experiment the size of the average error was about four-eighths of an inch. Figure 11.7 shows, however, that the performance of the Quantitative KR Group was vastly superior to that of the Qualitative KR Group. From this pattern of results, we can conclude that information, not reinforcement, was the crucial factor, and that the more precise, quantitative KR produced much better performance than the less precise, qualitative KR.

Knowledge of Performance

Often it is possible to give a participant many types of feedback besides how close the movement came to some goal. Consider, for example, the many useful pieces of information a coach might be able to give a pole-vaulter after each vault in practice. The coach might discuss various details related to the athlete's takeoff, approach, pole placement, ascent, limb positions, and so on, and each piece of information might help to improve the athlete's future performance. The delivery of such information about the components of a complex

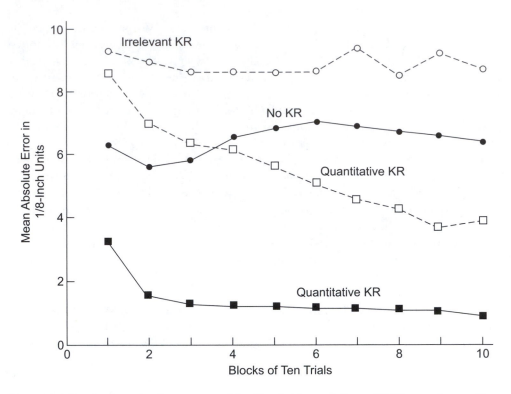

Figure 11.7 Results from the four groups of the Trowbridge and Cason (1932) experiment. (From Trowbridge, M.H., & Cason, H., 1932, An experimental study of Thorndike's theory of learning, *Journal of General Psychology, 7,* 245–260. Reproduced by permission of Taylor & Francis Ltd, www. taylorandfrancis.com.)

movement is called **knowledge of performance (KP)**. Many variations of KP can be used in the training of athletes. For instance, a discus thrower might be videotaped as he practices; later, his performance can be reviewed and compared to the motions of a computer-generated figure that demonstrates the movements that would maximize the distance the discus is thrown.

To study the effects of different types of KP, Kernodle and Carlton (1992) had participants in four groups learn to throw a ball with their nondominant hands (i.e., with the left hand for those who were naturally right-handed, and vice versa). The goal was to throw the ball in a straight line as far as possible. One group received normal KR: They were told the exact distance of each throw. A second group received KP: After each throw, they watched a video replay of their throwing motion on that trial. A third group also watched a video replay, but in addition they were told to focus their attention on a particular part of the throwing motion while watching the replay. During the training, they were told to focus on 10 different components of a good throw, such as "Focus on the hips during the throwing phase." A fourth group also received KP, but while watching the replay they were instructed on what to do to improve their motion on the next trial, such as "Stride forward with the right foot toward the target area." All four groups were given 12 training sessions over a 4-week

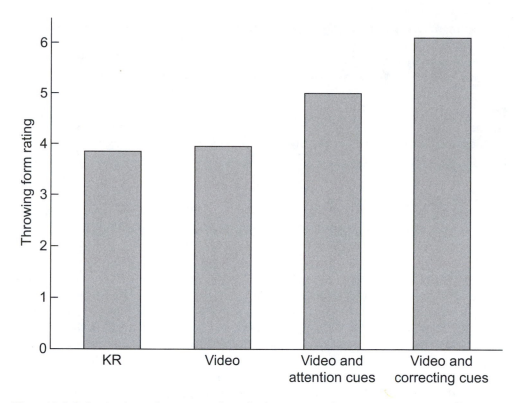

Figure 11.8 Judges' ratings of movement form for four groups of participants who received four different types of feedback when learning to throw a ball with their nondominant hands. (Based on Kernodle & Carlton, 1992)

period. This fourth group, which received KP plus instructions on how to improve, showed the greatest improvement, both in the length of their throws and in judges' ratings of their throwing form (Figure 11.8).

KP is not just helpful for athletes. Cirstea and Levin (2007) worked with patients to help them recover arm movements they had lost due to strokes. The patients tried to point their arms toward a target, and they were given KP consisting of information about the movements of the joints in their arms. After 10 sessions of therapy, the KP group achieved significant improvements in arm movements and coordination, whereas a group that received only KR showed no overall improvement.

Distribution of Practice

As a general rule, laboratory studies suggest that performance is better if rest periods are interspersed among fairly brief practice periods than if practice occurs in one continuous block. In short, **distributed practice** often seems to yield better results than **massed practice**. One explanation of this effect is that during continuous practice, a type of fatigue builds up that interferes with performance; this fatigue dissipates during rest periods, so overall performance is better if frequent rest periods are allowed. Indeed, in learning motor skills there is often an improvement in performance immediately after a rest period.

In some experiments, the advantages of distributed practice were only temporary: Participants who received massed practice did substantially worse during that practice, but after a rest period they performed about as well as those who had received distributed practice (Rider & Abdulahad, 1991). However, other studies have found long-term benefits to distributed practice (Dail & Christina, 2004). Overall, it seems that there may be some advantages to distributed practice in the learning of motor skills, but the effects are not always large or permanent.

Observational Learning of Motor Skills

Not surprisingly, simply observing someone else perform a motor skill is not as effective as practicing it yourself. Nevertheless, observational learning can be beneficial, especially when combined with direct practice. In one experiment, people could make the cursor on a computer screen move either left or right by pressing two different keys; their goal was to keep the cursor on a moving dot on the screen. A group of participants who practiced this task themselves performed better on the test day than participants who watched another person learning the task. However, those who only observed the task performed much better than control participants who neither practiced nor observed the task until the test day. Furthermore, participants who first observed the task and then practiced it themselves performed better than all the other groups on a transfer test where the movement of the dot was different than it was in training (Shea, Wright, Wulf, & Whitacre, 2000). In short, both individual practice and observation contributed to the participants' acquisition of this new skill.

Video self-modeling can also be an effective way to learn motor skills. In one example, adults learning to swim received feedback by watching videos of their swimming strokes, and these adults showed more improvement than those who watched videos of someone else swimming (Starek & McCullagh, 1999). In another study, children with coordination problems used video self-modeling to help them improve such skills as throwing or catching a ball, batting a ball, and jumping toward a target (Wilson, Thomas, & Maruff, 2002).

Transfer From Previous Training

In motor-skill research, transfer of training is similar to generalization in operant conditioning, except that there can be either positive or negative transfer from one skill to another. In **positive transfer**, practice on one task leads to faster learning on a similar task. Quite a few studies have found evidence for positive transfer. Latash (1999) had college students practice mirror writing, in which they had to write a sentence while looking in a mirror so that the words read correctly as seen in the mirror. After practicing this task for several days with their normal writing hands, the students showed large transfer effects when they had to switch to their other hands. Palmer and Meyer (2000) found positive transfer when experienced pianists first learned a new piece of music and then were asked to play a variation of the melody that required them to use different hand and finger movements. These researchers concluded that motor learning is not simply a matter of learning specific muscle movements because experienced learners can transfer their skills to new situations that require them to produce the same general patterns of movements using different muscle groups.

Negative transfer occurs when practicing one skill interferes with the learning of another skill. Somewhat surprisingly, there are not many reports of negative transfer in motor-skill tasks. When it is found, negative transfer is often very fleeting, sometimes lasting only a trial or two. However, one study that found strong negative transfer used a task that required moving both hands, but at different rates. For instance, in the initial task, a participant might learn to perform repetitive movements with both hands, but to make two movements of the left hand for every one movement of the right hand. The researchers found strong evidence for negative transfer when participants were required to switch hands—now making two right-hand cycles for every one left-hand movement (Vangheluwe, Suy, Wenderoth, & Swinnen, 2006).

It is often difficult to predict whether positive or negative transfer will occur, and sometimes there can be a mixture of both. In one study, participants in an experimental group practiced the skills of short tennis and lawn tennis for a few hours each, and a control group practiced lawn tennis only. Then both groups were tested in lawn tennis skills. The researchers found that the experimental participants were better at certain lawn tennis skills and the control participants were better at others, thereby providing evidence for both positive and negative transfer in the same experiment (Coldwells & Hare, 1994).

THEORIES OF MOTOR-SKILL LEARNING

So far we have considered some factors that determine how quickly and how well a new skill will be learned, but we have not discussed hypotheses about what takes place inside the individual during such learning episodes. We will now turn to some well-known theories that deal with this question.

Adams's Two-Stage Theory

Jack A. Adams (1971) developed one of the most influential theories of motor learning. According to **Adams's two-stage theory**, there are two phases in the learning of a typical motor skill. The first stage is called the *verbal-motor stage* because in this stage improvement depends on the delivery of feedback, usually in a verbal form. The verbal-motor stage is the time when improvement depends on constant feedback from the piano teacher, the pitching coach, or the gymnastics instructor. Without this feedback, the learner cannot tell whether the movement was good or what was wrong with it. Much of the learning in the verbal-motor stage involves the development of a *perceptual trace*—an internal sensation that allows the learner to discriminate a good movement from a bad one. For example, in Thorndike's line-drawing task, the blindfolded participant knows that the task is to draw a 3-inch line but initially does not know what it "feels like" to draw a line of this length. During the verbal-motor stage, the learner gradually develops a perceptual trace, so he or she can discriminate a good movement from a bad one based on the way it feels.

In the second stage of Adams's theory, called the *motor stage*, feedback from the piano teacher, the pitching coach, or the gymnastics instructor becomes less important. The learner can now improve through practice on his or her own by relying on internal feedback (the perceptual trace) in place of the coach's feedback. In this stage, the learner must continue to practice to develop the coordination of muscles that is needed to produce the desired movements reliably. For example, a beginning pianist may listen to a recording of a difficult piece again and again until she has a firm idea of what an excellent rendition sounds like. Having reached this point, however, it may take long hours of painstaking practice before she can even approximate a good rendition on her own. Similarly, an athlete may have a good perceptual trace for what it feels like to throw a good curve ball or to make a good golf swing, but it may require enormous amounts of practice before he can produce those movements consistently.

Many experiments have found support for different predictions of Adams's theory. For example, if KR is only delivered on occasional trials when a person is in the first stage of motor learning, the perceptual trace should be strengthened on trials when KR is delivered but then decay on trials without KR. Sparrow and Summers (1992) examined performance on a simple positioning task in which participants either received KR after every 5th trial or after every 10th trial. Figure 11.9 shows the type of patterns that Adams's theory predicts

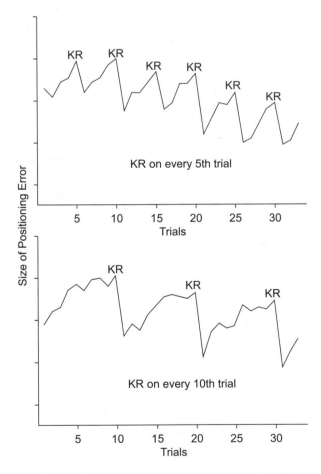

Figure 11.9 These graphs illustrate the variations in accuracy that are predicted by Adams's theory if KR is delivered on every 5th trial (top panel) or every 10th trial (bottom panel). Performance should improve on the trials immediately after KR is provided and then deteriorate on the trials when no KR is provided.

for this situation: Right after each trial with KR, there should be an improvement in accuracy (smaller error), and then performance should gradually get worse on successive trials without KR. After another trial with KR, errors should decrease again, and so on, resulting in the up-and-down pattern illustrated in Figure 11.9. In their experiment, Sparrow and Summers did find this type of improvement on the trials after KR was delivered, just as predicted by Adams's theory.

There is also good evidence that KR can become unnecessary later in training. The best evidence comes from studies in which KR is withdrawn at some point in the middle of the experiment. For example, Bilodeau, Bilodeau, and Schumsky (1959) had participants practice a discrete movement—moving a lever through an angle of 33 degrees—for 20 trials. One group received quantitative KR on all trials, one group received no KR, and two groups received quantitative KR for two or six trials before it was withdrawn. Figure 11.10 shows that in the group with constant KR, errors steadily decreased to a low level. Not surprisingly, the group with no KR did not improve at all. The results from the groups with two or six trials with KR are more interesting, because they appeared to derive some permanent benefits from the initial KR. There was some deterioration in performance when the KR was removed, but these groups continued to

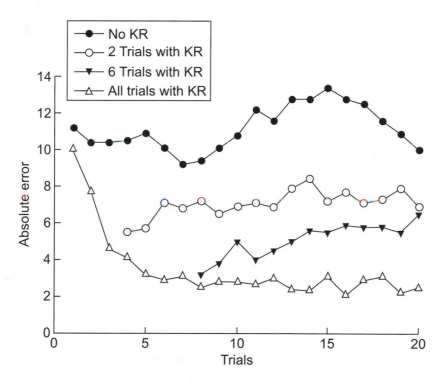

Figure 11.10 Results from the experiment of Bilodeau et al., where each group received a different number of trials with KR. (From Bilodeau, E.R., Bilodeau, I.M., & Schmusky, D.A., 1959, Some effects of introducing and withdrawing knowledge of results early and late in practice, *Journal of Experimental Psychology, 58,* 142–144. © American Psychological Association. Adapted with permission.)

perform better than the group that never received KR. According to Adams's theory, these groups were beginning to develop a perceptual trace. A similar experiment by Newell (1974) found that if participants receive more trials with KR, their performance may not deteriorate at all when KR is then removed (presumably because they had reached the second stage of Adams's theory).

Adams's theory has also been supported by other research (Badets & Blandin, 2010; Russell & Newell, 2007). Perhaps its most important contribution is that it distinguishes between the two types of learning that take place during the acquisition of most motor skills: learning to recognize what it feels like to make an accurate response and learning to produce such a response consistently.

Schmidt's Schema Theory

Adams's theory focuses on the acquisition of single, repetitive movements (such as shooting a foul shot in basketball, where the stimulus conditions and the required movement are exactly the same, trial after trial). The theory says nothing about how people can learn skills that require different responses on every trial to deal with different stimulus conditions. Think of a tennis player's response to an approaching ball, a hiker's response to the irregular terrain of a rocky hillside, or a driver's response to an unfamiliar winding road. In all of these cases and many others, the individual is confronted with new and different stimulus conditions and must generate a response to suit these conditions. To deal with these more flexible motor skills, Richard Schmidt (1975) developed his schema theory of motor-skill learning.

Stated simply, **Schmidt's schema theory** maintains that people can acquire general rules (schemas) as they practice. As a concrete example, we can consider how a golfer learns to putt a ball the appropriate distance. The golfer must learn to stroke the ball with different amounts of effort, depending on how far the ball is from the hole. During practice, the golfer may use different amounts of effort on different trials and observe the result (the distance the ball travels). This situation is illustrated in Figure 11.11a, where each point represents a

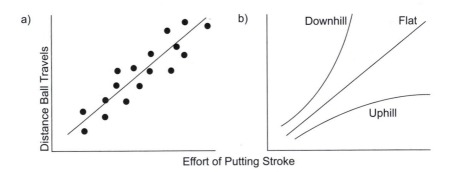

Figure 11.11 (a) A hypothetical illustration of how, according to Schmidt's schema theory, a person might learn a general rule or schema about the relationship between the effort of a putting stroke and the distance the golf ball moves. Each data point represents one practice trial, and the line represents the general rule the learner supposedly retains from these trials. (b) A successful golfer's schema for putting would have to include many different rules for downhill, flat, and uphill putts of different slopes.

single practice trial (the effort exerted by the golfer and the distance the ball travels). According to Schmidt, these individual data points are soon forgotten, but what the golfer develops and retains is a general rule, or *motor schema*, about the relationship between effort and the distance the ball moves (represented by the solid line in Figure 11.11a). Furthermore, motor schemas may consist of more than a single function because other factors, such as the slope of the green, can affect the results. Figure 11.11b shows a simplified illustration of the more complex motor schema a golfer might develop by practicing level, uphill, and downhill putts. The advantage of such a schema is that the individual can respond to new situations with a decent chance of success. A golfer may never have practiced a 22-foot putt on a moderately slow green with a downhill slope of 4 degrees, but the motor schema allows the golfer to generalize from similar past experiences and produce a reasonably suitable response.

The ability to deal with open-ended classes of movements, such as putting golf balls or shooting baskets from different parts of the court, makes Schmidt's theory more versatile than Adams's. But what scientific evidence is there that people do in fact learn such motor schemas? To test the theory, several different research strategies have been used. Some studies have tested whether people soon forget the specific examples that they practice but nevertheless retain a general schema (as illustrated in Figure 11.11). Chamberlin and Magill (1992) taught participants a timing task that involved pressing a sequence of three buttons that were 15 cm, 45 cm, or 135 cm apart. The participants were then tested 1 day later and again 1 week later on both these well-practiced distances and on new distances that they had never tried before (e.g., 30 cm and 90 cm). Chamberlin and Magill found that their participants were just as accurate with the new distances as with the well-practiced distances. This finding is consistent with the prediction of schema theory that people can learn a general rule for movement and not just individual movement patterns.

An important prediction of Schmidt's theory (but not Adams's theory) is that variability in one's practice routine is beneficial because it contributes to the development of the learner's perceptual and motor schemas. Several experiments have provided support for this prediction that variable practice is beneficial. For example, Kerr and Booth (1978) had children toss beanbags at a target without visual feedback, and they were given quantitative KR by the experimenter. One group of children received *specific training* in which they always aimed for a target that was 3 feet away. A second group received *variable training* in which the target was sometimes 2 feet away and sometimes 4 feet away. Both groups later received test trials with the 3-foot target distance, and the group that had received variable training performed more accurately, even though they had never practiced with the 3-foot distance. Kerr and Booth suggested that the variable training helped the children develop stronger schemas than did the specific training.

To summarize, Schmidt's schema theory provides a framework for understanding how people develop flexible motor skills that allow them to make successful responses when confronted with situations they have never experienced before. One of the theory's strengths is its prediction that variable practice can be more effective than constant practice, an idea that has received substantial empirical support. However, some research findings have posed problems for schema theory, and other theories of motor learning have been proposed to try to deal with these findings (Sanli & Lee, 2014; Sherwood & Fosler, 2013). Perhaps the fairest way to summarize Schmidt's theory is to say that it represents an important advance, but as the science of motor-skill learning advances, new and more refined theories will almost surely be developed.

BOX 11.2   APPLYING THE RESEARCH

What Is the Best Way to Practice?

A good general rule for learning motor skills is that more difficult practice sessions often produce better long-term performance. The advantage of variable training over specific training is one example of this principle. Discussing this principle in a more general way, Battig (1979) used the term **contextual interference** to refer to any features of the learning situation (the "context") that make performing the task more difficult (i.e., they "interfere" with the learner's performance during the acquisition of a new skill). Battig's theory was that high contextual interference during acquisition ultimately leads to better long-term performance. Some experiments have tested this idea by comparing blocked practice and random practice. In blocked practice, the learner practices the same variation of a skill for a block of trials then switches to a different variation for another block of trials, and so on. For example, a basketball player might practice 10 shots from a specific spot on the left side of the basket, then 10 shots from one spot in front of the basket, and then 10 shots from one spot on the right side of the basket. In random practice, the task requirements are changed every trial (e.g., the basketball player would randomly switch among the left, front, and right positions after every shot). According to Battig, contextual interference should be higher during random practice because the movements needed for a successful performance are constantly changing on each practice trial.

Some studies have found the predicted advantage for random practice over blocked practice. Shea and Morgan (1979) taught people to make three different patterns of rapid arm movements in response to three different signals, and their speed in completing the movements was measured. They found that performance during the acquisition phase was worse with random practice, which makes sense according to the theory because the task demands were more difficult when every trial was different from the last. However, the participants who had random practice performed better than those who had blocked practice when tested 10 minutes later and 10 days later. Similarly, Vera and Montilla (2003) found an advantage for random practice for 6-year-olds learning a throwing task during their physical education class.

Although variable practice is often better than specific practice and random practice is often better than blocked practice, there are exceptions to these rules. For example, on a task that required accuracy in both the amount of force used and in movement duration, Whitacre and Shea (2000) found that randomly varying the force requirements from trial to trial had a detrimental effect on the participants' timing. It could be that when a task places many demands on the learner, random variations along one dimension may make learning the task overwhelming. Exactly why random practice has an advantage in some situations but not others is not well understood.

LEARNING MOVEMENT SEQUENCES

In this section we will consider motor skills involving sequences of movements that must be performed in a specific order. Some skills of this type are walking, swimming, typing, or playing a musical instrument. Successful performance depends on producing the sequence of movements in the correct order and with the correct timing. For instance, in performing the breaststroke, a swimmer must coordinate the movements of the arms and legs to move through the water efficiently. A pianist must play the notes in the correct sequence and with the correct tempo. The challenge for motor-skill researchers is to explain why people become more skillful in performing such sequences of movement with practice.

The Response Chain Approach

One approach to the topic of movement sequences is based on the concept of a response chain, which was discussed in Chapter 5. A response chain was defined as a sequence of behaviors that must occur in a specific order, with a primary reinforcer following the completion of the last behavior of the chain. According to the standard analysis, what keeps the behaviors of the chain in their correct sequence is that each response produces a distinctive stimulus that acts as a discriminative stimulus for the next response of the chain. It is easy to see how this analysis could be applied to some skilled movement sequences, such as walking. Seeing or feeling one's right leg in front might serve as a discriminative stimulus to shift one's weight to this leg and bring the left leg forward. The opposite would be true when one's left leg is in front. The main idea is that the visual, tactile, or kinesthetic feedback from one movement serves as a discriminative stimulus for the next movement in the sequence.

   Why, according to this analysis, does a person's ability to perform a sequence of movements improve with practice? The answer is that the appropriate stimulus–response associations are strengthened by reinforcement. For instance, to achieve the maximum propulsion in the breaststroke, a swimmer must begin to move his or her hands forward at a particular point during each stroke. If we assume that swimming speed is the reinforcer, then through the process of successive approximations, the swimmer should eventually learn exactly what cues signal that the forward movement of the hands should begin.

   The response chain analysis of movement sequences is compatible with theories such as those of Adams and Schmidt, which emphasize the role of feedback in the control of movement. Yet although the response chain approach provides a satisfactory analysis for many response sequences, several types of evidence now suggest that it cannot account for all examples of movement sequences.

Motor Programs

Those who favor the concept of **motor programs** suggest that the response chain approach is incorrect (or at least incomplete) because some movement sequences do not depend on continual sensory feedback for their proper execution. Keele (1973) described the concept of a motor program as follows:

> If neither visual nor kinesthetic feedback is needed for the execution of patterns of movement, then the movement patterns must be represented centrally in the brain, or perhaps in some cases in the spinal cord. Such representation is called a motor program. As a motor program is executed, neural impulses are sent to the appropriate muscles in proper sequence, timing, and force, as predetermined by the program, and the neural impulses are largely uninfluenced by the resultant feedback.
>
> (p. 124)

To clarify the difference between a response chain and a motor program, we can take a concrete example of a movement sequence—the typing of the word *the*. A response chain analysis might proceed as follows: To start typing the word *the*, a typist responds by striking the *t* key with the left forefinger. This movement produces sensory feedback (kinesthetic feedback from the finger and perhaps auditory feedback from the keyboard) that serves as a discriminative stimulus to make the next response—striking the *h* key with the right forefinger. Sensory feedback from this response serves as a stimulus for the final response of striking the *e* key with the left middle finger.

Although this response chain analysis could be correct for a beginning typist, a skilled typist may have a motor program for producing this response sequence. The idea is that when a skilled typist needs to type the word *the*, this motor program is activated and sends a series of commands to the muscles of the left forefinger, the right forefinger, and the left middle finger. These commands are timed so that the three movements are performed in the correct sequence, but this timing does not depend on sensory feedback from each successive movement in the sequence. One obvious advantage of the motor program is an increase in speed: The typist can begin to produce the second keystroke before receiving sensory feedback from the first keystroke.

An early advocate of motor programs was Karl Lashley (1951), who presented several types of evidence that a response chain analysis cannot explain all movement sequences. For one thing, Lashley argued that human reaction times are too slow to support the idea that sensory feedback from one response can serve as the stimulus for the next response in a rapid sequence. Lashley noted that musicians can produce as many as 16 finger movements per second. His point is that this rate could never be achieved if the musician had to wait for sensory feedback from one movement before beginning the next. Similar arguments have been made for the skill of typing (Shaffer, 1978).

A second argument made by Lashley was that skilled movements and sequences of movements are still possible for individuals who have lost sensory feedback. He reported the case of a man who had lost all sensation in the area of the knee as a result of a gunshot wound. Despite the loss of sensation, the man could move and position his leg as accurately as an uninjured person. Other evidence that complex movements can continue in the absence of sensory feedback comes from animal studies in which sensory nerve fibers are severed before they enter the spinal cord. Taub and Berman (1968) surgically removed all sensory feedback from both forelimbs of several monkeys. After this surgery, the monkeys were still able to use these limbs to walk and climb (even when blindfolded, which removed the possible influence of visual feedback). The monkeys could coordinate the movements of their senseless forelimbs with their normal hindlimbs. This is evidence that sensory feedback is not always necessary for skilled movements.

Lashley's third argument for motor programs concerns the types of errors frequently found in rapid movement sequences. He noted that many typing mistakes are errors of anticipation or transposition. For instance, I sometimes type *hte* when I intend to type *the*. It is difficult to explain this sort of error with a response chain analysis. If the stimulus for striking the *h* key was the sensory feedback from the movement of striking the *t* key, the second movement should never precede the first. Instead, Lashley maintained that the separate movements were sequenced by a motor program but that the synchronization of the movements became distorted somewhere along the line from command to execution. In short, Lashley suggested that any errors that indicate the individual was planning ahead support the notion of a motor program but are inconsistent with the response chain approach.

A fourth type of evidence, not known to Lashley, is that the amount of time needed to begin a sequence of movements depends on the number of separate movements that are part of the sequence. For instance, a person needs more time to begin a sequence that involves four discrete motions than one that involves only two motions (Ulrich, Giray, & Schaffer, 1990). The explanation usually offered for this effect is that the person is constructing a motor program for all of the motions at the beginning, and it takes more time to preprogram four movements than two movements. If the individual was only planning the first movement before beginning, why would it take longer to plan this single movement in one case than in the other? Starting times are slower for longer movement sequences even when such sequences have been practiced extensively.

An experiment on handwriting found evidence of this last type (Portier, Van Galen, & Meulenbroek, 1990). Participants were taught to write six different patterns, each composed of three letter-like characters. Specialized recording equipment could detect the exact location of the pen at each instant. With practice, writing speed increased substantially for the second and third characters of each pattern, but writing speed for the first character did not increase very much. Why should it take participants so long to write the first character, which had a relatively simple shape? The experimenters concluded that this was because participants were not simply learning to write the three individual characters; they were developing motor programs for each pattern as a whole. The first character

---

PRACTICE QUIZ 2: CHAPTER 11

1. _____ is telling a person that a movement was right or wrong, and _____ is telling a person how far off target the movement was.
2. Giving a person tips on specific parts of a movement that need improvement is called _____.
3. According to Adams's theory, in the _____ stage, a person needs external feedback in order to improve a motor skill, but not in the _____ stage.
4. In Schmidt's theory, when a person learns how different movements produce different results, this is called a _____.
5. In a _____, feedback from each movement is not necessary for a person to produce a coordinated sequence of movements.

ANSWERS

1. qualitative KR, quantitative KR 2. knowledge of performance (KP) 3. verbal-motor, motor 4. motor schema 5. motor program

presumably took longer to write because participants were simultaneously planning the rest of the pattern.

SUMMARY

One theory of imitation states that it is an instinctive tendency, and there is evidence that animals and even newborn infants can learn by imitation. A second theory states that people imitate when they are reinforced for imitation. A third theory states that imitation is a generalized operant response: People imitate in situations that are similar to those where imitation has been reinforced in the past. Bandura's theory states that four factors determine whether imitative behavior will occur: attentional processes, retentional processes, motor abilities, and incentive and motivational processes. The idea that observational learning is a unique type of learning has been bolstered by the discovery of mirror neurons, which fire both when an individual makes a response and when the individual sees someone else make that response.

In modern society, observational learning can occur in many ways other than through direct personal contact, including through TV, video games, popular music, and the Internet. Research suggests that these media can have both positive and negative effects on children. Many different variations on modeling techniques have been used successfully in behavior therapy, including graduated modeling and video self-modeling. Through modeling, shy children can learn better social skills, adults can learn to be more assertive, children with autism can be taught to speak, and phobias can be eliminated.

Thorndike believed that reinforcement was an important variable in motor-skill learning, but later research showed that knowledge of results (KR) is really the critical variable. Giving participants more detailed information about specific parts of their performance (KP) can produce even better learning than simple KR. People learn motor skills more quickly with distributed practice than with massed practice, but the difference is not always large. Studies in which people are trained on one motor task and then tested on a different task have found evidence for both positive and negative transfer.

Adams's two-stage theory states that motor-skill learning first involves a verbal-motor stage in which feedback from a teacher or coach is essential and later a motor stage in which the learner can continue to improve without external feedback. Studies in which KR is either delivered intermittently or withdrawn at different points during training have provided support for Adams's theory. Schmidt's schema theory states that by practicing different variations of the same response, people develop general rules (schemas) that allow them to perform responses they have never practiced. Schema theory has been supported by various types of evidence, such as the finding that variable training often leads to better performance than practicing exactly the same movement over and over.

According to the response chain theory, in a sequence of movements, sensory feedback from one movement serves as a stimulus for the next response in the chain. Lashley presented several types of evidence against this theory, such as errors of anticipation that suggest a person is planning ahead. The theory of motor programs maintains that well-practiced sequences of movements can become a single unit that can be executed without sensory feedback from each individual response.

Review Questions

1. Explain the theory that imitation is a simple operant response and the theory that imitation is a generalized operant response. Which theory is better and why?

2. What are the four factors necessary for imitation, according to Bandura's theory? What are Bandura's main criticisms of the generalized operant theory of imitation? Are these criticisms convincing?

3. Give one specific example to show how modeling has been used in behavior therapy to effect the following: (a) facilitating low-probability behaviors, (b) acquiring new behaviors, and (c) eliminating unwanted behaviors.

4. What are the two stages of Adams's theory of motor-skill learning? What is Schmidt's schema theory and how does it differ from the theory of Adams? Describe some research that supports each theory.

5. Describe several different types of evidence that have been used to argue for the existence of motor programs.

REFERENCES

Adams, J.A. (1971). A closed-loop theory of motor learning. *Journal of Motor Behavior, 3*, 111–150.

Anderson, C.A., & Bushman, B.J. (2002). Media violence and the American public revisited. *American Psychologist, 57*, 448–450.

Anderson, C.A., Carnagey, N.L., & Eubanks, J. (2003). Exposure to violent media: The effects of songs with violent lyrics on aggressive thoughts and feelings. *Journal of Personality and Social Psychology, 84*, 960–971.

Badets, A., & Blandin, Y. (2010). Feedback schedules for motor-skill learning: The similarities and differences between physical and observational practice. *Journal of Motor Behavior, 42*, 257–268.

Baer, D.M., Peterson, R.F., & Sherman, J.A. (1967). The development of imitation by reinforcing behavioral similarity to a model. *Journal of the Experimental Analysis of Behavior, 10*, 405–416.

Bandura, A. (1965). Influence of models' reinforcement contingencies on the acquisition of imitative responses. *Journal of Personality and Social Psychology, 1*, 589–595.

Bandura, A. (1969). Principles of behavior modification. New York: Holt, Rinehart & Winston.

Bandura, A., Grusec, J.E., & Menlove, F.L. (1967). Vicarious extinction of avoidance behavior. *Journal of Personality and Social Psychology, 5*, 16–23.

Bandura, A., Ross, D., & Ross, S.A. (1963). Imitation of film-mediated aggressive models. *Journal of Abnormal and Social Psychology, 66*, 3–11.

Bandura, A., & Walters, R.H. (1963). *Social learning and personality development.* New York: Holt, Rinehart & Winston.

Battig, W.F. (1979). The flexibility of human memory. In L.S. Cermakl & F.I.M. Craik (Eds.), *Levels of processing in human memory* (pp. 23–44). Hillsdale, NJ: Erlbaum.

Bernier, R., & Dawson, G. (2009). The role of mirror neuron dysfunction in autism. In J.A. Pineda (Ed.), *Mirror neuron systems: The role of mirroring processes in social cognition* (pp. 261–286). Totowa, NJ: Humana Press.

Bilodeau, E.A., Bilodeau, I.M., & Schumsky, D.A. (1959). Some effects of introducing and withdrawing knowledge of results early and late in practice. *Journal of Experimental Psychology, 58*, 142–144.

Byrne, R.W., & Russon, A.E. (1998). Learning by imitation: A hierarchical approach. *Behavioral and Brain Sciences, 21*, 667–721.

Camòes-Costa, V., Erjavec, M., & Horne, P.J. (2011). The impact of body-part-naming training on the accuracy of imitative performances in 2- to 3-year-old children. *Journal of the Experimental Analysis of Behavior, 96*, 291–315.

Chamberlin, C.J., & Magill, R.A. (1992). The memory representation of motor skills: A test of schema theory. *Journal of Motor Behavior, 24*, 309–319.

Christensen, P., & Wood, W. (2007). Effects of media violence on viewers' aggression in unconstrained social interaction. In R.W. Preiss, B. Gayle, N. Burrell, M. Allen, & J. Bryant (Eds.), *Mass media effects research: Advances through meta-analysis* (pp. 145–168). Mahwah, NJ: Erlbaum.

Cirstea, M.C., & Levin, M.F. (2007). Improvement of arm movement patterns and endpoint control depends on type of feedback during practice in stroke survivors. *Neurorehabilitation and Neural Repair, 21*, 398–411.

Coldwells, A., & Hare, M.E. (1994). The transfer of skill from short tennis to lawn tennis. *Ergonomics, 37*, 17–21.

Cream, A., O'Brian, S., Onslow, M., Packman, A., & Menzies, R. (2009). Self-modelling as a relapse intervention following speech-restructuring treatment for stuttering. *International Journal of Language & Communication Disorders, 44*, 587–599.

Dail, T.K., & Christina, R.W. (2004). Distribution of practice and metacognition in learning and long-term retention. *Research Quarterly for Exercise and Sport, 75*, 148–155.

Davis, T., Ollendick, T.H., & Öst, L. (2009). Intensive treatment of specific phobias in children and adolescents. *Cognitive and Behavioral Practice, 16*, 294–303.

Di Pellegrino, G., Fadiga, L., Gallese, V., & Rizzolatti, G. (1992). Understanding motor events: A neurophysiological study. *Experimental Brain Research, 91*, 176–180.

Donohue, S.E., Woldorff, M.G., & Mitroff, S.R. (2010). Video game players show more precise multisensory temporal processing abilities. *Attention, Perception, & Psychophysics, 72*, 1120–1129.

Dowrick, P.W., & Raeburn, J.M. (1995). Selfmodeling: Rapid skill training for children with physical disabilities. *Journal of Developmental and Physical Disabilities, 7*, 25–37.

Eron, L.D., Huesmann, L.R., Lefkowitz, M.M., & Walder, L.O. (1972). Does television violence cause aggression? *American Psychologist, 27*, 253–263.

Fisch, S., & Truglio, R. (Eds.). (2001). *"G" is for "growing": Thirty years of Sesame Street research*. Mahwah, NJ: Lawrence Erlbaum.

Fitzpatrick, C., Barnett, T., & Pagani, L.S. (2012). Early exposure to media violence and later child adjustment. *Journal of Developmental and Behavioral Pediatrics, 33*, 291–297.

Friedrich-Cofer, L., & Huston, A.C. (1986). Television violence and aggression: The debate continues. *Psychological Bulletin, 100*, 364–371.

Gosch, E.A., Flannery-Schroeder, E., Mauro, C.F., & Compton, S.N. (2006). Principles of cognitive-behavioral therapy for anxiety disorders in children. *Journal of Cognitive Psychotherapy, 20*, 247–262.

Gunby, K.V., Carr, J.E., & Leblanc, L.A. (2010). Teaching abduction-prevention skills to children with autism. *Journal of Applied Behavior Analysis, 43*, 107–112.

Horne, P.J., & Erjavec, M. (2007). Do infants show generalized imitation of gestures? *Journal of the Experimental Analysis of Behavior, 87*, 63–87.

Johnson, J.G., Cohen, P., Smailes, E.M., Kasen, S., & Brook, J.S. (2002). Television viewing and aggressive behavior during adolescence and adulthood. *Science, 295*, 2468–2471.

Jostad, C.M., Miltenberger, R.G., Kelso, P., & Knudson, P. (2008). Peer tutoring to prevent firearm play: Acquisition, generalization, and long-term maintenance of safety skills. *Journal of Applied Behavior Analysis, 41*, 117–123.

Kawai, M. (1965). Newly acquired pre-cultural behavior of the natural troop of Japanese monkeys on Koshima Islet. *Primates, 6,* 1–30.

Keele, S.W. (1973). *Attention and human performance.* Pacific Palisades, CA: Goodyear Publishing.

Kernodle, M.W., & Carlton, L.G. (1992). Information feedback and the learning of multiple-degree-of-freedom activities. *Journal of Motor Behavior, 24,* 187–196.

Kerr, R., & Booth, B. (1978). Specific and varied practice of motor skill. *Perceptual and Motor Skills, 46,* 395–401.

Keysers, C., & Gazzola, V. (2010). Social neuroscience: Mirror neurons recorded in humans. *Current Biology, 20,* R353–R354.

Krcmar, M., Farrar, K., & McGloin, R. (2011). The effects of video game realism on attention, retention and aggressive outcomes. *Computers in Human Behavior, 27,* 432–439.

Kymissis, E., & Poulson, C.L. (1990). The history of imitation in learning theory: The language acquisition process. *Journal of the Experimental Analysis of Behavior, 54,* 113–127.

Lashley, K.S. (1951). The problem of serial order in behavior. In L.A. Jeffress (Ed.), *Cerebral mechanisms in behavior* (pp. 112–146). New York: Wiley.

Latash, M.L. (1999). Mirror writing: Learning, transfer, and implications for internal inverse models. *Journal of Motor Behavior, 31,* 107–111.

Linebarger, D.L., & Walker, D. (2005). Infants' and toddlers' television viewing and language outcomes. *American Behavioral Scientist, 48,* 624–645.

Marcus, A., & Wilder, D.A. (2009). A comparison of peer video modeling and self video modeling to teach textual responses in children with autism. *Journal of Applied Behavior Analysis, 42,* 335–341.

Markey, P.M., Markey, C.N., & French, J.E. (2014). Violent video games and real-world violence: Rhetoric versus data. *Psychology of Popular Media Culture,* August 18, 2014. doi:10.1037/ppm0000030

Mast, J.F., & McAndrew, F.T. (2011). Violent lyrics in heavy metal music can increase aggression in males. *North American Journal of Psychology, 13,* 63–64.

McGraw-Hunter, M.M., Faw, G.D., & Davis, P.K. (2006). The use of video self-modelling and feedback to teach cooking skills to individuals with traumatic brain injury: A pilot study. *Brain Injury, 20,* 1061–1068.

Mehta, U.M., Thirthalli, J., Aneelraj, D., Jadhav, P., Gangadhar, B.N., & Keshavan, M.S. (2014). Mirror neuron dysfunction in schizophrenia and its functional implications: A systematic review. *Schizophrenia Research, 160,* 9–19.

Meichenbaum, D.H., & Goodman, J. (1971). Training impulsive children to talk to themselves: A means of developing self-control. *Journal of Abnormal Psychology, 77,* 115–126.

Meltzoff, A.N., & Moore, M.K. (1977). Imitation of facial and manual gestures by human neonates. *Science, 198,* 75–78.

Middleton, M.B., & Cartledge, G. (1995). The effects of social skills instruction and parental involvement on the aggressive behaviors of African American males. *Behavior Modification, 19,* 192–210.

Miller, N.E., & Dollard, J. (1941). *Social learning and imitation.* New Haven, CT: Yale University Press.

Murray, J.P. (2008). Media violence: The effects are both real and strong. *American Behavioral Scientist, 51,* 1212–1230.

Nabeyama, B., & Sturmey, P. (2010). Using behavioral skills training to promote safe and correct staff guarding and ambulation distance of students with multiple physical disabilities. *Journal of Applied Behavior Analysis, 43,* 341–345.

Neuman, S.B. (1988). The displacement effect: Assessing the relation between television viewing and reading performance. *Reading Research Quarterly, 23,* 414–440.

Newell, K.M. (1974). Knowledge of results and motor learning. *Journal of Motor Behavior, 6,* 235–244.

O'Connor, R.D. (1969). Modification of social withdrawal through symbolic modeling. *Journal of Applied Behavior Analysis, 2,* 15–22.

Palmer, C., & Meyer, R.K. (2000). Conceptual and motor learning in music performance. *Psychological Science, 11*, 63–68.

Polman, H., de Castro, B., & van Aken, M.G. (2008). Experimental study of the differential effects of playing versus watching violent video games on children's aggressive behavior. *Aggressive Behavior, 34*, 256–264.

Portier, S.J., Van Galen, G.P., & Meulenbroek, R.G. (1990). Practice and the dynamics of handwriting performance: Evidence for a shift of motor programming load. *Journal of Motor Behavior, 22*, 474–492.

Prather, J.F., Peters, S.S., Nowicki, S.S., & Mooney, R.R. (2008). Precise auditory-vocal mirroring in neurons for learned vocal communication. *Nature, 451*, 305–310.

Rider, R.A., & Abdulahad, D.T. (1991). Effects of massed versus distributed practice on gross and fine motor proficiency of educable mentally handicapped adolescents. *Perceptual and Motor Skills, 73*, 219–224.

Rizzolatti, G., Craighero, L., & Fadiga, L. (2002). The mirror system in humans. In M.I. Stamenov, V. Gallese, M.I. Stamenov, & V. Gallese (Eds.), *Mirror neurons and the evolution of brain and language* (pp. 37–59). Amsterdam, Netherlands: John Benjamins Publishing Company.

Robert, M. (1990). Observational learning in fish, birds, and mammals: A classified bibliography spanning over 100 years of research. *Psychological Record, 40*, 289–311.

Rosenberg, D., Depp, C.A., Vahia, I.V., Reichstadt, J., Palmer, B.W., Kerr, J., & . . . Jeste, D.V. (2010). Exergames for subsyndromal depression in older adults: A pilot study of a novel intervention. *American Journal of Geriatric Psychiatry, 18*, 221–226.

Russell, D.M., & Newell, K.M. (2007). On No-KR tests in motor learning, retention and transfer. *Human Movement Science, 26*, 155–173.

Sanli, E.A., & Lee, T.D. (2014). What roles do errors serve in motor skill learning? An examination of two theoretical predictions. *Journal of Motor Behavior, 46*, 329–337.

Schmidt, R.A. (1975). A schema theory of discrete motor skill learning. *Psychological Review, 82*, 225–260.

Shaffer, L.H. (1978). Timing in the motor programming of typing. *Quarterly Journal of Experimental Psychology, 30*, 333–345.

Shea, C.H., Wright, D.L., Wulf, G., & Whitacre, C. (2000). Physical and observational practice afford unique learning opportunities. *Journal of Motor Behavior, 32*, 27–36.

Shea, J.B., & Morgan, R.L. (1979). Contextual interference effects on the acquisition, retention, and transfer of a motor skill. *Journal of Experimental Psychology: Human Learning and Memory, 5*, 179–187.

Sherwood, D.E., & Fosler, J. (2013). Blocked and alternating variable practice and unintended spatial variations in continuous aiming movements. *Perceptual and Motor Skills, 116*, 611–625.

Shukla-Mehta, S., Miller, T., & Callahan, K.J. (2010). Evaluating the effectiveness of video instruction on social and communication skills training for children with autism spectrum disorders: A review of the literature. *Focus on Autism and Other Developmental Disabilities, 25*, 23–36.

Sparrow, W.A., & Summers, J.J. (1992). Performance on trials without knowledge of results (KR) in reduced relative frequency presentations of KR. *Journal of Motor Behavior, 24*, 197–209.

Starek, J., & McCullagh, P. (1999). The effect of self-modeling on the performance of beginning swimmers. *Sport Psychologist, 13*, 269–287.

Taub, E., & Berman, A.J. (1968). Movement and learning in the absence of sensory feedback. In S.J. Freedman (Ed.), *The neuro-psychology of spatially oriented behavior* (pp. 172–193). Homewood, IL: Dorsey Press.

Thorndike, E.L. (1927). The law of effect. *American Journal of Psychology, 39*, 212–222.

Trowbridge, M.H., & Cason, H. (1932). An experimental test of Thorndike's theory of learning. *Journal of General Psychology, 7*, 245–260.

Ulrich, R., Giray, M., & Schaffer, R. (1990). Is it possible to prepare the second component of a movement before the first one? *Journal of Motor Behavior, 22*, 125–148.

Vangheluwe, S., Suy, E., Wenderoth, N., & Swinnen, S.P. (2006). Learning and transfer of bimanual multifrequency patterns: Effector–independent and effector-specific levels of movement representation. *Experimental Brain Research, 170*, 543–554.

Vera, J.G., & Montilla, M.M. (2003). Practice schedule and acquisition, retention, and transfer of a throwing task in 6-yr-old children. *Perceptual and Motor Skills, 96*, 1015–1024.

Whitacre, C.A., & Shea, C.H. (2000). Performance and learning of generalized motor programs: Relative (GMP) and absolute (parameter) errors. *Journal of Motor Behavior, 32*, 163–175.

Wilson, P.H., Thomas, P.R., & Maruff, P. (2002). Motor imagery training ameliorates motor clumsiness in children. *Journal of Child Neurology, 17*, 491–498.

Zhou, S., Hou, Z., & Bai, R. (2008). Effect of group assertiveness training on university students' assertive competence. *Chinese Journal of Clinical Psychology, 16*, 665–667.

CHAPTER 12

Choice

Learning Objectives

After reading this chapter, you should be able to

- describe the matching law, and explain how it has been applied to different choice situations
- describe optimization theory, and discuss studies that compare its predictions to those of the matching law
- describe momentary maximization theory, and explain how it differs from optimization theory
- define the self-control choice situation, and give examples from the laboratory and from everyday life
- discuss techniques people can use to improve their self-control
- explain the phenomenon of the "tragedy of the commons," and discuss ways that it can be avoided

It is not much of an exaggeration to say that all behavior involves choice. Even in the most barren experimental chamber, an animal can choose among performing the operant response, exploring, sitting, standing, grooming, sleeping, and so on. Outside the laboratory, the choices are much more numerous. At any moment, an individual can choose to either continue with its current behavior or switch to another. Because both people and animals are constantly making choices, understanding choice is an essential part of understanding behavior itself.

One of the most remarkable characteristics of behavior in choice situations is its orderliness and predictability. The choice behavior of animals in laboratory experiments is often so orderly that it can be described by simple mathematical equations. One such equation is the matching law, one of the best-known principles that has arisen from behavioral research on choice.

THE MATCHING LAW

Herrnstein's Experiment

Herrnstein (1961) conducted an experiment with pigeons in a chamber with two response keys, one red and one white. Each key was associated with its own VI schedule of reinforcement. For example, in one condition, pecks at the left key were reinforced on a VI 135-second schedule, and pecks at the right key were reinforced on a VI 270-second schedule, so the left key delivered about twice as many food reinforcers. (Technically, when two or more reinforcement schedules are presented simultaneously they are called a **concurrent schedule**.) Herrnstein's main question was this: After the birds have learned all that they can about this choice situation, how will they distribute their responses? He therefore gave them many days of training with the same two VI schedules and then measured their responses. As is typical on VI schedules, the birds made many responses for each reinforcer they received. What is most interesting, however, is that in this condition, where two thirds of the reinforcers came from the left key, the birds made approximately two thirds of their responses on the left key. That is, the proportion of responses on the left key equaled, or *matched*, the proportion of reinforcers delivered by the left key.

In another condition, two birds received only about 15% of their reinforcers from the left key, and they made about 15% of their responses on this key. Once again, the percentage of left-key responses approximately matched the percentage of left-key reinforcers. Based these results, Herrnstein proposed the following general principle, now known as the **matching law**:

$$\frac{B_1}{B_1 + B_2} = \frac{R_1}{R_1 + R_2} \tag{12.1}$$

B_1 is the number of responses of type 1 (left-key responses), and B_2 is the number of responses of type 2 (right-key responses). Similarly, R_1 is the number of reinforcers obtained by making response 1, and R_2 is the number of reinforcers obtained by making response 2. Equation 12.1 states that in a two-choice situation, the proportion of responses directed toward one alternative should equal the proportion of reinforcers delivered by that alternative.

Figure 12.1 plots the results from all of the conditions of Herrnstein's experiment. The x-axis represents the percentage of left-key reinforcers and the y-axis the percentage of left-key responses. According to the matching law, the data points should fall along the diagonal line because this is where these two percentages are equal. As can be seen, all the points are close to the line. The matching law provided a very good description of the pigeons' behavior.

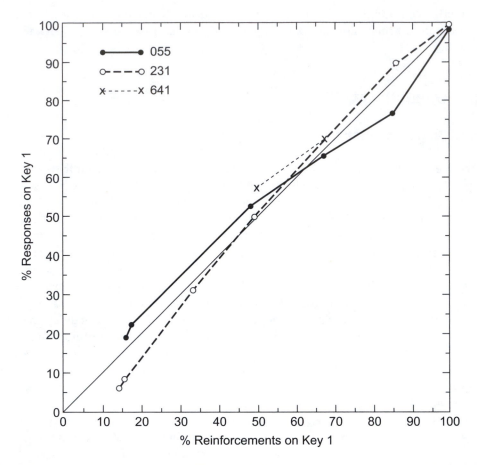

Figure 12.1 Results from three pigeons in Herrnstein's (1961) experiment on concurrent VI schedules. Each data point shows the results from a different condition. The diagonal line shows the predictions of the matching law, which predicts that response percentages will match reinforcement percentages. (From Herrnstein, R. J., Relative and absolute strength of response as a function of frequency of reinforcement, *Journal of the Experimental Analysis of Behavior, 4*, 267–272. Copyright 1961 by the Society for the Experimental Analysis of Behavior, Inc.)

Other Experiments on Matching

The matching law has been applied with reasonable success in a wide range of experiments with both animals and humans. One experiment found that the percentage of time people spent talking to another person in a group discussion approximately matched the percentage of verbal reinforcers delivered by that person (Conger & Killeen, 1974). Billington and DiTommaso (2003) showed how the matching law can be used to analyze classroom behavior. According to the matching law, the percentage of class time a child spends off-task versus on-task will depend on the relative amounts of reinforcement each provides. A teacher who wants to increase on-task behavior must find ways either to reduce the reinforcers for off-task behavior (which might be difficult) or to increase the reinforcers for on-task behavior (by providing praise, encouragement, special privileges, and so on). In other applications, the matching law has been used to analyze conflicts between career and family (Redmon & Lockwood, 1986) and to describe how consumers make choices when purchasing food items (Foxall, James, Oliveira-Castro, & Ribier, 2010).

The matching law has also been applied to choices made by individual athletes and entire teams. For example, Stilling and Critchfield (2010) examined the numbers of passing plays versus running plays used by different football teams during a season (which varied from team to team because of differences in talent, coaching strategies, etc.). They treated the choice of plays as the behaviors and yards gained as the reinforcers, and they found an approximate matching relation—the percentage of passing plays used by the different teams varied in accordance with the relative amounts of yardage the teams gained from these two types of plays.

Deviations From Matching

Not all experiments have produced results that are consistent with Equation 12.1. Baum (1974) listed three ways that the results of experiments have deviated from strict matching, each of which is depicted graphically in Figure 12.2. The most common of these deviations is **undermatching**, in which response proportions are consistently less extreme (i.e., closer to .5) than reinforcement proportions. In the example of undermatching shown in Figure 12.2, when the proportion of left reinforcers is .8, the proportion of left responses is only .6. When the proportion of left reinforcers is .3, the proportion of left responses is .45. In other words, undermatching describes the case where an individual's preferences are closer to indifference than they should be according to the matching law.

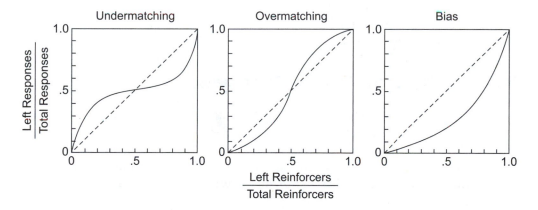

Figure 12.2 In each panel, the broken diagonal line shows where data points would fall if a subject's behavior conformed perfectly to the matching law (Equation 12.1). The solid curves illustrate three types of deviation from perfect matching.

One explanation of undermatching is that it can occur if the learner develops a habit of rapidly switching back and forth between the two options, a pattern that could be accidentally reinforced if food was delivered immediately after a switch. (To reduce the chance that switching behavior might be inadvertently reinforced, Herrnstein included a 1.5-second *changeover delay*—no food could be delivered during the first 1.5 seconds after a pigeon switched from one key to the other. This meant that a pigeon had to make two or more consecutive responses on the same key before collecting a reinforcer, thereby making the accidental reinforcement of switching behavior less likely.) Another hypothesis about undermatching is that animals may occasionally attribute a reinforcer to the wrong response (Davison & Jenkins, 1985). For instance, in the short time between making a response and collecting the reinforcer, a pigeon may forget which key it pecked.

The opposite of undermatching is **overmatching**, in which response proportions are more extreme than the reinforcement proportions. In the illustration of overmatching in Figure 12.2, a reinforcer proportion of .8 produces a response proportion of .9, and a reinforcer proportion of .3 produces a response proportion of .15. Overmatching is not as common as matching or undermatching, but it has been observed in situations where there is a penalty for switching between schedules. Baum (1982) found overmatching when pigeons had to walk around a barrier and over a hurdle to switch from one key to the other. As the effort involved in switching between keys was increased, the pigeons switched less and less and spent most of their time responding on the better VI schedule, which resulted in overmatching.

In the third type of deviation from matching, **bias**, an individual consistently spends more time on one alternative than predicted by the matching equation. The example in Figure 12.2 illustrates a bias for the right key: Regardless of the reinforcer proportion, there are more responses on the right key than predicted by the matching law. Many factors can produce a bias, such as a preference for a particular side of the chamber, for a particular response key (if one key requires a bit less effort than the other), or for a particular color (if the two response keys have different colors). In some cases, the reason for bias is easy to explain. In a study of college basketball players' choices between 2-point and 3-point shots, researchers found that the matching law described the players' shot selections quite well, except that there was a consistent bias for 3-point shots (Alferink, Critchfield, Hitt, & Higgins, 2009). The explanation for this bias is straightforward and obvious—3-point shots are worth more than 2-point shots.

Varying the Quality and Amount of Reinforcement

With some small modifications, the matching law can be used to measure an individual's preferences for reinforcers of different types. For instance, Miller (1976) presented pigeons with pairs of VI schedules that provided different types of grain as reinforcers. When the two reinforcers were wheat and buckwheat, the pigeons showed a strong preference (bias) for the wheat. Miller suggested that the matching equation could take this bias into account if it were modified in the following way:

$$\frac{B_1}{B_1 + B_2} = \frac{Q_1 R_1}{Q_1 R_1 + Q_2 R_2} \qquad (12.2)$$

where Q_1 and Q_2 stand for the qualities of the reinforcers available on the two keys. This equation states that a pigeon's behavior is determined by both the rate of reinforcement and the quality of reinforcement delivered by the different schedules. Miller arbitrarily assigned a value of 10 to Q_b, the quality of buckwheat, and he found that Equation 12.2 provided a good description of the results if Q_w, the quality of wheat, was given a value of about 14. He interpreted this number as meaning that each wheat reinforcer was worth about 1.4 times as much as each buckwheat reinforcer. Miller made similar calculations for conditions where the alternatives were hemp and buckwheat, and he estimated that Q_h, the quality of hemp, was about 9.1, or slightly less than that of buckwheat. Based on these numbers, Miller predicted that he should observe a preference (bias) of 14 to 9.1 when the pigeons had to choose between wheat and hemp, and this is approximately what he found. This experiment nicely demonstrates how the matching law can be used to scale animals' preferences for different types of reinforcers. The matching law has been used in other studies to measure preferences among reinforcers of different qualities, with subjects as different as humans (Neef, Mace, Shea, & Shade, 1992) and cows (Foster, Temple, Robertson, Nair, & Poling, 1996).

Besides the rate of reinforcement and the quality of reinforcement, another variable that can affect preference is the amount or size of each reinforcer. If one key delivers two food pellets as a reinforcer and the other key delivers only one, this should certainly affect a subject's choices. Baum and Rachlin (1969) suggested that when amount of reinforcement is the independent variable, it can be used in place of rate of reinforcement in the matching equation:

$$\frac{B_1}{B_1 + B_2} = \frac{A_1}{A_1 + A_2} \tag{12.3}$$

where A_1 and A_2 are the amounts of reinforcement delivered by the two alternatives. In some cases, Equation 12.3 has been quite accurate (Catania, 1963), but other studies have found substantial undermatching or overmatching when amount of reinforcement is varied (Davison & Hogsden, 1984).

MATCHING AND REINFORCEMENT RELATIVITY

The matching law makes a basic and important point about reinforcer effectiveness: We cannot predict how much behavior will be devoted to one option (e.g., on-task behavior by children in a classroom) just by knowing how much reinforcement is available for that behavior. We must also know how much reinforcement is available for other behaviors (e.g., off-task behaviors). Using a laboratory example, if pressing one lever delivers 20 reinforcers per hour, we cannot predict how much time a rat will spend pressing that lever unless we know whether pressing a second lever produces 60 reinforcers per hour or only 5 reinforcers per hour. The effects of reinforcement are relative: We must take into account the context— all the other reinforcers that are available for other behaviors.

As a real-world example, try to predict how a young child's behavior would be altered by giving him a new reinforcer—a yo-yo, for example. To make any sensible prediction, we need to know something about the context. If the yo-yo is given on an average rainy day in August, the child may play with the yo-yo for hours because he may be bored with all his other toys and indoor activities. On the other hand, if the yo-yo is given on Christmas and the context includes a host of new toys—trucks, video games, puzzles—the amount of time spent playing with the yo-yo will probably be small. The rich supply of other reinforcers will attract most of the child's time.

Other examples where the total reinforcement context plays a major role are easy to imagine. Many people claim that they tend to eat more when they are bored. This presumably happens not because the reinforcing value of food actually increases when one is bored, but rather because there are few reinforcers available to compete with eating. As another example, imagine that you are sitting in a reception area waiting for an appointment with someone who is running behind schedule (such as your mechanic or your optometrist). There is little to do but wait, and if you are like me, you may find yourself reading magazines you would not ordinarily spend your time on, such as 2-year-old issues of *Newsweek*, *Good Housekeeping*, or *Optometry Today*. What little reinforcement value these outdated magazines offer takes on added significance in the absence of any alternative sources of reinforcement.

THEORIES OF CHOICE BEHAVIOR

In many areas of science, it is important to distinguish between descriptions and explanations. For example, the statement that water increases in volume when it freezes is simply a description—it does not explain why this expansion occurs. Descriptive statements can be extremely useful in their own right because they can help us to predict and control future events (e.g., avoiding the bursting of outdoor water pipes by draining them before they freeze). On the other hand, a statement that attributes this expansion to the crystalline structure that hydrogen and oxygen molecules form when in a solid state can be called an explanation: It is a theory about the molecular events that underlie this phenomenon.

The matching equation can be viewed as either simply a description of choice behavior or a theory about the mechanisms of choice behavior. We have seen that as a description of behavior in certain choice situations, the matching equation is fairly accurate. We will now consider the possibility that the matching law is an explanatory theory and compare it to a few other theories that have been presented as possible explanatory theories of choice.

Matching as an Explanatory Theory

Herrnstein (1970) suggested that the matching equation is also a general explanatory theory of choice behavior. The theory is quite simple: It states that animals exhibit matching behavior because they are built to do so. That is, in any choice situation, an animal measures the value of the reinforcement it receives from each alternative (where "value" includes such factors as the rate, size, and quality of the reinforcers), and the animal then distributes its behavior in proportion to the values of the various alternatives. According this theory, matching is not just a description of behavior in concurrent VI schedules. It is a general principle that explains how animals and people make choices in all situations, in the laboratory and in the real world.

Optimization Theory

One major competitor for matching theory is **optimization theory**. As discussed in Chapter 8, some psychologists and economists have proposed that optimization theory is a general explanatory theory of choice for both humans and nonhumans, and many experiments have supported the predictions of this theory. Some psychologists have proposed that optimization theory can also explain why matching occurs on concurrent VI schedules (Silberberg, Thomas, & Berendzen, 1991). They propose that although the matching law may provide a satisfactory description of behavior in these situations, optimization theory actually provides an explanation of matching behavior.

To understand this logic, imagine a pigeon on a concurrent VI 30-second (left-key) VI 120-second (right-key) schedule. Rachlin, Green, Kagel, and Battalio (1976) used computer simulations to determine how different ways of distributing responses between the two keys would affect the total rate of reinforcement. The results of these simulations are presented in Figure 12.3. If a pigeon made all of its responses on the left key, it would obtain about 120 reinforcers per hour (which is shown by the point at the extreme right in Figure 12.3). If the pigeon responded only on the right key, it would collect about 30 per hour (the point at the extreme left in Figure 12.3). By making some responses on each

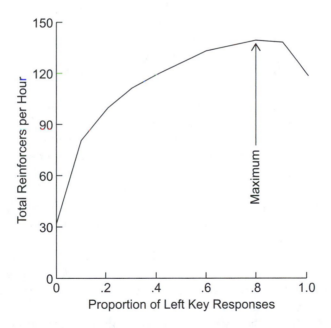

Figure 12.3 Predictions of the computer simulations of Rachlin et al. (1976) for a concurrent VI 30-second (left-key) VI 120-second (right-key) schedule. According to the predictions, a subject on this schedule would maximize the rate of reinforcement by making 80% of its responses on the left key.

key, however, the pigeon could collect many of the reinforcers from both schedules. The computer simulations showed that a pigeon could obtain the highest possible rate of reinforcement by making 80% of its responses to the left key, which is also the point of matching behavior (because in this example the left key delivers 80% of the reinforcers). Rachlin et al. claimed that with any typical pair of VI schedules, matching behavior will maximize the rate of reinforcement. To put it simply, they proposed that matching occurs with concurrent VI schedules because it is the optimal way to respond—matching produces the highest total rate of reinforcement.

Tests of Optimization Versus Matching

A common strategy when comparing scientific theories is to find a situation for which the theories make distinctly different predictions and then to conduct the appropriate experiment to see what actually happens. Quite a few experiments have examined choice situations for which the matching law makes one prediction and optimization theory makes a very different prediction.

An experiment with pigeons that I conducted was also designed to compare the two theories (Mazur, 1981). In many ways, my experiment was similar to Herrnstein's (1961) original experiment on matching. Pigeons could peck at either of two keys, one red and one green. Occasionally, a peck on one of the keys would cause the key lights to go off, and food was presented for 3 seconds. One main difference in my procedure, however, was that a single VI schedule randomly assigned the food deliveries to the two keys, whereas Herrnstein used two separate VI schedules. This was an important difference because whenever food was assigned to one key, the VI clock stopped until the food was collected. This meant that a pigeon had to respond on both keys frequently to keep the VI clock moving. Therefore, the optimal strategy was for the pigeon to make half of its responses on each key, switching back and forth frequently, because this kept the clock moving and kept the food deliveries coming.

In one condition, where the food deliveries per hour were equal for the two keys, the pigeons did perform optimally, making about 50% of their responses on each key (which was also matching, of course). However, a second condition provided the critical test between optimization and matching. In this condition, 90% of the food deliveries for the red key were replaced with "dark-key periods"—the keys went dark for 3 seconds, but no food was delivered. Despite this change, the optimal strategy was still to switch back and forth between the two keys frequently, making about 50% of one's responses on each key. This strategy would ensure that the VI timer would be running most of the time. However, the matching law predicted that the pigeons should now make many more responses on the green key, since this key now provided about 10 times as many food reinforcers. That is what happened: The pigeons shifted most of their responses to the green key and made an average of 86% of their responses on the green key (which delivered about 92% of the reinforcers). However, because they responded so little on the red key, the VI clock was often stopped, and as a result, the pigeons lost about 29% of their potential reinforcers. In other conditions, the pigeons lost three quarters or more of their potential reinforcers by matching rather than optimizing.

The procedure of this experiment may seem complex, but the results can be stated simply: Although optimization theory predicted that the birds should always make about 50% of their responses on each key, they consistently showed a preference for whichever key delivered more reinforcers, as predicted by the matching law. But by doing so, they slowed down the VI clock and lost many potential reinforcers, which is exactly the opposite of what optimization theory predicted should happen.

Psychologists have used a variety of other experimental procedures to compare the predictions of the matching law and optimization theory. For example, in choice situations involving both a VI schedule and a VR schedule, optimization theory predicts that animals should make most of their responses on the VR schedule because most of the responses on any VI schedule are wasted, whereas every response on a VR schedule brings the animal closer to reinforcement. Several experiments with animals failed to support this prediction, and the results were consistent with the predictions of the matching law (DeCarlo, 1985; Vyse & Belke, 1992). Similar results were obtained in a study with college students working for money: The students spent more time on the VI schedule than predicted by optimization theory, and their choices were closer to the predictions of the matching law (Savastano & Fantino, 1994).

Many other experiments, some with animals and some with humans, have been conducted to test the predictions of the matching law and optimization theory. Some have found evidence supporting the matching law and inconsistent with optimization theory (Jacobs & Hackenberg, 2000; Heyman & Herrnstein, 1986). However, others have supported optimization theory (MacDonall, Goodell, & Juliano, 2006; Sakagami, Hursh, Christensen, & Silberberg, 1989). With some evidence supporting each theory, some psychologists continue to favor optimization theory, whereas others favor matching theory.

Because they deal with an individual's overall distribution of responses over long periods of time (e.g., over an entire experimental session), matching theory and optimization theory can both be classified as molar theories (see Chapter 6). Some researchers now believe that more complete explanations of choice behavior will be found in molecular theories, which attempt to predict moment-to-moment behavior and which assume that short-term consequences have large effects on choice. One molecular theory of choice is presented in the next section.

Momentary Maximization Theory

Stated simply, the basic premise of **momentary maximization theory** is that at each moment, an individual will select whichever alternative has the highest value at that moment. Although both momentary maximization theory and optimization theory state that people and animals attempt to maximize the value of their choices, the two theories often make different predictions because the best choice in the short run is not always the best choice in the long run. As a simple example, consider a dieter who must choose between low-fat yogurt and a strawberry sundae for dessert. The strawberry sundae may appear more attractive at the moment, but the yogurt might be the better alternative for the dieter in the long run. Choices that involve a conflict between short-term and long-term benefits will be examined later in the chapter, but for now the point is that the strategies of momentary maximization and overall optimization may lead to very different decisions.

To understand how momentary maximizing theory works, a concrete example may help. Before reading further, try playing the hypothetical gambling game described in Box 12.1.

BOX 12.1   APPLYING THE RESEARCH

Can You Use a Momentary Maximizing Strategy?

Imagine that you are allowed to play this game for nine trials. You are seated in front of a panel with two small doors, and on each trial you are allowed to open one of the two doors. There may be a dollar behind the door (which you win) or there may be no money. The following rules determine whether a dollar is deposited behind a door or not: Behind the panel and out of sight, there is a modified roulette wheel for each door, which is spun before each trial begins. The probability of winning is 10% on the roulette wheel for Door 1 and 20% on the wheel for Door 2. Therefore, on Trial 1 of the game, there may be a dollar behind both doors, behind one door, or behind neither door, depending on the outcome of spinning the wheel for each door. Which door would you choose on Trial 1?

Two additional rules apply for the next eight trials:

1. Once a dollar is deposited behind a door, it will remain there until you collect it. So if a dollar is deposited behind Door 1 on Trial 4, it will remain there until the next time you choose Door 1.
2. There will never be more than one dollar behind a door at one time. For instance, if a dollar is deposited behind Door 1 on Trial 4 and you do not collect it until Trial 7, the spinning of the wheel is irrelevant on Trials 5, 6, and 7, since no more dollars will be deposited behind Door 1. However, the spinning of the wheel for Door 2 will continue to be important on these trials since it might pay off on any trial. In other words, Door 2 is not affected by what is happening at Door 1, and vice versa.

In the table below, decide what door you would choose on each of the nine trials:

Trial 1:	Door 1	or	Door 2
Trial 2:	Door 1	or	Door 2
Trial 3:	Door 1	or	Door 2
Trial 4:	Door 1	or	Door 2
Trial 5:	Door 1	or	Door 2
Trial 6:	Door 1	or	Door 2
Trial 7:	Door 1	or	Door 2
Trial 8:	Door 1	or	Door 2
Trial 9:	Door 1	or	Door 2

For many people, choosing the momentary maximizing strategy is not easy. Return to the text to get an explanation of the strategy for this game.

For situations like the game described in Box 12.1, momentary maximization theory predicts that the player will choose whichever alternative has the higher probability of reinforcement on each trial. On the first two trials, Door 2 has the higher probability of reinforcement, and so it should be chosen. However, it can be shown (using some elementary rules of probability theory that will not be explained here) that after two choices of Door 2, the probability of a dollar behind Door 2 is still 20%, but the probability of a dollar behind Door 1 is 27.1% (because there are now three trials on which a dollar might have been deposited at Door 1). A momentary maximizer would therefore choose Door 1 on Trial 3. After checking Door 1 on Trial 3, it is best to go back to Door 2 on Trial 4 because now its winning probability is again greater than for Door 1. The pattern followed by a momentary maximizer on the nine trials would be 2, 2, 1, 2, 2, 1, 2, 2, 1. How close did your choices come to the momentary maximizing strategy?

This hypothetical gambling game is quite similar to concurrent VI schedules. The two roulette wheels are similar to two independent VI timers, and like VI clocks, the roulette wheels will only store one reinforcer at a time. Therefore, you can probably see what momentary maximizing theory predicts for concurrent VI schedules: There should be an orderly and cyclical pattern to an animal's moment-by-moment choices. Of course, those who advocate momentary maximizing theory do not expect an animal's performance to show perfect momentary maximizing, but they do predict that animals will show at least some tendency to choose the alternative that has the higher probability of reinforcement. For example, after an animal has made several consecutive responses on the better of two VI schedules, it should show a tendency to switch to the other VI (because a reinforcer may have been stored on this VI during the interim). According to momentary maximizing theory, matching behavior is simply an incidental by-product of an animal's orderly moment-by-moment choices. In contrast, molar theories do not predict that an animal's moment-to-moment behavior will exhibit any orderly patterns because these theories assume that an animal's behavior is controlled by variables (e.g., total reinforcement rate) that do not change from moment to moment.

When animals exhibit matching behavior, are there orderly moment-by-moment patterns in their behavior? It seems that sometimes there are but not always. Some studies have found evidence for the sort of moment-by-moment changes predicted by momentary maximizing theory (Shimp, 1966; Silberberg, Hamilton, Ziriax, & Casey, 1978), but others have not (Heyman, 1979; Nevin, 1969). In one interesting study, Hinson and Staddon (1983) continuously recorded the time since a pigeon sampled (pecked at) each of two VI keys. They reasoned that time is the critical independent variable since on VI schedules it is the passage of time and not the number of responses that actually determines the availability of a reinforcer. They showed that their pigeons could follow a momentary maximizing strategy if they used a fairly simple rule: If schedule 1 delivers, for example, three times as many reinforcers as schedule 2, you should check schedule 2 if the time since you last checked it is more than three times longer than the time since you last checked schedule 1. Hinson and Staddon showed that their pigeons' behaviors were by no means perfect from the standpoint of momentary maximization theory, but a majority of their responses did follow this rule.

More recently, many other studies have found additional evidence that animals' moment-to-moment choices are influenced by a variety of short-term factors, such as the time since their last response (Brown & Cleaveland, 2009) or which response has just delivered a reinforcer (Aparicio & Baum, 2009). These results do not necessarily support momentary maximizing theory, but they conclusively show that animals' moment-tomoment choices are affected by molecular events, not just the molar reinforcement contingencies.

Over the years, many other behavioral theories of choice have been proposed, some of which might be called *hybrid theories* because they assume that both molar and molecular variables affect choice (Fantino & Silberberg, 2010; Grace, 1994; Killeen, 1982). These theories are mathematically quite complex, and we will not examine them here. Regardless of which theory of choice proves to be most accurate, no one can dispute the more general claim of molecular theories that short-term factors have a large effect on choice behavior. The next section shows that when a small but immediate reinforcer is pitted against a large but delayed reinforcer, the small, immediate reinforcer is frequently chosen.

PRACTICE QUIZ 1: CHAPTER 12

1. According to the matching law, if an animal receives 75% of its reinforcers from one schedule, it will make _____ of its responses on that schedule.
2. If an animal receives 20% of its reinforcers from one schedule, but makes 30% of its responses on that schedule, this is called _____.
3. _____ theory states that individuals will make choices that give them the greatest value in the long run.
4. In experiments designed to compare the predictions of optimization theory and the matching law, the results have usually supported _____.
5. According to _____ theory, an individual will choose whichever alternative has the highest value at that moment.

ANSWERS

1. 75% 2. undermatching 3. optimization 4. the matching law 5. momentary maximization

---

SELF-CONTROL CHOICES

Every day, people make many choices that involve a conflict between their short-term and long-term interests. Think of a college student who has a class that meets early Monday morning, and in this course it is important to attend each lecture. On Sunday evening, the student sets her alarm clock so that she can awaken early enough to get to class on time. She has chosen going to class (and the improved chances for a good grade this will bring) over an hour of extra sleep. This sounds like a prudent choice, but unfortunately she has plenty of time to change her mind. When the alarm clock rings on Monday morning, the warmth and comfort of the bed are more appealing than going to class, and the student turns off the alarm and goes back to sleep. Later in the day, she will probably regret her choice and vow not to miss class again.

This example is a typical **self-control choice** situation, that is, one involving a choice between a small immediate reinforcer and a larger but more distant reinforcer. The small reinforcer is the extra hour of sleep, and the larger, delayed reinforcer is the better grade that will probably result from going to class. An important characteristic of self-control situations is that a person's preferences can change systematically as time passes. On Sunday evening, the young woman evidently preferred going to class (and its long-term benefits) over an extra hour of sleep, since she set the alarm for the appropriate time. The next morning, her preference had changed, and she chose the extra hour of sleep. Later that day, she regrets this choice and decides to make a different decision in the future.

In case you are not convinced that self-control situations are commonplace, consider the following everyday decisions. You should be able to identify the small, more immediate reinforcer and larger, delayed reinforcer in each case:

1. To smoke a cigarette or not to smoke.
2. To keep the thermostat at 65°F during the winter months or set it at a higher temperature and face a larger fuel bill at the end of the month.
3. When on a diet, to choose between low-fat yogurt or ice cream for dessert.
4. To shout at your roommate in anger or control your temper and avoid saying something you do not really mean.
5. To save money for some big item you want (e.g., a car) or spend it on parties each weekend.

For each example, you should also be able to see how one's preference might change over time. It is easy to say you will begin a diet—tomorrow. On Monday or Tuesday, it is easy to decide you will have a frugal weekend and begin saving for that car. It is much harder, however, to keep these commitments when the time comes to make your final choice. Herrnstein and Mazur (1987) argued that this tendency to switch preferences over time in self-control choices is one of the strongest pieces of evidence against optimization theory. If people followed the strategy that optimized their satisfaction in the long run, they would consistently choose one alternative or the other.

BOX 12.2   SPOTLIGHT ON RESEARCH

Measuring Delay Discounting

Self-control choices illustrate quite dramatically how the strength or value of a reinforcer decreases as its delay increases. This effect is called **delay discounting**. To get an idea of how delay discounting works, imagine that you have won a prize in a lottery, and you can choose to receive either $1,000 in one year or a smaller amount of money today. Before reading further, take a moment to answer the questions below. There are no right or wrong answers; just try to answer as if these choices were real.

For each choice below, pick either A or B. Which would you rather have:

A. $1000 today	or	B. $1000 in 1 year
A. $950 today	or	B. $1000 in 1 year
A. $900 today	or	B. $1000 in 1 year
A. $800 today	or	B. $1000 in 1 year
A. $700 today	or	B. $1000 in 1 year

A. $600 today   or   B. $1000 in 1 year
A. $500 today   or   B. $1000 in 1 year
A. $400 today   or   B. $1000 in 1 year
A. $300 today   or   B. $1000 in 1 year
A. $200 today   or   B. $1000 in 1 year
A. $100 today   or   B. $1000 in 1 year
A. $50 today   or   B. $1000 in 1 year

When given a series of hypothetical choices like these, most people start by choosing Option A, but at some point their preference switches to Option B. For instance, suppose that a college student selected Option A when it was $700 today, but for the next question ($600 today), he chose Option B ($1000 in a year). Because his preference switched between $700 and $600, we can conclude that somewhere in between these two values there is an **indifference point**—a combination of delays and amounts that the student finds equally preferable. For this student, we could estimate that receiving $650 today would be about equal in value to receiving $1,000 in 1 year (because $650 is half-way between $700 and $600).

Questions like these have been used in numerous studies to measure delay discounting to estimate how the value of a reinforcer like money decreases with delay. Green, Fry, and Myerson (1994) compared three different age groups and found that the rates of delay discounting were fastest for 12-year-old children, slower for 20-year-old college students, and slowest for adults in their 60s. In other words, the older people were more willing to wait for the larger, delayed reward than were the younger people. Other studies have found faster rates of delay discounting for smokers than for nonsmokers (Mitchell, 1999), and it is also faster for individuals with addictions to drugs or alcohol (Bickel, Koffarnus, Moody, & Wilson, 2014) and for pathological gamblers (MacKillop et al., 2014). Many factors can affect the rate of delay discounting, and it varies both from person to person and from situation to situation (Odum, 2011).

The Ainslie–Rachlin Theory

The concept of delay discounting is not hard to understand, but we need to take this idea one step further to explain why a person's choices change as time passes. Why does a student set the alarm in the evening for an early morning class but then stay in bed the next morning and skip class? To answer questions like this, George Ainslie (1975) and Howard Rachlin (1970) independently developed similar ideas about self-control, which are known as the **Ainslie–Rachlin theory**.

Relying on the concept of delay discounting, the theory assumes that the value of a reinforcer decreases as the delay between making a choice and receiving the reinforcer increases. The upper panel of Figure 12.4 shows that the value of a good grade is high at the end of the term, but on the Sunday and Monday in question, its value is much lower because it is so far in the future. In the lower panel, the value of an hour of extra sleep at different points in time is also shown, and the same principle of delay discounting applies to this reinforcer: Its value decreases as its delay increases. The second assumption of the theory is that an individual will choose whichever reinforcer has the higher value at the moment a choice is made. Notice that the way the curves are drawn in Figure 12.4, the value of the good grade is higher on Sunday evening, which explains why the student sets the alarm with the intention of going to class. On Monday morning, however, the value of an hour of extra sleep has increased substantially because of its proximity. Because it is now greater than that of the good grade, the student chooses the more immediate reinforcer.

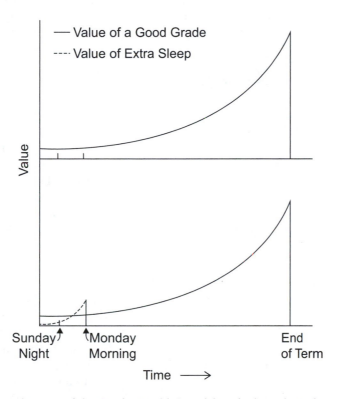

Figure 12.4 An application of the Ainslie–Rachlin model to the hypothetical example described in the text. The top panel shows how the subjective value of a good grade increases as the time of its delivery gets closer. The bottom panel shows that the value of a bit of extra sleep also increases as the time of its delivery gets closer. Because of these changes in value, a person may prefer the good grade at some times (e.g., Sunday evening) and the extra sleep at other times (say, Monday morning).

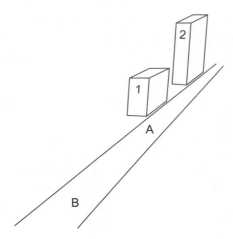

Figure 12.5 For a person standing at point A, building 1 subtends a larger visual angle than building 2. The opposite is true for a person standing at point B. This situation is somewhat analogous to a self-control situation if we replace physical distance with time and think of the large, distant building as a large, delayed reinforcer and the small, closer building as a small, more immediate reinforcer.

If you find the curves in Figure 12.5 difficult to understand, it may help to draw an analogy between time and distance. Figure 12.5 is a sketch of a long street with two buildings on the left. The buildings are analogous to the two reinforcers in a self-control situation. Building 2 is clearly larger, but for a person standing at point A, building 1 would subtend a greater visual angle. We might say that from the perspective of point A, building 1 appears larger. However, if the person walked to point B, both buildings would appear smaller, but now the visual angle subtended by building 2 would be the larger of the two. By stepping back from both buildings, a person can get a better perspective on their relative sizes. Similarly, by examining two reinforcers (say, an extra hour of sleep and a better grade) from a distance (e.g., the night before a class), a person "gets a better perspective" on the values of the two reinforcers and is more likely to choose the "larger" one.

As you can probably see, the student's problem is that she is free to change her mind on Monday morning, when the proximity of the extra hour of sleep gives her a distorted perspective on its value. One strategy for avoiding this problem is called **precommitment**: The individual makes a decision in advance, which is difficult or impossible to change at a later time. For example, on Sunday evening the student might ask a friend from the same class to come and get her on the way to class Monday morning and not to take "no" for an answer. This would make it more difficult and more embarrassing to stay in bed. In short, the student could make a precommitment to go to class by having a friend pick her up. The technique is a very effective way to avoid making an impulsive choice.

Animal Studies on Self-Control

Some of the research supporting the Ainslie–Rachlin theory has used animal subjects. A study by Green, Fischer, Perlow, and Sherman (1981) demonstrated the sort of preference reversals we would expect if the Ainslie–Rachlin theory is correct. Pigeons received many trials each day, and on each trial a bird made its choice by pecking just once at one of two keys. A peck at the red key delivered 2 seconds of grain, and a peck at the green key delivered 6 seconds of grain. There was, however, a short delay between a peck and the delivery of the grain. For example, in one condition there was a 2-second delay for the 2-second reinforcer and a 6-second delay for the 6-second reinforcer (Figure 12.6). In this condition, the birds showed impulsive behavior on nearly every trial, choosing the 2-second reinforcer. This choice did not speed up future trials because the trials occurred every 40 seconds regardless of which choice was made. This behavior is certainly inconsistent with optimization theory because the optimal solution would be to choose the 6-second reinforcer on every trial. By consistently choosing the smaller but more immediate reinforcer, the birds lost about two thirds of their potential access to grain. In another condition, the experimenters simply added 18 seconds to the delay for each reinforcer, so the delays were now 20 seconds and 24 seconds. When they had to choose so far in advance (similar to making a precommitment), the birds' behaviors were more nearly optimal: They chose the 6-second reinforcer on more than 80% of the trials. This shift in preference when both reinforcers are farther away is exactly what the Ainslie–Rachlin model predicts.

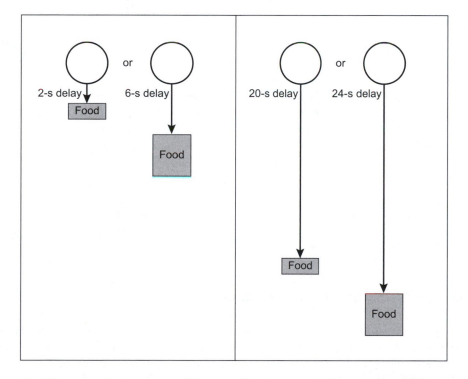

Figure 12.6 The procedure in two conditions used by Green et al. (1981). When the delays to the small and large reinforcers were 2 s and 6 s, pigeons usually chose the small reinforcer (left panel). When 18 additional seconds of delay were added to both options (right panel), pigeons usually chose the larger reinforcer.

When the alternatives in a self-control situation are punishers rather than reinforcers, they have the reverse effect on choice. In one study, rats tended to choose a large, delayed shock over a smaller but more immediate one. However, when they could make a precommitment a few seconds before the trial began to the smaller but more immediate shock, they frequently did so (Deluty, Whitehouse, Mellitz, & Hineline, 1983). This study provides one more example of how reinforcers and punishers have symmetrical but opposite effects on behavior.

Other research with animals has examined factors that may make them more or less likely to choose a more preferred but delayed reinforcer. Grosch and Neuringer (1981) gave pigeons choices between two different types of grain: A pigeon could either wait 15 seconds and then eat a preferred grain or peck a key and receive a less preferred type of grain immediately. The pigeons must have had a strong preference for the delayed reinforcer because Grosch and Neuringer found that they would wait for this reinforcer on about 80% of the trials. The experimenters then made one small change in the procedure: The two types of food were now placed where they were visible to the pigeons (behind a transparent barrier) throughout the waiting period. With the food in plain sight, the pigeons became much more impulsive, and they waited for the preferred type of grain on only about 15% of the trials. The sight of the food evidently provided too much of a temptation to resist. In another study, Grosch and Neuringer found that stimuli associated with the food reinforcers had a similar effect. In this case, no food was visible during the waiting interval, but the food hoppers were lit with the same colored lights that normally accompanied the presentation of food. Like the presence of food itself, the colored lights made the pigeons more likely to choose the immediate, less desirable grain.

Grosch and Neuringer (1981) also found that their pigeons were more likely to wait for the delayed reinforcer if they had the opportunity to engage in some other activity during the delay. They taught the birds to peck on a key in the rear of the chamber, which at first delivered food on an FR 20 schedule. Not surprisingly, the birds found it easier to wait for preferred grain when they could spend the delay working on the FR 20 schedule. More surprisingly, when the rear key no longer delivered any reinforcers, the birds continued to peck at it during the delays for the rest of the experiment with no signs of extinction.

These studies illustrate a few of the factors that have been found to affect the self-control choices of animal subjects. The next section shows that these same factors affect children's choices.

Factors Affecting Self-Control in Children

The experiments of Grosch and Neuringer were patterned after a series of experiments conducted with children by Walter Mischel and his colleagues. In one experiment (Mischel & Ebbesen, 1970), preschool children (tested one at a time) were given a choice between waiting 15 minutes for a preferred reinforcer (e.g., pretzels) versus receiving a less preferred reinforcer (e.g., cookies) immediately. During the 15-minute wait, a child could terminate the trial at any time and get the less preferred snack. Like the pigeons of Grosch and Neuringer, the children found it much more difficult to wait when the reinforcers were visible (in an open cake tin in front of the child). In another study, Mischel, Ebbesen, and Zeiss (1972) told some children that they could "think about the marshmallow and the pretzel for as long as you want." Other children were given no such instructions. The children who were encouraged to think about the reinforcers chose to terminate the trial and obtain the less preferred reinforcer more frequently. The researchers also found that children were more likely to wait for the preferred reinforcer when given an activity to engage in during the delay (some children were given a toy).

Just as with adults, there are substantial individual differences among children in their self-control abilities: Some children will wait for quite a while for a delayed reinforcer and others will not. It seems that some 2- or 3-year-olds have already learned the strategy of diverting their attention away from the desired objects as a way of avoiding an impulsive choice (Cournoyer & Trudel, 1991). Researchers have found that the tendency to wait for a large delayed reinforcer is related to a child's age, IQ, and other factors. One study reported that the quality of a toddler's interactions with his or her mother is related to self-control ability 4 years later. Children who had "responsive, cognitively stimulating parent–toddler interactions" (p. 317) at age 2 tended to be less impulsive at age 6 (Olson, Bates, & Bayles, 1990).

Mischel (1966) found that a child's behavior in a self-control situation can be influenced by observational learning. When choosing between an inferior product they could have immediately and a better product after a two-week delay, fourth and fifth graders tended to select whichever they saw an adult model choose. Fading procedures can also be used to help children learn to tolerate delays to reinforcement. Schweitzer and Sulzer-Azaroff (1988) taught a group of impulsive preschoolers to wait for a larger, delayed reinforcer by beginning with very short delays and progressively increasing the delays as the training proceeded. Similar procedures have been used for children with hyperactivity and attention-deficit disorder (Bloh, 2010) and for adults with developmental disabilities (Dixon, Rehfeldt, & Randich, 2003).

Techniques for Improving Self-Control

Behavior therapists can offer quite a few suggestions to clients who wish to avoid impulsive behaviors in such varied realms as dieting, maintaining an exercise program, studying regularly, saving money, and avoiding excessive drinking or smoking. The strategy of precommitment can be used in many self-control situations. People who wish to lose weight are advised to shop for food when they are not hungry and to purchase only foods that are low in calories and require some preparation before they can be eaten. (You cannot impulsively eat some high-calorie snack if there are no such snacks in the house.) People who habitually spend money impulsively are advised to make a list before they go shopping, to take only enough money to buy what they need, to destroy their credit cards, and to avoid going to a shopping mall without some definite purpose in mind. Similarly, people prone to excessive gambling should bring only a limited amount of money to the casino or use debit cards that set limits on how much they can lose before they are forced to stop (Nower & Blaszczynski, 2010). All of these strategies make it more difficult for the person to spend money on the spur of the moment because it seems appealing at the time (Figure 12.7).

Figure 12.7 Making arrangements to work out with friends is a type of precommitment which makes it less likely that you will back out at the last moment. (Visionsi/Shutterstock.com)

Anything that either increases the value of the delayed alternative or decreases the value of the immediate alternative should make the choice of the delayed reinforcer more likely. One useful strategy, therefore, is to provide an additional, immediate reward for choosing the large, delayed reinforcer. For instance, a dieter may make an agreement with himself that he will watch his favorite evening television program only if he skips dessert. A college student may allow herself to go out with friends for a snack only after she has studied in the library for two solid hours. A common problem with this strategy, however, is that it is easy to "cheat"—to give yourself the reinforcer even when you have failed to perform the appropriate behavior. For this reason, it is advisable to enlist the help of a friend or family member. The dieter's wife might make sure he only watches his television program if he did not have dessert. The college student may go to the library with a conscientious roommate who makes sure she has spent 2 hours studying before they go out for a snack.

The complementary strategy is to decrease the value of the impulsive option by attaching some form of punishment to it. Ross (1974) reported a case in which this technique was used to cure a woman of an impulsive nail-biting habit. As part of her treatment, the woman gave the therapist a deposit of $50 and agreed that the money would be donated to an organization she intensely disliked if her nails did not grow a certain length each week. Another strategy makes use of rule-governed behavior (see Chapter 6). The basic idea is that people can be taught to use verbal rules to guide their choices toward the larger, delayed reinforcer. For example, Benedick and Dixon (2009) taught individuals with developmental disabilities to exhibit more self-control simply by having them read out loud a card stating that it was better to pick the larger, delayed option.

Other strategies have a more cognitive flavor, because people are taught to use specific thought processes to improve their self-control. For instance, a person on a diet may be advised to visualize the attractive, healthy body he or she is striving for before sitting down to eat. A similar tactic is to tape on the refrigerator door a picture of an attractive person in a swimsuit to remind you of your long-term goal each time you have the urge for a snack. The idea behind this approach is that a picture or visual image somehow bridges the gap between the present and the long-term goal, thereby increasing the subjective value of that goal. Conversely, research on the treatment of drug addictions suggests that distracting the individual can be helpful, presumably because thinking about something else reduces the subjective value of the drug (Ashe, Newman, & Wilson, 2015).

All of these strategies show that there is more to self-control than simple determination and willpower. People who blame their impulsive behaviors on a lack of willpower may actually be lacking only the knowledge of how to apply the appropriate strategies.

OTHER CHOICE SITUATIONS

To conclude this chapter on choice behavior, we will examine a few other situations where people's or animals' decisions seem paradoxical. In some cases, their decisions appear to be inconsistent; in others, they are self-defeating.

Risk Taking

In many everyday decisions, the outcomes are not certain. If you invest in a company, you cannot be certain whether its stock will increase or decrease in value. If you leave home without your umbrella, you cannot be certain that it will not rain. If you go to a party, you cannot be certain whether you will enjoy yourself. An interesting fact about choices involving uncertain consequences is that sometimes people seem to prefer a risky alternative, and sometimes they prefer a safe alternative instead. The same has been found for animals. Researchers have tried to understand why individuals are sometimes risk prone (preferring a risky alternative) and sometimes risk averse (preferring a safer alternative).

In one experiment on this topic, Caraco, Martindale, and Whittam (1980) presented juncos (small birds) choices of the following type. Every trial, a junco could go to one of two feeding sites. If it went to one feeding site, it would receive one millet seed every time. If it went to the other feeding site, the bird had a 50% chance of finding two seeds and a 50% chance of finding none. If the trials followed one another rapidly (so there were plenty of opportunities to obtain food), the birds preferred the single, guaranteed millet seed. However, if the trials were separated by longer delays (so there were fewer opportunities to obtain food), the birds preferred the 50% chance of getting two seeds. Caraco concluded that these strategies maximize a junco's chances of survival in the wild. When food is plentiful, there is no need to take a risk because choosing small but certain food sources will guarantee that the bird has enough to eat. When food is scarce and the safe food sources do not provide enough food, the bird will choose riskier options with larger possible payoffs because the bird has nothing to lose—getting lucky with the risky option is the bird's only chance of survival.

Humans who need to earn a certain amount of money also tend to be risk prone when their resources are scarce and risk averse when their resources are plentiful (Pietras, Searcy, Huitema, & Brandt, 2008). March and Shapira (1992) suggested that both individuals (e.g., politicians) and groups (e.g., companies) are likely to take large risks when their survival (in a political campaign, in the marketplace) is at stake. However, they also proposed that besides being concerned merely with survival, individuals and groups also have aspiration levels (goals they wish to achieve), and their level of risk taking may depend on how close they are to their goals. For instance, a company may take large risks if its profits for the year are far below its goal, but if its profits are close to the goal, it may behave more conservatively. If the company's profits have exceeded the goal by a comfortable margin, the company may start to take greater risks once again. March and Shapira also proposed that other factors affect the level of risk taking by an individual or group, such as past habits, previous successes or failures, and self-confidence. Considering all of these factors, it is no wonder that it can be difficult to predict how a person will behave in a risky situation.

When it comes to games of chance, risk taking is always involved. Many people enjoy gambling—in casinos, in office pools, in state lotteries. Betting a few dollars a week may be harmless, but for some people gambling becomes excessive, and they create financial ruin for themselves and their families because of their gambling losses. Excessive betting on lotteries or in casinos makes little financial sense because the average gambler has to lose money (since state lotteries and casinos always make a profit). Why do people gamble, sometimes heavily, despite the fact that the odds are against them in the long run? Rachlin (1990) suggested that the preference for gambling is based on the possibility of obtaining an immediate reward. Consider the "instant lottery" games found in some states, in which you have a chance of winning money immediately (usually a fairly small amount) each time you buy a ticket. If you buy a ticket every day, you may sometimes go for weeks before you get a winner. But there is always a chance that you will win the very next time you play. Rachlin proposed that buying a lottery ticket is an attractive option for some people for the same reason that VR or VI schedules produce steady and persistent responding in the laboratory: In both cases, there is a chance that a reinforcer will be delivered almost immediately. As in so many choice situations, the power of immediate reinforcement is a crucial factor.

The Tragedy of the Commons

In an article entitled "The Tragedy of the Commons," Garrett Hardin (1968) described a situation that has far too many parallels in modern society. In many villages of colonial America, the commons was a grassland owned by the village, where residents could allow their cows to graze freely. The commons was therefore a public resource that benefited everyone as long as the number of grazing animals did not grow too large. This might not happen for decades or for centuries, but according to Hardin, it was inevitable that eventually there would be more animals than the commons could support. Then, because of over-grazing, the grass becomes scarce, erosion occurs, and the commons is destroyed, to the detriment of everyone.

Why did Hardin believe this unhappy scenario was inevitable? His reasoning was that it is to each herder's benefit to have as many cows as possible, for this will maximize one's income. Suppose a herder must decide whether to add one more cow to the herd. What are the benefits and costs to consider? The benefits are the profits to be earned from this cow, which go entirely to the owner of the cow. The cost is the extra strain imposed on the commons, but one additional cow will not make much of a difference, and besides, this cost is shared by everyone who uses the commons. Hardin therefore concluded that the herder will experience a net gain by adding the additional cow to the herd, and by adding a second cow, and so on: "But this is the conclusion reached by each and every rational herdsman sharing a commons. Therein is the tragedy. Each man is locked into a system that compels him to increase his herd without limit—in a world that is limited. Ruin is the destination toward which all men rush, each pursuing his own best interest in a society that believes in the freedom of the commons. Freedom in a commons brings ruin to all" (Hardin, 1968, p. 1244).

The **tragedy of the commons** is a scenario that has been acted out many times in our civilization. The buffalo herds on the American plains were hunted nearly to the point of extinction. Excessive fishing has ruined many of the world's richest fishing areas. With every acre of forestland that is turned into a highway or a shopping mall, there is less wilderness for everyone to enjoy.

Most problems of pollution have a similar structure. A company that must pollute the air in order to manufacture its product cheaply keeps the profits of its enterprise to itself; the air pollution is shared by everyone. Before we condemn big business, however, we should realize that individual people frequently make equally selfish decisions. Every person who drives to work in a large city (rather than walking, riding a bike, or taking public transportation) contributes to the air pollution of that city. The reason that many people behave selfishly in this situation is obvious: The driver alone receives the benefits of convenience and comfort that come from driving one's own car. If the driver chose to walk, the reduction in air pollution would be so slight as to be undetectable.

The tragedy of the commons can also be seen on a global level in the struggles among nations to develop international policies to deal with climate change (Murphy & Murphy, 2012). Even if national leaders are convinced that human activities are contributing to climate change, they may not want to change their own country's policies on greenhouse gases and other pollutants because this might hurt their country's economic prosperity. The short-term economic well-being of the country can seem more important than long-term global climate changes.

Another instance of the commons tragedy can be seen in the annual trade deficit of the United States, a consequence of the large amounts of foreign products that Americans buy. Most people know that the trade deficit hurts the economy and that it would be eliminated if people bought fewer foreign goods. Nevertheless, when an individual consumer is deciding which product to purchase, alleviating the trade deficit usually seems far less important than getting the best buy, regardless of whether the product is domestic or foreign.

Although there are many examples of the tragedy of the commons in modern life, Hardin (1968) and others have suggested several ways in which the tragedy can be averted (Platt, 1973; Sasaki, Brännström, Dieckmann, Sigmund, & Wachter, 2012). These suggestions will probably sound familiar, because in recent years our society has focused a good deal of attention on the problems of pollution, the extinction of wildlife, and the like, as well as on potential solutions. What is interesting, however, is the strong resemblance these remedies bear to the strategies that individuals can use to avoid impulsiveness in a self-control situation.

We saw that one powerful technique for improving self-control is the precommitment strategy in which an individual takes some action in advance that makes it difficult or impossible to make an impulsive choice later. Similarly, a society can decide to make it difficult or impossible for individuals to act selfishly. For example, a society can pass legislation that simply makes it illegal to dump dangerous chemicals where they might seep into the water supply, to pollute the air, or to kill a member of an endangered species.

Less coercive strategies for self-control situations are those that either attach a punisher to the small, immediate alternative or attach an additional (often immediate) reinforcer to the large, delayed alternative. These strategies do not make an impulsive choice impossible, only less likely. In a similar fashion, a city with traffic and pollution problems can punish the behavior of driving one's own car by prohibiting parking on city streets and by making it expensive to park in garages. Based on what we know about punishment, however, there should also be reinforcement for a desirable alternative behavior. For instance, the city should do all that it can to make public transportation convenient, reliable, safe, and inexpensive.

Finally, we should not underestimate the capacity of human beings to attend to and be influenced by the long-term consequences of their behaviors for society. Just as a picture on the refrigerator can remind a dieter of his or her long-term goal, educational programs and advertising campaigns can encourage individuals to alter their behaviors for the long-term benefits of the community (Figure 12.8). A good example is the personal sacrifices

Figure 12.8 Something as simple as a sign in a parking lot can help people make choices that are better for everyone in the long run.

civilians were willing to make for the war effort during World War II, not to mention the soldiers who gave their lives in the name of freedom. In some fishing communities, overfishing is avoided by informal agreements among individuals to limit their catches for the good of all (Leal, 1998). From a logical perspective, such behaviors may seem puzzling: Why should people behave in a way that is helpful to others but is harmful to them personally? One solution to this puzzle is simply to assert that, at least in certain circumstances, behaviors that benefit others can be inherently reinforcing for many people (just as eating, reading a novel, or exercising can be inherently reinforcing). Admittedly, this is not much of an explanation. But given the many examples of selfish behaviors we have been forced to consider, it is refreshing to remember that people will often make sacrifices when the only personal benefit from their behavior is the knowledge that they are promoting the common good.

PRACTICE QUIZ 2: CHAPTER 12

1. An individual who chooses a _____ reinforcer over a _____ reinforcer is said to be making an impulsive choice.
2. Making a choice of a large, delayed reinforcer in advance, so that later it is difficult to choose a smaller, more immediate reinforcer, is called _____.
3. In a self-control choice situation where the actual reinforcers are visible during a delay, both children and animals are more likely to choose the _____ reinforcer.
4. The rate of delay discounting is usually _____ for children than for adults.
5. If a person chooses an option with an uncertain outcome over one with a guaranteed outcome, the person is said to be _____.

ANSWERS

1. small, immediate; large, delayed   2. precommitment   3. smaller, more immediate   4. faster   5. risk prone

---

SUMMARY

The matching law states that the proportion of responses on each schedule tends to match the proportion of reinforcers delivered by that schedule. This law has been demonstrated with many different species of subjects, including people. However, three different types of deviations from exact matching are often found: undermatching, overmatching, and bias. The matching law has also been applied to other variables, such as reinforcer quality and amount. It follows from the matching law that the effects of a reinforcer on behavior are relative—they depend on what reinforcers are available for other behaviors.

Herrnstein proposed that matching is a fundamental property of behavior. A very different theory, optimization theory, states that individuals will distribute their responses in whatever way will maximize the reinforcement they receive. Most studies that compared the predictions of the matching law and optimization theory have favored the matching law; that is, subjects exhibited approximate matching even when this behavior decreased the overall amount of reinforcement. Momentary maximization theory states that, at each moment, an individual chooses whichever behavior has the highest value at that moment. Some experiments have found such moment-to-moment patterns in choice behavior that are predicted by this theory, but others have not.

In a self-control choice situation, an individual must choose between a small, fairly immediate reinforcer and a larger, more delayed reinforcer. Individuals frequently choose the small, immediate reinforcer, even though the larger reinforcer would be better in the long run. Studies with animals and children have demonstrated several factors that can affect choice in these situations. Making a precommitment to choose the larger, delayed reinforcer is an effective self-control strategy, as are adding additional reinforcers to the long-term alternative, adding punishers to the short-term alternative, or using cognitive strategies to focus attention on the long-term consequences of one's choices.

The effects of delay can also be seen in other choice situations, such as in risk-prone behavior (e.g., gambling when the odds are against winning). The tragedy of the commons occurs when individuals make decisions that benefit them in the short run but are harmful to society as a whole in the long run. Strategies similar to those used to improve self-control may also be helpful in such cases.

Review Questions

1. What is the matching law? Describe Herrnstein's experiment on matching, and discuss three ways that behavior can deviate from perfect matching.
2. Summarize the main differences between the matching law, optimization theory, and momentary maximizing theory. What has research found about the strengths and weaknesses of these competing theories?
3. Describe the Ainslie–Rachlin theory, and use an everyday example to show how it accounts for the reversals in preference that occur in self-control choices.
4. Describe several techniques a person could use to help him avoid eating foods that are high in fat and cholesterol.
5. What is the tragedy of the commons? Give a few modern-day examples of this problem and describe some strategies that can be used to overcome the problem.

REFERENCES

Ainslie, G. (1975). Specious reward: A behavioral theory of impulsiveness and impulse control. *Psychological Bulletin, 82,* 463–496.

Alferink, L.A., Critchfield, T.S., Hitt, J.L., & Higgins, W.J. (2009). Generality of the matching law as a descriptor of basketball shot selection. *Journal of Applied Behavior Analysis, 42,* 592–605.

Aparicio, C.F., & Baum, W.M. (2009). Dynamics of choice: Relative rate and amount affect local preference at three different time scales. *Journal of the Experimental Analysis of Behavior, 91,* 293–317.

Ashe, M.L., Newman, M.G., & Wilson, S.J. (2015). Delay discounting and the use of mindful attention versus distraction in the treatment of drug addiction: A conceptual review. *Journal of the Experimental Analysis of Behavior, 103,* 234–248.

Baum, W.M. (1974). On two types of deviation from the matching law: Bias and undermatching. *Journal of the Experimental Analysis of Behavior, 22,* 231–242.

Baum, W.M. (1982). Choice, changeover, and travel. *Journal of the Experimental Analysis of Behavior, 38,* 35–49.

Baum, W.M., & Rachlin, H.C. (1969). Choice as time allocation. *Journal of the Experimental Analysis of Behavior, 12,* 861–874.

Benedick, H., & Dixon, M.R. (2009). Instructional control of self-control in adults with co-morbid developmental disabilities and mental illness. *Journal of Developmental and Physical Disabilities, 21,* 457–471.

Bickel, W.K., Koffarnus, M.N., Moody, L., & Wilson, A.G. (2014). The behavioral- and neuro-economic process of temporal discounting: A candidate behavioral marker of addiction. *Neuropharmacology, 76*(Part B), 518–527.

Billington, E.J., & DiTommaso, N.M. (2003). Demonstrations and applications of the matching law in education. *Journal of Behavioral Education, 12,* 91–104.

Bloh, C. (2010). Assessing self-control training in children with attention deficit hyperactivity disorder. *Behavior Analyst Today, 10,* 357–363.

Brown, E., & Cleaveland, J. (2009). An application of the active time model to multiple concurrent variable-interval schedules. *Behavioural Processes, 81,* 250–255.

Caraco, T., Martindale, S., & Whittam, T.S. (1980). An empirical demonstration of risk-sensitive foraging preferences. *Animal Behavior, 28,* 820–830.

Catania, A.C. (1963). Concurrent performances: A baseline for the study of reinforcement magnitude. *Journal of the Experimental Analysis of Behavior, 6,* 299–300.

Conger, R., & Killeen, P. (1974). Use of concurrent operants in small group research. *Pacific Sociological Review, 17,* 399–416.

Cournoyer, M., & Trudel, M. (1991). Behavioral correlates of self-control at 33 months. *Infant Behavior and Development, 14,* 497–503.

Davison, M., & Hogsden, I. (1984). Concurrent variable-interval schedule performance: Fixed versus mixed reinforcer durations. *Journal of the Experimental Analysis of Behavior, 41,* 169–182.

Davison, M., & Jenkins, P.E. (1985). Stimulus discriminability, contingency discriminability, and schedule performance. *Animal Learning and Behavior, 13,* 77–84.

DeCarlo, L.T. (1985). Matching and maximizing with variable-time schedules. *Journal of the Experimental Analysis of Behavior, 43,* 75–81.

Deluty, M.Z., Whitehouse, W.G., Mellitz, M., & Hineline, P.N. (1983). Self-control and commitment involving aversive events. *Behaviour Analysis Letters, 3,* 213–219.

Dixon, M.R., Rehfeldt, R.A., & Randich, L. (2003). Enhancing tolerance for delayed reinforcers: The role of intervening activities. *Journal of Applied Behavior Analysis, 36,* 263–266.

Fantino, E., & Silberberg, A. (2010). Revisiting the role of bad news in maintaining human observing behavior. *Journal of the Experimental Analysis of Behavior, 93,* 157–170.

Foster, T.M., Temple, W., Robertson, B., Nair, V., & Poling, A. (1996). Concurrent-schedule performance in dairy cows: Persistent undermatching. *Journal of the Experimental Analysis of Behavior, 65,* 57–80.

Foxall, G.R., James, V.K., Oliveira-Castro, J.M., & Ribier, S. (2010). Product substitutability and the matching law. *Psychological Record, 60,* 185–216.

Grace, R.C. (1994). A contextual choice model of concurrent-chains choice. *Journal of the Experimental Analysis of Behavior, 61,* 113–129.

Green, L., Fischer, E.B., Perlow, S., & Sherman, L. (1981). Preference reversal and self control: Choice as a function of reward amount and delay. *Behavior Analysis Letters, 1,* 43–51.

Green, L., Fry, A.F., & Myerson, J. (1994). Discounting of delayed rewards: A life-span comparison. *Psychological Science, 5,* 33–36.

Grosch, J., & Neuringer, A. (1981). Self-control in pigeons under the Mischel paradigm. *Journal of the Experimental Analysis of Behavior, 35,* 3–21.

Hardin, G. (1968). The tragedy of the commons. *Science, 162*, 1243–1248.

Herrnstein, R. J. (1961). Relative and absolute strength of response as a function of frequency of reinforcement. *Journal of the Experimental Analysis of Behavior, 4*, 267–272.

Herrnstein, R. J. (1970). On the law of effect. *Journal of the Experimental Analysis of Behavior, 13*, 243–266.

Herrnstein, R. J., & Mazur, J. E. (1987). Making up our minds: A new model of economic behavior. *The Sciences, 27*, 40–47.

Heyman, G. M. (1979). A Markov model description of changeover probabilities on concurrent variableinterval schedules. *Journal of the Experimental Analysis of Behavior, 31*, 41–51.

Heyman, G. M., & Herrnstein, R. J. (1986). More on concurrent interval-ratio schedules: A replication and review. *Journal of the Experimental Analysis of Behavior, 46*, 331–351.

Hinson, J. M., & Staddon, J. E. R. (1983). Hillclimbing by pigeons. *Journal of the Experimental Analysis of Behavior, 39*, 25–47.

Jacobs, E. A., & Hackenberg, T. D. (2000). Human performance on negative slope schedules of points exchangeable for money: A failure of molar maximization. *Journal of the Experimental Analysis of Behavior, 73*, 241–260.

Killeen, P. R. (1982). Incentive theory: II. Models for choice. *Journal of the Experimental Analysis of Behavior, 38*, 217–232.

Leal, D. R. (1998). Community-run fisheries: Avoiding the "tragedy of the commons". *Population and Environment: A Journal of Interdisciplinary Studies, 19*, 225–245.

MacDonall, J. S., Goodell, J., & Juliano, A. (2006). Momentary maximizing and optimal foraging theories of performance on concurrent VR schedules. *Behavioural Processes, 72*, 283–299.

MacKillop, J., Miller, J. D., Fortune, E., Maples, J., Lance, C. E., Campbell, W. K., & Goodie, A. S. (2014). Multidimensional examination of impulsivity in relation to disordered gambling. *Experimental and Clinical Psychopharmacology, 22*, 176–185.

March, J. G., & Shapira, Z. (1992). Variable risk preferences and the focus of attention. *Psychological Review, 99*, 172–183.

Mazur, J. E. (1981). Optimization theory fails to predict performance of pigeons in a two-response situation. *Science, 214*, 823–825.

Miller, H. L. (1976). Matching-based hedonic scaling in the pigeon. *Journal of the Experimental Analysis of Behavior, 26*, 335–347.

Mischel, W. (1966). Theory and research on the antecedents of self-imposed delay of reward. *Progress in Experimental Personality Research, 3*, 85–132.

Mischel, W., & Ebbesen, E. B. (1970). Attention in delay of gratification. *Journal of Personality and Social Psychology, 16*, 329–337.

Mischel, W., Ebbesen, E. B., & Zeiss, A. R. (1972). Cognitive and attentional mechanisms in delay of gratification. *Journal of Personality and Social Psychology, 21*, 204–218.

Mitchell, S. H. (1999). Measures of impulsivity in cigarette smokers and non-smokers. *Psychopharmacology, 146*, 455–464.

Murphy, R., & Murphy, M. (2012). The tragedy of the atmospheric commons: Discounting future costs and risks in pursuit of immediate fossil-fuel benefits. *Canadian Review of Sociology, 49*, 247–270.

Neef, N. A., Mace, F. C., Shea, M. C., & Shade, D. (1992). Effects of reinforcer rate and reinforcer quality on time allocation: Extensions of matching theory to educational settings. *Journal of Applied Behavior Analysis, 25*, 691–699.

Nevin, J. A. (1969). Interval reinforcement of choice behavior in discrete trials. *Journal of the Experimental Analysis of Behavior, 12*, 875–885.

Nower, L., & Blaszczynski, A. (2010). Gambling motivations, money-limiting strategies, and precommitment preferences of problem versus non-problem gamblers. *Journal of Gambling Studies, 26*, 361–372.

Odum, A.L. (2011). Delay discounting: I'm a k, you're a k. *Journal of the Experimental Analysis of Behavior, 96*, 427–439.

Olson, S.L., Bates, J.E., & Bayles, K. (1990). Early antecedents of childhood impulsivity: The role of parent-child interaction, cognitive competence, and temperament. *Journal of Abnormal Child Psychology, 18*, 317–334.

Pietras, C.J., Searcy, G.D., Huitema, B.E., & Brandt, A.E. (2008). Effects of monetary reserves and rate of gain on human risky choice under budget constraints. *Behavioural Processes, 78*, 358–373.

Platt, J. (1973). Social traps. *American Psychologist, 28*, 641–651.

Rachlin, H. (1970). *Introduction to modern behaviorism.* San Francisco, CA: W.H. Freeman.

Rachlin, H. (1990). Why do people gamble and keep gambling despite heavy losses. *Psychological Science, 1*, 294–297.

Rachlin, H., Green, L., Kagel, J.H., & Battalio, R.C. (1976). Economic demand theory and psychological studies of choice. In G. H. Bower (Ed.), *The psychology of learning and motivation* (Vol. 10, pp. 129–154). New York: Academic Press.

Redmon, W.K., & Lockwood, K. (1986). The matching law and organizational behavior. *Journal of Organizational Behavior Management, 8*, 57–72.

Ross, J.A. (1974). The use of contingency contracting in controlling adult nailbiting. *Journal of Behavior Therapy and Experimental Psychiatry, 5*, 105–106.

Sakagami, T., Hursh, S.R., Christensen, J., & Silberberg, A. (1989). Income maximizing in concurrent interval-ratio schedules. *Journal of the Experimental Analysis of Behavior, 52*, 41–46.

Sasaki, T., Brännström, A., Dieckmann, U., Sigmund, K., & Wachter, K. (2012). The take-it-or-leave-it option allows small penalties to overcome social dilemmas. *PNAS Proceedings of the National Academy of Sciences of the United States of America, 109*, 1165–1169.

Savastano, H.I., & Fantino, E. (1994). Human choice in concurrent ratio-interval schedules of reinforcement. *Journal of the Experimental Analysis of Behavior, 61*, 453–463.

Schweitzer, J.B., & Sulzer-Azaroff, B. (1988). Self-control: Teaching tolerance for delay in impulsive children. *Journal of the Experimental Analysis of Behavior, 50*, 173–186.

Shimp, C.P. (1966). Probabilistically reinforced choice behavior in pigeons. *Journal of the Experimental Analysis of Behavior, 9*, 443–455.

Silberberg, A., Hamilton, B., Ziriax, J.M., & Casey, J. (1978). The structure of choice. *Journal of Experimental Psychology: Animal Behavior Processes, 4*, 368–398.

Silberberg, A., Thomas, J.R., & Berendzen, N. (1991). Human choice on concurrent variable-interval, variable-ratio schedules. *Journal of the Experimental Analysis of Behavior, 56*, 575–584.

Stilling, S.T., & Critchfield, T.S. (2010). The matching relation and situation-specific bias modulation in professional football play selection. *Journal of the Experimental Analysis of Behavior, 93*, 435–454.

Vyse, S.A., & Belke, T.W. (1992). Maximizing versus matching on concurrent variable-interval schedules. *Journal of the Experimental Analysis of Behavior, 58*, 325–334.

Glossary

a-process In the opponent-process theory, an initial fast-acting emotional response to a stimulus, which is later followed by the b-process, leading to the opposite emotion.

ABAB design A design for behavioral treatment where each "A" phase is a baseline phase in which the patient's behavior is recorded but no treatment is given, and each "B" phase is a treatment phase.

absolute theory of stimulus control A theory about how animals learn about reinforced and nonreinforced stimuli. The theory states that animals simply learn about the two stimuli separately but learn nothing about the relation between the two.

acquisition The learning of a new behavior or skill, or the time period over which this learning occurs.

acquisition phase The period in the learning process when an individual is learning a new behavior.

Adams's two-stage theory A theory of motor-skill learning that consists of a verbal-motor stage in which improvement depends on the delivery of feedback from the teacher, followed by a motor stage in which the learner can continue to improve without the teacher's feedback.

adjunctive behaviors Stereotyped behaviors that arise when food or some other reinforcer is delivered at regular intervals.

Ainslie–Rachlin theory A theory of self-control choices that explains why an individual's preference can shift from a larger, delayed reinforcer to a smaller, more immediate reinforcer as the time of reinforcer delivery approaches.

analogy A statement in the form "A is to B as C is to D." To test the ability to understand analogies, the subject is given two or more choices for D and asked which is correct.

animal cognition Also called comparative cognition, a field of psychology that compares the cognitive processes and abilities of different species, including humans.

Associationists Philosophers who developed early theories about how people learn to associate separate thoughts or ideas as a result of their experiences.

associative rehearsal A type of rehearsal that strengthens the information in long-term memory.

attribute conditioning A type of classical conditioning in which the attributes or characteristics of one stimulus are transferred to another stimulus.

automatic reinforcement Reinforcement of a behavior derived from the sensory stimulation that occurs as a result of performing the behavior itself.

aversive counterconditioning   A treatment for alcoholism and other addictions in which the addictive substance is paired with an aversive stimulus, such as an illness-inducing drug, designed to condition an aversive response to the addictive substance.

avoidance   A type of negative reinforcement in which performing a response prevents an aversive stimulus from occurring in the first place.

avoidance paradox   The puzzle about how the nonoccurrence of an aversive event can serve as a reinforcer for an avoidance response.

axon   A long branch-like part of a neuron that transmits electrical pulses, or action potentials, when the neuron is stimulated. Enlarged structures at the ends of the axons, the axon terminals, release chemical transmitters that stimulate the dendrites of other neurons.

b-process   In the opponent-process theory, an emotional response that is the opposite of the a-process. The b-process is supposedly activated only in response to the activity of the a-process, and it is more sluggish both to rise and to decay.

backward conditioning   A classical conditioning procedure in which the conditioned stimulus is presented after the unconditioned stimulus.

Bandura's theory of imitation   A theory that four factors are needed for imitation to occur: attentional processes, retentional processes, motor reproductive processes, and incentive and motivational processes.

behavior decelerator   Any procedure that leads to a slowing, reduction, or elimination of an unwanted behavior.

behavior-systems analysis   The view that different reinforcers evoke different systems or collections of species-typical behaviors, which can account for the types of behaviors seen in autoshaping, classical conditioning, and some operant conditioning situations.

behavioral contrast   A phenomenon in which responding in the presence of one stimulus changes as a result of a change in the reinforcement conditions during another stimulus.

behavioral economics   A field that uses principles from both behavioral psychology and economics to predict people's choices and behaviors.

behavioral momentum   An operant behavior's resistance to change when the reinforcement conditions change (e.g., when free reinforcers are delivered or when the schedule changes to extinction).

behavioral skills training   A method for teaching new behaviors that includes techniques such as modeling, verbal instruction, prompting, guided practice, and feedback.

behaviorism   An approach to psychology and the field of learning that emphasizes the study of external events (observable stimuli and responses) and avoids speculation about processes inside the organism.

bias   In choice behavior, a deviation from matching in which a subject consistently allocates more time or responding to one alternative than predicted by the matching equation.

biofeedback   A procedure that provides a person with amplified feedback about some bodily function, usually presented with the intention of increasing the individual's control over that bodily function to treat some medical problem.

blocking   In classical conditioning, the finding that there is little or no conditioning to a stimulus if it is presented along with a previously conditioned stimulus on conditioning trials.

British Associationists   British philosophers who proposed early theories about how the ideas in memory are formed from a person's experiences.

cell body   The part of a neuron that contains the nucleus, which regulates the basic metabolic functions of the cell.

central instance   In research of concept formation, an example from a natural category that people tend to judge as a "good," or "typical," example.

cerebellum   A part of the brain, located in the back of the head beneath the cerebral cortex, that is important for many skilled movements.

chunk   A group of items that the learner combines into a single unit (e.g., a group of letters that form a word), which makes learning easier than if all the items had to be learned individually.

classical conditioning   The procedure of repeatedly pairing an initially neutral stimulus (the conditioned stimulus) and an unconditioned stimulus, through which the conditioned stimulus develops the capacity to elicit a conditioned response.

cognitive map   According to Tolman, a mental map that an animal develops of its environment by exploring or observing its surroundings (as when a rat learns a maze).

cognitive psychology   An approach to psychology that, unlike behaviorism, makes use of theories about processes that take place inside the head (memory, attention, rehearsal, etc.) that cannot be observed directly.

cognitive theory of avoidance   The theory that avoidance responses will occur when the individual has expectations that (1)

an aversive event will occur if no response is made and (2) the aversive event will be avoided if a response is made. Avoidance responding will continue until one or both of these expectations are violated.

comparative cognition   A field of psychology that compares the cognitive processes and abilities of different species, including humans.

comparator   In control systems theory, a device that compares its goal state (the reference input) and the current situation (the actual input) and signals that action is necessary if the two are not equal.

comparator theory   A theory of classical conditioning that states that the strength of a conditioned response depends on a comparison of the likelihood of an unconditioned stimulus in the presence of the conditioned stimulus versus its absence.

complex idea   A term used by James Mill, a British Associationist, to describe what happens when two or more simple ideas are combined.

compound CS   In classical conditioning, the simultaneous presentation of two or more conditioned stimuli.

concurrent schedule   A situation in which two or more reinforcement schedules are available at the same time, each requiring its own responses and delivering its own reinforcers.

conditioned compensatory response   In classical conditioning, a conditioned response that is the opposite of the unconditioned response.

conditioned inhibitor (CS–)   In classical conditioning, a conditioned stimulus that prevents the occurrence of a conditioned response or reduces the size of the conditioned response from what it would otherwise be. It is also called an *inhibitory CS*.

conditioned opponent theory   A theory of classical conditioning that states that the later portions of an unconditioned response (which are often opposite in form to the early portions) become associated with the conditioned stimulus. The theory accounts for conditioned responses that appear to be the opposite of the unconditioned response.

conditioned reinforcer   A previously neutral stimulus that has acquired the capacity to strengthen responses because it has been repeatedly paired with a primary reinforcer.

conditioned response (CR)   The response that is elicited by a conditioned stimulus after classical conditioning has taken place.

conditioned stimulus (CS)   An initially neutral stimulus that develops the capacity to elicit a conditioned response after it is paired with an unconditioned stimulus.

conditioned suppression   A classical conditioning procedure in which the conditioned stimulus signals that an aversive event is coming. The measure of conditioning is the suppression of ongoing behavior (e.g., pressing a lever to obtain food) when the conditioned stimulus is presented.

context-shift effect   The finding that if one learns information in a particular context, recall of that information will be better if one is tested in the same context than if the testing occurs in a different context.

contextual interference   Any features of the learning situation that make learning a new task more difficult but that may lead to better performance in the long run.

contextual stimuli   The sights, sounds, and smells of a creature's environment.

contiguity   One of Aristotle's principles of association stating that two ideas will be associated if they tend to occur together in space or time. In modern psychology, contiguity between stimuli is an important factor in classical conditioning, and contiguity between a response and its consequences is important in operant conditioning.

contingency contract   A written agreement used in behavior therapy that lists the duties (behaviors) required of each party and the privileges (reinforcers) that will result if the duties are performed.

contingency-shaped behavior   Behavior that is controlled by the schedule of reinforcement or punishment (as opposed to rule-governed behavior, which is controlled by a verbal or mental rule about how to behave).

continuous reinforcement (CRF)   A reinforcement schedule that delivers a reinforcer after every occurrence of a specific response.

contrast   One of Aristotle's principles of association stating that the thought of one concept often leads to the thought of the opposite concept.

control systems theory   A branch of science that analyzes goal-directed behaviors in both living creatures and inanimate objects.

CS preexposure effect   The finding that classical conditioning proceeds more slowly if the conditioned stimulus is repeatedly presented by itself before it is paired with the unconditioned stimulus.

cue exposure treatment   In the treatment of drug addictions, exposing the individual to stimuli that are normally associated with the drug, so that conditioned drug cravings can be extinguished.

cumulative recorder   A simple mechanical device that records responses in a way that plots time on the horizontal axis and cumulative responses on the vertical axis. It allows the observer to see at a glance the moment-to-moment patterns of a subject's behavior.

delay discounting A decrease in the strength or value of a reinforcer as its delay increases.

delayed matching to sample (DMTS) A procedure used to measure short-term memory, or working memory. First, a sample stimulus is presented, followed by a delay with no stimuli; then two comparison stimuli are presented, and a choice of the comparison that matches the sample is reinforced.

demand curve A graph that plots the demand for a product as a function of its price.

dendrite A branch-like structure on the receptive side of a neuron that is sensitive to transmitters released by the axon terminals of other neurons.

differential reinforcement of alternative behavior (DRA) A technique for reducing unwanted behaviors by using extinction combined with reinforcement of more desirable behaviors.

differential reinforcement of high rates (DRH) schedule A reinforcement schedule in which a reinforcer is delivered if a certain number of responses have occurred within a fixed amount of time.

differential reinforcement of low rates (DRL) schedule A reinforcement schedule in which a reinforcer is delivered if a certain amount of time has elapsed between two responses.

directed forgetting A procedure for studying memory and forgetting in which the learner (either human or animal) is taught that on some trials it is important to remember a stimulus and on other trials it is safe to forget the stimulus.

discrimination In either classical or operant conditioning, learning to respond to one stimulus but not to another similar stimulus.

discrimination hypothesis An explanation of the partial reinforcement effect, which states that the rate of decrease in responding depends on how quickly the subject can discriminate the change from reinforcement to extinction.

discriminative stimulus In operant conditioning, a stimulus that indicates whether or not responding will lead to reinforcement.

disinhibition In classical conditioning, the reappearance of a conditioned response to a stimulus that has undergone extinction that can occur if a novel stimulus is presented shortly before the extinguished stimulus.

distributed practice In motor-skill learning, a training procedure in which fairly brief practice periods alternate with rest periods, which may lead to better learning than massed practice.

drive-reduction theory A theory proposed by Hull that any decrease in a biological drive (the hunger drive, the sex drive, etc.) will serve as a reinforcer.

duplex idea A term developed by James Mill, a British Associationist, to describe what happens when complex ideas are combined.

elastic demand In economics, demand for a product that exhibits large changes as the price increases or decreases.

empiricism The philosophical position that all knowledge is obtained through experience.

equipotentiality premise The hypothesis that a stimulus or response that is difficult to condition in one context should also be difficult to condition in all other contexts.

errless discrimination learning A procedure for teaching discriminations developed by Herbert Terrace; errorless discrimination learning begins with stimuli that are easy for the subject to discriminate and progresses to more difficult ones, so the subject makes very few errors during the course of learning.

escape A type of negative reinforcement in which performing a response leads to the termination of an aversive stimulus.

escape extinction A procedure used to eliminate an unwanted behavior that has been previously reinforced by escape from an unpleasant situation; escape is prevented if the unwanted behavior occurs.

evaluative conditioning A form of second-order classical conditioning with human subjects in which neutral stimuli are paired with a positive or negative stimuli; then the subjects are asked to rate how much they like or dislike the stimuli.

excitatory CS (CS+) In classical conditioning, a conditioned stimulus that regularly elicits a conditioned response.

exemplar theory A theory of concept learning that states that one's ability to categorize objects depends on one's memory of specific examples.

extinction In classical conditioning, presenting the conditioned stimulus without the unconditioned stimulus. In operant conditioning, no longer presenting the reinforcer when the operant response is made. In both cases, responding decreases and eventually disappears.

fading A behavior modification procedure in which a prompt for a desired behavior is gradually withdrawn, thereby teaching the learner to produce the behavior without the prompt.

feature detector A neuron that responds to a specific type of visual stimulus.

feature theory A theory of concept learning that states that one judges whether a given instance is a member of a category by checking for specific features.

fixed action pattern An innate sequence of behaviors that is elicited by a specific stimulus and, once started, continues to its end whether or not the behaviors are appropriate in the current situation.

fixed-interval (FI) schedule A reinforcement schedule in which the first response after a fixed amount of time has elapsed is reinforced.

fixed-ratio (FR) schedule A reinforcement schedule that delivers a reinforcer after a fixed number of responses.

flooding A treatment for phobias in which a patient is presented with a highly feared object or situation that is not removed until the patient's fear diminishes.

forgetting curve A graph showing how performance on a memory task declines with the passage of time since learning.

free-operant avoidance Another name for the Sidman avoidance task.

free-operant procedure A procedure developed by Skinner in which, unlike a discrete trial procedure, the operant response can occur at any time and can occur repeatedly for as long as the subject remains in the experimental chamber.

functional analysis A method in which stimuli and/or reinforcers are systematically varied so that a therapist can determine which are maintaining a patient's behavior.

functional magnetic resonance imaging (fMRI) A brain-imaging technique that can show, in real time, which parts of a person's brain are currently most active.

generalization   The transfer of a learned response from one stimulus to another similar stimulus.

generalization decrement hypothesis   An explanation of the partial reinforcement effect, which states that responding during extinction will be rapid if the stimuli present during extinction are different from those that occurred during reinforcement, but it will be slow if the stimuli are similar to those that occurred during reinforcement.

generalization gradient   A graphic representation of generalization in which the x-axis plots some dimension along which the test stimuli are varied and the y-axis shows the strength of conditioned responding to the different stimuli.

generalized imitation   The idea that people will imitate in situations that are similar to those where imitation has been reinforced in the past.

generalized reinforcer   A conditioned reinforcer that has been associated with a large number of different primary reinforcers.

graduated modeling   A type of modeling in which the model's behaviors steadily progress from simple to more difficult behaviors.

habituation   A decrease in the strength of a reflexive response after repeated presentation of the stimulus that elicits the response.

human universals   Abilities or behaviors that are found in all known human cultures.

Humphreys's paradox   Another name for the partial reinforcement effect, or the seemingly paradoxical finding that a response that is only intermittently reinforced is more resistant to extinction than a response that is reinforced every time it occurs.

indifference point   In choice behavior, a pair of alternatives that an individual finds equally preferable, or chooses equally often.

inelastic demand   In economics, demand for a product that shows relatively little change as the price increases or decreases.

inhibitory CS   In classical conditioning, a conditioned stimulus that prevents the occurrence of a conditioned response or reduces the size of the conditioned response from what it would otherwise be. It is also called a *conditioned inhibitor.*

instinctive drift   In operant conditioning, innate behaviors that are related to the type of reinforcer being used that cause an animal's performance to drift away from the reinforced behavior and toward instinctive behaviors.

interim behavior   A behavior pattern that occurs in the early parts of each interval when food or some other primary reinforcer is delivered at regular intervals.

intermediate-size problem   A discrimination problem in which the subject learns to choose the middle stimulus along some dimension (e.g., a medium-sized circle) and is then tested when this stimulus is no longer the medium one (e.g., it is now the smallest of three circles).

interresponse time (IRT) reinforcement theory   The theory that responding is faster on variable-ratio schedules than on variable-interval schedules because long IRTs (long pauses between responses) are more frequently reinforced on variable-interval schedules.

intervening variable   A theoretical concept that cannot be observed directly but is used in science to predict the relationship between independent and dependent variables.

kinesis   A tropism in which the direction of the movement is random in relation to the stimulus.

knowledge of performance (KP)   In motor-skill learning, detailed feedback given to the learner, such as information about which parts of the movement were performed well and how other parts of the movement could be improved.

knowledge of results (KR)   In motor-skill learning, feedback given to the learner about how close his or her movement came to the goal.

latent learning   Tolman's term for the hidden learning that occurs on trials when no reinforcer is delivered; it can only be seen in the subject's behavior once trials with reinforcement begin.

Law of Effect   Thorndike's version of the principle of reinforcement, which states that responses that are followed by pleasant or satisfying stimuli will be strengthened and will occur more often in the future.

learned helplessness   Seligman's term for the impaired ability to learn an avoidance response that occurs after a subject has been exposed to inescapable aversive stimuli.

learned optimism   Seligman's term for the ability to think about potentially bad situations in positive ways.

long-delay conditioning   A type of classical conditioning in which the onset of the conditioned stimulus precedes that of the unconditioned stimulus by at least several seconds and continues until the unconditioned stimulus is presented.

long-term memory   A part of memory that has a very large capacity and can retain information for months, years, or longer, although some information is lost through interference or forgetting.

long-term potentiation   An increase in the strengths of connections between neurons, which can last for weeks or months, caused by electrical stimulation.

maintenance rehearsal   A type of rehearsal that retains information in short-term memory but does not necessarily strengthen information in long-term memory.

massed practice   In motor-skill learning, a training procedure in which practice takes place in one continuous block without rest periods, which may lead to worse learning than distributed practice.

matching law   Herrnstein's general principle of choice behavior that states that in a two-choice situation, the percentage of responses directed toward one alternative will equal the percentage of reinforcers delivered by that alternative.

metacognition   The ability to reflect on one's memories and thought processes and make judgments about them.

mirror neurons   Neurons that respond both when an individual makes a certain movement and when the individual observes someone else make that movement.

molar theory   A theory of behavior that focuses on the long-term relationships between behaviors and their consequences.

molecular theory   A theory of behavior that focuses on the moment-by-moment relationships between behaviors and their consequences.

momentary maximization theory   A theory of choice behavior that states that at each moment, a creature will select whichever alternative has the highest value at that moment, even though it may not be the best choice in the long run.

motor program   A brain or spinal cord mechanism that controls a sequence of movements and does not rely on sensory feedback from one movement to initiate the next movement in the sequence.

multiple schedule   A procedure in which two or more reinforcement schedules are presented one at a time in an alternating pattern, and each schedule is signaled by a different discriminative stimulus.

narrowing   A technique of stimulus control that involves gradually reducing the range of situations in which an unwanted behavior is allowed to occur.

Nativism   The hypothesis that some ideas are innate (inborn) and do not depend on an individual's past experience.

need-reduction theory   A theory proposed by Hull that all primary reinforcers are stimuli that reduce some biological need, and all stimuli that reduce a biological need will act as reinforcers.

negative contrast   A type of behavioral contrast in which there is a decrease in responding in the presence of one stimulus due to an increase in the reinforcement conditions for another stimulus.

negative punishment   A behavior reduction procedure, more commonly called omission, in which a desired stimulus is removed or omitted if the behavior occurs.

negative reinforcement   A behavior strengthening procedure in which an aversive stimulus is removed or omitted if the behavior occurs.

negative transfer   In motor-skill learning, when practice of one task interferes with learning or performance on another task.

neurofeedback   A type of biofeedback in which a person receives feedback about some brainwave pattern for the purpose of changing or controlling that pattern.

neurogenesis   The growth of new neurons.

object permanence   An understanding that objects continue to exist even when they are not visible. Researchers have studied how and when young children develop the concept of object permanence and whether different species of animals can also develop this concept.

omission   A behavior reduction procedure in which a desired stimulus is removed or omitted if the unwanted behavior occurs.

one-factor theory   A theory of avoidance that states that avoidance of an aversive stimulus, such as a shock, can in itself serve as a reinforcer and that the classical conditioning component of two-factor theory is not necessary.

opponent-process theory   Solomon and Corbit's theory that states that many emotional responses include an initial emotional reaction followed by an after-reaction of the opposite emotion.

optimization theory   A theory of choice behavior that states that people tend to make decisions that maximize their satisfaction.

organizational behavior management   A field of applied behavior analysis that uses the principles of behavioral psychology to improve human performance in the workplace.

orienting response   An innate reaction to a sudden or unexpected stimulus in which an animal stops its current activity to look at or listen to the novel stimulus.

overcorrection   A behavior reduction procedure in which the individual is required to make several repetitions of an alternate, more desirable behavior if an undesired behavior occurs.

overexpectation effect   A decrease in the strength of responding to two conditioned stimuli that have been trained separately that occurs if they are presented as a compound CS and followed by the usual unconditioned stimulus.

overlearning   Continuing to practice a response after performance is apparently perfect, which often results in stronger or more accurate performance in a delayed test.

overmatching   A deviation from matching in which response percentages are consistently more extreme than reinforcement percentages in a choice situation.

overshadowing   In classical conditioning, the finding that there is less conditioning to a weak conditioned stimulus if it is presented along with a more intense conditioned stimulus.

partial reinforcement effect   The finding that responses are more rapidly extinguished after continuous reinforcement than after a schedule of intermittent reinforcement.

peak procedure   A procedure for studying animal timing abilities in which the time of its peak response rate shows how accurately the animal can time the intervals.

peak shift   After discrimination training with a reinforced stimulus and an unreinforced stimulus, a shift in the peak of a generalization gradient from the reinforced stimulus in a direction away from the unreinforced stimulus.

percentile schedule   A reinforcement schedule in which a given response is reinforced if it is better than a certain percentage of the last several responses the learner has made.

peripheral instance   In research of concept formation, an example from a natural category that people tend to judge as a "bad" or "atypical" example.

positive contrast   A type of behavioral contrast in which there is an increase in responding in the presence of one stimulus due to a decrease in the reinforcement conditions for another stimulus.

positive reinforcement   A behavior-strengthening procedure in which the occurrence of a behavior is followed by a desired stimulus, or reinforcer.

positive transfer   In motor-skill learning, when practice of one task improves learning or performance on a similar task.

positron emission tomography (PET)   A brain-imaging technique that can show which parts of a person's brain are currently most active.

postreinforcement pause   A pause in responding that usually occurs after each reinforcer in fixed-ratio schedules.

precommitment   A technique for improving self-control in which the individual makes a choice in advance that is difficult or impossible to change at a later time.

Premack's principle   The theory that more probable behaviors will act as reinforcers for less probable behaviors and that less probable behaviors will act as punishers for more probable behaviors.

prepared association   An association between stimuli, or between stimuli and responses, in which members of a particular species have an innate tendency to learn quickly and easily.

primary reinforcer   A stimulus that naturally strengthens any response it follows (e.g., food, water, sexual pleasure, and comfort).

proactive interference   When previously learned material impairs the learning of new material.

prompt   In behavior modification, a stimulus that makes a desired response very likely to occur and is gradually removed (faded out) as training proceeds.

prototype theory   A theory of concept learning that states that one's ability to categorize objects depends on forming a prototype or ideal example, to which new examples are compared.

punishment   A behavior reduction procedure in which the occurrence of a behavior is followed by an aversive stimulus.

puzzle box   A type of experimental chamber used by Thorndike in which an animal had to make a certain response in order to open the door and obtain food that was available outside.

radial-arm maze   A maze for animals in which eight or more arms radiate from a central starting area, and each of the arms may contain food at the end.

rapid reacquisition   Learning in a second acquisition phase that follows extinction that occurs more quickly than in the initial acquisition phase.

ratio strain   A general weakening of responding that is found when a fixed-ratio schedule requires a very large number of responses.

reaction chain   An innate sequence of behaviors in which the progression from one behavior to the next depends on the presence of the appropriate external stimulus. Portions of the sequence may be skipped or omitted depending on which stimuli are presented and which are not.

receptor   A specialized neuron that responds to sensory stimulation, either from the traditional "five senses" or from internal bodily sensations such as muscle tension and balance.

reciprocal contingency   A procedure that ensures that two behaviors occur in a fixed proportion by requiring the individual to perform fixed amounts of the two behaviors in alternation.

reflex   An innate movement that can be reliably elicited by presenting the appropriate stimulus.

rehearsal   An active processing of stimuli or events after they have occurred, which can keep information active in short-term memory and promote its transfer into long-term memory.

reinforcement schedule   A rule that states under what conditions a reinforcer will be delivered.

reinforcer   A stimulus that strengthens behavior if it is delivered after the behavior occurs.

relational theory of stimulus control   The theory that animals can learn to respond to relationships between stimuli (e.g., larger, redder, or brighter). The opposite is the absolute theory of stimulus control, which assumes that animals cannot learn such relationships.

Rescorla–Wagner model   A mathematical theory of classical conditioning that states that the amount of conditioning depends on the associative strengths of all the conditioned stimuli that are present and on the intensity of the unconditioned stimulus.

response blocking   A behavior reduction procedure in which the individual is physically prevented from making an unwanted response. In extinction of avoidance responding, response blocking can teach the individual that the avoidance response is no longer necessary.

response chain   A sequence of learned behaviors that must occur in a specific order, with a primary reinforcer delivered only after the final response.

response cost   A behavior reduction procedure in which the individual is penalized by the loss of reinforcers if an undesired behavior occurs.

response deprivation theory   A theory of reinforcement that states that any contingency that deprives an animal of its preferred level of a behavior will cause that behavior to act as a reinforcer for less restricted behaviors.

response–reinforcer correlation theory   The theory that responding is faster on variable-ratio schedules than on variable-interval schedules because faster responding leads to more reinforcers on variable-ratio schedules but not on variable-interval schedules.

retroactive interference   When the presentation of new material interferes with the memory of something that was learned earlier.

rule-governed behavior   Behavior that is controlled by a verbal or mental rule about how to behave (as opposed to contingency-shaped behavior, which is controlled by the schedule of reinforcement or punishment).

Schmidt's schema theory   A theory of motor-skill learning that states that as people practice a task, they acquire general rules (schemas) about how to recognize the correct response and how to produce it.

second-order conditioning   A classical conditioning procedure in which a conditioned response is transferred from one stimulus to another by pairing a neutral stimulus with a previously conditioned stimulus.

self-control choice   A choice between a small, more immediate reinforcer and a larger but more delayed reinforcer.

shaping (or method of successive approximations)   A procedure for teaching a new behavior in which closer and closer approximations to the desired behavior are reinforced.

short-delay conditioning   A classical conditioning procedure in which the conditioned stimulus begins a second or so before the unconditioned stimulus.

short-term memory   A type of memory that can only hold information for a matter of seconds and has a very limited capacity.

shuttle box   An experimental chamber with two rectangular compartments. An animal may be required to move from one compartment to the other to escape or avoid an aversive stimulus, such as shock.

Sidman avoidance task   An avoidance procedure in which shocks occur at regular intervals if the subject does not respond, but a response postpones the next shock for a fixed period of time.

sign stimulus   A stimulus that initiates a fixed action pattern.

sign-tracking theory   A theory of classical conditioning that states that animals tend to orient themselves toward, approach, and explore any stimuli that are good predictors of important events, such as the delivery of food.

similarity   One of Aristotle's principles of association stating that the thought of one concept often leads to the thought of similar concepts.

simple cell   A type of neuron in the visual cortex, discovered by Hubel and Wiesel, which fires most rapidly when a line is presented at a specific angle in a specific part of the visual field.

simple systems approach   In physiological research, the strategy of studying primitive creatures, which have smaller and less complex nervous systems.

simultaneous conditioning   A type of classical conditioning in which the conditioned stimulus and unconditioned stimulus begin at the same moment.

skin conductance response (SCR)   A change in the electrical conductivity of the skin due to an emotional reaction, which can be measured by sensors attached to the palm.

sometimes opponent process (SOP)   A general theory of classical conditioning, developed by Allan Wagner, which speculates about why some conditioned responses are similar in form and others are opposite in form to the unconditioned response.

species-specific defense reaction (SSDR)   An innate defensive reaction that occurs when an animal encounters any kind of new or sudden stimulus in the wild. SSDRs usually fall into the categories of freezing, fleeing, or fighting.

spinal reflex arc   Neural pathways that produce the reflexive withdrawal of one's hand from a painful stimulus. The arc consists of pain-sensitive neurons in the hand with axons that extend into the spinal cord, interneurons, and motor neurons that activate the muscles of the arm.

spontaneous recovery   In classical or operant conditioning, the reappearance of a response that has undergone extinction after a passage of time without further conditioning trials.

stimulus control   The general topic of how behaviors can be controlled by the stimuli that precede them.

stimulus equivalence   A situation in which an individual learns to respond to all stimuli in a category as if they are interchangeable even though the individual has been taught only a few relations between these stimuli, not all the possible relations.

stimulus satiation   A behavior reduction procedure in which the reinforcer is presented in such great quantities that it loses its effectiveness.

stimulus substitution theory   Pavlov's theory of classical conditioning, which states that the conditioned stimulus becomes a substitute for the unconditioned stimulus and elicits the same response.

stop-action principle   A principle of reinforcement that states that the precise movements being performed at the moment of reinforcer delivery will be strengthened and be more likely to occur in the future.

subject effect   The finding that when people know they are participating in an experiment, their behaviors may change or improve, even if they are in a control group and receive no special treatment.

superstition experiment   Skinner's classic experiment in which food was delivered to pigeons every 15 seconds no matter what they were doing, and most pigeons developed distinctive behaviors that they performed repeatedly between food presentations.

superstitious behavior   A behavior that occurs because, by accident or coincidence, it has previously been followed by a reinforcer.

synapse   A small gap between the axon terminal of one neuron and the dendrite of another neuron into which transmitters are released.

systematic desensitization   A behavioral treatment for phobias that involves slowly presenting the patient with increasingly strong fear-provoking stimuli while keeping the patient in a very relaxed state.

taxis   A tropism in which the eliciting stimulus determines the direction of the creature's movement.

temporal coding hypothesis   The hypothesis that in classical conditioning, the individual learns about the timing of the CS and US, not just an association between them.

terminal behavior   A behavior pattern that occurs near the end of each interval when food or some other primary reinforcer is delivered at regular intervals.

three-term contingency   A contingency involving a discriminative stimulus, a response, and a reinforcer or punisher. The contingency states that in the presence of a specific discriminative stimulus, a specific response will lead to specific consequences.

time-out   A behavior reduction procedure in which one or more desirable stimuli are temporarily removed if the individual performs some unwanted behavior.

token system   A behavior modification system, often used with groups of people, in which each person can earn tokens by performing specific behaviors and can later exchange these tokens for a variety of primary reinforcers.

tolerance   A decrease in the effects of a drug that is observed after repeated use of the drug.

trace conditioning   A classical conditioning procedure in which the conditioned stimulus and the unconditioned stimulus are separated by some time interval in which neither stimulus is present.

tragedy of the commons   A situation in which people, acting in their individual short-term interests, make choices that are detrimental to society as a whole.

transitive inference   Learning a rule about the relation between three stimuli, such as the following: If A < B and B < C, then A < C.

transmitter   A chemical released into the synapse by the axon terminals of a neuron, to which cell bodies and dendrites of other neurons are sensitive.

transposition   A case in which a subject receives reinforcers for choosing one of two stimuli in a discrimination task (e.g., choosing a 2-inch circle rather than a 1-inch circle), but later chooses a more extreme stimulus along the same dimension rather than the previously reinforced stimulus (e.g., choosing a 3-inch circle rather than the 2-inch circle).

trans-situationality   The theory that once a stimulus is determined to be a reinforcer in one situation, it will also serve as a reinforcer in other situations.

tropism   An innate movement of a creature's entire body in response to a specific stimulus. The two major categories of tropisms are kineses and taxes.

true imitation   Imitation of a behavior pattern that is very unusual or improbable for the species so that it would seldom be learned through trial and error.

two-factor theory (or two-process theory)   The theory that both classical conditioning (learning to fear a stimulus) and operant conditioning (escape from the fear-eliciting stimulus) are required for avoidance responding.

unconditioned response (UR)   In classical conditioning, an innate response that is elicited by an unconditioned stimulus.

unconditioned stimulus (US)   In classical conditioning, a stimulus that naturally elicits a specific response (an unconditioned response).

undermatching   A deviation from matching in which response percentages are consistently less extreme than reinforcement percentages in a choice situation.

variable–interval (VI) schedule   A reinforcement schedule in which reinforcers become available after variable and unpredictable time intervals. Once a reinforcer becomes available, a single response is required to collect it.

variable–ratio (VR) schedule   A reinforcement schedule that delivers a reinforcer after a variable and unpredictable number of responses.

video self-modeling   A behavior modification technique in which clients watch videos of themselves correctly performing the desired behaviors.

virtual reality therapy   A type of systematic desensitization in which a patient wears a headset that displays realistic visual images that change with every head movement, simulating a three-dimensional environment.

Weber's law   A principle of perception that states that the just noticeable difference (the smallest difference between two stimuli that can be detected) is proportional to the sizes of the stimuli.

working memory   A type of memory that holds information for a short period of time, has a limited capacity, and is assumed to guide whatever tasks an individual is currently performing.

Author Index

Subject Index